Contents

Schweser Video Class Workbook

2013 CFA Level I

Volume 1

SCHWESER VIDEO CLASS WORKBOOK, VOLUME 1 (2013 CFA LEVEL I)

Published in November 2012 by Kaplan Schweser.
Printed in the United States of America.

ISBN: 978-1-4277-4250-6 / 1-4277-4250-2

PPN: 3200-2888

Study Session 1

Ethics and Professional Standards

Ethical and Professional Standards

1. Code of Ethics and Standards of Professional Conduct
2. Guidance for Standards I – VII

Ethical and Professional Standards

LOS 1.a Describe
CFAI p. 8, Schweser p. 13

Code of Ethics and Standards of Professional Conduct

CFA Institute Professional Conduct Program

- **Disciplinary Review Committee** of CFA Institute Board of Governors has responsibility for the Professional Conduct Program and for enforcement of the Code and Standards
- CFA Institute Designated Officer, through Professional Conduct staff, conducts **inquiries related to professional conduct**

 2

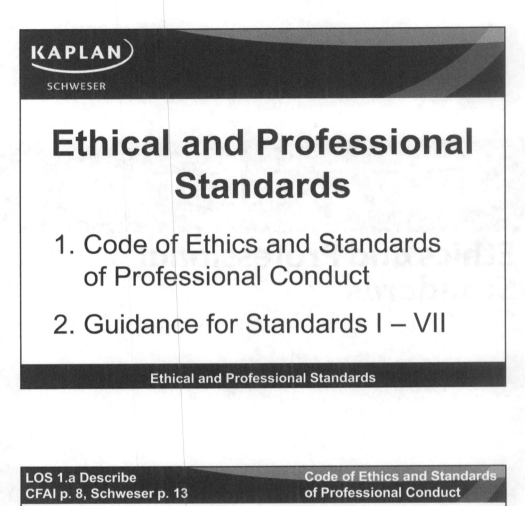

LOS 1.a Describe
CFAI p. 8, Schweser p. 13

Code of Ethics and Standards of Professional Conduct

CFA Institute Professional Conduct Program

Inquiry can be prompted by:

- **Self-disclosure** by members or candidates
- **Written complaints** about a member or candidate's professional conduct
- **Evidence of misconduct** by a member or candidate
- Report by a **CFA exam proctor**

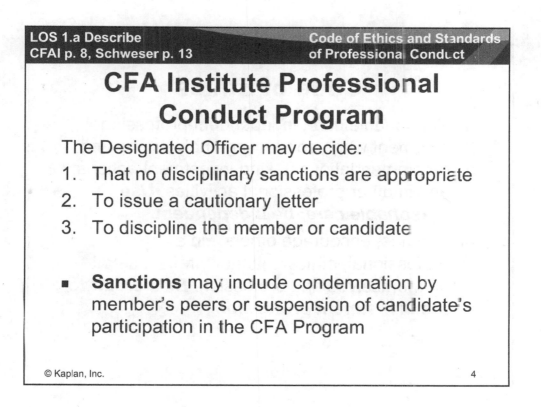

LOS 1.a Describe
CFAI p. 8, Schweser p. 13

Code of Ethics and Standards of Professional Conduct

CFA Institute Professional Conduct Program

The Designated Officer may decide:

1. That no disciplinary sanctions are appropriate
2. To issue a cautionary letter
3. To discipline the member or candidate

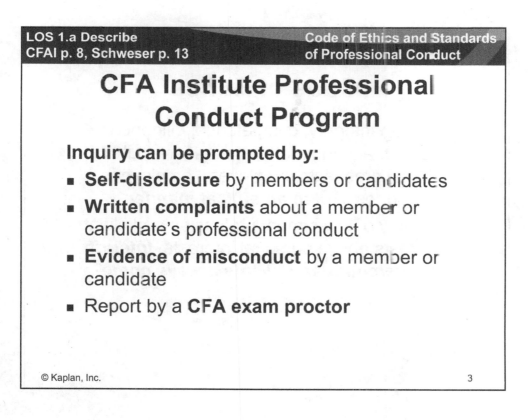

- **Sanctions** may include condemnation by member's peers or suspension of candidate's participation in the CFA Program

LOS 1.b State
CFAI p. 14, Schweser p. 14

Code of Ethics and Standards of Professional Conduct

Code of Ethics

- Act with integrity, competence, diligence, respect, and in an ethical manner—public, clients, prospects, employers, employees, colleagues. ***Act in an ethical manner.***
- Integrity of investment profession and client interests above personal interests. ***Integrity is paramount and clients always come first.***

 5

LOS 1.b State
CFAI p. 14, Schweser p. 14

Code of Ethics and Standards of Professional Conduct

Code of Ethics

- Reasonable care, independent professional judgment when conducting analysis, making recommendations, taking investment actions, and in other professional activities. ***Use reasonable care; be independent.***
- Practice, encourage others…in a professional, ethical manner…reflect credit on themselves and profession. ***Be a credit to the investment profession.***

 6

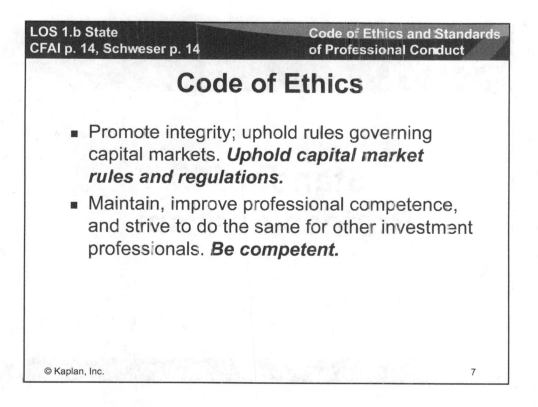

LOS 1.b State
CFAI p. 14, Schweser p. 14

Code of Ethics and Standards of Professional Conduct

Code of Ethics

- Promote integrity; uphold rules governing capital markets. ***Uphold capital market rules and regulations.***
- Maintain, improve professional competence, and strive to do the same for other investment professionals. ***Be competent.***

 7

LOS 1.c Explain
CFAI p. 14, Schweser p. 15

Code of Ethics and Standards of Professional Conduct

Standards of Professional Conduct

I. Professionalism
II. Integrity of Capital Markets
III. Duties to Clients
IV. Duties to Employers
V. Investment Analysis, Recommendations, and Actions
VI. Conflicts of Interest
VII. Responsibilities as a CFA Institute Member or CFA Candidate

 8

Standard I: Professionalism

Ethical and Professional Standards

LOS 2.a,b,c Demonstrate/Distinguish/ Recommend; CFAI p. 19, Schweser p. 18

Code of Ethics and Standards of Professional Conduct

Standard I: Professionalism

The Standard

A. Knowledge of the Law

- Understand and comply with all laws, rules, and regulations (including Code and Standards) of any government, regulatory agency, or association governing professional activities
- Comply with *more strict* law, rule, and regulation
- Do not knowingly assist in violation, otherwise dissociate from activity

10

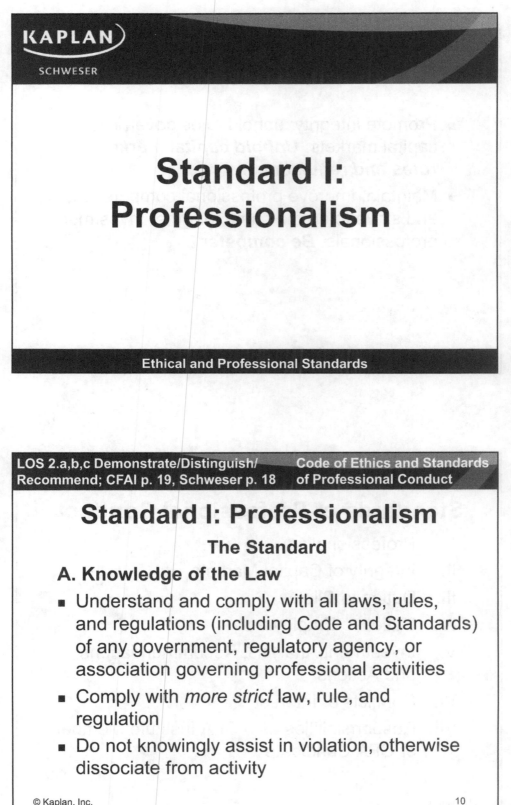

LOS 2.a,b,c Demonstrate/Distinguish/ Recommend; CFAI p. 19, Schweser p. 18

Code of Ethics and Standards of Professional Conduct

Standard I: Professionalism

Guidance

A. Knowledge of the Law

- Most strict
- First, notify supervisor or compliance
- May confront wrongdoer directly
- Dissociate if necessary
- Inaction may be construed as participation
- No requirement to report violations to governmental authorities, but this may be appropriate in certain cases

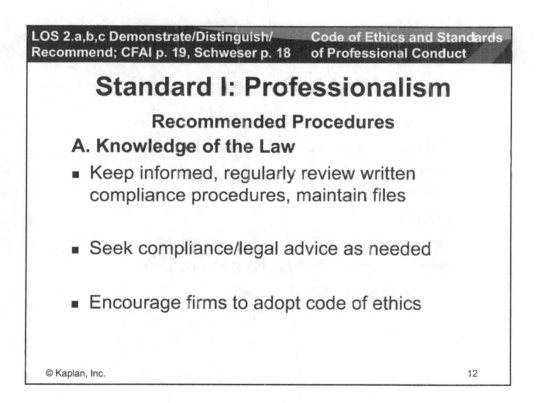

 11

LOS 2.a,b,c Demonstrate/Distinguish/ Recommend; CFAI p. 19, Schweser p. 18

Code of Ethics and Standards of Professional Conduct

Standard I: Professionalism

Recommended Procedures

A. Knowledge of the Law

- Keep informed, regularly review written compliance procedures, maintain files
- Seek compliance/legal advice as needed
- Encourage firms to adopt code of ethics

 12

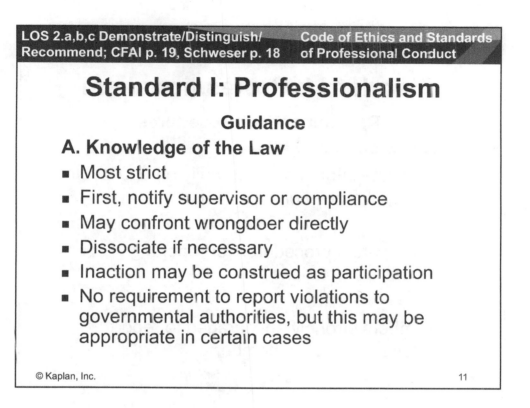

LOS 2.a,b,c Demonstrate/Distinguish/ Recommend; CFAI p. 19, Schweser p. 18

Code of Ethics and Standards of Professional Conduct

Standard I: Professionalism

Recommended Procedures

A. Knowledge of the Law

- Distribute information internally on applicable laws and regulations
- Have written procedures for reporting suspected violations
- Members strongly encouraged to report violations by other members

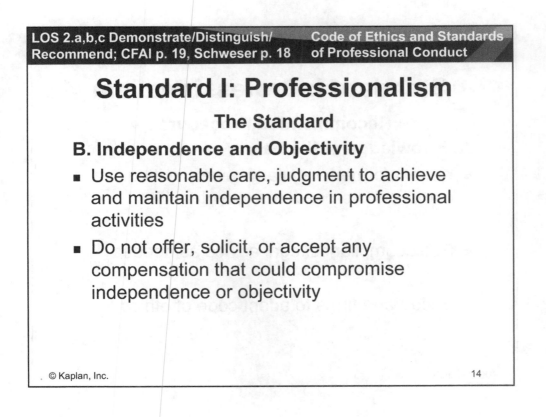

 13

LOS 2.a,b,c Demonstrate/Distinguish/ Recommend; CFAI p. 19, Schweser p. 18

Code of Ethics and Standards of Professional Conduct

Standard I: Professionalism

The Standard

B. Independence and Objectivity

- Use reasonable care, judgment to achieve and maintain independence in professional activities
- Do not offer, solicit, or accept any compensation that could compromise independence or objectivity

 14

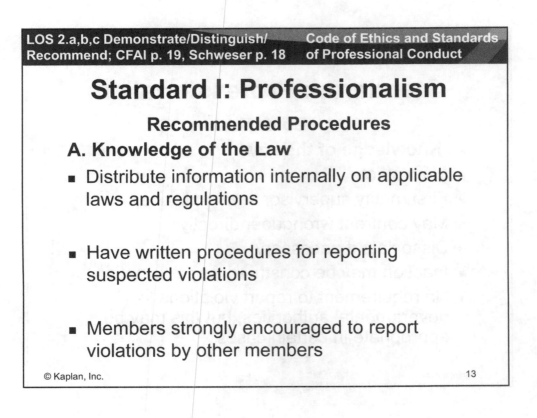

LOS 2.a,b,c Demonstrate/Distinguish/ Recommend; CFAI p. 19, Schweser p. 18

Code of Ethics and Standards of Professional Conduct

Standard I: Professionalism

Guidance

B. Independence and Objectivity

- Modest gifts okay
- Distinguish between gifts from clients and gifts from entities trying to influence a member's behavior
- May accept gift from clients—disclose to employer—get permission if gift is for future performance

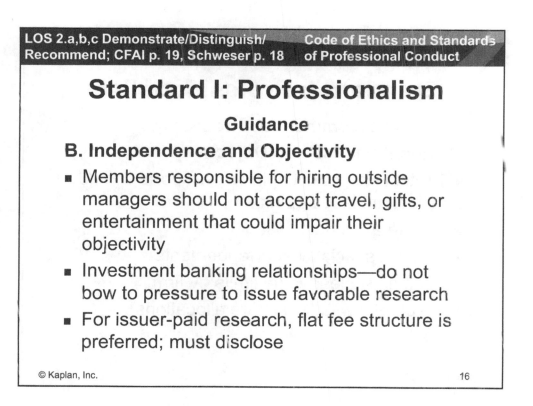

 15

LOS 2.a,b,c Demonstrate/Distinguish/ Recommend; CFAI p. 19, Schweser p. 18

Code of Ethics and Standards of Professional Conduct

Standard I: Professionalism

Guidance

B. Independence and Objectivity

- Members responsible for hiring outside managers should not accept travel, gifts, or entertainment that could impair their objectivity
- Investment banking relationships—do not bow to pressure to issue favorable research
- For issuer-paid research, flat fee structure is preferred; must disclose

 16

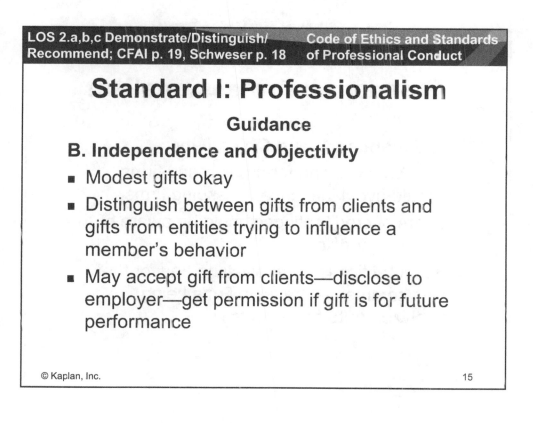

LOS 2.a,b,c Demonstrate/Distinguish/ Recommend; CFAI p. 19, Schweser p. 18

Code of Ethics and Standards of Professional Conduct

Standard I: Professionalism

Guidance

B. Independence and Objectivity

- Members working for credit rating firms should avoid influence by issuing firms
- Users of credit ratings should be aware of this potential conflict
- Best practice is for analysts to pay for their own commercial travel to firms being analyzed or to firm events

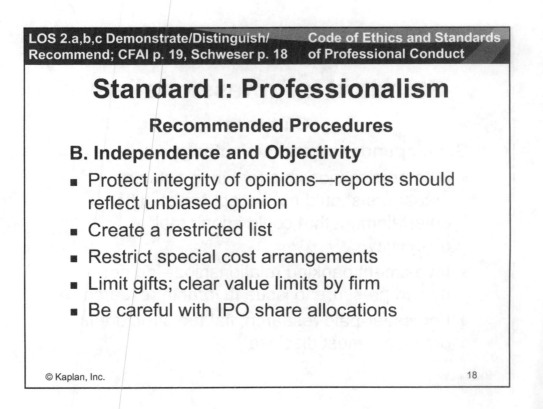

17

LOS 2.a,b,c Demonstrate/Distinguish/ Recommend; CFAI p. 19, Schweser p. 18

Code of Ethics and Standards of Professional Conduct

Standard I: Professionalism

Recommended Procedures

B. Independence and Objectivity

- Protect integrity of opinions—reports should reflect unbiased opinion
- Create a restricted list
- Restrict special cost arrangements
- Limit gifts; clear value limits by firm
- Be careful with IPO share allocations

18

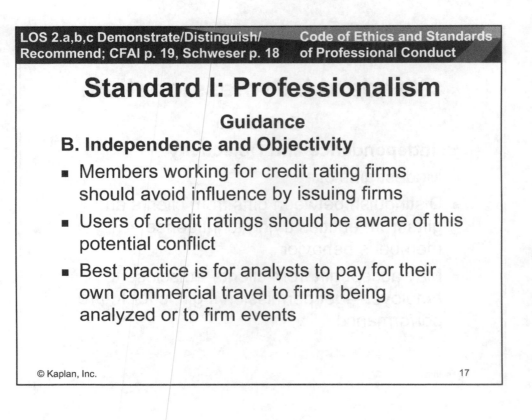

LOS 2.a,b,c Demonstrate/Distinguish/ Recommend; CFAI p. 19, Schweser p. 18

Code of Ethics and Standards of Professional Conduct

Standard I: Professionalism

The Standard

C. Misrepresentation

- Do not make misrepresentations relating to investment analysis, recommendations, actions, or other professional activities

LOS 2.a,b,c Demonstrate/Distinguish/ Recommend; CFAI p. 19, Schweser p. 18

Code of Ethics and Standards of Professional Conduct

Standard I: Professionalism

Guidance

C. Misrepresentation

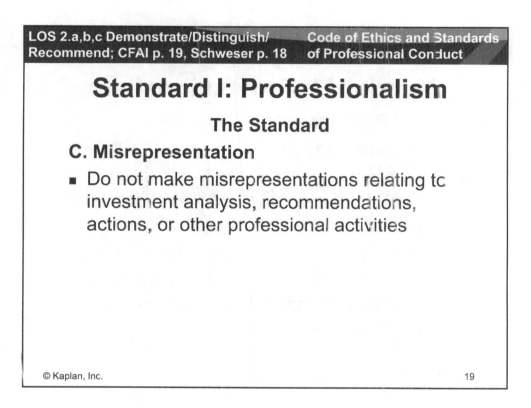

- Standard covers oral, written, or electronic communications
- Do not misrepresent qualifications, services of self or firm, or performance record, characteristics of an investment
- Do not guarantee a certain return
- No plagiarism—written, oral, or electronic communications

LOS 2.a,b,c Demonstrate/Distinguish/ Recommend; CFAI p. 19, Schweser p. 18 | Code of Ethics and Standards of Professional Conduct

Standard I: Professionalism

Recommended Procedures

C. Misrepresentation

- Firms can assist employees by providing written list of the firm's available services and a description of the firm's qualifications
- Maintain records of materials used to prepare research reports, and quote source, except for "recognized financial and statistical reporting services"

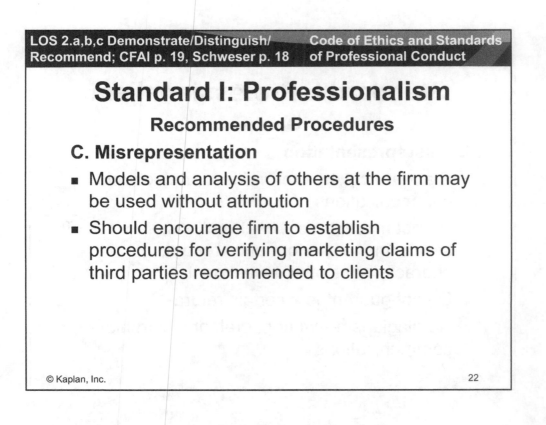

 21

LOS 2.a,b,c Demonstrate/Distinguish/ Recommend; CFAI p. 19, Schweser p. 18 | Code of Ethics and Standards of Professional Conduct

Standard I: Professionalism

Recommended Procedures

C. Misrepresentation

- Models and analysis of others at the firm may be used without attribution
- Should encourage firm to establish procedures for verifying marketing claims of third parties recommended to clients

 22

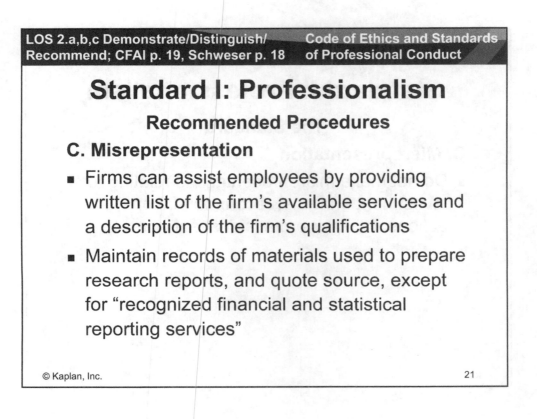

LOS 2.a,b,c Demonstrate/Distinguish/ Recommend; CFAI p. 19, Schweser p. 18

Code of Ethics and Standards of Professional Conduct

Standard I: Professionalism

The Standard

D. Misconduct

- Do not engage in any professional conduct involving dishonesty, fraud, deceit, or commit any act that reflects adversely on professional reputation, integrity, or competence

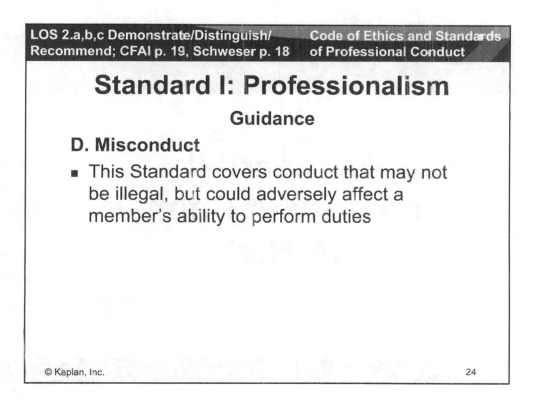

 23

LOS 2.a,b,c Demonstrate/Distinguish/ Recommend; CFAI p. 19, Schweser p. 18

Code of Ethics and Standards of Professional Conduct

Standard I: Professionalism

Guidance

D. Misconduct

- This Standard covers conduct that may not be illegal, but could adversely affect a member's ability to perform duties

 24

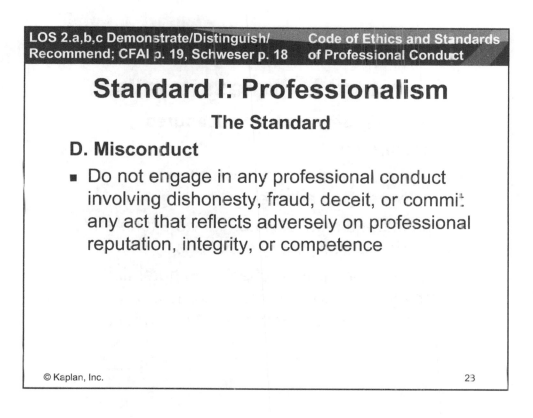

LOS 2.a,b,c Demonstrate/Distinguish/ Recommend; CFAI p. 19, Schweser p. 18 — Code of Ethics and Standards of Professional Conduct

Standard I: Professionalism

Recommended Procedures

D. Misconduct

- Adopt a code of ethics to which every employee must adhere
- Disseminate a list of potential violations and associated disciplinary sanctions
- Conduct background checks on potential employees—look for good character and eligibility to work in the investment industry

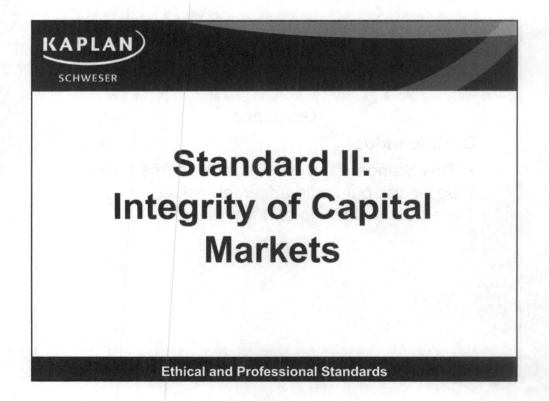

 25

Standard II: Integrity of Capital Markets

Ethical and Professional Standards

LOS 2.a,b,c Demonstrate/Distinguish/ Recommend; CFAI p. 19, Schweser p. 18 — Code of Ethics and Standards of Professional Conduct

Standard II: Integrity of Capital Markets

The Standard

A. Material Nonpublic Information

- Members in possession of nonpublic information that could affect an investment's value must not act or cause someone else to act on the information

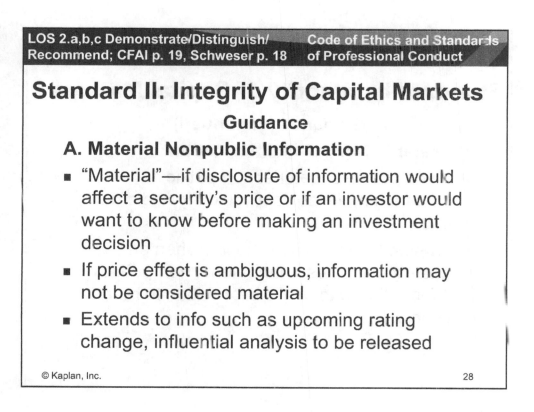

 27

LOS 2.a,b,c Demonstrate/Distinguish/ Recommend; CFAI p. 19, Schweser p. 18 — Code of Ethics and Standards of Professional Conduct

Standard II: Integrity of Capital Markets

Guidance

A. Material Nonpublic Information

- "Material"—if disclosure of information would affect a security's price or if an investor would want to know before making an investment decision
- If price effect is ambiguous, information may not be considered material
- Extends to info such as upcoming rating change, influential analysis to be released

 28

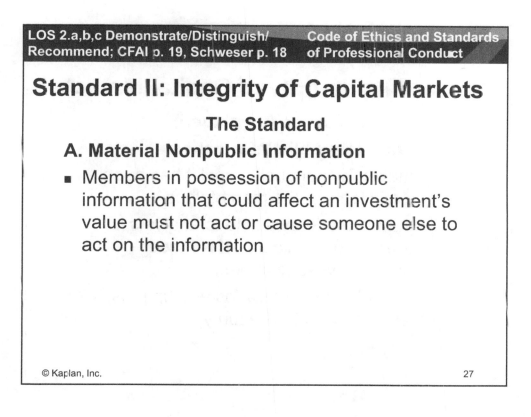

LOS 2.a,b,c Demonstrate/Distinguish/ Recommend; CFAI p. 19, Schweser p. 18 | Code of Ethics and Standards of Professional Conduct

Standard II: Integrity of Capital Markets

Guidance (continued)

A. Material Nonpublic Information

- Information is "nonpublic" until it has been made available to the marketplace
- Information made available to analysts is considered nonpublic until it is made available to investors in general
- "Act" includes related swaps and options, mutual funds with the security

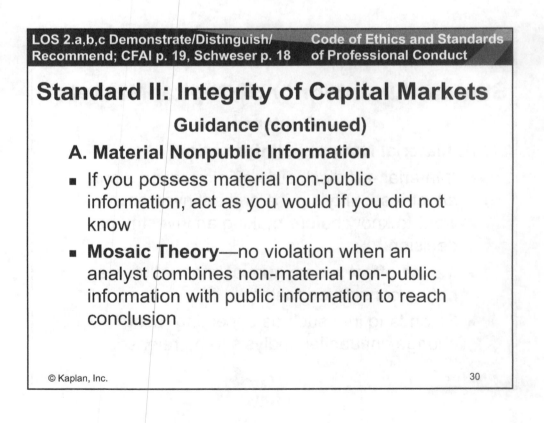

 29

LOS 2.a,b,c Demonstrate/Distinguish/ Recommend; CFAI p. 19, Schweser p. 18 | Code of Ethics and Standards of Professional Conduct

Standard II: Integrity of Capital Markets

Guidance (continued)

A. Material Nonpublic Information

- If you possess material non-public information, act as you would if you did not know
- **Mosaic Theory**—no violation when an analyst combines non-material non-public information with public information to reach conclusion

 30

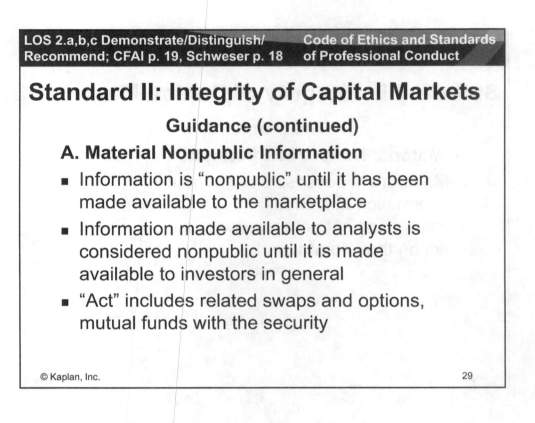

LOS 2.a,b,c Demonstrate/Distinguish/ Recommend; CFAI p. 19, Schweser p. 18

Code of Ethics and Standards of Professional Conduct

Standard II: Integrity of Capital Markets

Recommended Procedures

A. Material Nonpublic Information

- Information barrier or "firewall" is recommended to control interdepartmental communications
- Information barrier includes use of restricted list
- Review employee trades

 31

LOS 2.a,b,c Demonstrate/Distinguish/ Recommend; CFAI p. 19, Schweser p. 18

Code of Ethics and Standards of Professional Conduct

Standard II: Integrity of Capital Markets

Recommended Procedures

A. Material Nonpublic Information

- Increase review/restrict proprietary trading while firm is in possession of material nonpublic information

 32

LOS 2.a,b,c Demonstrate/Distinguish/ Recommend; CFAI p. 19, Schweser p. 18 — Code of Ethics and Standards of Professional Conduct

Standard II: Integrity of Capital Markets

The Standard

B. Market Manipulation

- Do not engage in practices that distort prices or artificially inflate trading volume with **intent to mislead** market participants

 33

LOS 2.a,b,c Demonstrate/Distinguish/ Recommend; CFAI p. 19, Schweser p. 18 — Code of Ethics and Standards of Professional Conduct

Standard II: Integrity of Capital Markets

Guidance

B. Market Manipulation

- Do not engage in transaction-based manipulation—give false impression of activity/price movement; gain dominant position in an asset to manipulate price of the asset or a related derivative
- Do not distribute false, misleading information

 34

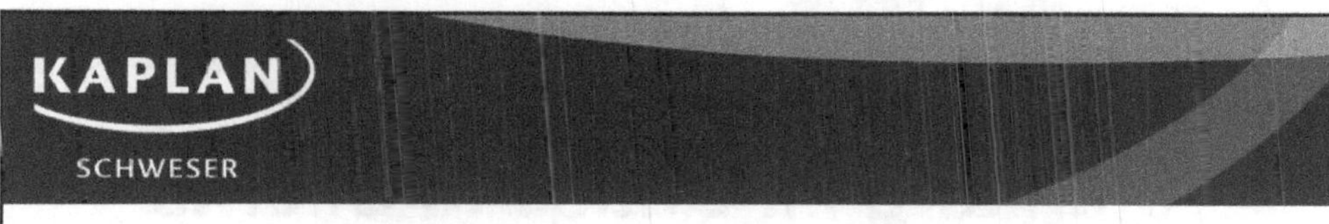

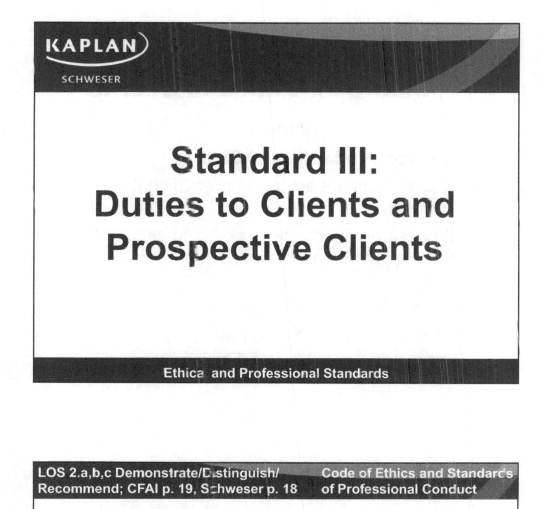

Standard III: Duties to Clients and Prospective Clients

Ethics and Professional Standards

LOS 2.a,b,c Demonstrate/Distinguish/Recommend; CFAI p. 19, Schweser p. 18

Code of Ethics and Standards of Professional Conduct

Standard III: Duties to Clients

The Standard

A. Loyalty, Prudence, and Care

- Duty of loyalty to clients—act with reasonable care and exercise prudent judgment
- Act for benefit of clients and place their interests before employer's or own interests
- Determine and comply with any applicable fiduciary duty

LOS 2.a,b,c Demonstrate/Distinguish/ Recommend; CFAI p. 19, Schweser p. 18 — Code of Ethics and Standards of Professional Conduct

Standard III: Duties to Clients

Guidance

A. Loyalty, Prudence, and Care

- Take investment actions in client's best interests
- Exercise prudence, care, skill, and diligence that a person familiar with such matters would use
- Follow applicable fiduciary duty
- "Client" may be investing public

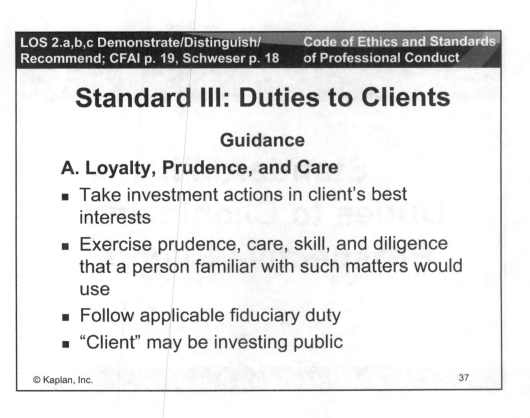

 37

LOS 2.a,b,c Demonstrate/Distinguish/ Recommend; CFAI p. 19, Schweser p. 18 — Code of Ethics and Standards of Professional Conduct

Standard III: Duties to Clients

Guidance (continued)

A. Loyalty, Prudence, and Care

- Manage pools of client assets according to terms of governing documents
- Make investment decisions in context of total portfolio
- Vote proxies responsibly and disclose proxy voting policies to clients
- "Soft dollars" must benefit client

 38

LOS 2.a,b,c Demonstrate/Distinguish/ Recommend; CFAI p. 19, Schweser p. 18 — Code of Ethics and Standards of Professional Conduct

Standard III: Duties to Clients

Recommended Procedures

A. Loyalty, Prudence, and Care

- Follow rules and laws
- Establish client investment objectives
- Diversify
- Deal fairly with clients—investment actions
- Disclose all possible conflicts
- Vote proxies in best interest of clients and ultimate beneficiaries

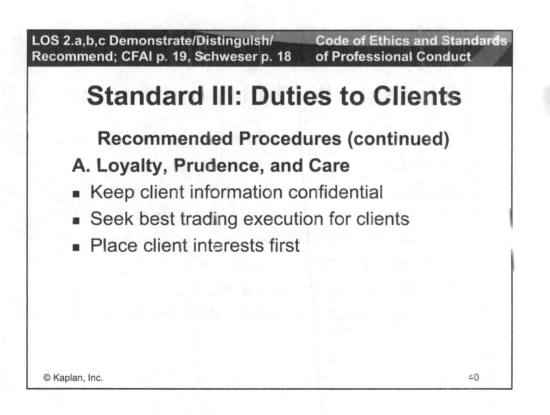

 39

LOS 2.a,b,c Demonstrate/Distinguish/ Recommend; CFAI p. 19, Schweser p. 18 — Code of Ethics and Standards of Professional Conduct

Standard III: Duties to Clients

Recommended Procedures (continued)

A. Loyalty, Prudence, and Care

- Keep client information confidential
- Seek best trading execution for clients
- Place client interests first

 40

LOS 2.a,b,c Demonstrate/Distinguish/ Recommend; CFAI p. 19, Schweser p. 18 — Code of Ethics and Standards of Professional Conduct

Standard III: Duties to Clients

The Standard

B. Fair Dealing

- Deal fairly and objectively with all clients when:
  - Providing investment analysis
  - Making investment recommendations
  - Taking investment action
  - Engaging in other professional activities

 41

LOS 2.a,b,c Demonstrate/Distinguish/ Recommend; CFAI p. 19, Schweser p. 18 — Code of Ethics and Standards of Professional Conduct

Standard III: Duties to Clients

Guidance

B. Fair Dealing

- No discrimination against any clients when disseminating investment recommendations or taking investment action
- *Fair* does not mean *equal*
- Different levels of service are okay as long as disclosed and do not disadvantage any clients

 42

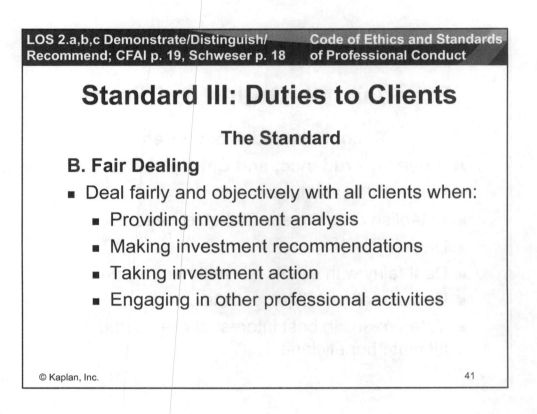

LOS 2.a,b,c Demonstrate/Distinguish/ Recommend; CFAI p. 19, Schweser p. 18 — Code of Ethics and Standards of Professional Conduct

Standard III: Duties to Clients

Guidance (continued)

B. Fair Dealing

- Investment recommendations:
  - All clients must have fair chance to act on every recommendation
  - If client is unaware of recommendation change, advise before accepting trade order

 43

LOS 2.a,b,c Demonstrate/Distinguish/ Recommend; CFAI p. 19, Schweser p. 18 — Code of Ethics and Standards of Professional Conduct

Standard III: Duties to Clients

Guidance (continued)

B. Fair Dealing

- Investment actions:
  - Treat all clients fairly—consider investment objectives and circumstances
  - Disclose written allocation procedures
  - Do not disadvantage any clients when distributing "hot" issues

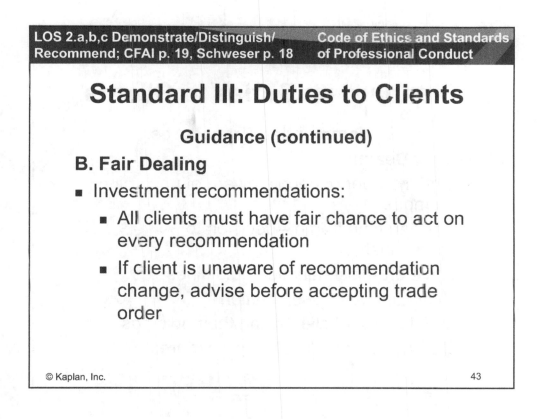

 44

LOS 2.a,b,c Demonstrate/Distinguish/ Recommend; CFAI p. 19, Schweser p. 18

Code of Ethics and Standards of Professional Conduct

Standard III: Duties to Clients

Recommended Procedures

B. Fair Dealing

- Limit number of people aware of upcoming changes
- Shorten time frame—decision to dissemination
- Have pre-dissemination guidelines
- Simultaneous dissemination
- Maintain list of clients and their holdings
- Disclose trade allocation procedures

45

LOS 2.a,b,c Demonstrate/Distinguish/ Recommend; CFAI p. 19, Schweser p. 18

Code of Ethics and Standards of Professional Conduct

Standard III: Duties to Clients

Recommended Procedures (continued)

B. Fair Dealing

- Review accounts regularly to ensure fair client treatment
- If firm offers different levels of service, disclose this fact to all clients
- Deviations from strict pro rata allocation of IPO is sometimes okay (e.g., minimum block sizes)

46

LOS 2.a,b,c Demonstrate/Distinguish/ Recommend; CFAI p. 19, Schweser p. 18 | Code of Ethics and Standards of Professional Conduct

Standard III: Duties to Clients

The Standard

C. Suitability

- When in advisory relationship with a client:
  - Make reasonable inquiry as to client's investment experience, risk/return objectives, financial constraints prior to making any recommendation, or taking investment action
  - Update information regularly

 47

LOS 2.a,b,c Demonstrate/Distinguish/ Recommend; CFAI p. 19, Schweser p. 18 | Code of Ethics and Standards of Professional Conduct

Standard III: Duties to Clients

The Standard (continued)

C. Suitability

- When in advisory relationship with client:
  - Ensure investment is suitable to client's situation and consistent with written objectives before recommending an investment or taking investment action
  - Look at suitability in a portfolio context

 48

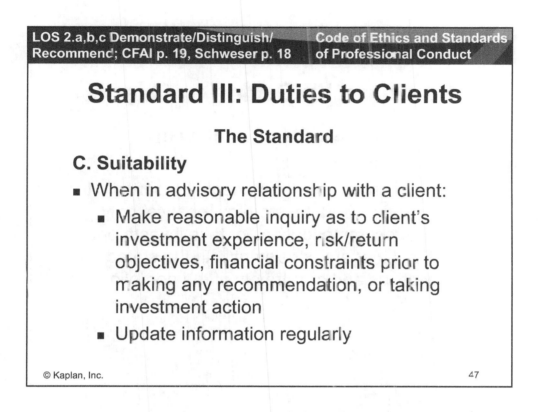

LOS 2.a,b,c Demonstrate/Distinguish/ Recommend; CFAI p. 19, Schweser p. 18

Code of Ethics and Standards of Professional Conduct

Standard III: Duties to Clients

The Standard (continued)

C. Suitability

- When responsible for managing a portfolio to a specific mandate, strategy, or style, only make recommendations or take investment actions that are consistent with the stated objectives and constraints of the portfolio

49

LOS 2.a,b,c Demonstrate/Distinguish/ Recommend; CFAI p. 19, Schweser p. 18

Code of Ethics and Standards of Professional Conduct

Standard III: Duties to Clients

Guidance

C. Suitability

- When in advisory relationship, gather client information at the outset and prepare IPS
- Update IPS at least annually
- Consider whether leverage (derivatives) is suitable for client
- If managing a fund to an index or other mandate, invest according to mandate

50

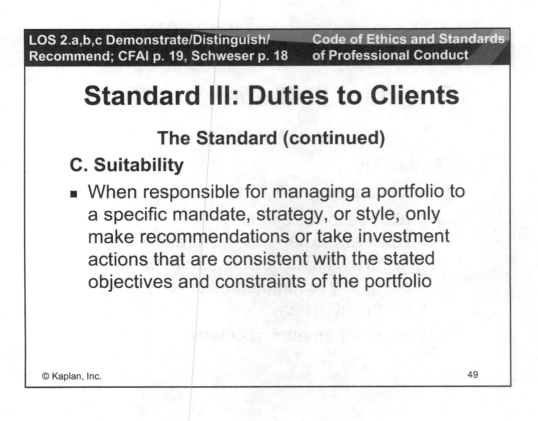

LOS 2.a,b,c Demonstrate/Distinguish/ Recommend; CFAI p. 19, Schweser p. 18 | Code of Ethics and Standards of Professional Conduct

Standard III: Duties to Clients

Recommended Procedures

C. Suitability

- When formulating IPS for client, know the client's:
  - Return objectives
  - Risk tolerance

 51

LOS 2.a,b,c Demonstrate/Distinguish/ Recommend; CFAI p. 19, Schweser p. 18 | Code of Ethics and Standards of Professional Conduct

Standard III: Duties to Clients

Recommended Procedures (continued)

C. Suitability

- Determine the client's constraints:
  - Liquidity needs
  - Expected cash flows, investable funds
  - Time horizon, tax considerations
  - Regulatory/legal constraints
  - Unique circumstances/needs

 52

LOS 2.a,b,c Demonstrate/Distinguish/ Recommend; CFAI p. 19, Schweser p. 18 | Code of Ethics and Standards of Professional Conduct

Standard III: Duties to Clients

The Standard

D. Performance Presentation

- When communicating investment performance information, make reasonable efforts to ensure that it is fair, accurate, and complete
- Can make brief presentation, note limited nature, and make detailed information available on request

 53

LOS 2.a,b,c Demonstrate/Distinguish/ Recommend; CFAI p. 19, Schweser p. 18 | Code of Ethics and Standards of Professional Conduct

Standard III: Duties to Clients

Guidance

D. Performance Presentation

- Do not misstate performance or mislead clients about investment performance
- Do not misrepresent past performance
- Provide fair and complete performance information
- Do not state or imply ability to achieve returns similar to those achieved in the past

 54

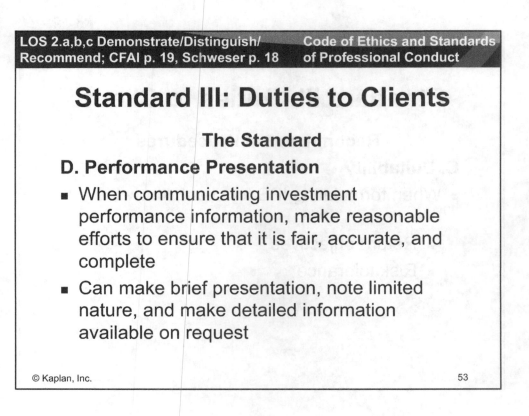

LOS 2.a,b,c Demonstrate/Distinguish/ Recommend; CFAI p. 19, Schweser p. 18 — Code of Ethics and Standards of Professional Conduct

Standard III: Duties to Clients

Recommended Procedures

D. Performance Presentation

- Consider audience sophistication when presenting performance
- Use performance of the weighted composite of similar portfolios
- Include terminated accounts as part of historical performance
- Make all disclosures and maintain records

 55

LOS 2.a,b,c Demonstrate/Distinguish/ Recommend; CFAI p. 19, Schweser p. 18 — Code of Ethics and Standards of Professional Conduct

Standard III: Duties to Clients

The Standard

E. Preservation of Confidentiality

- Keep current and prospective client information confidential, unless:
  - Illegal activities are suspected
  - Disclosure is required by law
  - Client or prospect allows disclosure of the information

 56

LOS 2.a,b,c Demonstrate/Distinguish/ Recommend; CFAI p. 19, Schweser p. 18

Code of Ethics and Standards of Professional Conduct

Standard III: Duties to Clients

Guidance

E. Preservation of Confidentiality

- In some cases it may be required by law to report activities to relevant authorities
- This Standard extends to former clients
- Exception: May provide confidential information to CFA Institute for an investigation under Professional Conduct Program

 57

LOS 2.a,b,c Demonstrate/Distinguish/ Recommend; CFAI p. 19, Schweser p. 18

Code of Ethics and Standards of Professional Conduct

Standard III: Duties to Clients

Recommended Procedures

E. Preservation of Confidentiality

- Avoid discussing any information received from a client except to colleagues working on the same project
- Follow firm's electronic data storage procedures; recommend adoption of procedures if none exist

 58

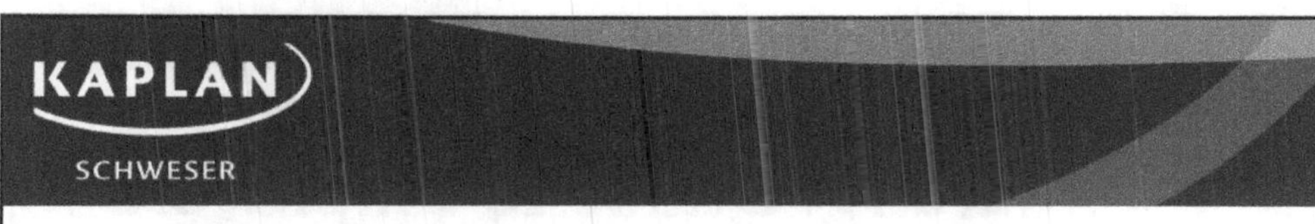

Standard IV: Duties to Employers

Ethical and Professional Standards

LOS 2.a,b,c Demonstrate/Distinguish/ Recommend; CFAI p. 19, Schweser p. 18

Code of Ethics and Standards of Professional Conduct

Standard IV: Duties to Employers

The Standard

A. Loyalty

- On matters related to employment, act for benefit of employer and do not deprive employer of the advantage of skills/abilities, divulge confidential information, or otherwise cause harm to employer

 60

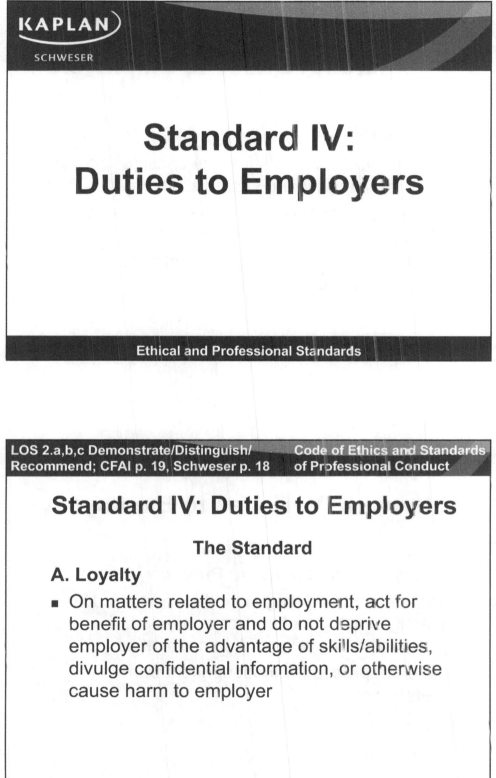

LOS 2.a,b,c Demonstrate/Distinguish/ Recommend; CFAI p. 19, Schweser p. 18 | Code of Ethics and Standards of Professional Conduct

Standard IV: Duties to Employers

Guidance

A. Loyalty

- Place client interests first but consider effects on firm integrity and sustainability
- Members encouraged to give employer a copy of the Code and Standards
- No incentive or compensation structure that encourages unethical behavior

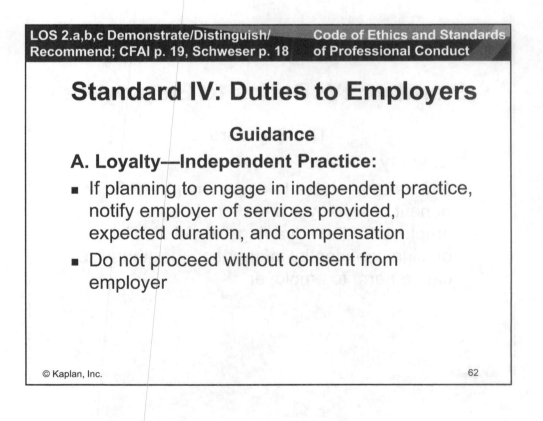

 61

LOS 2.a,b,c Demonstrate/Distinguish/ Recommend; CFAI p. 19, Schweser p. 18 | Code of Ethics and Standards of Professional Conduct

Standard IV: Duties to Employers

Guidance

A. Loyalty—Independent Practice:

- If planning to engage in independent practice, notify employer of services provided, expected duration, and compensation
- Do not proceed without consent from employer

 62

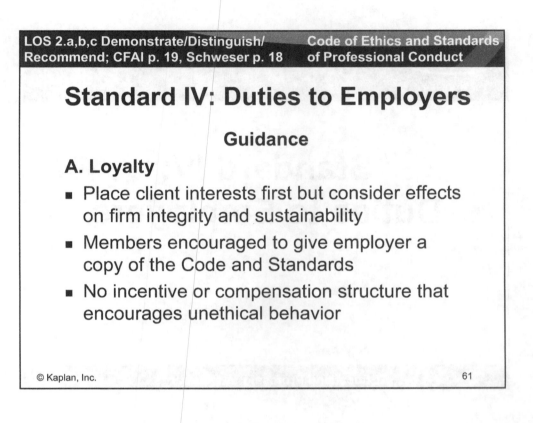

LOS 2.a,b,c Demonstrate/Distinguish/ Recommend; CFAI p. 19, Schweser p. 18 | Code of Ethics and Standards of Professional Conduct

Standard IV: Duties to Employers

Guidance (continued)

A. Loyalty—Leaving an Employer:

- Act in best interest of employer until resignation is effective
- Employer records on any medium (e.g., cell phone, PDA, home computer) are property of the firm
- Simple knowledge of names of former clients is okay; don't solicit prior to leaving
- No prohibition on use of experience or knowledge gained at former employer

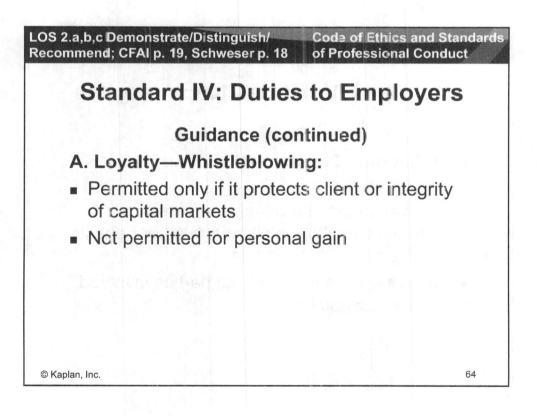

 63

LOS 2.a,b,c Demonstrate/Distinguish/ Recommend; CFAI p. 19, Schweser p. 18 | Code of Ethics and Standards of Professional Conduct

Standard IV: Duties to Employers

Guidance (continued)

A. Loyalty—Whistleblowing:

- Permitted only if it protects client or integrity of capital markets
- Not permitted for personal gain

 64

LOS 2.a,b,c Demonstrate/Distinguish/ Recommend; CFAI p. 19, Schweser p. 18

Code of Ethics and Standards of Professional Conduct

Standard IV: Duties to Employers

The Standard

B. Additional Compensation Arrangements

- Do not accept gifts, benefits, compensation, or consideration that competes with, or creates a conflict of interest with, employer's interest unless written consent is obtained from all parties involved

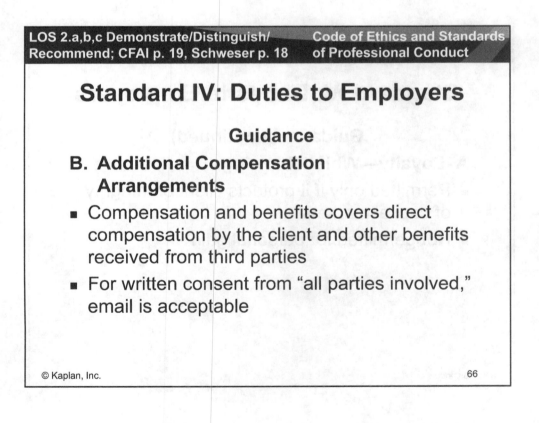

65

LOS 2.a,b,c Demonstrate/Distinguish/ Recommend; CFAI p. 19, Schweser p. 18

Code of Ethics and Standards of Professional Conduct

Standard IV: Duties to Employers

Guidance

B. Additional Compensation Arrangements

- Compensation and benefits covers direct compensation by the client and other benefits received from third parties
- For written consent from "all parties involved," email is acceptable

66

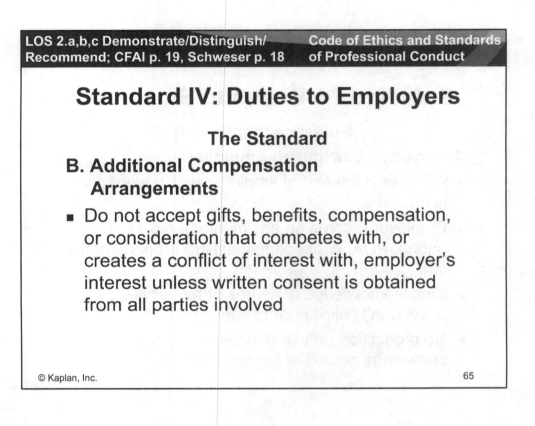

LOS 2.a,b,c Demonstrate/Distinguish/ Recommend; CFAI p. 19, Schweser p. 18

Code of Ethics and Standards of Professional Conduct

Standard IV: Duties to Employers

Recommended Procedures

B. Additional Compensation Arrangements

- Written report to employer with details of proposed compensation in addition to normal compensation and benefits
- Details of incentives verified by offering party
- Include nature of compensation, amount, and duration of agreement

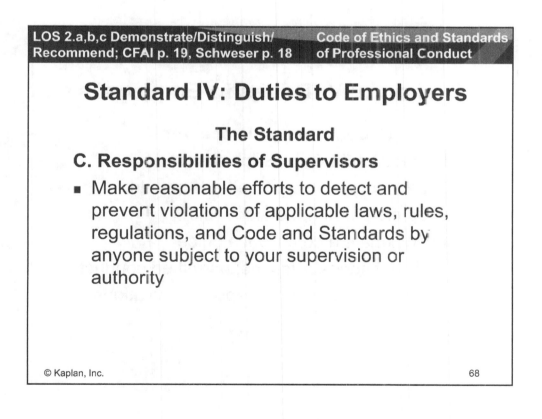

 67

LOS 2.a,b,c Demonstrate/Distinguish/ Recommend; CFAI p. 19, Schweser p. 18

Code of Ethics and Standards of Professional Conduct

Standard IV: Duties to Employers

The Standard

C. Responsibilities of Supervisors

- Make reasonable efforts to detect and prevent violations of applicable laws, rules, regulations, and Code and Standards by anyone subject to your supervision or authority

 68

LOS 2.a,b,c Demonstrate/Distinguish/ Recommend; CFAI p. 19, Schweser p. 18 | Code of Ethics and Standards of Professional Conduct

Standard IV: Duties to Employers

Guidance

C. Responsibilities of Supervisors

- Supervisors must take steps to prevent employees from violating laws, rules, regulations, or the Code and Standards
- Supervisors must make reasonable efforts to detect violations
- Should enforce non-investment rules as well (e.g., mandatory vacations)

 69

LOS 2.a,b,c Demonstrate/Distinguish/ Recommend; CFAI p. 19, Schweser p. 18 | Code of Ethics and Standards of Professional Conduct

Standard IV: Duties to Employers

Recommended Procedures

C. Responsibilities of Supervisors

Adequate compliance procedures should:

- Be clear and understandable
- Designate a compliance officer
- Have checks/balances; permitted conduct
- Have procedures for reporting violations

 70

LOS 2.a,b,c Demonstrate/Distinguish/ Recommend; CFAI p. 19, Schweser p. 18

Code of Ethics and Standards of Professional Conduct

Standard IV: Duties to Employers

Recommended Procedures (continued)

C. Responsibilities of Supervisors

- Supervisor and compliance officer should:
  - Distribute procedures; update periodically
  - Continually educate staff
  - Review employee actions
  - Promptly initiate procedures once a violation has occurred

 71

LOS 2.a,b,c Demonstrate/Distinguish/ Recommend; CFAI p. 19, Schweser p. 18

Code of Ethics and Standards of Professional Conduct

Standard IV: Duties to Employers

Recommended Procedures (continued)

C. Responsibilities of Supervisors

- Once a violation has occurred, a supervisor should:
  - Respond promptly
  - Conduct a thorough investigation
  - Place appropriate limitations on the wrongdoer until investigation is complete

 72

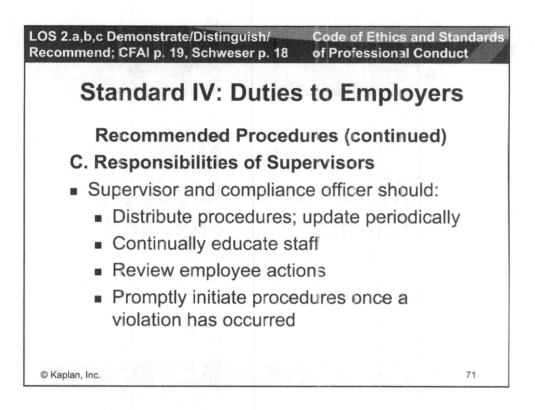

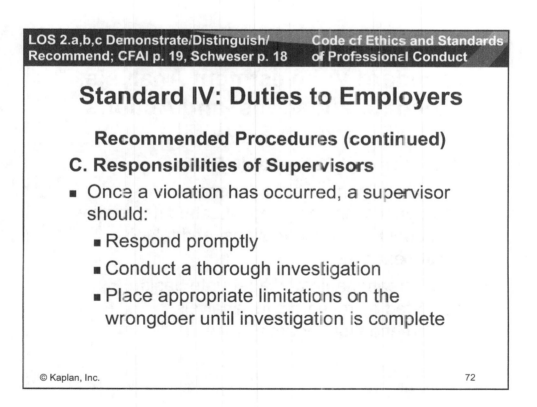

Standard V: Investment Analysis, Recommendations, and Action

Ethical and Professional Standards

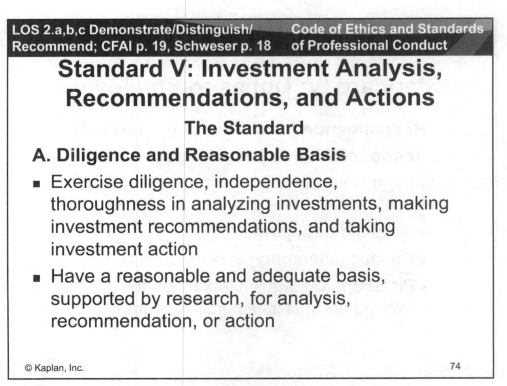

LOS 2.a,b,c Demonstrate/Distinguish/ Recommend; CFAI p. 19, Schweser p. 18

Code of Ethics and Standards of Professional Conduct

Standard V: Investment Analysis, Recommendations, and Actions

The Standard

A. Diligence and Reasonable Basis

- Exercise diligence, independence, thoroughness in analyzing investments, making investment recommendations, and taking investment action
- Have a reasonable and adequate basis, supported by research, for analysis, recommendation, or action

74

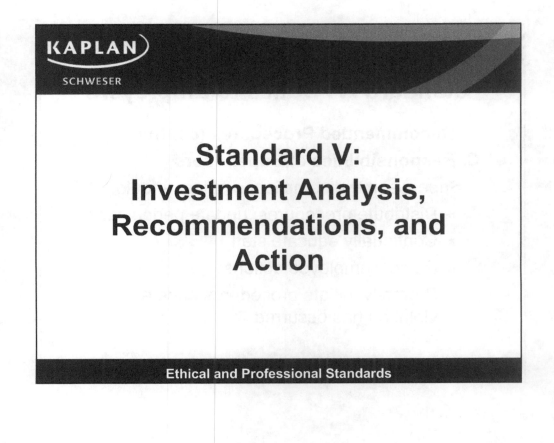

LOS 2.a,b,c Demonstrate/Distinguish/ Recommend; CFAI p. 19, Schweser p. 18 | Code of Ethics and Standards of Professional Conduct

Standard V: Investment Analysis, Recommendations, and Actions

Guidance

A. Diligence and Reasonable Basis

- Make reasonable efforts to cover all relevant issues when arriving at an investment recommendation
- Level of diligence will depend on product or service offered

 75

LOS 2.a,b,c Demonstrate/Distinguish/ Recommend; CFAI p. 19, Schweser p. 18 | Code of Ethics and Standards of Professional Conduct

Standard V: Investment Analysis, Recommendations, and Actions

Guidance (continued)

A. Diligence and Reasonable Basis

Using secondary or third-party research:

- Determine soundness of the research—review assumptions, rigor, timeliness, and independence of analysis
- Encourage firm to adopt policy of periodic review of quality of third-party research regarding assumptions, timeliness, rigor, objectivity, and independence

 76

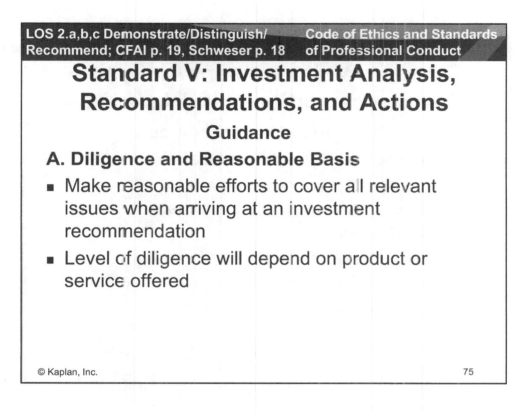

LOS 2.a,b,c Demonstrate/Distinguish/ Recommend; CFAI p. 19, Schweser p. 18 — Code of Ethics and Standards of Professional Conduct

Standard V: Investment Analysis, Recommendations, and Actions

Recommended Procedures

A. Diligence and Reasonable Basis

- Establish policy that research and recommendations should have reasonable and adequate basis
- Review/approve research reports and recommendations prior to external circulation

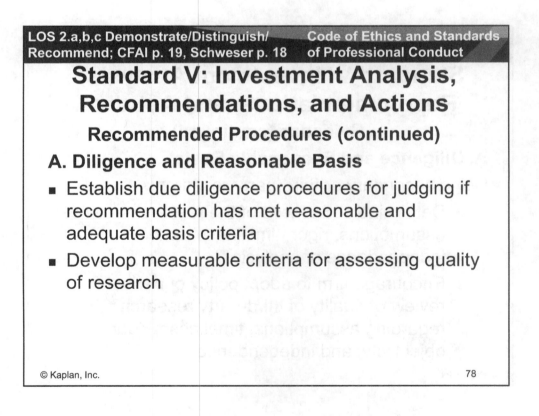

 77

LOS 2.a,b,c Demonstrate/Distinguish/ Recommend; CFAI p. 19, Schweser p. 18 — Code of Ethics and Standards of Professional Conduct

Standard V: Investment Analysis, Recommendations, and Actions

Recommended Procedures (continued)

A. Diligence and Reasonable Basis

- Establish due diligence procedures for judging if recommendation has met reasonable and adequate basis criteria
- Develop measurable criteria for assessing quality of research

 78

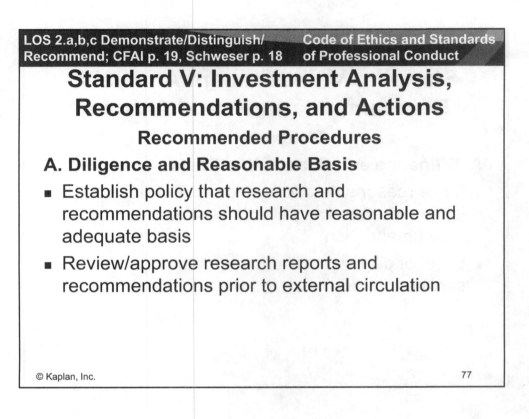

LOS 2.a,b,c Demonstrate/Distinguish/ Recommend; CFAI p. 19, Schweser p. 18 — Code of Ethics and Standards of Professional Conduct

Standard V: Investment Analysis, Recommendations, and Actions

Recommended Procedures (continued)

A. Diligence and Reasonable Basis

- Consider scenarios outside recent experience to assess downside risk of quantitative models
- Make sure firm has procedures to evaluate external advisers they use or promote, including how often to review

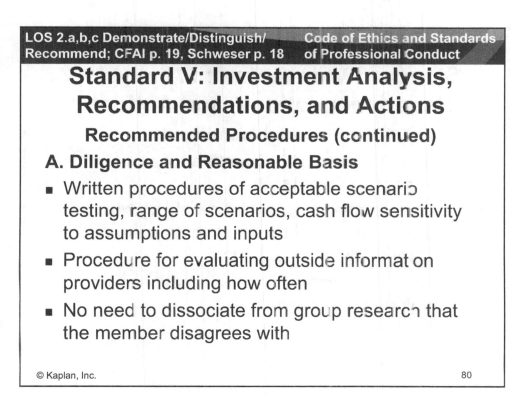

 79

LOS 2.a,b,c Demonstrate/Distinguish/ Recommend; CFAI p. 19, Schweser p. 18 — Code of Ethics and Standards of Professional Conduct

Standard V: Investment Analysis, Recommendations, and Actions

Recommended Procedures (continued)

A. Diligence and Reasonable Basis

- Written procedures of acceptable scenario testing, range of scenarios, cash flow sensitivity to assumptions and inputs
- Procedure for evaluating outside information providers including how often
- No need to dissociate from group research that the member disagrees with

 80

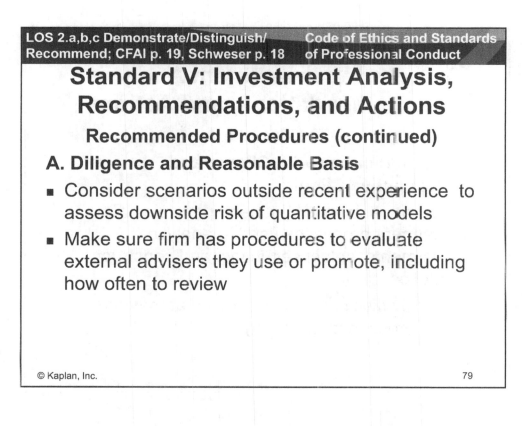

LOS 2.a,b,c Demonstrate/Distinguish/ Recommend; CFAI p. 19, Schweser p. 18

Code of Ethics and Standards of Professional Conduct

Standard V: Investment Analysis, Recommendations, and Actions

The Standard

B. Communication with Clients and Prospective Clients

- Disclose basic format/general principles of investment processes used to analyze investments, select securities, and construct portfolios
- Promptly disclose any changes that may affect those processes materially

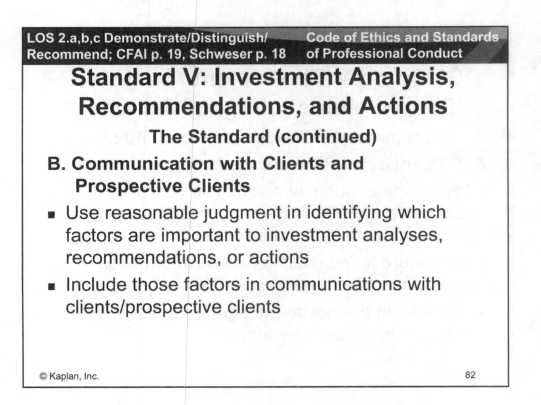

81

LOS 2.a,b,c Demonstrate/Distinguish/ Recommend; CFAI p. 19, Schweser p. 18

Code of Ethics and Standards of Professional Conduct

Standard V: Investment Analysis, Recommendations, and Actions

The Standard (continued)

B. Communication with Clients and Prospective Clients

- Use reasonable judgment in identifying which factors are important to investment analyses, recommendations, or actions
- Include those factors in communications with clients/prospective clients

82

LOS 2.a,b,c Demonstrate/Distinguish/ Recommend; CFAI p. 19, Schweser p. 18 — Code of Ethics and Standards of Professional Conduct

Standard V: Investment Analysis, Recommendations, and Actions

The Standard (continued)

B. Communication with Clients and Prospective Clients

- Distinguish between fact and opinion in presentation of investment analysis and investment recommendations
- Clearly communicate potential gains and losses on an investment

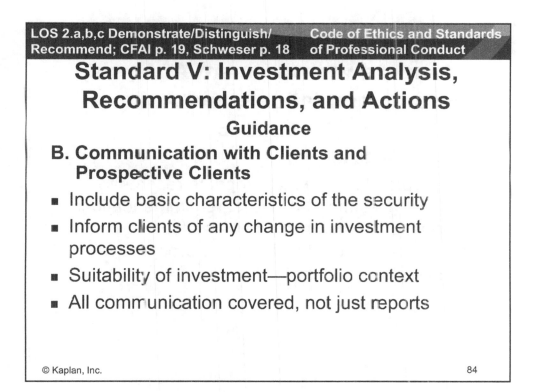

 83

LOS 2.a,b,c Demonstrate/Distinguish/ Recommend; CFAI p. 19, Schweser p. 18 — Code of Ethics and Standards of Professional Conduct

Standard V: Investment Analysis, Recommendations, and Actions

Guidance

B. Communication with Clients and Prospective Clients

- Include basic characteristics of the security
- Inform clients of any change in investment processes
- Suitability of investment—portfolio context
- All communication covered, not just reports

 84

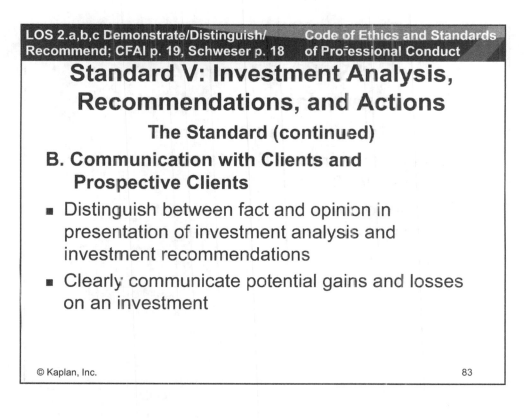

LOS 2.a,b,c Demonstrate/Distinguish/ Recommend; CFAI p. 19, Schweser p. 18 — Code of Ethics and Standards of Professional Conduct

Standard V: Investment Analysis, Recommendations, and Actions

Recommended Procedures

B. Communication with Clients and Prospective Clients

- The inclusion or exclusion of information depends on a case-by-case review
- Maintain records

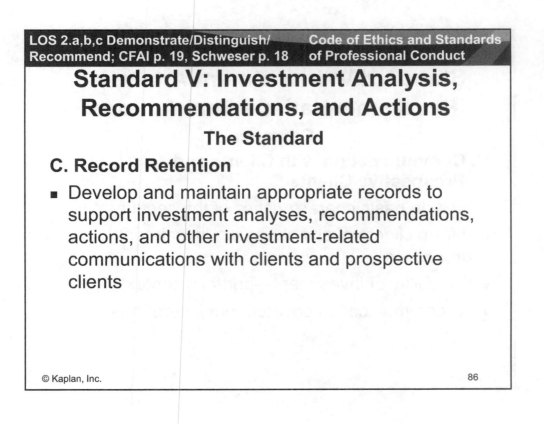

 85

LOS 2.a,b,c Demonstrate/Distinguish/ Recommend; CFAI p. 19, Schweser p. 18 — Code of Ethics and Standards of Professional Conduct

Standard V: Investment Analysis, Recommendations, and Actions

The Standard

C. Record Retention

- Develop and maintain appropriate records to support investment analyses, recommendations, actions, and other investment-related communications with clients and prospective clients

 86

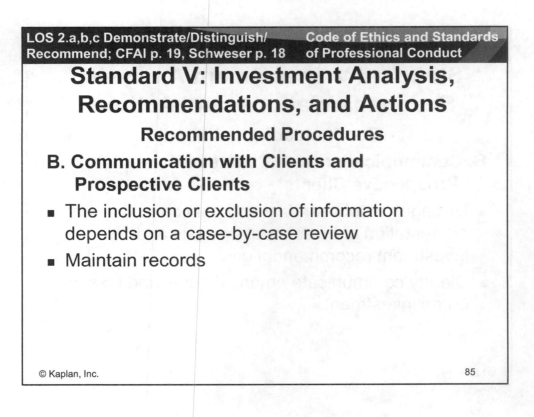

LOS 2.a,b,c Demonstrate/Distinguish/ Recommend; CFAI p. 19, Schweser p. 18

Code of Ethics and Standards of Professional Conduct

Standard V: Investment Analysis, Recommendations, and Actions

Guidance

C. Record Retention

- Maintain records to support research, and the rationale for conclusions and actions
- Records are firm's property and cannot be taken when member leaves without firm's consent
- If no regulatory requirement, CFA Institute recommends retention period of 7 years

 87

LOS 2.a,b,c Demonstrate/Distinguish/ Recommend; CFAI p. 19, Schweser p. 18

Code of Ethics and Standards of Professional Conduct

Standard V: Investment Analysis, Recommendations, and Actions

Recommended Procedures

C. Record Retention

- Responsibility to maintain records generally falls with the firm
- However, individuals must retain documents that support investment-related communications

 88

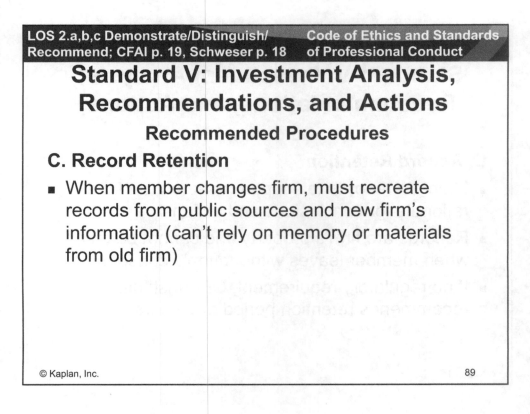

LOS 2.a,b,c Demonstrate/Distinguish/ Recommend; CFAI p. 19, Schweser p. 18 — Code of Ethics and Standards of Professional Conduct

Standard V: Investment Analysis, Recommendations, and Actions

Recommended Procedures

C. Record Retention

- When member changes firm, must recreate records from public sources and new firm's information (can't rely on memory or materials from old firm)

 89

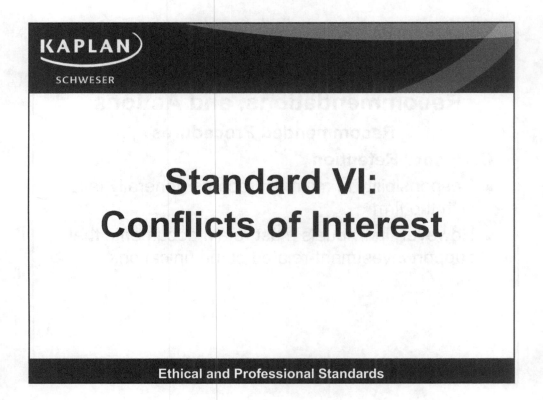

Standard VI: Conflicts of Interest

Ethical and Professional Standards

LOS 2.a,b,c Demonstrate/Distinguish/ Recommend; CFAI p. 19, Schweser p. 18

Code of Ethics and Standards of Professional Conduct

Standard VI: Conflicts of Interest

The Standard

A. Disclosure of Conflicts

- Make full, fair disclosure of all matters that could reasonably be expected to impair independence/objectivity, or interfere with duties to clients, prospects, or employer
- Ensure disclosures are prominent, delivered in plain language

 91

LOS 2.a,b,c Demonstrate/Distinguish/ Recommend; CFAI p. 19, Schweser p. 18

Code of Ethics and Standards of Professional Conduct

Standard VI: Conflicts of Interest

Guidance

A. Disclosure of Conflicts

- Disclose to clients:
  - All matters that could impair objectivity—allow clients to judge motives, biases
  - For example, between member or firm and issuer, investment banking relations, broker/dealer market-making activities, significant stock ownership, board service

 92

LOS 2.a,b,c Demonstrate/Distinguish/ Recommend; CFAI p. 19, Schweser p. 18 — Code of Ethics and Standards of Professional Conduct

Standard VI: Conflicts of Interest

Guidance (continued)

A. Disclosure of Conflicts

- Disclose to employers:
  - Conflicts of interest—ownership of stock analyzed/recommended, board participation, financial and other pressures that may influence decisions
  - Also covers conflicts that could be damaging to employer's business

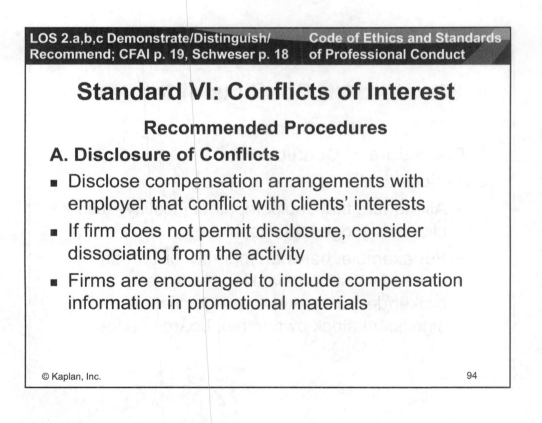

 93

LOS 2.a,b,c Demonstrate/Distinguish/ Recommend; CFAI p. 19, Schweser p. 18 — Code of Ethics and Standards of Professional Conduct

Standard VI: Conflicts of Interest

Recommended Procedures

A. Disclosure of Conflicts

- Disclose compensation arrangements with employer that conflict with clients' interests
- If firm does not permit disclosure, consider dissociating from the activity
- Firms are encouraged to include compensation information in promotional materials

 94

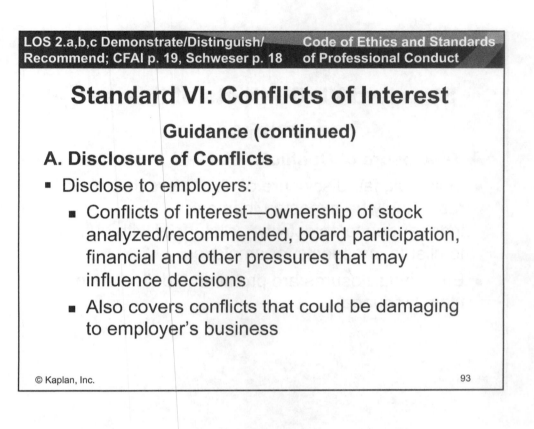

LOS 2.a,b,c Demonstrate/Distinguish/ Recommend; CFAI p. 19, Schweser p. 18 — Code of Ethics and Standards of Professional Conduct

Standard VI: Conflicts of Interest

The Standard

B. Priority of Transactions

- Investment transactions for clients and employers must have priority over transactions in which a member or candidate is the beneficial owner
- Do not use knowledge of pending trades for personal gain

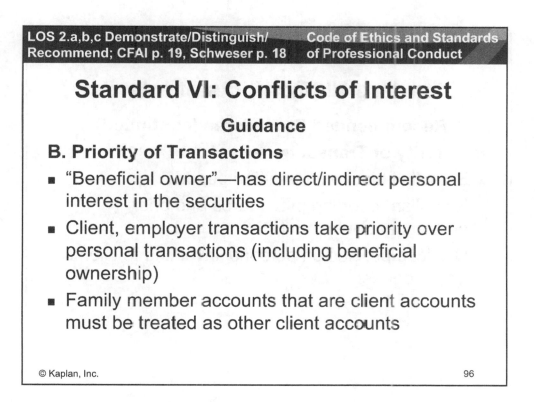

 95

LOS 2.a,b,c Demonstrate/Distinguish/ Recommend; CFAI p. 19, Schweser p. 18 — Code of Ethics and Standards of Professional Conduct

Standard VI: Conflicts of Interest

Guidance

B. Priority of Transactions

- "Beneficial owner"—has direct/indirect personal interest in the securities
- Client, employer transactions take priority over personal transactions (including beneficial ownership)
- Family member accounts that are client accounts must be treated as other client accounts

 96

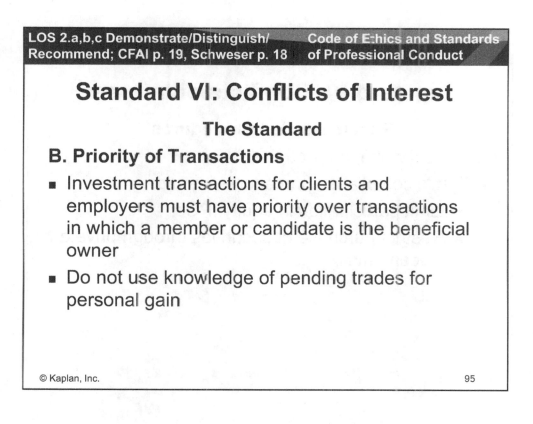

LOS 2.a,b,c Demonstrate/Distinguish/ Recommend; CFAI p. 19, Schweser p. 18 — Code of Ethics and Standards of Professional Conduct

Standard VI: Conflicts of Interest

Recommended Procedures

B. Priority of Transactions

- Firm's compliance procedures should:
  - Limit participation in equity IPOs
  - Restrict purchase of securities through private placements

© Kaplan, Inc. 97

LOS 2.a,b,c Demonstrate/Distinguish/ Recommend; CFAI p. 19, Schweser p. 18 — Code of Ethics and Standards of Professional Conduct

Standard VI: Conflicts of Interest

Recommended Procedures (continued)

B. Priority of Transactions

- Establish blackout/restricted periods
- Establish reporting procedures and prior clearance requirements
- Disclose policies on personal investing to clients, upon request

© Kaplan, Inc. 98

LOS 2.a,b,c Demonstrate/Distinguish/ Recommend; CFAI p. 19, Schweser p. 18

Code of Ethics and Standards of Professional Conduct

Standard VI: Conflicts of Interest

The Standard

C. Referral Fees

- Disclose to employer, clients, and prospective clients, as appropriate, any compensation, consideration, benefit received from, or paid to, others for the recommendation of products or services

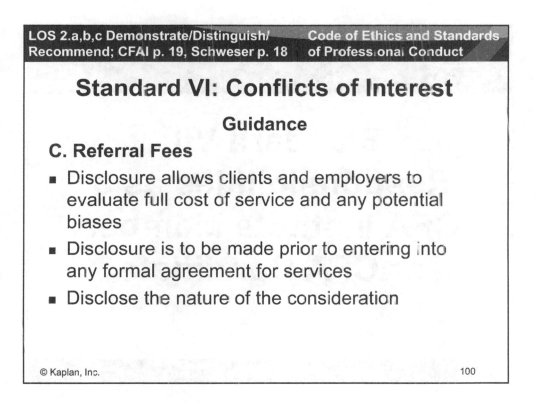

LOS 2.a,b,c Demonstrate/Distinguish/ Recommend; CFAI p. 19, Schweser p. 18

Code of Ethics and Standards of Professional Conduct

Standard VI: Conflicts of Interest

Guidance

C. Referral Fees

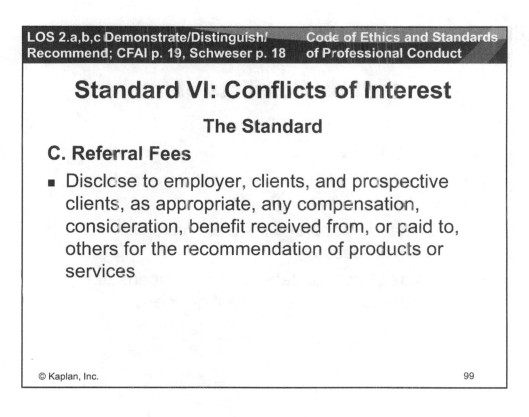

- Disclosure allows clients and employers to evaluate full cost of service and any potential biases
- Disclosure is to be made prior to entering into any formal agreement for services
- Disclose the nature of the consideration

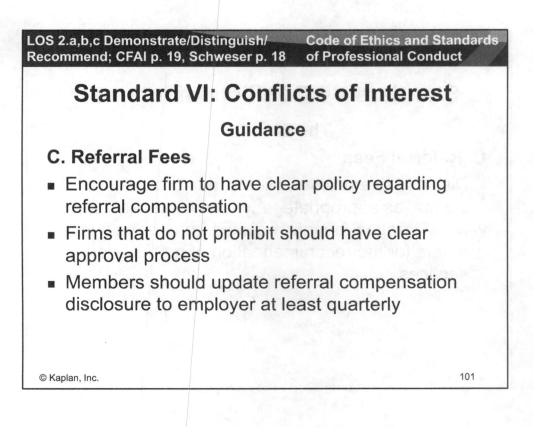

LOS 2.a,b,c Demonstrate/Distinguish/ Recommend; CFAI p. 19, Schweser p. 18 — Code of Ethics and Standards of Professional Conduct

Standard VI: Conflicts of Interest

Guidance

C. Referral Fees

- Encourage firm to have clear policy regarding referral compensation
- Firms that do not prohibit should have clear approval process
- Members should update referral compensation disclosure to employer at least quarterly

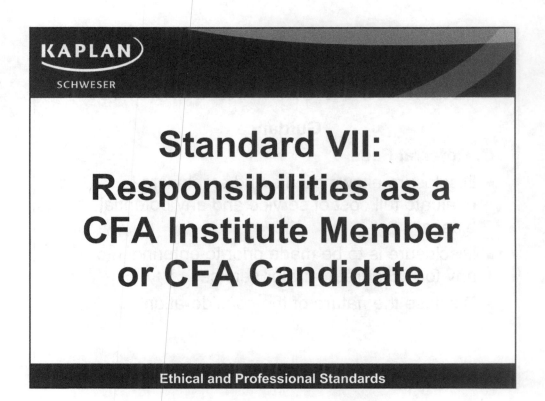

 101

Standard VII: Responsibilities as a CFA Institute Member or CFA Candidate

Ethical and Professional Standards

LOS 2.a,b,c Demonstrate/Distinguish/ Recommend; CFAI p. 19, Schweser p. 18 — Code of Ethics and Standards of Professional Conduct

Standard VII: Responsibilities as CFA Institute Member or Candidate

The Standard

A. Conduct as Members and Candidates in CFA Program

- Do not engage in any conduct that compromises the reputation or integrity of CFA Institute or CFA designation, or the integrity, validity, or security of the CFA examinations

 103

LOS 2.a,b,c Demonstrate/Distinguish/ Recommend; CFAI p. 19, Schweser p. 18 — Code of Ethics and Standards of Professional Conduct

Standard VII: Responsibilities as CFA Institute Member or Candidate

Guidance

A. Conduct as Members and Candidates in CFA Program

- Conduct includes:
  - Cheating on the exam
  - Disregarding rules and policies or security measures related to exam administration
  - Giving confidential information to candidates or public

 104

LOS 2.a,b,c Demonstrate/Distinguish/Recommend; CFAI p. 19, Schweser p. 18 — Code of Ethics and Standards of Professional Conduct

Standard VII: Responsibilities as CFA Institute Member or Candidate

Guidance

A. Conduct as Members and Candidates in CFA Program

- Don't disclose:
  - Formulas tested or not tested on exam
  - Specific question information
  - Topic emphasis on the exam or topics tested

 105

LOS 2.a,b,c Demonstrate/Distinguish/Recommend; CFAI p. 19, Schweser p. 18 — Code of Ethics and Standards of Professional Conduct

Standard VII: Responsibilities as CFA Institute Member or Candidate

Guidance (continued)

A. Conduct as Members and Candidates in CFA Program

- Conduct includes (continued):
  - Improper use of CFA designation to further personal and professional objectives
  - Misrepresenting the CFA Institute Professional Development Program or the Professional Conduct Statement

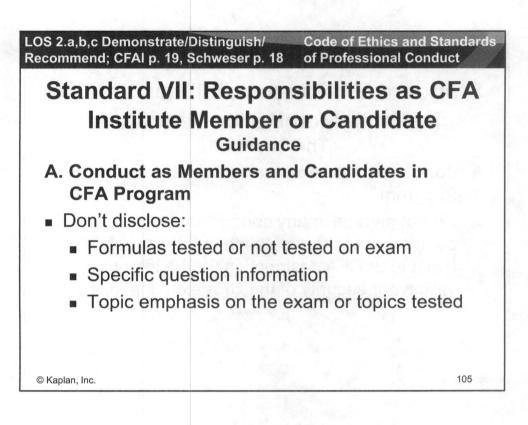

 106

LOS 2.a,b,c Demonstrate/Distinguish/ Recommend; CFAI p. 19, Schweser p. 18 — Code of Ethics and Standards of Professional Conduct

Standard VII: Responsibilities as CFA Institute Member or Candidate

The Standard

B. Reference to CFA Institute, the CFA Designation, and the CFA Program

- When referring to CFA Institute, membership, designation, or candidacy, do not misrepresent or exaggerate the meaning or implications of membership in CFA Institute, holding the CFA designation, or candidacy in the CFA program

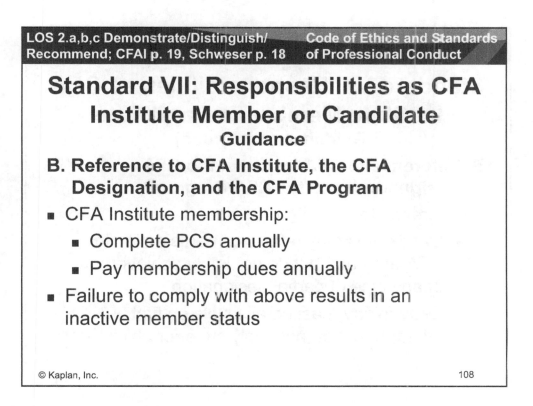

 107

LOS 2.a,b,c Demonstrate/Distinguish/ Recommend; CFAI p. 19, Schweser p. 18 — Code of Ethics and Standards of Professional Conduct

Standard VII: Responsibilities as CFA Institute Member or Candidate

Guidance

B. Reference to CFA Institute, the CFA Designation, and the CFA Program

- CFA Institute membership:
  - Complete PCS annually
  - Pay membership dues annually
- Failure to comply with above results in an inactive member status

 108

LOS 2.a,b,c Demonstrate/Distinguish/ Recommend; CFAI p. 19, Schweser p. 18 — Code of Ethics and Standards of Professional Conduct

Standard VII: Responsibilities as CFA Institute Member or Candidate

Guidance (continued)

B. Reference to CFA Institute, the CFA Designation, and the CFA Program

- Using the CFA designation:
  - Use the marks "Chartered Financial Analyst" or "CFA" in a manner that does not misrepresent or exaggerate the meaning or implications of holding the CFA designation

 109

LOS 2.a,b,c Demonstrate/Distinguish/ Recommend; CFAI p. 19, Schweser p. 18 — Code of Ethics and Standards of Professional Conduct

Standard VII: Responsibilities as CFA Institute Member or Candidate

Guidance (continued)

B. Reference to CFA Institute, the CFA Designation, and the CFA Program

- Reference to the CFA program:
  - Candidates may reference participation in CFA program, but do not imply achievement of any type of partial designation
  - Okay to say "passed all levels on first attempt," but do not imply superior ability

 110

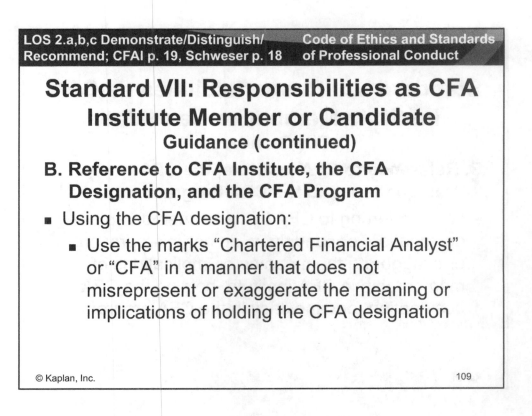

LOS 2.a,b,c Demonstrate/Distinguish/ Recommend; CFAI p. 19, Schweser p. 18 — Code of Ethics and Standards of Professional Conduct

Standard VII: Responsibilities as CFA Institute Member or Candidate

Guidance (continued)

B. Reference to CFA Institute, the CFA Designation, and the CFA Program

- Improper use of the CFA marks:
  - The "Chartered Financial Analyst" and "CFA" marks must always be used either after a charterholder's name or as adjectives, not as nouns

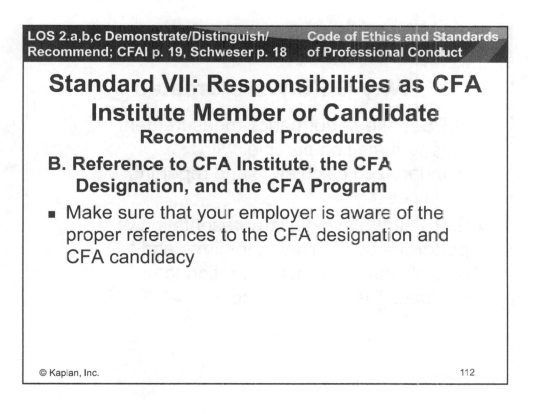

 111

LOS 2.a,b,c Demonstrate/Distinguish/ Recommend; CFAI p. 19, Schweser p. 18 — Code of Ethics and Standards of Professional Conduct

Standard VII: Responsibilities as CFA Institute Member or Candidate

Recommended Procedures

B. Reference to CFA Institute, the CFA Designation, and the CFA Program

- Make sure that your employer is aware of the proper references to the CFA designation and CFA candidacy

 112

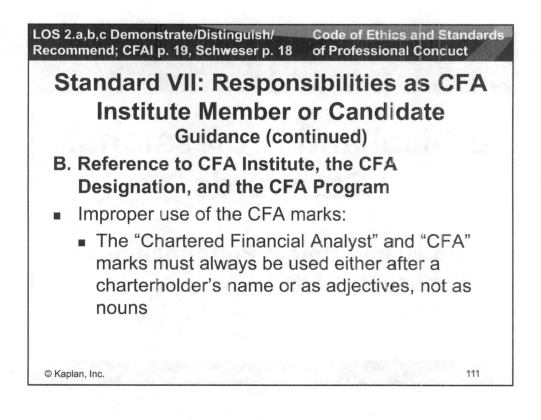

Ethical and Professional Standards

3. Global Investment Performance Standards (GIPS®)

Ethical and Professional Standards

LOS 3.a Explain
CFAI p. 163, Schweser p. 82

Global Investment Performance Standards

Why GIPS Were Created

- GIPS make performance measurement among firms comparable, with standardized calculation and reporting practices
- GIPS aim to avoid misrepresentation of performance of investment firms and to give clients relevant information to evaluate past performance

114

LOS 3.a Explain
CFAI p. 163, Schweser p. 82

Global Investment Performance Standards

Parties Affected by GIPS

- **Firms**—the GIPS apply to investment management firms
- **Prospective and current clients**—intended to serve prospective and current clients of investment management firms

 115

LOS 3.b Explain
CFAI p. 165, Schweser p. 83

Global Investment Performance Standards

Composites: Construction and Purpose

- **Composite**—grouping of individual discretionary portfolios with same investment strategy, objective, or mandate
- A composite must include all portfolios (current and past) that the firm has managed in accordance with this particular strategy
- Groupings must be pre-identified

 116

LOS 3.c Explain
CFAI p. 165, Schweser p. 83

Global Investment Performance Standards

Purpose of Verification

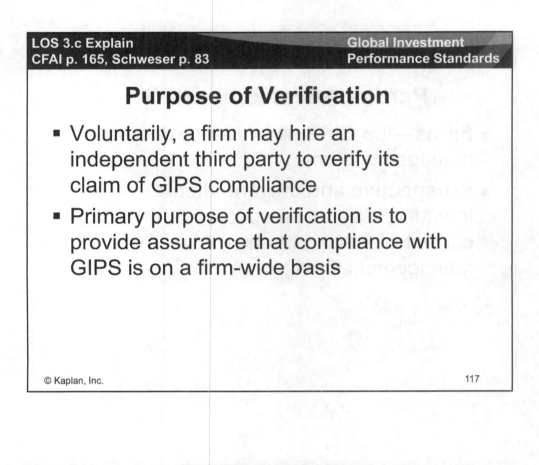

- Voluntarily, a firm may hire an independent third party to verify its claim of GIPS compliance
- Primary purpose of verification is to provide assurance that compliance with GIPS is on a firm-wide basis

117

LOS 3.c Explain
CFAI p. 165, Schweser p. 83

Global Investment Performance Standards

Requirements – Verification of Compliance

- Must be performed by a third party, on a firm-wide basis
- Verifier must attest that firm has complied with GIPS requirements for composite construction, and firm's processes/procedures are established to present performance in accordance with proper calculation methods, data, and format

118

LOS 4.a Describe
CFAI p. 170, Schweser p. 84

Global Investment Performance Standards

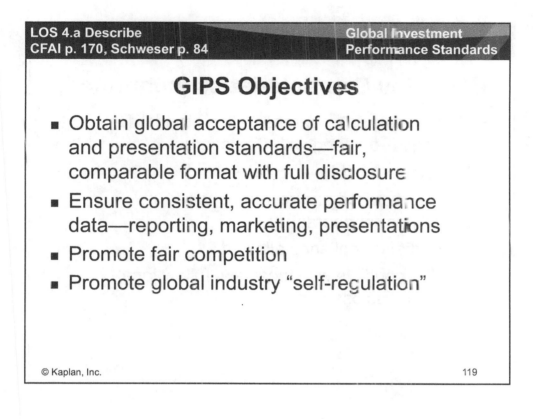

GIPS Objectives

- Obtain global acceptance of calculation and presentation standards—fair, comparable format with full disclosure
- Ensure consistent, accurate performance data—reporting, marketing, presentations
- Promote fair competition
- Promote global industry "self-regulation"

 119

LOS 4.a Describe
CFAI p. 170, Schweser p. 84

Global Investment Performance Standards

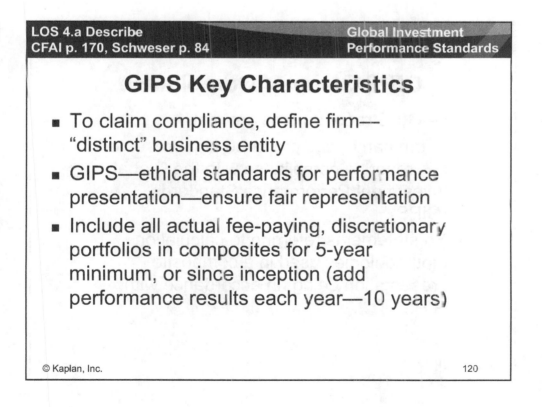

GIPS Key Characteristics

- To claim compliance, define firm—"distinct" business entity
- GIPS—ethical standards for performance presentation—ensure fair representation
- Include all actual fee-paying, discretionary portfolios in composites for 5-year minimum, or since inception (add performance results each year—10 years)

 120

LOS 4.a Describe
CFAI p. 170, Schweser p. 84

Global Investment Performance Standards

GIPS Key Characteristics (continued)

- Certain calculation/presentation standards are required, along with disclosures
- Input data must be accurate
- GIPS—required and recommended provisions (encouraged)
- No partial compliance allowed
- If GIPS conflicts with local law, follow local law, but disclose conflict

 121

LOS 4.a Describe
CFAI p. 170, Schweser p. 84

Global Investment Performance Standards

GIPS Claim of Compliance

- Once GIPS requirements are met:
  - "[Firm name] has prepared and presented this report in compliance with the Global Investment Performance Standards (GIPS)"
  - No statements referring to calculation methodologies used in a composite presentation being "in accordance with GIPS"

 122

LOS 4.a Describe
CFAI p. 170, Schweser p. 84

Global Investment Performance Standards

GIPS Firm's Fundamental Responsibilities

- Provide compliant presentation to all prospects
- Provide composite list/description to all prospects who make a request
- On client request, provide compliant presentation and composite description
- Joint marketing, separate non-compliant firm

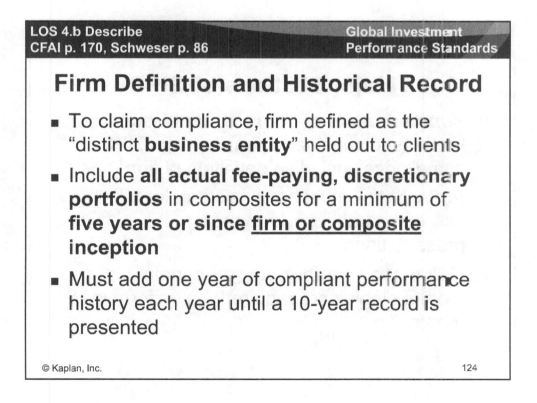

 123

LOS 4.b Describe
CFAI p. 170, Schweser p. 86

Global Investment Performance Standards

Firm Definition and Historical Record

- To claim compliance, firm defined as the "distinct **business entity**" held out to clients
- Include **all actual fee-paying, discretionary portfolios** in composites for a minimum of **five years or since <u>firm or composite</u> inception**
- Must add one year of compliant performance history each year until a 10-year record is presented

 124

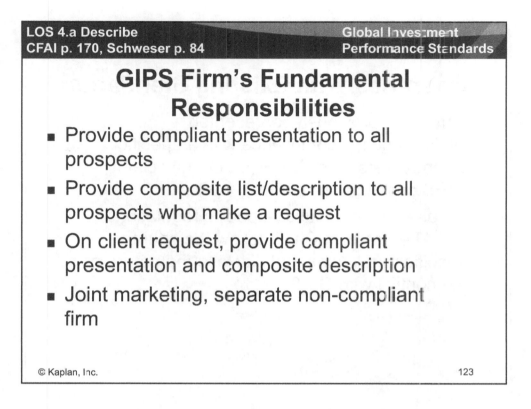

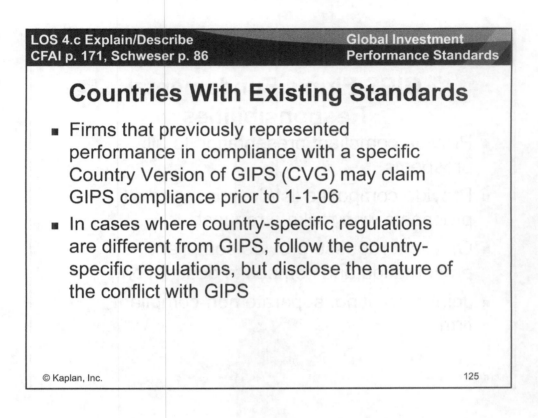

LOS 4.c Explain/Describe
CFAI p. 171, Schweser p. 86

Global Investment
Performance Standards

Countries With Existing Standards

- Firms that previously represented performance in compliance with a specific Country Version of GIPS (CVG) may claim GIPS compliance prior to 1-1-06
- In cases where country-specific regulations are different from GIPS, follow the country-specific regulations, but disclose the nature of the conflict with GIPS

125

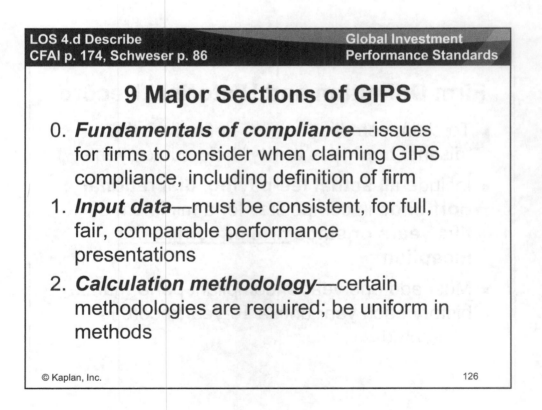

LOS 4.d Describe
CFAI p. 174, Schweser p. 86

Global Investment
Performance Standards

9 Major Sections of GIPS

0. ***Fundamentals of compliance***—issues for firms to consider when claiming GIPS compliance, including definition of firm
1. ***Input data***—must be consistent, for full, fair, comparable performance presentations
2. ***Calculation methodology***—certain methodologies are required; be uniform in methods

126

LOS 4.d Describe
CFAI p. 174, Schweser p. 86

Global Investment Performance Standards

9 Major Sections of GIPS (continued)

3. ***Composite construction***—create meaningful, asset-weighted composites
4. ***Disclosures***—certain info must be disclosed about presentation/policies
5. ***Presentation and reporting***—present investment performance according to GIPS requirements

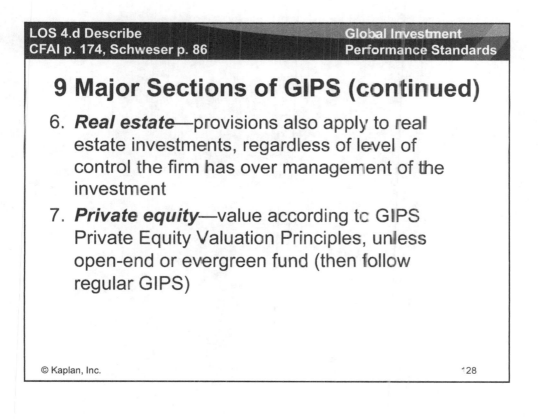

 127

LOS 4.d Describe
CFAI p. 174, Schweser p. 86

Global Investment Performance Standards

9 Major Sections of GIPS (continued)

6. ***Real estate***—provisions also apply to real estate investments, regardless of level of control the firm has over management of the investment
7. ***Private equity***—value according to GIPS Private Equity Valuation Principles, unless open-end or evergreen fund (then follow regular GIPS)

 128

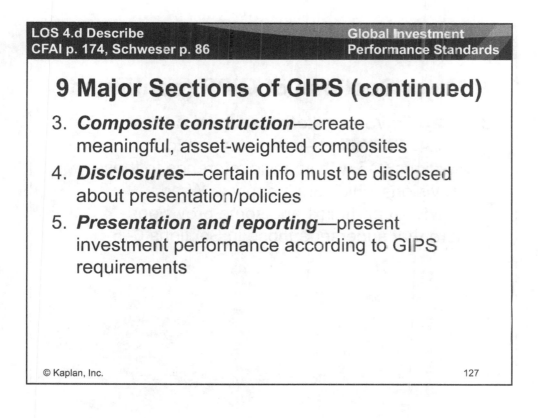

LOS 4.d Describe
CFAI p. 174, Schweser p. 86

Global Investment
Performance Standards

9 Major Sections of GIPS (continued)

8. ***Wrap Fee/Separately Managed Account (SMA) Portfolios***—a supplement to Sections 0–5 with specific reference to those provisions which don't apply to Wrap Fee/SMA portfolios and some provisions here that supersede those in Sections 0–5

129

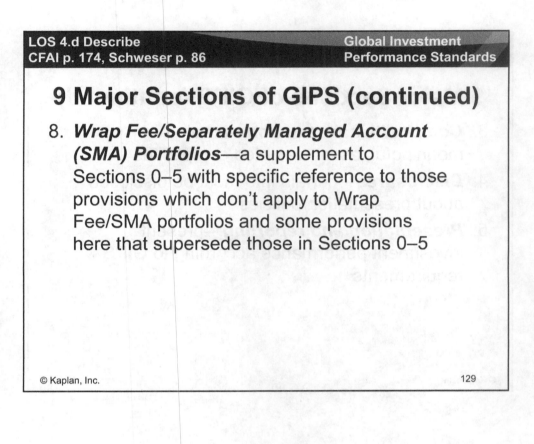

Study Session 2

Quantitative Methods: Basic Concepts

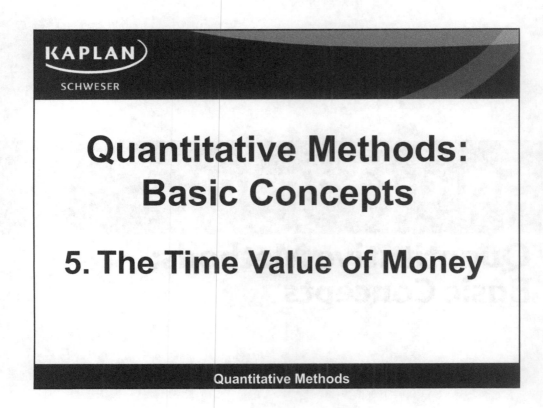

Quantitative Methods: Basic Concepts

5. The Time Value of Money

Quantitative Methods

LOS 5.a Interpret
CFAI p. 244, Schweser p. 100

The Time Value of Money

Interpreting Interest Rates

- Equilibrium interest rates are the **required rate of return** for a particular investment
- Interest rates are also referred to as **discount rates**
- We can also view interest rates as the **opportunity cost** of current consumption because future consumption could be **i%** higher

2

LOS 5.b Explain
CFAI p. 244, Schweser p. 101
The Time Value of Money

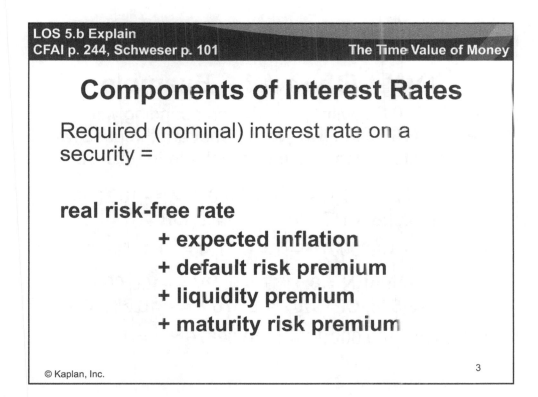

Components of Interest Rates

Required (nominal) interest rate on a security =

real risk-free rate
+ expected inflation
+ default risk premium
+ liquidity premium
+ maturity risk premium

3

LOS 5.c Calculate/Interpret
CFAI p. 253, Schweser p. 101
The Time Value of Money

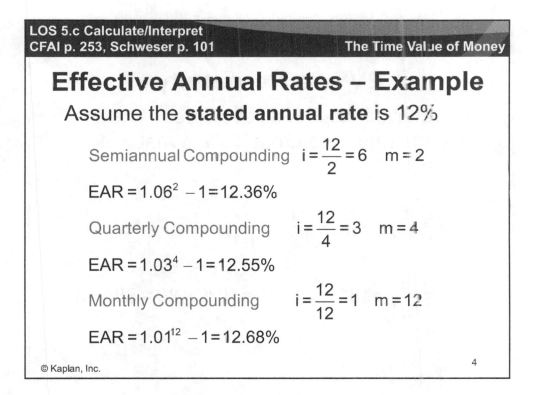

Effective Annual Rates – Example

Assume the **stated annual rate** is 12%

Semiannual Compounding $i = \frac{12}{2} = 6 \quad m = 2$

$EAR = 1.06^2 - 1 = 12.36\%$

Quarterly Compounding $i = \frac{12}{4} = 3 \quad m = 4$

$EAR = 1.03^4 - 1 = 12.55\%$

Monthly Compounding $i = \frac{12}{12} = 1 \quad m = 12$

$EAR = 1.01^{12} - 1 = 12.68\%$

4

LOS 5.d Solve
CFAI p. 250, Schweser p. 103 The Time Value of Money

TVM With m ≠ 1 – Example

A $100,000 CD with quarterly compounding will return $123,528 in two years. What are the effective annual rate and the stated annual rate for this CD?

Effective annual: N = 2, PMT = 0, PV = –100,000, FV = 123,528, CPT→I/Y = 11.14%, **OR**

$(123,528 / 100,000)^{1/2} - 1 = 0.1114 = 11.14\%$

Stated annual: N = 8, PMT = 0, PV = –100,000, FV = 123,528, CPT→I/Y = 2.676 × 4 = 10.7%, **OR**

$(123,528 / 100,000)^{1/8} - 1 = 0.02676 \times 4 = 10.7\%$

 5-4

LOS 5.e Calculate/Interpret
CFAI p. 245, Schweser p. 104 The Time Value of Money

PV of a Perpetuity

A preferred stock will pay $8/year forever, and the rate of return is 10%. What is its value?

$$PV = \frac{8}{1.1} + \frac{8}{1.1^2} + \frac{8}{1.1^3} + \frac{8}{1.1^4} + \ldots$$

$$PV = \frac{8}{0.1} = \$80 \qquad PMT = 10\% \times 80 = \$8/\text{year}$$

 6-2

LOS 5.e,f Calculate/Interpret/Demonstrate
CFAI p. 245, Schweser p. 104 The Time Value of Money

FV of Single Sum

What is the future value of $200 invested today in two years when the interest rate is 10%?

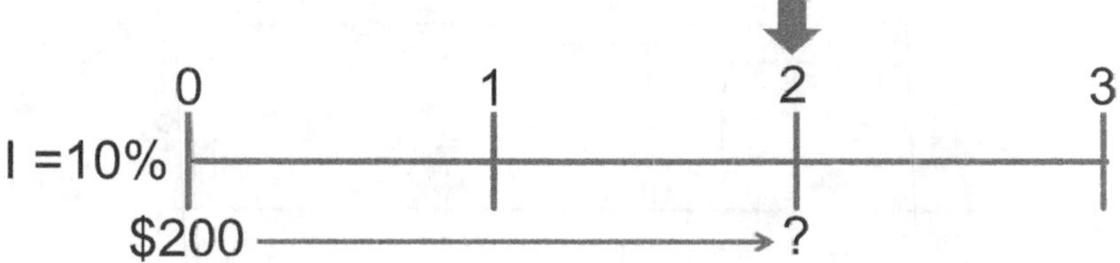

N = 2; I/Y = 10; PV = 200; PMT = 0;

CPT → FV = –242.00 **or**

$200 (1.1) (1.1) = 200(1.1^2) = 242$

7-2

LOS 5.e,f Calculate/Interpret/Demonstrate
CFAI p. 245, Schweser p. 104 The Time Value of Money

PV of Single Sum

What is the present value of $200 to be received in two years when the interest rate is 10%

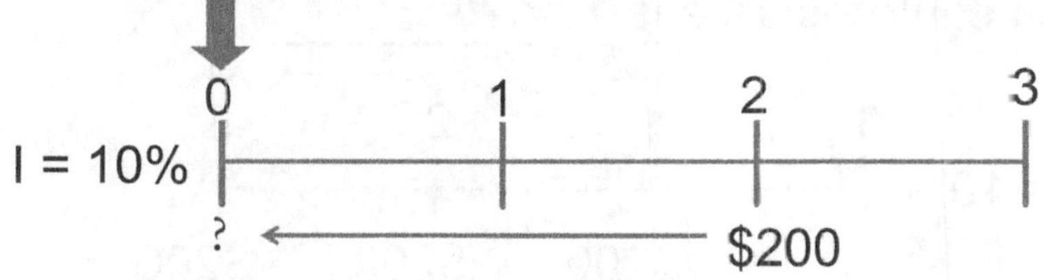

N = 2; I/Y = 10; FV = –200; PMT = 0; CPT → PV = $165.29

or

$$PV = \frac{FV}{(1+i)^n} \qquad \frac{200}{1.1^2} = \$165.29$$

8-2

LOS 5.e,f Calculate/Interpret/Demonstrate
CFAI p. 245, Schweser p. 104 The Time Value of Money

PV of an Ordinary Annuity

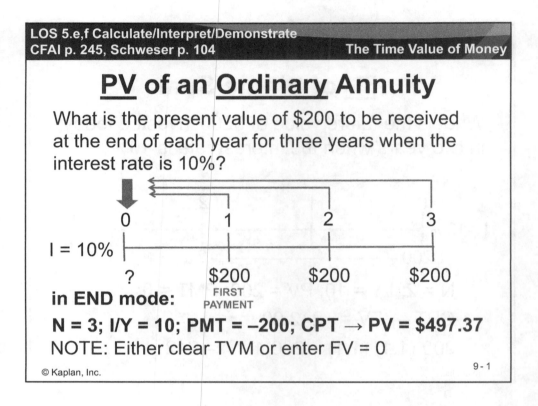

What is the present value of $200 to be received at the end of each year for three years when the interest rate is 10%?

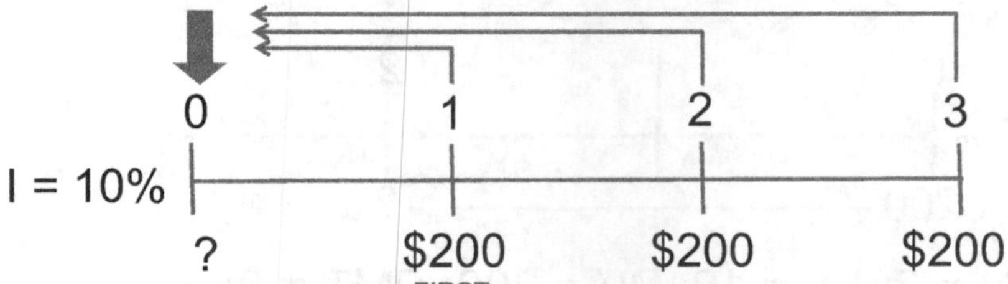

in END mode:

N = 3; I/Y = 10; PMT = –200; CPT → PV = $497.37

NOTE: Either clear TVM or enter FV = 0

 9-1

LOS 5.e,f Calculate/Interpret/Demonstrate
CFAI p. 245, Schweser p. 104 The Time Value of Money

FV of an Ordinary Annuity

What is the value in three years of $200 to be received at the end of each year for three years when the interest rate is 10%?

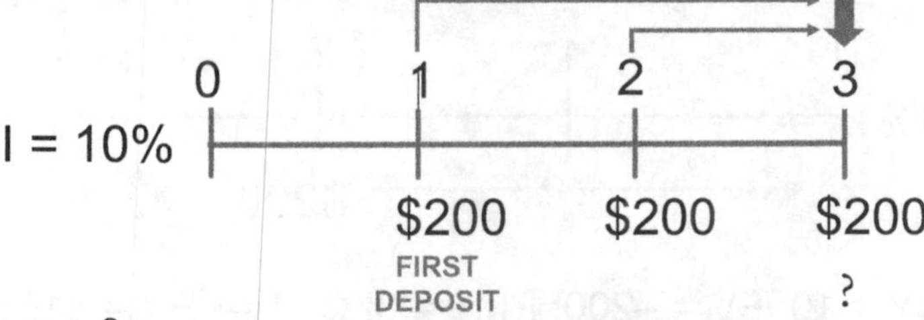

$$200 \times 1.1^2 + 200 \times 1.1 + 200 = 662$$

N = 3; I/Y = 10; PMT = –200; CPT → FV = 662.00

NOTE: Either clear TVM or enter PV = 0

 10-2

LOS 5.e,f Calculate/Interpret/Demonstrate
CFAI p. 245, Schweser p. 104 The Time Value of Money

PV of an Annuity Due

What is the present value of $200 to be received at the start of each year for three years when the interest rate is 10%?

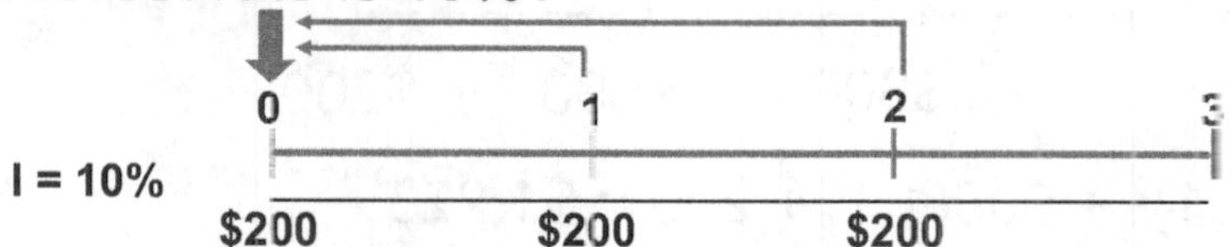

Annuity Due: CFs at the beginning of each period
200 + 200 / 1.1 + 200 / 1.1² = $547.11, or:

Method 1: N = 2; I/Y = 10; PMT = –200; FV = 0;
CPT→PV = $347.11 + $200 = $547.11

Method 2: Put calculator in **BGN** mode:
N = 3; I/Y = 10; PMT = –200; FV = 0; CPT→PV = $547.11

 11 - 3

LOS 5.e,f Calculate/Interpret/Demonstrate
CFAI p. 245, Schweser p. 104 The Time Value of Money

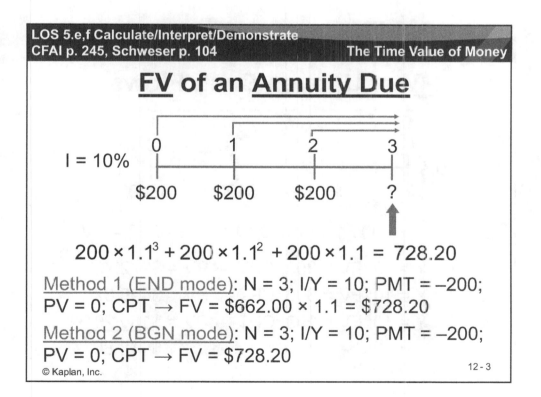

FV of an Annuity Due

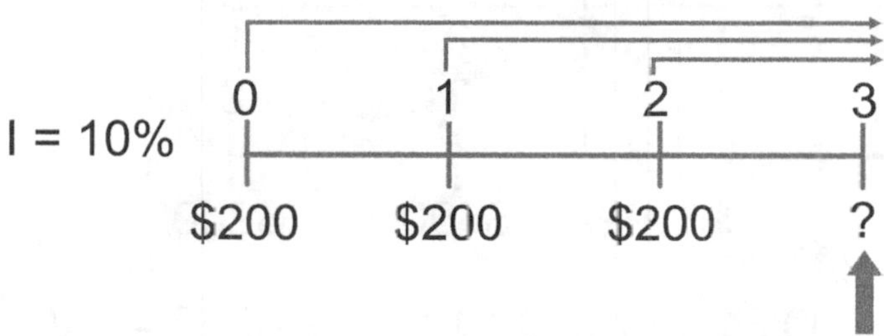

$$200 \times 1.1^3 + 200 \times 1.1^2 + 200 \times 1.1 = 728.20$$

Method 1 (END mode): N = 3; I/Y = 10; PMT = –200;
PV = 0; CPT → FV = $662.00 × 1.1 = $728.20

Method 2 (BGN mode): N = 3; I/Y = 10; PMT = –200;
PV = 0; CPT → FV = $728.20

 12 - 3

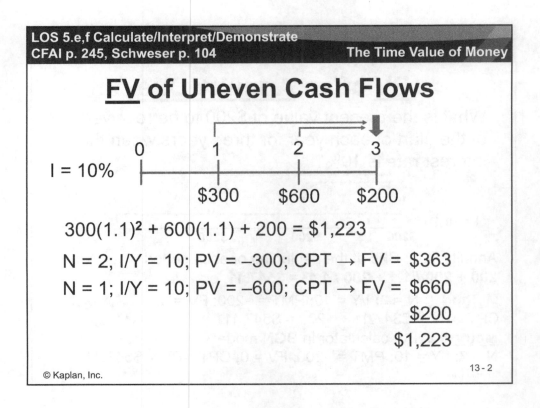

LOS 5.e,f Calculate/Interpret/Demonstrate
CFAI p. 245, Schweser p. 104
The Time Value of Money

FV of Uneven Cash Flows

I = 10%

0	1	2	3
	\$300	\$600	\$200

$300(1.1)^2 + 600(1.1) + 200 = \$1,223$

N = 2; I/Y = 10; PV = –300; CPT → FV = \$363
N = 1; I/Y = 10; PV = –600; CPT → FV = \$660
\$200
\$1,223

13 - 2

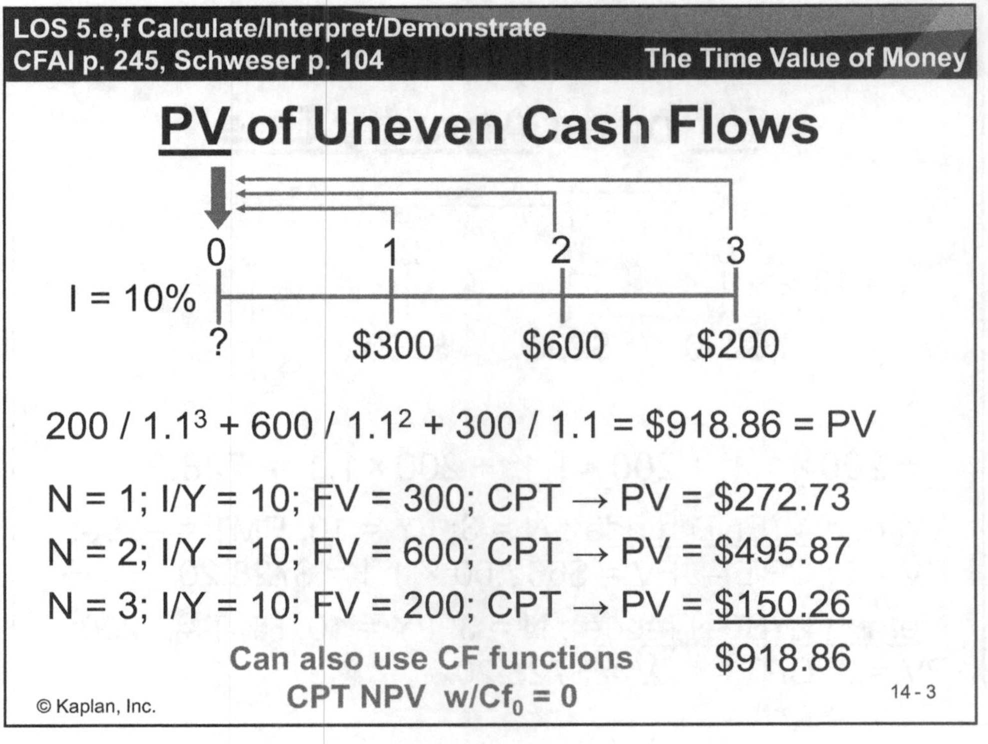

LOS 5.e,f Calculate/Interpret/Demonstrate
CFAI p. 245, Schweser p. 104
The Time Value of Money
PV of Uneven Cash Flows
0
1
2
3
I = 10%
?
\$300
\$600
\$200
200 / 1.1³ + 600 / 1.1² + 300 / 1.1 = \$918.86 = PV
N = 1; I/Y = 10; FV = 300; CPT → PV = \$272.73
N = 2; I/Y = 10; FV = 600; CPT → PV = \$495.87
N = 3; I/Y = 10; FV = 200; CPT → PV = \$150.26
\$918.86
Can also use CF functions
CPT NPV w/Cf0 = 0
© Kaplan, Inc.
14 - 3

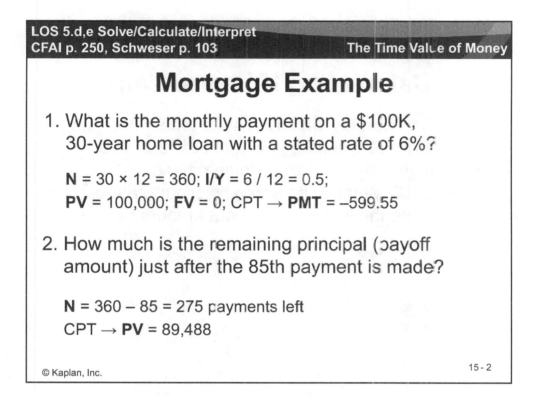

LOS 5.d,e Solve/Calculate/Interpret
CFAI p. 250, Schweser p. 103

The Time Value of Money

Mortgage Example

1. What is the monthly payment on a $100K, 30-year home loan with a stated rate of 6%?

   N = 30 × 12 = 360; **I/Y** = 6 / 12 = 0.5;
   PV = 100,000; **FV** = 0; CPT → **PMT** = –599.55

2. How much is the remaining principal (payoff amount) just after the 85th payment is made?

   N = 360 – 85 = 275 payments left
   CPT → **PV** = 89,488

15 - 2

The Time Value of Money

Retirement Savings – Problem

Client has $75,000 in savings now, will retire 20 years from today, and needs 25 payments of $62,000/year to begin then. Account is expected to earn 7%/year. What annual deposit must she make at the end of each year for 20 years to reach her goal?

Step 1:

Step 2:

16 - 4

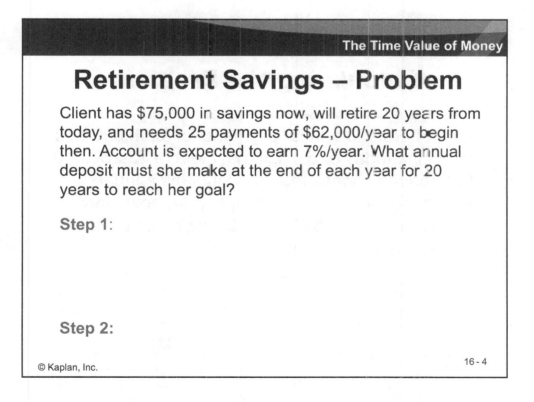

The Time Value of Money

Calculating I/Y – Problem

Elmer has won his $4 million state lottery and has been offered 20 annual payments of $200,000 each beginning today or a single payment of $2,267,000. What is the annual discount rate used to calculate the lump-sum payout amount?

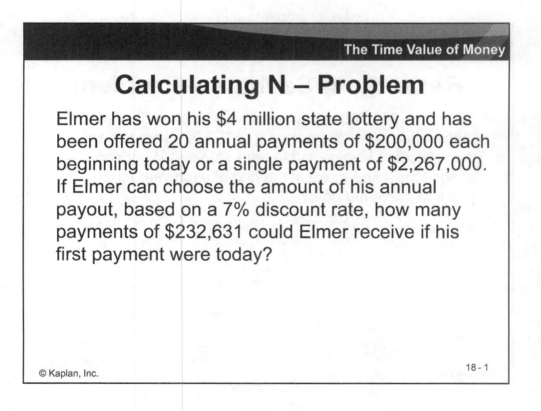

17 - 1

The Time Value of Money

Calculating N – Problem

Elmer has won his $4 million state lottery and has been offered 20 annual payments of $200,000 each beginning today or a single payment of $2,267,000. If Elmer can choose the amount of his annual payout, based on a 7% discount rate, how many payments of $232,631 could Elmer receive if his first payment were today?

18 - 1

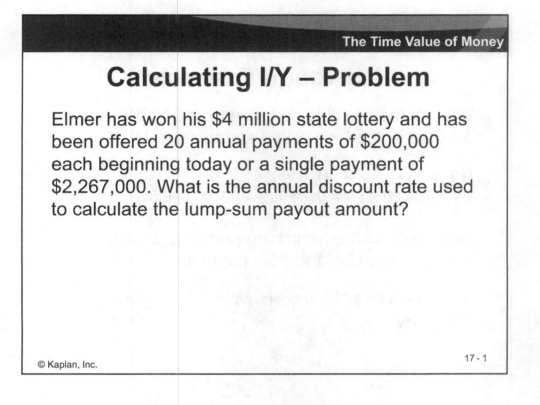

Quantitative Methods: Basic Concepts

6. Discounted Cash Flow Applications

Quantitative Methods

LOS 6.a Calculate/Interpret
CFAI p. 294, Schweser p. 138

Discounted Cash Flow Applications

Net Present Value (NPV)

The sum of the present values of a series of cash flows

$$NPV = CF_0 + \frac{CF_1}{(1+k)^1} + \frac{CF_2}{(1+k)^2} + \ldots + \frac{CF_n}{(1+k)^n}$$

NPV can be computed using your financial calculator

20

LOS 6.a Calculate/Interpret
CFAI p. 294, Schweser p. 138

Discounted Cash Flow Applications

Net Present Value (NPV)

Example using a 9% discount rate

End of Year	Project X	Discounted Cash Flow
0	–$100	–$100.00
1	25	22.94
2	50	42.08
3	75	57.91

–100.00
+ 22.94
+ 42.08
+ 57.91
NPV = $22.93

NPV is the change in wealth in present value terms from a series of cash flows

21

LOS 6.a Calculate/Interpret
CFAI p. 294, Schweser p. 138

Discounted Cash Flow Applications

Internal Rate of Return (IRR)

- IRR is the discount rate that equates the PV of a series of cash flows to their cost
- The IRR is the discount rate that makes the NPV = 0

$$\boxed{NPV = 0} = CF_0 + \frac{CF_1}{(1+IRR)^1} + \frac{CF_2}{(1+IRR)^2} + \ldots + \frac{CF_n}{(1+IRR)^n}$$

22

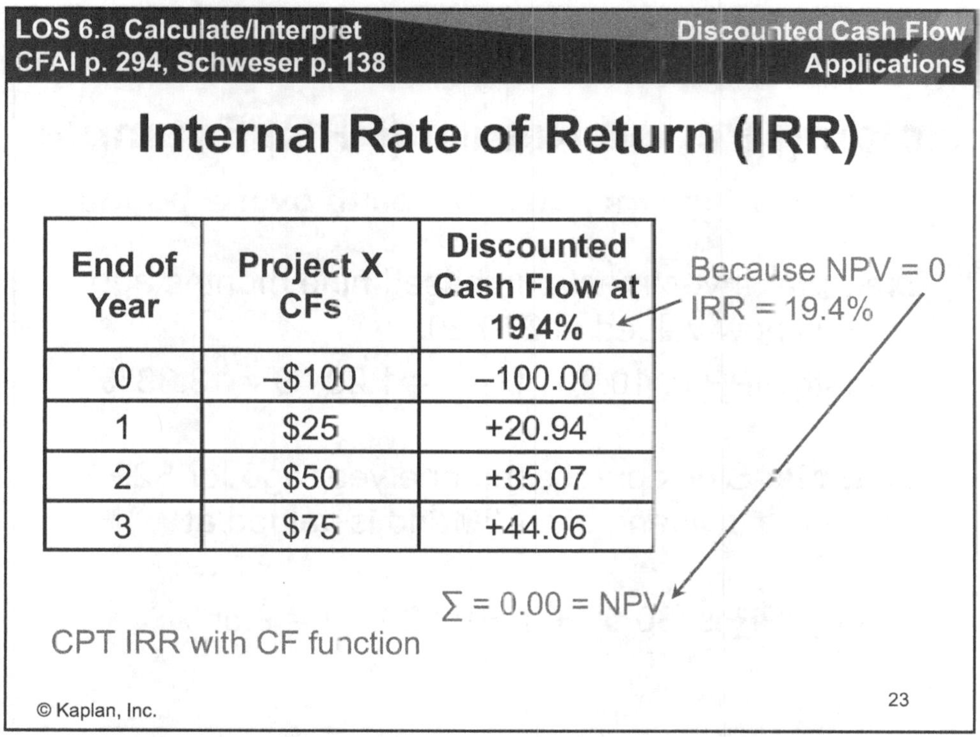

End of Year	Project X CFs	Discounted Cash Flow at 19.4%
0	–$100	–100.00
1	$25	+20.94
2	$50	+35.07
3	$75	+44.06

LOS 6.b Contrast/Identify
CFAI p. 298, Schweser p. 141

Discounted Cash Flow Applications

Possible Problems With IRR

1. When a series of cash flows goes from negative to positive, then back to negative again, there can be more than one IRR

2. Series of cash flows can be ranked by their NPVs, but IRR rankings can differ

More on NPV and IRR in Corporate Finance

24

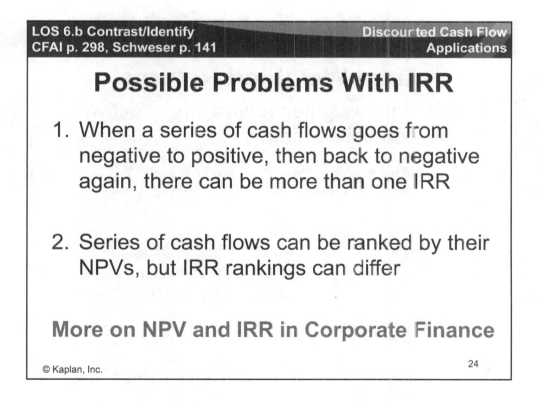

LOS 6.c Calculate/Interpret
CFAI p. 301, Schweser p. 143

Discounted Cash Flow Applications

Holding Period Return (HPR) Example

The percentage increase in wealth over a period

Example: Investment purchased nine months ago for \$9 is now valued at \$10.20.

9-month HPR is 10.20 / 9 – 1 = 1.20 / 9 = 13.33%

Example: Stock purchased one year ago for \$29 just paid a dividend of \$1.30 and is valued at \$30.50.

1-year HPR is (30.50 + 1.30) / 29 – 1 = 9.66%

25-2

LOS 6.d Calculate/Compare/Evaluate
CFAI p. 301, Schweser p. 143

Discounted Cash Flow Applications

Time-Weighted Returns

Annual time-weighted returns are effective annual compound returns.

$$TWR = \left[\left(\frac{\text{End Value}_1}{\text{Begin Value}_1}\right)\left(\frac{\text{End Value}_2}{\text{Begin Value}_2}\right)\cdots\left(\frac{\text{End Value}_N}{\text{Begin Value}_N}\right)\right]^{\frac{1}{\#YEARS}} - 1$$

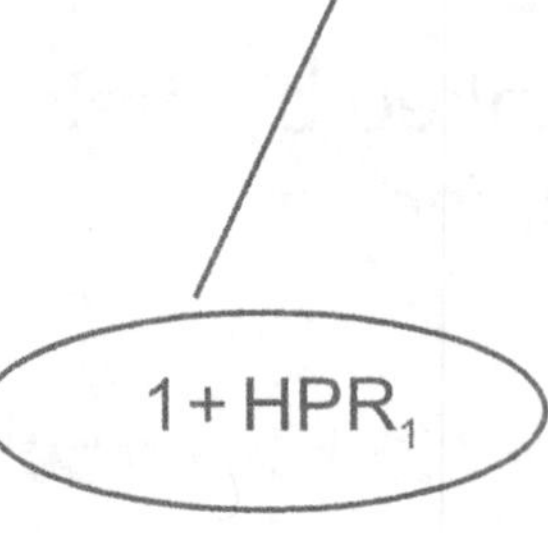

Periods can be any length

Calculate HPRs for periods between significant cash flows

26

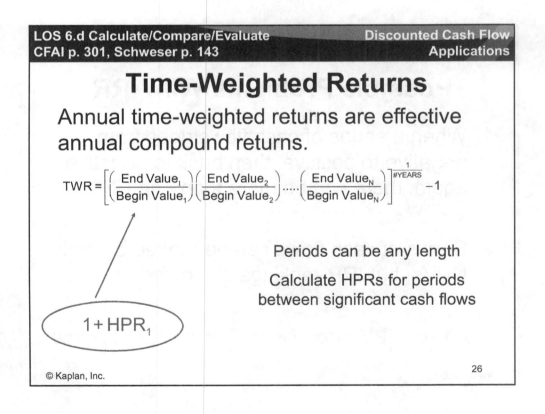

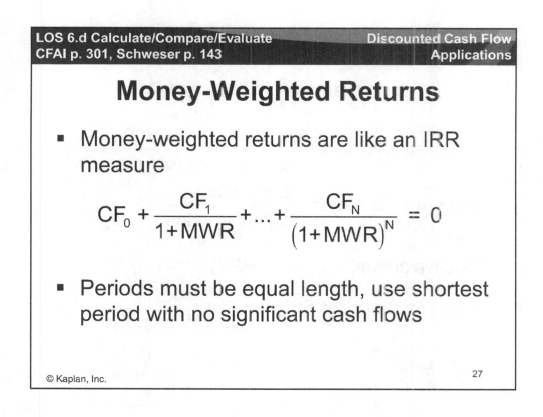

LOS 6.d Calculate/Compare/Evaluate
CFAI p. 301, Schweser p. 143

Discounted Cash Flow Applications

Money-Weighted Returns

- Money-weighted returns are like an IRR measure

$$CF_0 + \frac{CF_1}{1+MWR} + \ldots + \frac{CF_N}{(1+MWR)^N} = 0$$

- Periods must be equal length, use shortest period with no significant cash flows

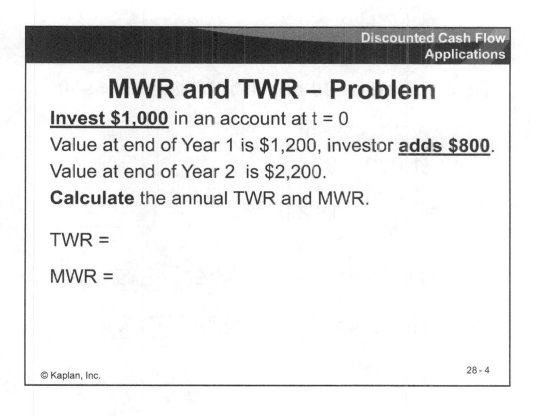

 27

Discounted Cash Flow Applications

MWR and TWR – Problem

Invest $1,000 in an account at t = 0

Value at end of Year 1 is $1,200, investor **adds $800**.

Value at end of Year 2 is $2,200.

Calculate the annual TWR and MWR.

TWR =

MWR =

 28 - 4

LOS 6.e Calculate/Interpret
CFAI p. 307, Schweser p. 147

Discounted Cash Flow Applications

BDY, HPY, EAY, MMY

$$\text{Bank discount yield} = \frac{\text{Discount}}{\text{Face}} \times \frac{360}{\text{days to maturity}}$$

$$\text{Holding period yield} = \frac{\text{Ending value}}{\text{Beginning value}} - 1$$

$$\text{Effective annual yield} = (1 + \text{HPY})^{\frac{365}{\text{days}}} - 1$$

$$\text{Money market yield} = \text{HPY} \times \frac{360}{\text{days to maturity}}$$

29

LOS 6.e Calculate/Interpret
CFAI p. 307, Schweser p. 147

Discounted Cash Flow Applications

Yield Example: 90-day T-bill Priced at $980

$$\text{BDY} = \frac{20}{1,000} \times \frac{360}{90} = 8\%$$

Simple annualized discount

$$\text{HPY} = \frac{1,000}{980} - 1 = 2.04\%$$

90-day HPY

$$\text{EAY} = (1.0204)^{\frac{365}{90}} - 1 = 8.53\%$$

Effective rate

$$\text{MMY} = 0.0204 \times \frac{360}{90} = 8.16\%$$

Simple annualized

30

LOS 6.f Convert
CFAI p. 307, Schweser p. 150

Discounted Cash Flow Applications

Bond Equivalent Yield (BEY)

BEY is two times the effective semi-annual yield

Annual effective yield is 8%, calculate BEY

Effective semi-annual yield is $1.08^{1/2} - 1 = 3.92\%$

BEY = 2 × 3.92 = 7.84%

Monthly effective yield is 0.75%, calculate BEY

Effective semi-annual yield is $1.0075^{6} - 1 = 4.59\%$

BEY = 2 × 4.59 = 9.18%

31 - 4

Discounted Cash Flow Applications

Yield Measures – Problem

A 90-day T-bill is purchased for $997.40. What are the discount yield, holding period yield, money market yield, and the effective yield?

Discount yield:

90-day HPY:

Money market yield:

Effective annual yield:

32 - 4

Quantitative Methods: Basic Concepts

7. Statistical Concepts and Market Returns

Quantitative Methods

LOS 7.a Distinguish
CFAI p. 325, Schweser p. 163

Statistical Concepts and Market Returns

Statistics

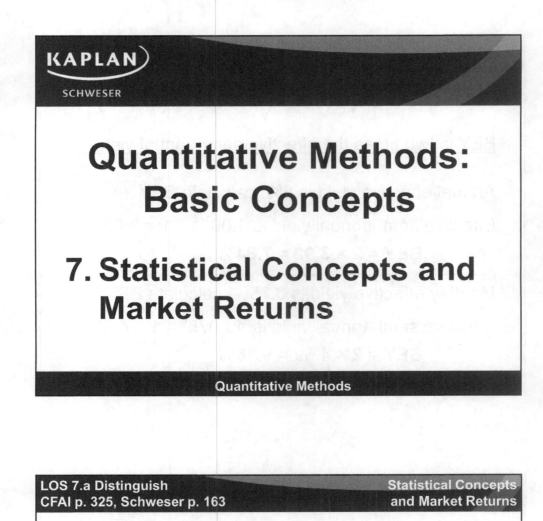

- **Descriptive statistics** describe the properties of a large data set
- **Inferential statistics** use a sample from a population to make probabilistic statements about the characteristics of a population
- A **population** is a complete set of outcomes
- A **sample** is a subset of outcomes drawn from a population

 34

LOS 7.a Distinguish
CFAI p. 325, Schweser p. 163

Statistical Concepts and Market Returns

Measurement Scales (NOIR)

- **Nominal** – only names make sense
  (e.g., robin, parrot, seagull)
- **Ordinal** – order makes sense
  (e.g., large-cap, mid-cap, small-cap)
- **Interval** – intervals make sense
  (e.g., 40°F is 10° greater than 30°F)
- **Ratio** – ratios make sense (absolute zero)
  (e.g., $200 is twice as much as $100)

35

LOS 7.b Define
CFAI p. 325, Schweser p. 164

Statistical Concepts and Market Returns

Statistics Terms

- A **parameter** describes a characteristic of a population
- A **sample statistic** describes a characteristic of a sample (drawn from a population)
- A **frequency distribution** is a table that summarizes a large data set by assigning the observations to intervals

36

LOS 7.c Calculate/Interpret
CFAI p. 330, Schweser p. 166

Statistical Concepts and Market Returns

Statistics Terms

- A **relative frequency distribution** shows the percentage of a distribution's outcomes in each interval
- A **cumulative frequency distribution** shows the percentage of observations less than the upper bound of each interval

37

LOS 7.d Describe
CFAI p. 335, Schweser p. 168

Statistical Concepts and Market Returns

A Histogram

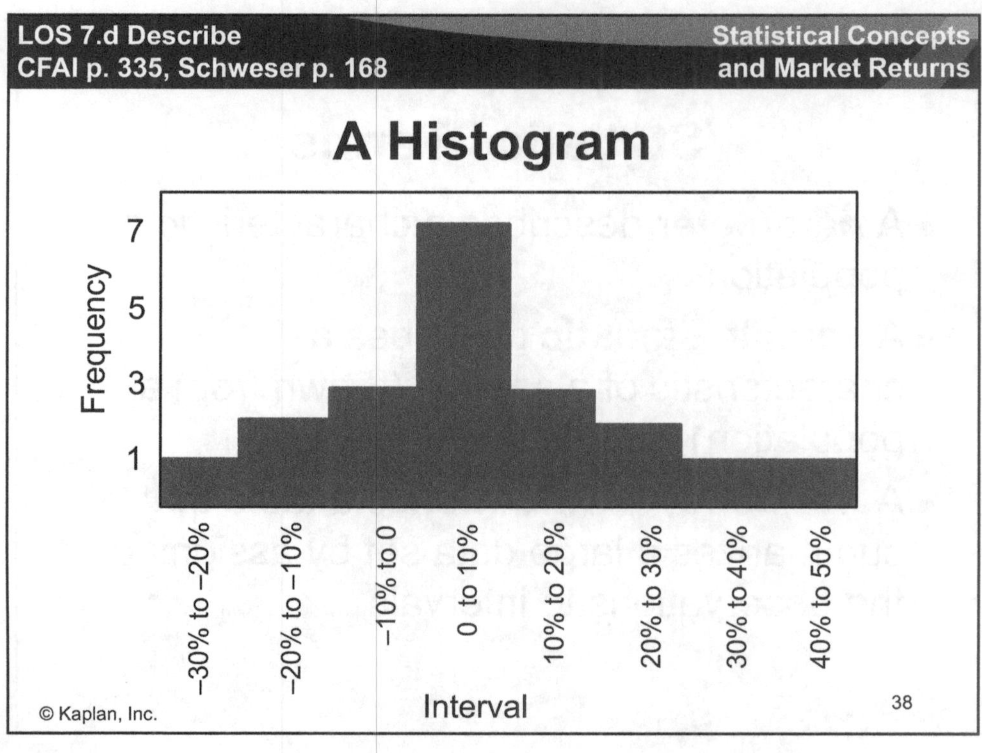

38

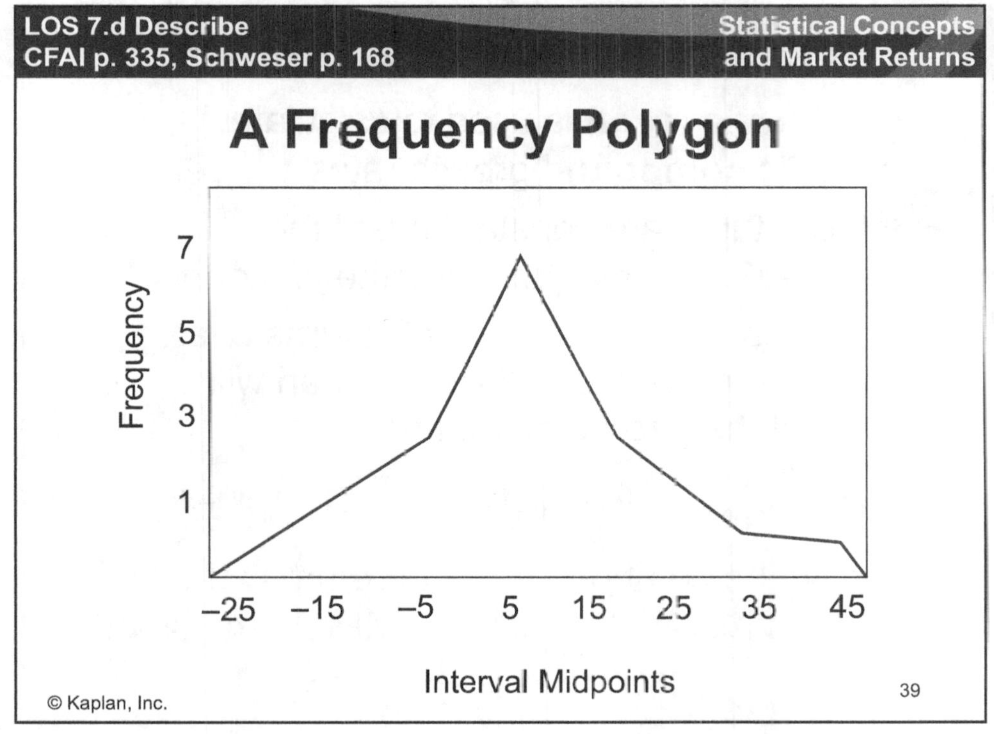

LOS 7.e Calculate/Interpret
CFAI p. 339, Schweser p. 169

Statistical Concepts and Market Returns

Measures of Central Tendency: Population and Sample Means

Population and sample means have different symbols but are both arithmetic means

$$\text{Population Mean: } \mu = \frac{\sum_{i=1}^{N} X_i}{N}$$

$$\text{Sample Mean: } \overline{X} = \frac{\sum_{i=1}^{n} X_i}{n}$$

40

LOS 7.e Calculate/Interpret
CFAI p. 339, Schweser p. 169

Statistical Concepts and Market Returns

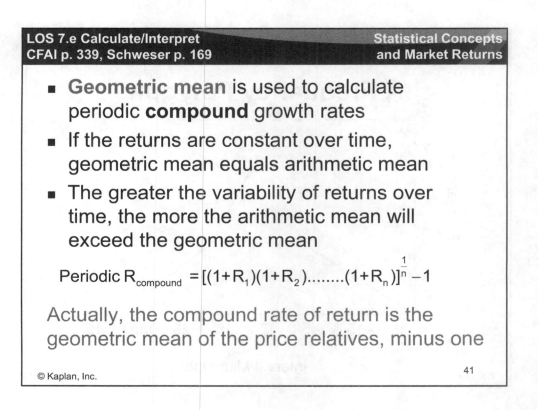

- **Geometric mean** is used to calculate periodic **compound** growth rates
- If the returns are constant over time, geometric mean equals arithmetic mean
- The greater the variability of returns over time, the more the arithmetic mean will exceed the geometric mean

$$\text{Periodic } R_{compound} = [(1+R_1)(1+R_2)........(1+R_n)]^{\frac{1}{n}} - 1$$

Actually, the compound rate of return is the geometric mean of the price relatives, minus one

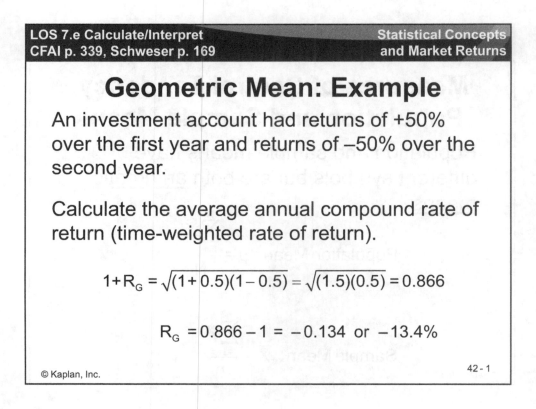

 41

LOS 7.e Calculate/Interpret
CFAI p. 339, Schweser p. 169

Statistical Concepts and Market Returns

Geometric Mean: Example

An investment account had returns of +50% over the first year and returns of –50% over the second year.

Calculate the average annual compound rate of return (time-weighted rate of return).

$$1+R_G = \sqrt{(1+0.5)(1-0.5)} = \sqrt{(1.5)(0.5)} = 0.866$$

$$R_G = 0.866 - 1 = -0.134 \text{ or } -13.4\%$$

 42 - 1

LOS 7.e Calculate/Interpret
CFAI p. 339, Schweser p. 169

Statistical Concepts and Market Returns

Weighted Mean

A mean in which different observations have different proportional influence on the mean

$$\overline{X}_W = \sum_{i=1}^{n} w_i R_i = w_1 R_1 + w_2 R_2 + \ldots + w_n R_n$$

where:

$R_1, R_2, \ldots, R_n$ are the returns for assets $1, 2, \ldots, n$

and $w_1, w_2, \ldots, w_n$ are the portfolio weights, so that

$w_1 + w_2 + \ldots + w_n = 1$

LOS 7.e Calculate/Interpret
CFAI p. 339, Schweser p. 169

Statistical Concepts and Market Returns

Harmonic Mean

Used to find the **average cost per share** of stock purchased over time in constant dollar amounts

$$\overline{X}_{Harmonic} = \frac{N}{\sum_{i=1}^{N} \frac{1}{X_i}}$$

where: N = number of purchases (equal \$ amounts)

X_i = share price for each purchase

© Kaplan, Inc.

LOS 7.e Calculate/Interpret
CFAI p. 339, Schweser p. 169

Statistical Concepts and Market Returns

Harmonic Mean – Example

Investor buys \$3,000 of a stock at the end of month 1 at \$20 a share, and \$3,000 at the end of month 2 at \$25 per share.

What is the average cost per share of stock?

$$\frac{2(3{,}000)}{3{,}000/20 + 3{,}000/25} = \frac{2}{1/20 + 1/25} = \$22.22 \text{ per share}$$

45 - 1

LOS 7.e Calculate/Interpret
CFAI p. 339, Schweser p. 169

Statistical Concepts and Market Returns

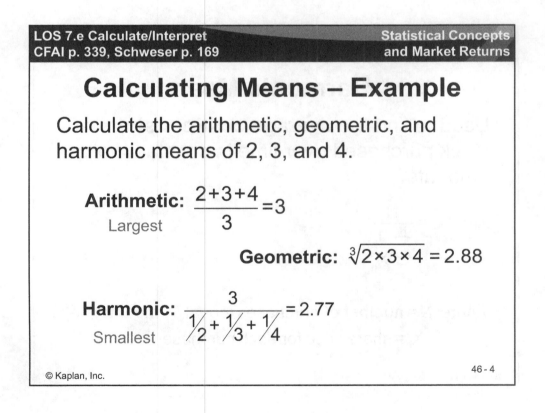

Calculating Means – Example

Calculate the arithmetic, geometric, and harmonic means of 2, 3, and 4.

Arithmetic: $\frac{2+3+4}{3} = 3$

Largest

Geometric: $\sqrt[3]{2\times3\times4} = 2.88$

Harmonic: $\frac{3}{1/2 + 1/3 + 1/4} = 2.77$

Smallest

46 - 4

LOS 7.e Calculate/Interpret
CFAI p. 339, Schweser p. 169

Statistical Concepts and Market Returns

Portfolio Return – Example

Dr. Hoover had the following portfolio at the beginning of the year: cash = $4 million, bonds = $6 million, equities = $10 million.

If returns were 5% on cash, 7% on bonds, and 12% on equities, what was the portfolio return?

	Return		Weight		
Cash	5%	×	4/20	=	1.00%
Bonds	7%	×	6/20	=	2.10%
Stocks	12%	×	10/20	=	6.00%
					9.10%

Same method works for expected portfolio returns!

 47 - 2

LOS 7.e Calculate/Interpret
CFAI p. 339, Schweser p. 169

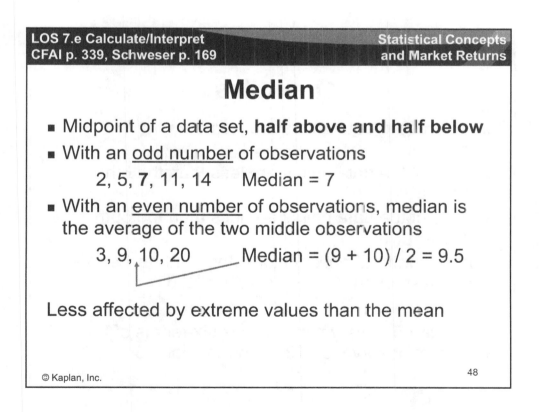

Statistical Concepts and Market Returns

Median

- Midpoint of a data set, **half above and half below**
- With an odd number of observations

  2, 5, **7**, 11, 14 Median = 7
- With an even number of observations, median is the average of the two middle observations

  3, 9, 10, 20 Median = (9 + 10) / 2 = 9.5

Less affected by extreme values than the mean

 48

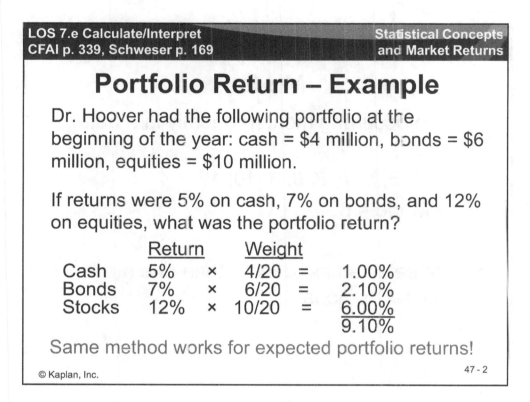

LOS 7.e Calculate/Interpret
CFAI p. 339, Schweser p. 169

Statistical Concepts and Market Returns

Mode

- Value occurring most frequently in a data set
  - 2, 4, 5, 5, 7, ***8, 8, 8***, 10, 12
    - Mode = 8
- Data sets can have more than one mode (bimodal, trimodal, etc.)

49

LOS 7.f Calculate/Interpret
CFAI p. 355, Schweser p. 174

Statistical Concepts and Market Returns

Quantiles

- 75% of the data points are less than the 3rd **quartile**
- 60% of the data points are less than the 6th **decile**
- 50% of the data points are less than the 50th **percentile**

For data with 17 observations, the 70th **percentile** is at observation (17 + 1) × 0.70 = 12.6

For ordered observations, this is six-tenths of the way from observation 12 to observation 13

50 - 1

LOS 7.g Calculate/Interpret
CFAI p. 361, Schweser p. 175

Statistical Concepts and Market Returns

Range and MAD

Annual returns data: 15%, –5%, 12%, 22%

Range (the difference between the largest and smallest value in a data set) = 22% – (–5%) = 27%

Mean Absolute Deviation (MAD): Average of the absolute values of deviations from the mean

Mean = (15 – 5 + 12 + 22) / 4 = 11%

MAD = (|15 – 11| + |–5 – 11| + |12 – 11| + |22 – 11|) / 4
= 32 / 4 = 8%

LOS 7.g Calculate/Interpret
CFAI p. 361, Schweser p. 175

Statistical Concepts and Market Returns

Population Variance and Standard Deviation

Variance is the average of the squared deviations from the mean	Standard deviation is the square root of variance

$$\sigma^2 = \frac{\sum_{i=1}^{N} (X_i - \mu)^2}{N} \qquad \sigma = \sqrt{\sigma^2}$$

LOS 7.g Calculate/Interpret
CFAI p. 361, Schweser p. 175

Statistical Concepts and Market Returns

Sample Variance (s^2) and Sample Standard Deviation (s)

$$s^2 = \frac{\sum_{i=1}^{n}(X_i - \bar{X})^2}{n-1} \qquad s = \sqrt{\frac{\sum_{i=1}^{n}(X_i - \bar{X})^2}{n-1}}$$

Note that for sample variance, the sum of the squared deviations is **divided by n – 1 instead of *n***

53

LOS 7.g Calculate/Interpret
CFAI p. 361, Schweser p. 175

Statistical Concepts and Market Returns

Variance (σ^2) – Example

Returns on four stocks are 15%, –5%, 12%, and 22%. What are the population and sample standard deviation?

Population Mean (μ) = 11%

$$\sigma^2 = \frac{(15-11)^2 + (-5-11)^2 + (12-11)^2 + (22-11)^2}{4} = 98.5$$

$\sigma =$ 9.9%

$$s^2 = \frac{(15-11)^2 + (-5-11)^2 + (12-11)^2 + (22-11)^2}{3} = 131.3$$

$s_x =$ 11.5%

54 - 8

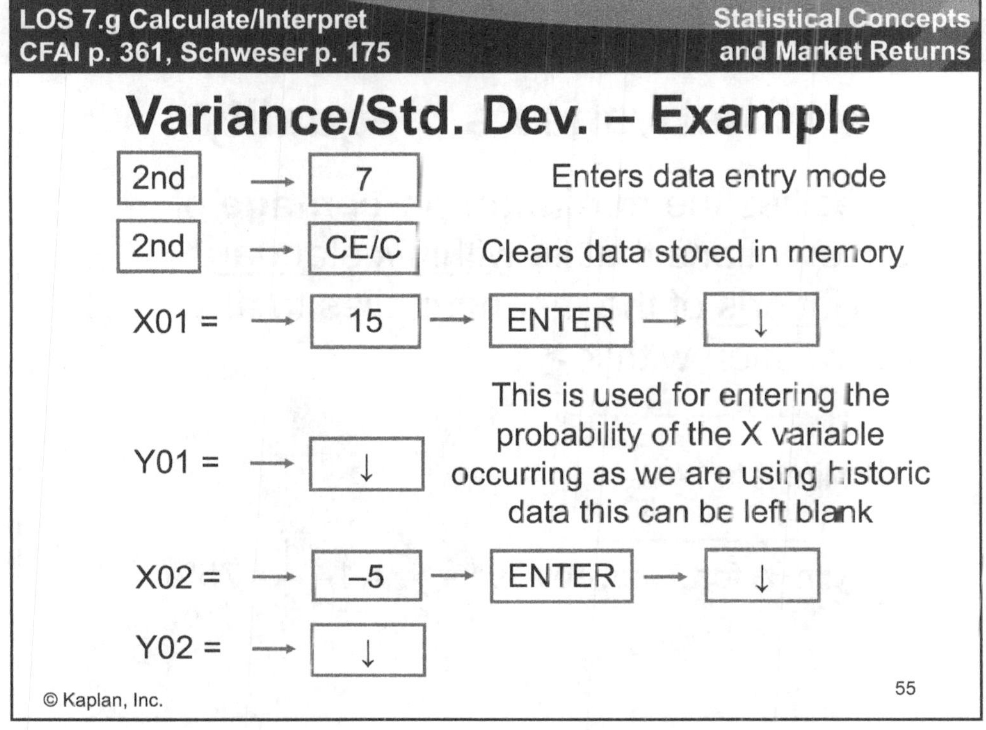

LOS 7.g Calculate/Interpret
CFAI p. 361, Schweser p. 175

Statistical Concepts and Market Returns

Variance/Std. Dev. – Example

X03 = → 12 → ENTER → ↓

Y03 = → ↓

X04 = → 22 → ENTER → ↓

2nd → 8 Enters statistics mode

2nd → ENTER Keep pressing until **1-V** appears

1-V = 1 Variable

↓ Pressing down arrow repeatedly now allows you to review the statistics for the data you entered

56

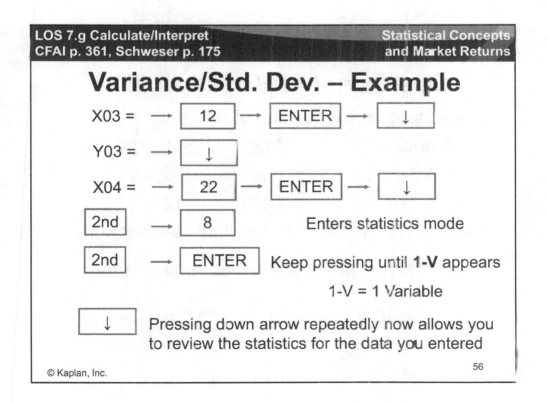

LOS 7.h Calculate/Interpret
CFAI p. 371, Schweser p. 179

Statistical Concepts and Market Returns

Chebyshev's Inequality

Specifies the **minimum percentage** of observations that lie within *k* standard deviations of the mean; applies to any distribution with k > 1

$$\text{Min.\% is } 1-\frac{1}{k^2}$$

$$\text{Min.\% for 2 std. dev. is } 1-\frac{1}{2^2}=1-\frac{1}{4}=75\%$$

57

LOS 7.i Calculate/Interpret
CFAI p. 372, Schweser p. 180

Statistical Concepts and Market Returns

Coefficient of Variation (CV)

A measure of risk per unit of return

Example:	Mean	Std. Dev.
Asset A	5%	10%
Asset B	8%	12%

Asset B has higher std. dev. and higher return

Lower CV is better, less risk per unit of return

$$CV=\frac{s}{\overline{X}} \quad CV_A=\frac{10}{5}=2 \quad CV_B=\frac{12}{8}=1.5$$

58

LOS 7.i Calculate/Interpret
CFAI p. 372, Schweser p. 180

Statistical Concepts and Market Returns

Sharpe Ratio

Excess return per unit of risk (CV measures risk per unit of return); **higher is better**

Example: Mean portfolio return = 17%, standard deviation = 9%, average risk-free rate = 5%.

What is the Sharpe ratio for the portfolio?

$$\text{Sharpe ratio} = \frac{\overline{R}_P - \overline{R}_F}{\sigma_P} = \frac{17-5}{9} = 1.33$$

Sharpe Ratio is Safety-first with R_f for target return

 59

LOS 7.j,k Explain/Describe
CFAI p. 377, Schweser p. 182

Statistical Concepts and Market Returns

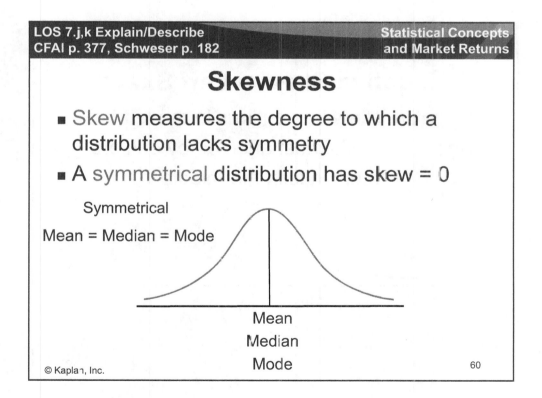

Skewness

- Skew measures the degree to which a distribution lacks symmetry
- A symmetrical distribution has skew = 0

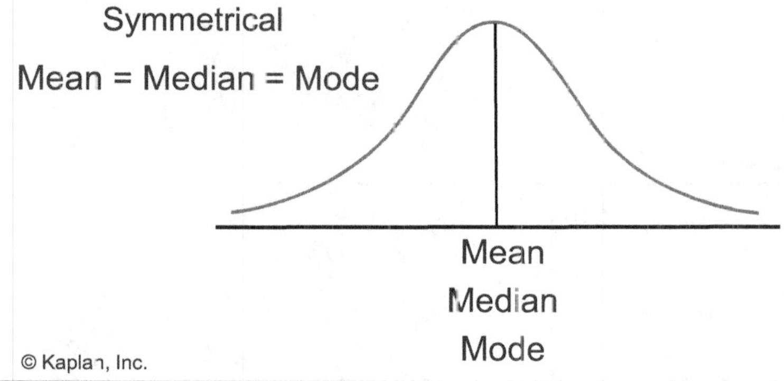

 60

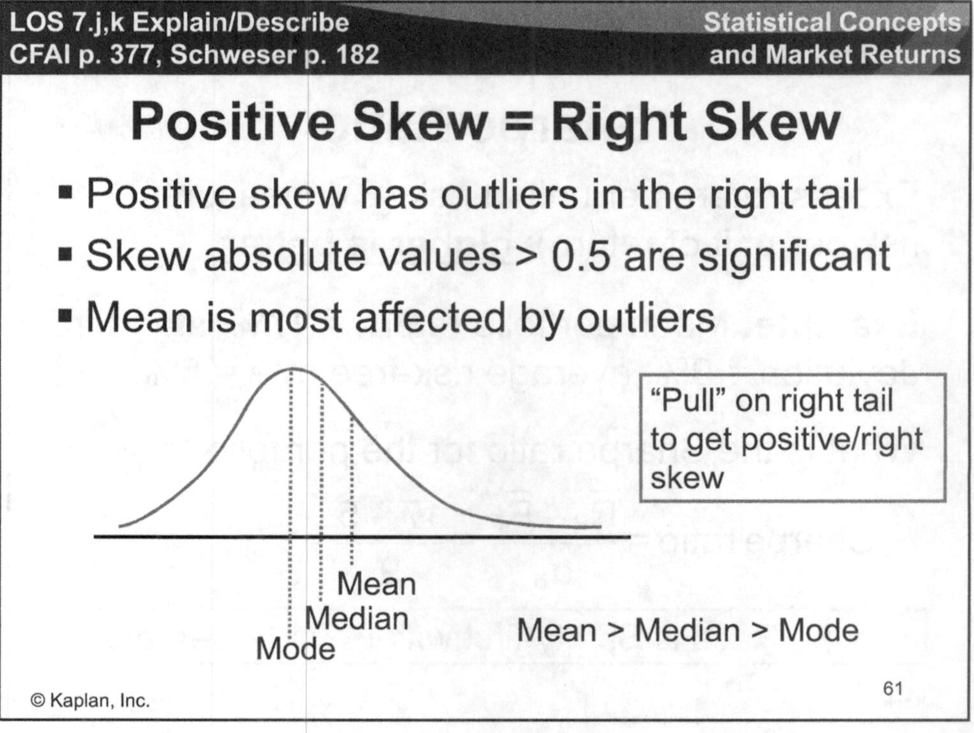
LOS 7.j,k Explain/Describe
CFAI p. 377, Schweser p. 182
Statistical Concepts
and Market Returns
Positive Skew = Right Skew
▪ Positive skew has outliers in the right tail
▪ Skew absolute values > 0.5 are significant
▪ Mean is most affected by outliers
"Pull" on right tail to get positive/right skew
Mean
Median
Mode
Mean > Median > Mode
© Kaplan, Inc.
61

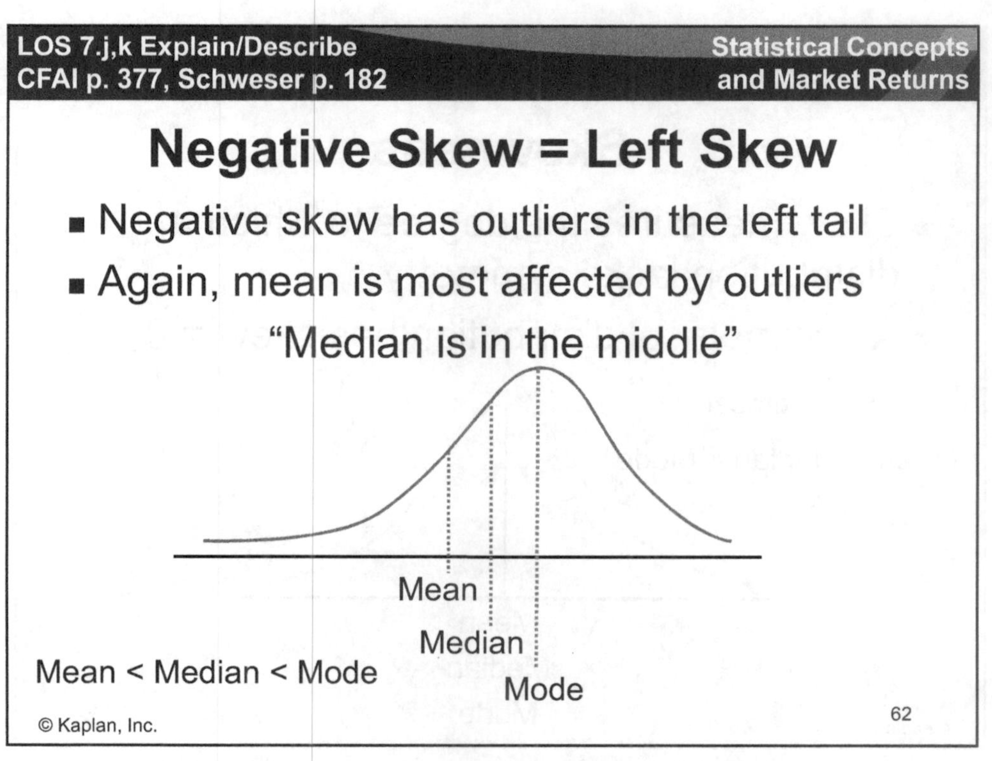
LOS 7.j,k Explain/Describe
CFAI p. 377, Schweser p. 182
Statistical Concepts
and Market Returns
Negative Skew = Left Skew
▪ Negative skew has outliers in the left tail
▪ Again, mean is most affected by outliers
"Median is in the middle"
Mean
Median
Mode
Mean < Median < Mode
© Kaplan, Inc.
62

LOS 7.l Explain
CFAI p. 380, Schweser p. 184

Statistical Concepts and Market Returns

Kurtosis

- Measures the degree to which a distribution is more or less peaked than a normal distribution
- *Leptokurtic* (kurtosis > 3) is **more peaked** with **fatter tails** (more extreme outliers)

Leptokurtic

Higher probability in tails with higher kurtosis

Normal Distribution

63

LOS 7.l Explain
CFAI p. 380, Schweser p. 184

Statistical Concepts and Market Returns

Kurtosis

- **Kurtosis for a normal distribution is 3.0**
- **Excess** kurtosis is kurtosis minus 3
- **Excess** kurtosis is *0 for a normal distribution*
- **Excess** kurtosis greater than 1.0 in absolute value is considered significant

64

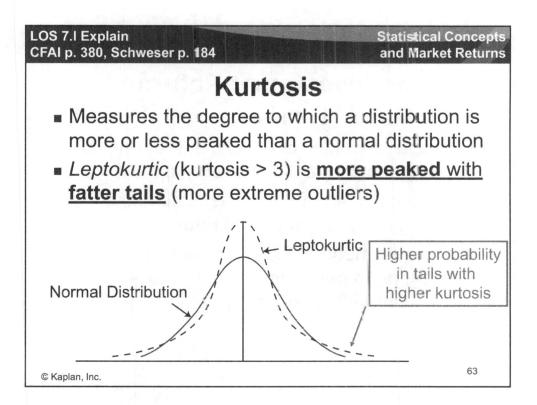

LOS 7.m Explain
CFAI p. 386, Schweser p. 186

Statistical Concepts and Market Returns

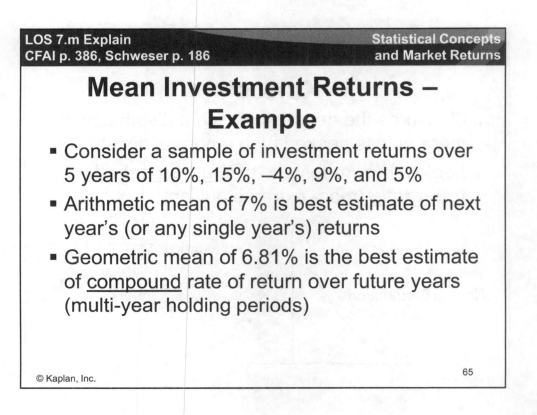

Mean Investment Returns – Example

- Consider a sample of investment returns over 5 years of 10%, 15%, –4%, 9%, and 5%
- Arithmetic mean of 7% is best estimate of next year's (or any single year's) returns
- Geometric mean of 6.81% is the best estimate of compound rate of return over future years (multi-year holding periods)

65

Quantitative Methods: Basic Concepts

8. Probability Concepts

Quantitative Methods

LOS 8.a Define
CFAI p. 412, Schweser p. 201

Probability Concepts

Probability Terminology

- **Random variable**: Uncertain number
- **Outcome**: Realization of random variable
- **Event**: Set of one or more outcomes
- **Mutually exclusive**: Cannot both happen
- **Exhaustive**: Set of events includes all possible outcomes

67

LOS 8.b State/Distinguish
CFAI p. 413, Schweser p. 201 Probability Concepts

Two Properties of Probability

Probability of an event, $P(E_i)$, is between 0 and 1

$$0 \leq P(E_i) \leq 1$$

For a set of events that are mutually exclusive and exhaustive, the **sum of probabilities is 1**

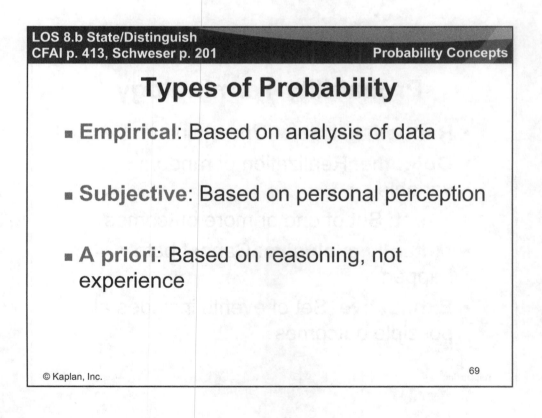

$$\Sigma P(E_i) = 1$$

 68

LOS 8.b State/Distinguish
CFAI p. 413, Schweser p. 201 Probability Concepts

Types of Probability

- **Empirical**: Based on analysis of data
- **Subjective**: Based on personal perception
- **A priori**: Based on reasoning, not experience

 69

LOS 8.c State
CFAI p. 414, Schweser p. 202
Probability Concepts

Odds For or Against

Probability that a horse will win a race = 20%

Odds for: 0.20 / (1 – 0.20) = 1/4
= one-to-four

Odds against: (1 – 0.20) / 0.20 = 4/1
= four-to-one

70 - 2

LOS 8.d Distinguish
CFAI p. 416, Schweser p. 203
Probability Concepts

Conditional vs. Unconditional

Two types of probability:

Unconditional: P(A), the probability of an event regardless of the outcomes of other events (e.g., probability market will be up for the day)

Conditional: P(A|B), the probability of A given that B has occurred (e.g., probability that the market will be up for the day, given that the Fed raises interest rates)

71

LOS 8.e Explain
CFAI p. 417, Schweser p. 203
Probability Concepts

Probability Rules

Use **addition rule** for probability of A or B occurring

P(A or B) = P(A) + P(B) – P(AB)

Use **multiplication rule** for joint probability

Prob(AB) = Prob(A|B) × Prob(B)

Multiplication rule for independent probabilities

Prob(AB) = Prob (A) × Prob(B)

72

LOS 8.e Explain
CFAI p. 417, Schweser p. 203
Probability Concepts

Probability Rules

Total probability rule

$$\text{Prob}(A) = \text{Prob}(A|B) \times \text{Prob}(B) + \text{Prob}(A|B^C) \times \text{Prob}(B^C)$$

or

$$\text{Prob}(A) = \text{Prob}(A|S_1) \times \text{Prob}(S_1) + \text{Prob}(A|S_2) \times \text{Prob}(S_2) + \ldots + \text{Prob}(A|S_n) \times \text{Prob}(S_n)$$

where $\text{Prob}(S_1) + \text{Prob}(S_2) + \ldots + \text{Prob}(S_n) = 1$

73

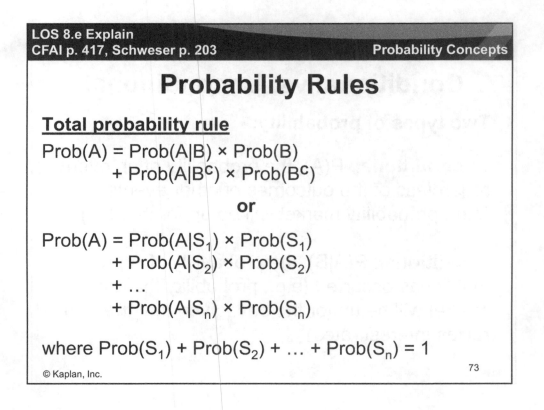

LOS 8.f Calculate/Interpret
CFAI p. 417, Schweser p. 204

Probability Concepts

Joint Probability

The probability that **both** of two events will occur is their **joint probability**

Example using conditional probability:

P (interest rates will increase) = P(I) = 40%

P (recession *given* a rate increase) = P(R|I) = 70%

Probability of a recession **and** an increase in rates, P(RI) = P(R|I) × P(I) = 0.7 × 0.4 = 28%

74

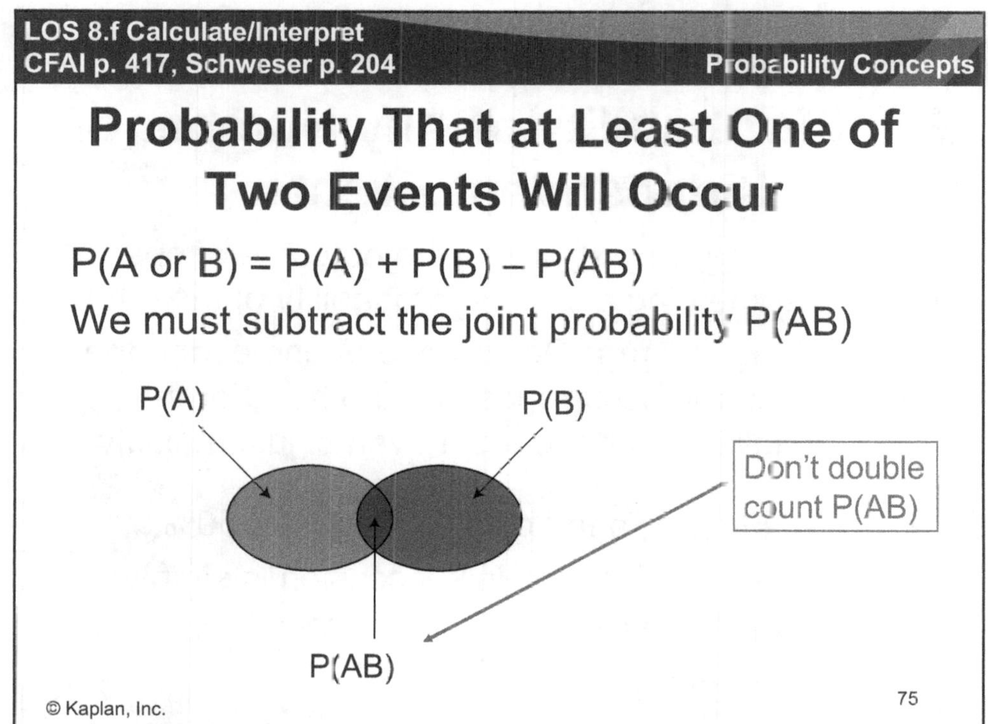
LOS 8.f Calculate/Interpret
CFAI p. 417, Schweser p. 204
Probability Concepts
Probability That at Least One of Two Events Will Occur
P(A or B) = P(A) + P(B) – P(AB)
We must subtract the joint probability P(AB)
P(A)
P(B)
Don't double count P(AB)
P(AB)
© Kaplan, Inc.
75

LOS 8.f Calculate/Interpret
CFAI p. 417, Schweser p. 204

Probability Concepts

Addition Rule – Example

P(I) = probability of rising interest rates is 40%

P(R) = probability of recession is 34%

Joint probability P(RI) = 0.28 (calculated earlier)

What is the probability of either rising interest rates **or** recession?

$$P(R \text{ or } I) = P(R) + P(I) - P(RI)$$
$$= 0.34 + 0.40 - 0.28 = 0.46$$

For mutually exclusive events, the joint probability P(AB) = 0 so:

$$P(A \text{ or } B) = P(A) + P(B)$$

76 - 3

LOS 8.g Distinguish
CFAI p. 420, Schweser p. 207

Probability Concepts

Joint Probability of Any Number of Independent Events

Dependent events: Knowing the outcome of one tells you something about the probability of the other

Independent events: Occurrence of one event does not influence the occurrence of the other. For the joint probability of independent events, just multiply

Example: Flipping a fair coin, P (heads) = 50%

The probability of 3 heads in succession is simply:

$0.5 \times 0.5 \times 0.5 = 0.5^3 = 0.125$, or 12.5%

77

LOS 8.h Calculate/Interpret
CFAI p. 423, Schweser p. 208

Probability Concepts

Calculating Unconditional Probability

P (Interest rate increase) = P(I) = 0.4

P (No interest rate increase) = $P(I^C)$ = 1 – 0.4 = 0.6

P (Recession | Increase) = P(R|I) = 0.70

P (Recession | No Increase) = $P(R|I^C)$ = 0.10

What is the (unconditional) probability of recession?

$$P(R) = P(R|I) \times P(I) + P(R|I^C) \times P(I^C)$$
$$= 0.70 \times 0.40 + 0.10 \times 0.60 = 0.34$$

78 - 1

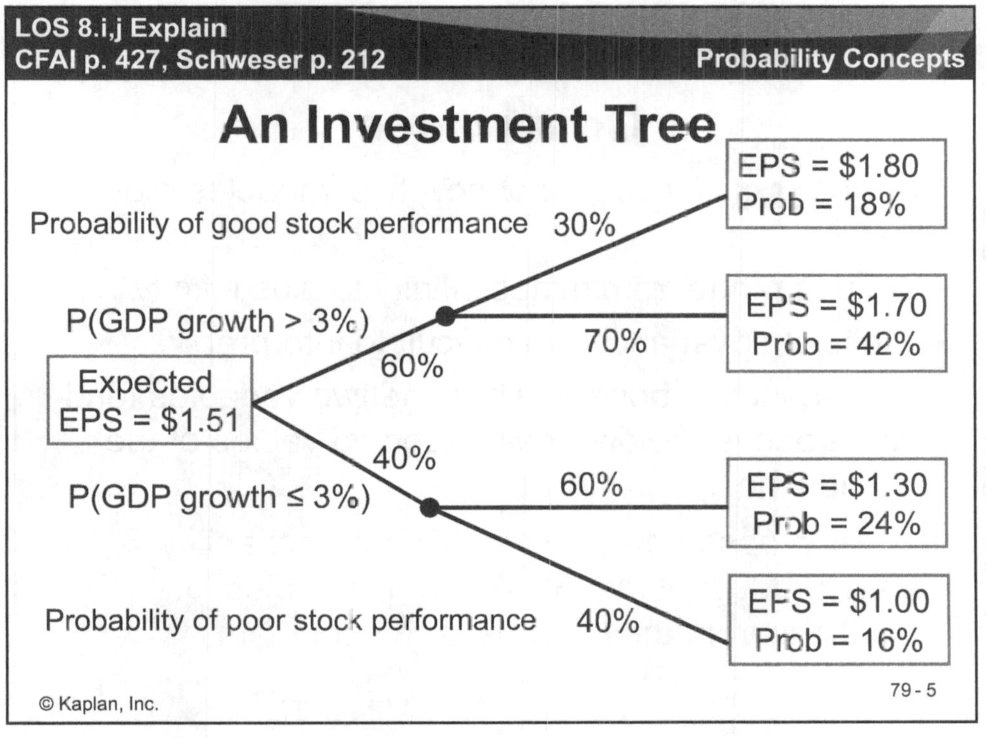

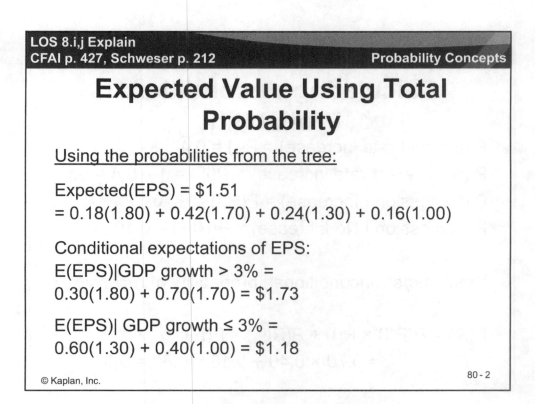

LOS 8.i,j Explain
CFAI p. 427, Schweser p. 212

Probability Concepts

Expected Value Using Total Probability

Using the probabilities from the tree:

Expected(EPS) = \$1.51
= 0.18(1.80) + 0.42(1.70) + 0.24(1.30) + 0.16(1.00)

Conditional expectations of EPS:
E(EPS)|GDP growth > 3% =
0.30(1.80) + 0.70(1.70) = \$1.73

E(EPS)| GDP growth ≤ 3% =
0.60(1.30) + 0.40(1.00) = \$1.18

80 - 2

LOS 8.k Calculate/Interpret
CFAI p. 434, Schweser p. 213

Probability Concepts

Covariance

Covariance: A measure of how two variables move together

- Values range from minus infinity to plus infinity
- Units of covariance are difficult to interpret
- Covariance is positive when the two variables tend to be above (below) their expected values at the same time

For each observation, multiply each probability by the product of the two random variables' deviations from their means, and sum them

81

LOS 8.k Calculate/Interpret
CFAI p. 434, Schweser p. 213 Probability Concepts

Correlation

- Correlation: A standardized measure of the linear relationship between two variables

$$\text{Corr}(R_i, R_j) = \frac{\text{Cov}(R_i, R_j)}{\sigma(R_i)\sigma(R_j)}$$

- Values range from +1, perfect positive correlation, to –1, perfect negative correlation
- r is sample correlation coefficient
- ρ is population correlation coefficient

Also covered in SS12

 82

LOS 8.k Calculate/Interpret
CFAI p. 434, Schweser p. 213 Probability Concepts

Correlation – Example

The covariance between two assets is 0.0046, $\sigma_A = 0.0623$ and $\sigma_B = 0.0991$. What is the correlation between the two assets (ρ_{AB})?

$$\rho_{AB} = \frac{\text{Cov}_{AB}}{\sigma_A \sigma_B} = \frac{0.0046}{0.0623 \times 0.0991} = 0.745$$

 83 - 1

LOS 8.I Calculate/Interpret
CFAI p. 425, Schweser p. 217
Probability Concepts

Expected Value, Variance, and Standard Deviation (Probability Model)

Expected Value: $E(X) = \Sigma P(x_i)x_i$

Economy	$P(x_i)$	Return (X_i)	$P(x_i)x_i$
Recession	0.25	–0.10	–0.025
Normal	0.50	0.08	0.040
Boom	0.25	0.22	0.055
			E(X) = 0.070

84

LOS 8.I Calculate/Interpret
CFAI p. 425, Schweser p. 217
Probability Concepts

Expected Return, Variance, and Standard Deviation (Probability Model)

- **Variance:** $\sigma^2_X = \Sigma P(x_i)[x_i - E(X)]^2$

Economy	$P(x_i)$	Return(X_i)	$P(x_i)x_i$	$P(x_i)[x_i - E(X)]^2$
Recession	0.25	–0.10	–0.025	0.00723
Normal	0.50	0.08	0.040	0.00005
Boom	0.25	0.22	0.055	0.00563
			E(X) = 0.070	0.01290 = σ^2

- **Standard deviation:** Square root of σ^2 = 0.1136

85

LOS 8.l Calculate/Interpret
CFAI p. 425, Schweser p. 217

Probability Concepts

Portfolio Expected Return

Expected return on a portfolio is a weighted average of the expected returns on the assets in the portfolio where the weights are proportions of portfolio value.

Also covered in SS12

86

LOS 8.l Calculate/Interpret
CFAI p. 425, Schweser p. 217

Probability Concepts

Portfolio Variance and Standard Deviation

- Portfolio variance also uses the weights of the assets in the portfolio, use either formula

$$\text{Var}(R_p) = \sigma_A^2 w_A^2 + \sigma_B^2 w_B^2 + 2w_A w_B \text{Cov}_{AB}$$

$$\text{Note: } \text{Cov}_{AB} = \rho_{AB}\sigma_A\sigma_B$$

$$\text{Var}(R_p) = \sigma_A^2 w_A^2 + \sigma_B^2 w_B^2 + 2w_A w_B \rho_{AB}\sigma_A\sigma_B$$

Also covered in SS12

87

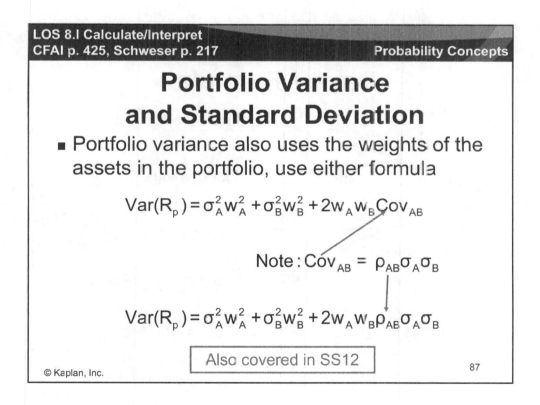

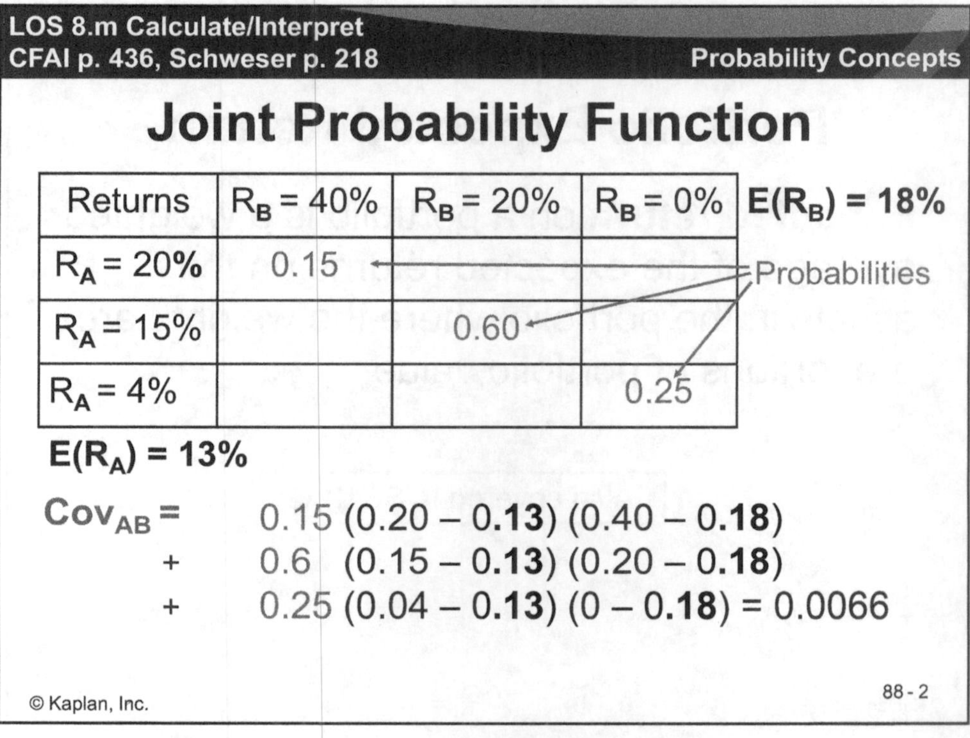
LOS 8.m Calculate/Interpret
CFAI p. 436, Schweser p. 218
Probability Concepts
Joint Probability Function
Returns
R_B = 40%
R_B = 20%
R_B = 0%
$E(R_B)$ = 18%
R_A = 20%
0.15
Probabilities
R_A = 15%
0.60
R_A = 4%
0.25
$E(R_A)$ = 13%
Cov_{AB} = 0.15 (0.20 – 0.13) (0.40 – 0.18)
+ 0.6 (0.15 – 0.13) (0.20 – 0.18)
+ 0.25 (0.04 – 0.13) (0 – 0.18) = 0.0066
© Kaplan, Inc.
88 - 2

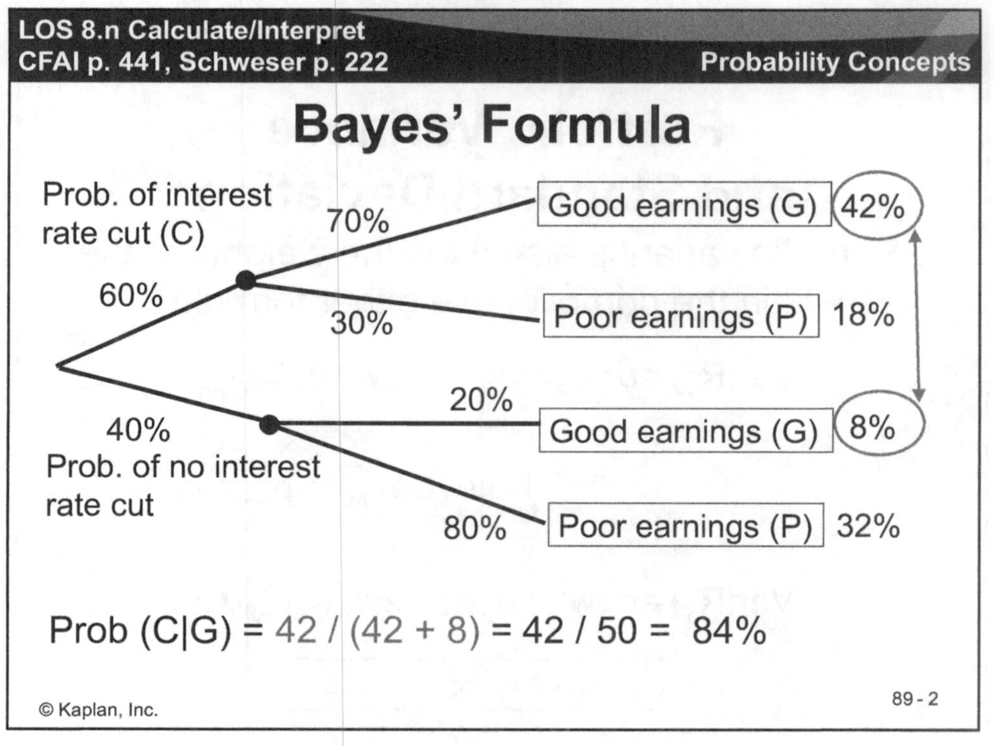
LOS 8.n Calculate/Interpret
CFAI p. 441, Schweser p. 222
Probability Concepts
Bayes' Formula
Prob. of interest rate cut (C)
60%
70%
Good earnings (G)
42%
30%
Poor earnings (P)
18%
40%
Prob. of no interest rate cut
20%
Good earnings (G)
8%
80%
Poor earnings (P)
32%
Prob (C|G) = 42 / (42 + 8) = 42 / 50 = 84%
© Kaplan, Inc.
89 - 2

LOS 8.o Identify/Solve
CFAI p. 444, Schweser p. 224

Probability Concepts

Factorial for Labeling

Example: Out of 10 stocks, 5 will be rated buy, 3 will be rated hold, and 2 will be rated sell. How many ways are there to do this?

$$\frac{10!}{5!\times 3!\times 2!} = 2{,}520$$

90 - 1

LOS 8.o Identify/Solve
CFAI p. 444, Schweser p. 224

Probability Concepts

Choosing *r* Objects From *n* Objects

When order does not matter and with just two possible labels, we can use the **combination formula** (binomial formula).

Example: You have 5 stocks and want to place orders to sell 3 of them. How many different combinations of 3 stocks are there?

$${}_nC_r = \frac{n!}{(n-r)!r!} = \frac{5!}{(5-3)!\times 3!} = 10$$

91 - 1

LOS 8.o Identify/Solve
CFAI p. 444, Schweser p. 224
Probability Concepts

Choosing *r* Objects From *n* Objects

When order <u>does</u> matter, we use the **permutation formula**:

$$nPr = \frac{n!}{(n-r)!}$$

Example: You have 5 stocks and want to sell 3, one at a time. The order of the stock sales matters. How many ways are there to choose the 3 stocks to sell in order?

$$\frac{5!}{(5-3)!} = 60$$

92 - 1

LOS 8.o Identify/Solve
CFAI p. 444, Schweser p. 224
Probability Concepts

Calculator Solutions: nCr and nPr

- How many ways to choose 3 from 5, order doesn't matter? **5 → 2nd → nCr → 3 → = 10**

- How many ways to choose 3 from 5, order does matter? **5 → 2nd → nPr → 3 → = 60**

Functions only on BAII Plus (and Professional)

93

The Time Value of Money

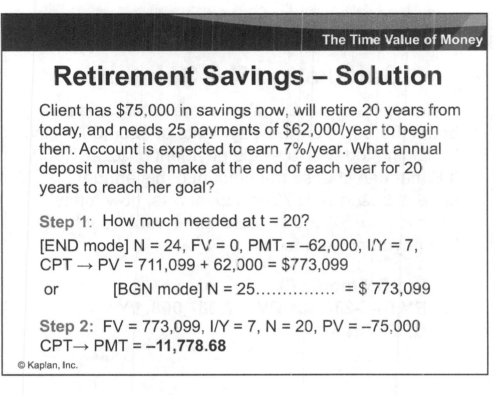

Retirement Savings – Solution

Client has $75,000 in savings now, will retire 20 years from today, and needs 25 payments of $62,000/year to begin then. Account is expected to earn 7%/year. What annual deposit must she make at the end of each year for 20 years to reach her goal?

Step 1: How much needed at t = 20?

[END mode] N = 24, FV = 0, PMT = –62,000, I/Y = 7, CPT → PV = 711,099 + 62,000 = $773,099

or [BGN mode] N = 25.............. = $ 773,099

Step 2: FV = 773,099, I/Y = 7, N = 20, PV = –75,000 CPT→ PMT = **–11,778.68**

The Time Value of Money

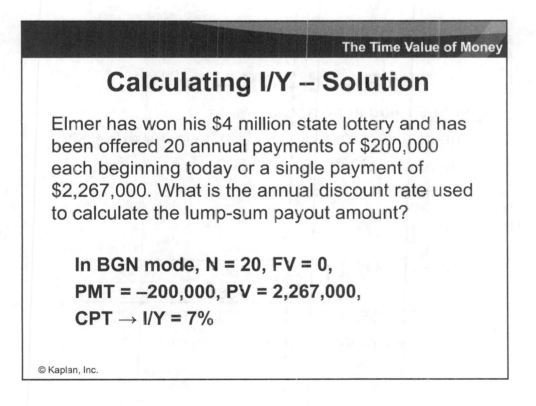

Calculating I/Y – Solution

Elmer has won his $4 million state lottery and has been offered 20 annual payments of $200,000 each beginning today or a single payment of $2,267,000. What is the annual discount rate used to calculate the lump-sum payout amount?

In BGN mode, N = 20, FV = 0,
PMT = –200,000, PV = 2,267,000,
CPT → I/Y = 7%

The Time Value of Money

Calculating N – Solution

Elmer has won his $4 million state lottery and has been offered 20 annual payments of $200,000 each beginning today or a single payment of $2,267,000. If Elmer can choose the amount of his annual payout, based on a 7% discount rate, how many payments of $232,631 could Elmer receive if his first payment were today?

In BGN mode, FV = 0,
PMT = –232,631,PV = 2,267,000, I/Y = 7%,
CPT → N = 15

Discounted Cash Flow Applications

MWR and TWR – Solution

Invest $1,000 in an account at t = 0

Value at end of Year 1 is $1,200, investor **adds $800**.

Value at end of Year 2 is $2,200.

Calculate the annual TWR and MWR.

TWR = $[(1.2)(1.1)]^{1/2} - 1 = 14.89\%$

MWR = 13.623% $-1{,}000 + \frac{-800}{1.13623} + \frac{2{,}200}{1.13623^2} = 0$

$CF_0 = -1{,}000$ $CF_1 = -800$ $CF_2 = 2{,}200$ IRR = 13.623%

MWR places more weight on second period returns

Discounted Cash Flow Applications

Yield Measures – Solution

A 90-day T-bill is purchased for $997.40. What are the discount yield, holding period yield, money market yield, and the effective yield?

Discount yield: [(1,000 – 997.40) / 1,000] × 4 = 1.04%

90-day HPY: 1,000 / 997.4 – 1 = 0.2607%

Money market yield: 0.2607 (360 / 90) = 1.0428%

Effective annual yield: $(1{,}000 / 997.4)^{365/90} - 1 =$ 1.0614%

Study Session 3

Quantitative Methods: Application

Quantitative Methods: Application

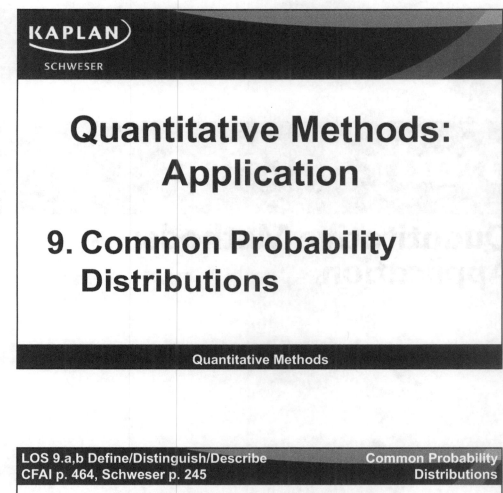

9. Common Probability Distributions

Quantitative Methods

LOS 9.a,b Define/Distinguish/Describe
CFAI p. 464, Schweser p. 245

Common Probability Distributions

Discrete and Continuous Probability Distributions

- A **probability distribution** gives the probabilities of all possible outcomes for a random variable
- A **discrete distribution** has a finite number of possible outcomes
- A **continuous distribution** has an infinite number of possible outcomes

2

LOS 9.a,b Define/Distinguish/Describe
CFAI p. 464, Schweser p. 245

Common Probability Distributions

Probability Functions

- The number of days next week on which it will rain is a **discrete random variable** that can take on the values {0,1,2,3,4,5,6,7}
- The amount of rain that will fall next week is a **continuous random variable**
- A **probability function**, **p(x),** gives the probability that a discrete random variable will take on the value x

  [e.g., p(x) = x / 15 for X = {1,2,3,4,5} → p(3) = 20%]

3

LOS 9.c,d Calculate/Interpret
CFAI p. 466, Schweser p. 247

Common Probability Distributions

Cumulative Distribution Function

A **cumulative distribution function** (cdf), F(x), gives the probability that a random variable will be less than or equal to a given value.

For the probability function:
p(x) = x / 15 for X = {1,2,3,4,5}

F(3) = 1 / 15 + 2 / 15 + 3 / 15 = 6 / 15 = 40%

4

LOS 9.c,d Calculate/Interpret
CFAI p. 466, Schweser p. 247

Common Probability Distributions

CDF for a Continuous Distribution

Example: The %ROE, x, for a firm is defined over (–20, +30) and has a CDF of F(x) = (x + 20) / 50. What is the probability that the ROE will be positive and less than or equal to 15?

Prob ($0 \leq x < 15$) = F(15) – F(0)
Prob ($x \leq 15$) = F(15) = (15 + 20) / 50 = 70%
Prob ($x \leq 0$) = F(0) = 20 / 50 = 40%
70 – 40 = 30%

 5-4

LOS 9.e Define
CFAI p. 466, Schweser p. 248

Common Probability Distributions

Discrete Uniform

- A <u>**discrete uniform distribution**</u> has a finite number of possible outcomes, all of which are equally likely

  For example, p(x) = 0.2 for X = {1,2,3,4,5}
  p(2) = 20%
  F(3) = 60%
  Prob($2 \leq X \leq 4$) = 60%

 6

LOS 9.e Define
CFAI p. 466, Schweser p. 248

Common Probability Distributions

Binomial Random Variable

- The probability of exactly <u>*x* successes</u> in *n* trials, given just two possible outcomes (success and failure)
- Probability of success on each trial (*p*) is constant, and trials are independent

$$p(x) = \left(\frac{n!}{(n-x)!x!}\right)p^x(1-p)^{n-x}$$

$$= nCx\ p^x(1-p)^{n-x}$$

 7

LOS 9.f Calculate/Interpret
CFAI p. 466, Schweser p. 248

Common Probability Distributions

Binomial – Example

What is the probability of drawing exactly two white marbles from a bowl of white and black marbles in six tries if the probability of selecting white is 0.4 each time?

$x = 2,\ p = 0.4,\ n = 6$

$$p(x) = (nCx)p^x(1-p)^{n-x} = \left(\frac{n!}{(n-x)!x!}\right)p^x(1-p)^{n-x}$$

$$p(2) = 15(0.4)^2(1-0.4)^{6-2} = 0.31$$

 8 - 3

LOS 9.g Construct
CFAI p. 476, Schweser p. 251

Common Probability Distributions

Binomial Tree

Two possible outcomes each period, up or down

Prob (up move) + Prob (down move) = 1
Up factor (U) > 1 Down factor (D) = 1/U

Example:
Beginning stock price (S_0) = $20
Prob up = 60% Prob down = 40%
Up factor = 1.12 Down factor 1 / 1.12

9

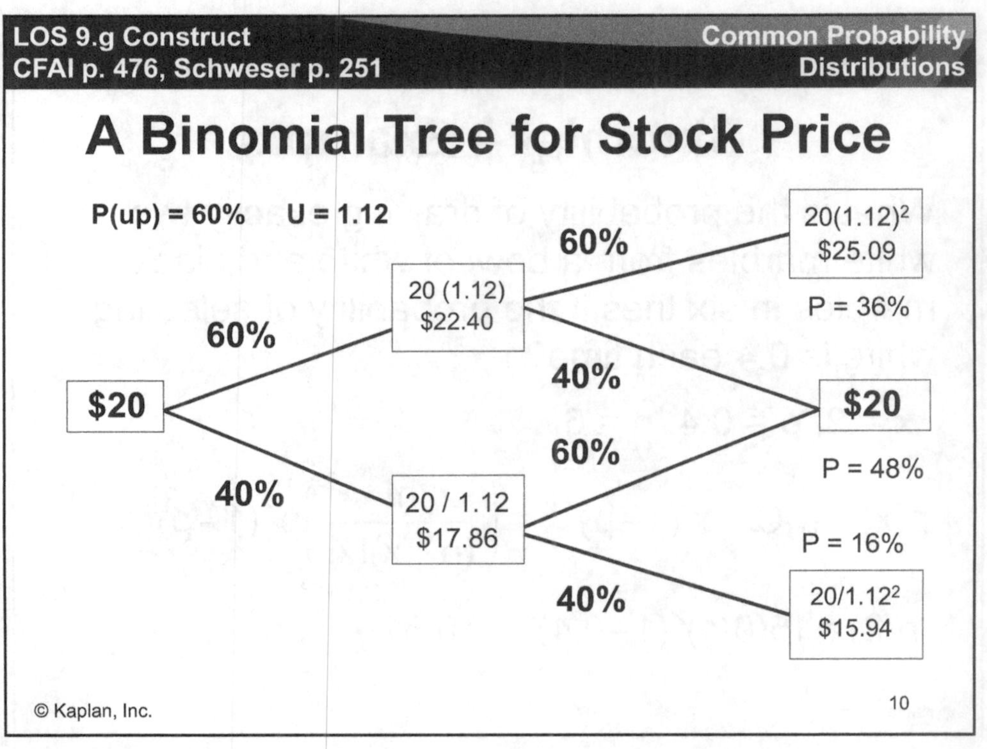

LOS 9.h Calculate/Interpret
CFAI p. 473, Schweser p. 253

Common Probability Distributions

Tracking Error

Tracking error = Total return on portfolio – total return on benchmark portfolio or index

Example:

U.S. stock portfolio total return = 4%

S&P 500 total return = 7%

Tracking error = –3%

 11

LOS 9.i Define/Calculate/Interpret
CFAI p. 477, Schweser p. 253

Common Probability Distributions

Continuous Uniform Distribution

Probability distributed evenly over an interval

Example: Random variable is continuous uniform over the interval 2 to 10.

$P(X < 2) = 0$ $P(X > 10) = 0$

$P(3 \leq X \leq 5) = (5 - 3) / (10 - 2) = 2 / 8 = 25\%$

 12 - 1

LOS 9.j,k Explain/Distinguish
CFAI p. 481, Schweser p. 255

Common Probability Distributions

Properties of Normal Distribution

- Completely described by **mean and variance**
- **Symmetric** about the mean (skewness = 0)
- **Kurtosis** (a measure of peakedness) = 3
- Linear combination of normally distributed random variables is also normally distributed
- Probabilities decrease further from the mean, but the **tails go on forever**

Multivariate normal: more than one random variable, need means, variances, and correlation coefficients

13

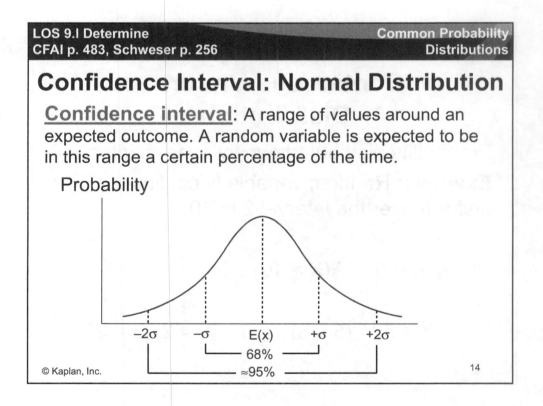

Confidence Interval: Normal Distribution

Confidence interval: A range of values around an expected outcome. A random variable is expected to be in this range a certain percentage of the time.

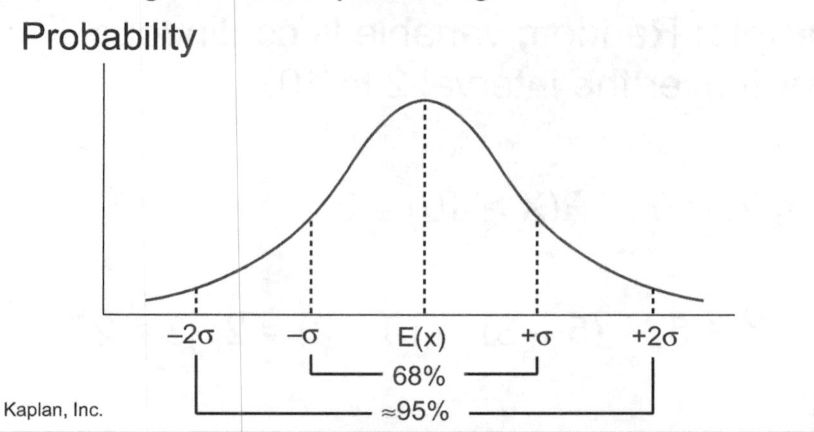

14

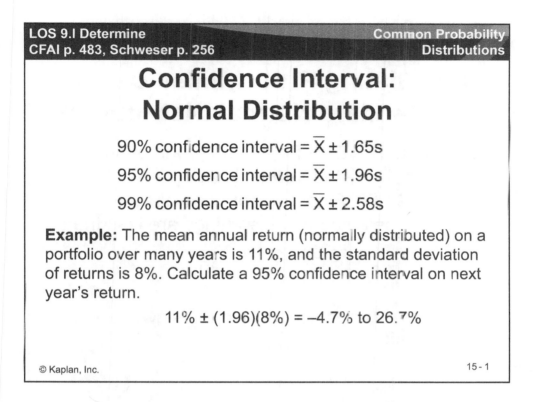

LOS 9.l Determine
CFAI p. 483, Schweser p. 256

Common Probability Distributions

Confidence Interval: Normal Distribution

$$90\% \text{ confidence interval} = \overline{X} \pm 1.65s$$

$$95\% \text{ confidence interval} = \overline{X} \pm 1.96s$$

$$99\% \text{ confidence interval} = \overline{X} \pm 2.58s$$

Example: The mean annual return (normally distributed) on a portfolio over many years is 11%, and the standard deviation of returns is 8%. Calculate a 95% confidence interval on next year's return.

$$11\% \pm (1.96)(8\%) = -4.7\% \text{ to } 26.7\%$$

15 - 1

LOS 9.m Define/Explain/Calculate/Interpret
CFAI p. 484, Schweser p. 258

Common Probability Distributions

Standard Normal Distribution

- A normal distribution that has been standardized so that **mean = 0 and standard deviation = 1**
- To standardize a random variable, calculate the z-value
- Subtract the mean (so mean = 0) and divide by standard deviation (so σ = 1)

$$z = \frac{X - \mu}{\sigma}$$

Z is the number of standard deviations from the mean

16

LOS 9.m Define/Explain/Calculate/Interpret
CFAI p. 484, Schweser p. 258
Common Probability Distributions

Calculating Probabilities Using the Standard Normal Distribution

Example: The EPS for a large group of firms are normally distributed and have **μ = $4.00** and **σ = $1.50**. Find the probability that a randomly selected firm's earnings are less than $3.70.

$$z = \frac{3.70 - 4.00}{1.50} = -0.20$$

3.70 is 0.20 standard deviations below the mean of 4.00

17 - 2

LOS 9.m Define/Explain/Calculate/Interpret
CFAI p. 484, Schweser p. 258
Common Probability Distributions

Calculating Probabilities Using the Standard Normal Distribution

$$z = \frac{3.70 - 4.00}{1.50} = -0.20$$

For negative z-value, calculate 1 – table value

N(–0.2) = 1 – N(0.2) = 1 – 0.5793 = 0.4207 = **42.07%**

Z	.00	0.01
0.0	0.5000	0.5040
0.1	0.5398	0.5438
0.2	0.5793	0.5832

18 - 2

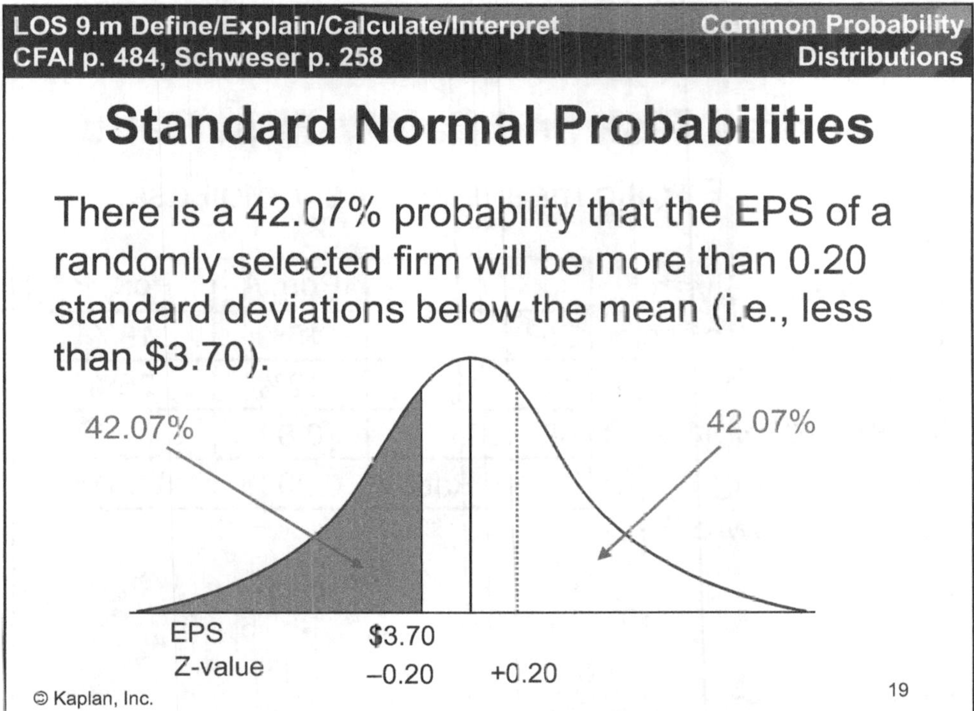

LOS 9.m Define/Explain/Calculate/Interpret
CFAI p. 484, Schweser p. 258
Common Probability Distributions
Standard Normal Probabilities
There is a 42.07% probability that the EPS of a randomly selected firm will be more than 0.20 standard deviations below the mean (i.e., less than $3.70).
42.07%
42.07%
EPS
Z-value
$3.70
–0.20
+0.20
© Kaplan, Inc.
19

LOS 9.n Define/Calculate/Select
CFAI p. 487, Schweser p. 261

Common Probability Distributions

Shortfall Risk and Safety-First Ratio

Shortfall risk: Probability that a portfolio return or value will be below a target return or value

Roy's Safety-First Ratio: Number of std. dev. target is below the expected return/value

$$\text{SF Ratio} = \frac{[E(R_P) - R_L]}{\sigma_P}, \text{ where } R_L = \text{threshold/target return}$$

If R_L = Risk-free rate, SF Ratio is the same as Sharpe ratio

20

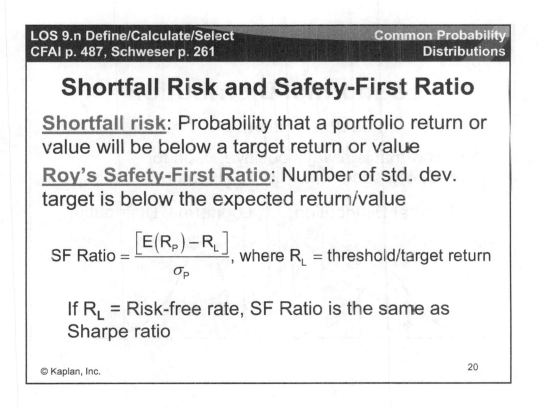

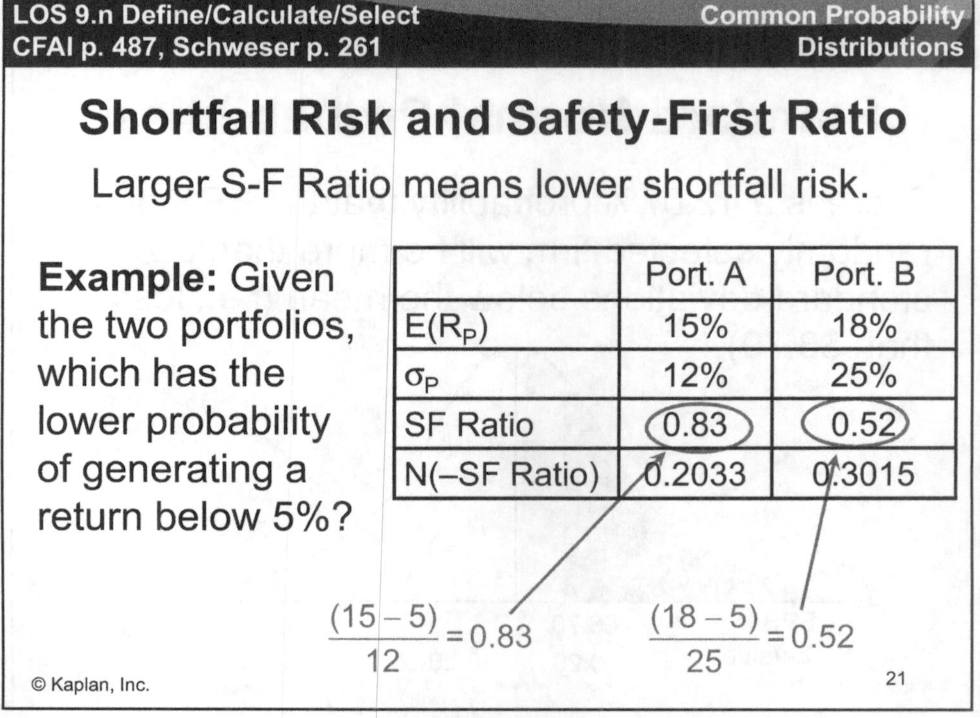
LOS 9.n Define/Calculate/Select
CFAI p. 487, Schweser p. 261
Common Probability Distributions
Shortfall Risk and Safety-First Ratio
Larger S-F Ratio means lower shortfall risk.
Example: Given the two portfolios, which has the lower probability of generating a return below 5%?
Port. A
Port. B
E(R_P)
15%
18%
σ_P
12%
25%
SF Ratio
0.83
0.52
N(–SF Ratio)
0.2033
0.3015
(15 – 5) / 12 = 0.83
(18 – 5) / 25 = 0.52
© Kaplan, Inc.
21

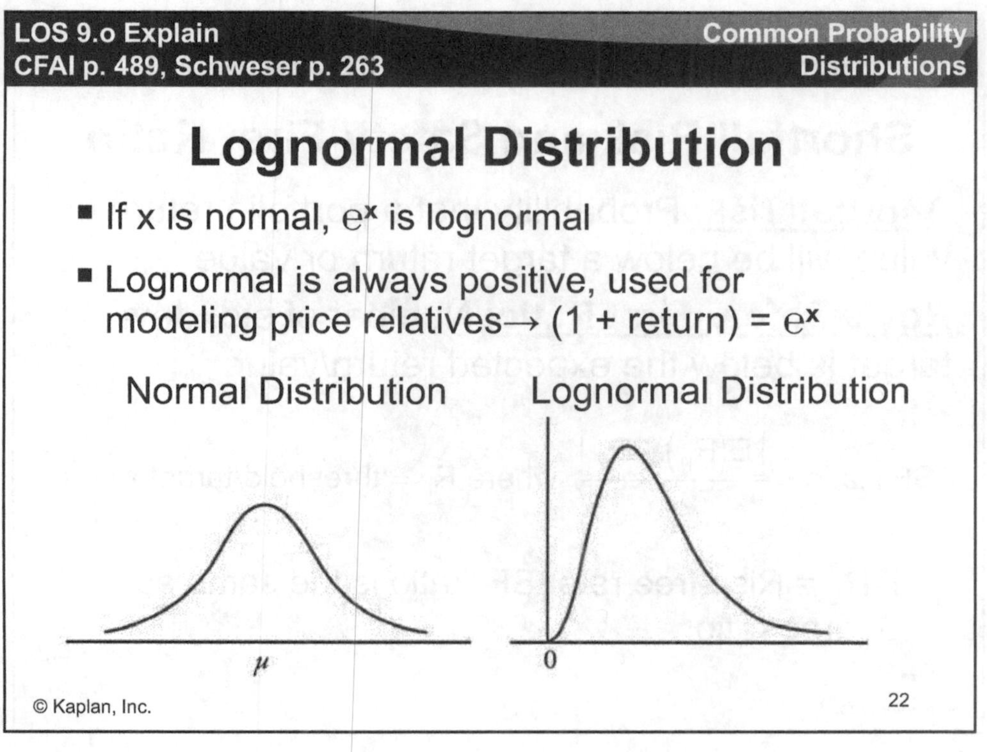
LOS 9.o Explain
CFAI p. 489, Schweser p. 263
Common Probability Distributions
Lognormal Distribution
If x is normal, e^x is lognormal
Lognormal is always positive, used for modeling price relatives→ (1 + return) = e^x
Normal Distribution
Lognormal Distribution
μ
0
© Kaplan, Inc.
22

LOS 9.p Distinguish/Calculate/Interpret
CFAI p. 491, Schweser p. 264

Common Probability Distributions

Continuous Compounding

- Continuously compounded rate = ln(1 + HPR)
- EAY with continuous compounding = $e^i - 1$

Example: 1-year holding period return = 8%

Continuously compounded rate of return =

ln (1.08) = 7.7%   ln (108 / 100) = 7.7%

7.7% rate with continuous compounding,

EAY = $e^{0.077} - 1 = 8\%$

23 - 3

Common Probability Distributions

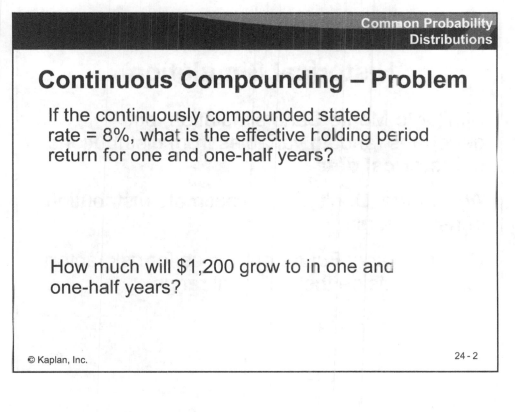

Continuous Compounding – Problem

If the continuously compounded stated rate = 8%, what is the effective holding period return for one and one-half years?

How much will $1,200 grow to in one and one-half years?

24 - 2

LOS 9.q Explain/Describe
CFAI p. 494, Schweser p. 266

Common Probability Distributions

Monte Carlo Simulation

Simulation can be used to estimate a distribution of derivatives prices or of NPVs

1. Specify distributions of random variables such as interest rates, underlying stock prices
2. Use computer random generation of variables
3. Value the derivative using those values
4. Repeat steps 2 and 3 1,000s of times
5. Calculate mean/variance of all values

25

LOS 9.r Compare
CFAI p. 500, Schweser p. 267

Common Probability Distributions

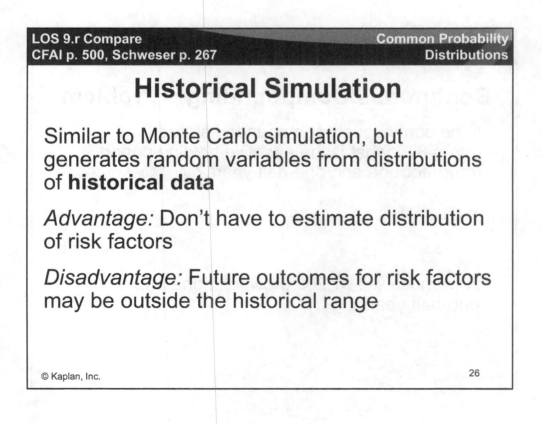

Historical Simulation

Similar to Monte Carlo simulation, but generates random variables from distributions of **historical data**

Advantage: Don't have to estimate distribution of risk factors

Disadvantage: Future outcomes for risk factors may be outside the historical range

26

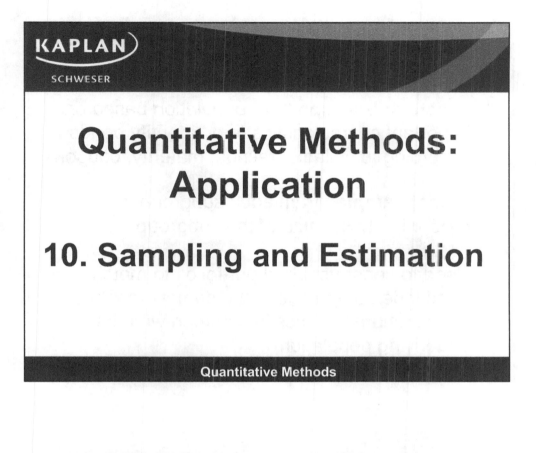

Quantitative Methods: Application

10. Sampling and Estimation

Quantitative Methods

LOS 10.a,b Define/Explain
CFAI p. 514, Schweser p. 280

Sampling and Estimation

Sampling

- To make inferences about the parameters of a population, we will use a **sample**
- A **simple random sample** is one where every population member has an equal chance of being selected
- A **sampling distribution** is the distribution of sample statistics for repeated samples of size *n*
- **Sampling error** is the difference between a sample statistic and true population parameter (e.g., $\bar{x} - \mu$)

28

LOS 10.c Distinguish
CFAI p. 515, Schweser p. 281 Sampling and Estimation

Stratified Random Sampling

1. **Create subgroups** from population based on important characteristics (e.g., identify bonds according to callable, ratings, maturity, coupon)

2. **Select samples** from each subgroup in proportion to the size of the subgroup

Used to construct bond portfolios to match a bond index or to construct a sample that has certain characteristics in common with the underlying population

 29

LOS 10.d Distinguish
CFAI p. 517, Schweser p. 282 Sampling and Estimation

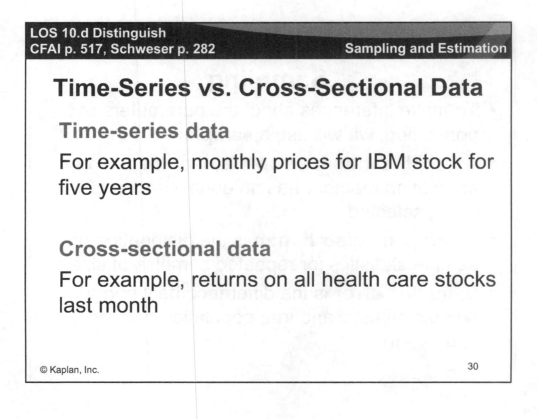

Time-Series vs. Cross-Sectional Data

Time-series data

For example, monthly prices for IBM stock for five years

Cross-sectional data

For example, returns on all health care stocks last month

 30

LOS 10.e Explain
CFAI p. 520, Schweser p. 282
Sampling and Estimation

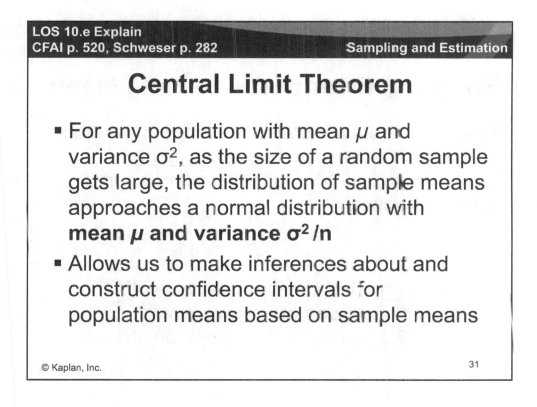

Central Limit Theorem

- For any population with mean μ and variance σ^2, as the size of a random sample gets large, the distribution of sample means approaches a normal distribution with **mean μ and variance σ^2/n**
- Allows us to make inferences about and construct confidence intervals for population means based on sample means

31

LOS 10.f Calculate/Interpret
CFAI p. 520, Schweser p. 283
Sampling and Estimation

Standard Error of the Sample Mean

Standard error of sample mean is the standard deviation of the distribution of sample means.

- When the population σ is **known**:

$$\sigma_{\bar{x}} = \frac{\sigma}{\sqrt{n}}$$

- When the population σ is **unknown**:

$$s_{\bar{x}} = \frac{s}{\sqrt{n}}$$

32

LOS 10.f Calculate/Interpret
CFAI p. 520, Schweser p. 283

Sampling and Estimation

Standard Error of the Sample Mean

Example: The mean P/E for a sample of 41 firms is **19.0**, and the standard deviation of the population is **6.6**. What is the standard error of the **sample mean**?

$$\sigma_{\bar{x}} = \frac{\sigma}{\sqrt{n}} = \frac{6.6}{\sqrt{41}} = 1.03$$

Interpretation: For samples of size n = 41, the distribution of the **sample means** would have a mean of 19.0 and a standard deviation of 1.03.

33

LOS 10.g Identify/Describe
CFAI p. 523, Schweser p. 285

Sampling and Estimation

Desirable Estimator Properties

1. **Unbiased** – expected value equal to parameter
2. **Efficient** – sampling distribution has smallest variance of all unbiased estimators
3. **Consistent** – larger sample → better estimator
   Standard error of estimate decreases with larger sample size

34

LOS 10.h Distinguish
CFAI p. 523, Schweser p. 285 Sampling and Estimation

Point Estimate and Confidence Interval

Example: The mean P/E (point estimate) for a sample of 41 firms is **19.0**, the standard error of the sample mean is **1.03**, and the population is normal

90% confidence interval is 19 +/– 1.65 (1.03)

17.3 < mean < 20.7

95% confidence interval is 19 +/– 1.96 (1.03)

17.0 < mean < 21.0

95% confidence interval for a randomly chosen firm 19 +/–1.96(6.6) or 6.06 < mean < 31.94

 35 - 5

LOS 10.i Describe/Calculate/Interpret
CFAI p. 527, Schweser p. 285 Sampling and Estimation

Student's *t*-Distribution and Degrees of Freedom

Properties of Student's *t*-Distribution

- Symmetrical (bell shaped)
- Fatter tails than a normal distribution
- Defined by single parameter, degrees of freedom (df), where df = n – 1
- As df increase, *t*-distribution approaches normal distribution

 36

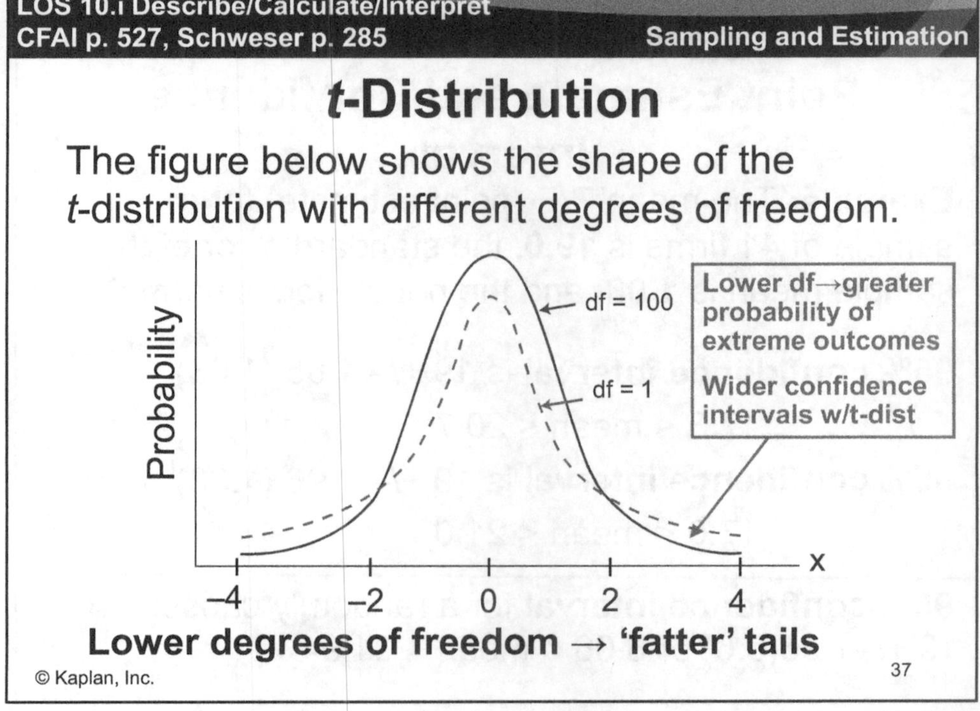

LOS 10.j Calculate/Interpret
CFAI p. 525, Schweser p. 287 — Sampling and Estimation

Constructing Confidence Intervals

- Confidence interval for a normal random variable is **mean +/– (reliability factor) standard deviation**
- Reliability factor depends on distribution

For normal distribution with mean = 3 and s.d. = 2

- For **90%** confidence interval:
  3 – **1.65**(2) to 3 + **1.65**(2) = –0.3 to 6.3
- For **95%** confidence interval:
  3 – **1.96**(2) to 3 + **1.96**(2) = –0.92 to 6.92

 38

LOS 10.j Calculate/Interpret
CFAI p. 525, Schweser p. 287 Sampling and Estimation

Confidence Intervals for Mean

When sampling from a:		Reliability Factors	
Distribution	**Variance**	**Small Sample ($n < 30$)**	**Large Sample ($n > 30$)**
Normal	Known	*z*-statistic	*z*-statistic
Normal	Unknown	*t*-statistic	*t*-statistic*
Nonnormal	Known	Not available	*z*-statistic
Nonnormal	Unknown	Not available	*t*-statistic*

***The *z*-statistic is theoretically acceptable here, but use of the *t*-statistic is more conservative.**

 39

LOS 10.j Calculate/Interpret
CFAI p. 525, Schweser p. 287 Sampling and Estimation

Confidence Interval for Mean:

Normal distribution, unknown variance

Example: The sample mean is 19.0, the sample standard deviation is 6.6, and n = 41. Establish a 90% confidence interval for the population mean.

$$t\text{-table reliability factor is } 1.684 \text{ (df} = 40, \alpha/2 = 0.05)$$

$$\text{standard error of mean} = \frac{s}{\sqrt{n}} = \frac{6.6}{\sqrt{41}} = 1.03$$

$$19.0 \pm 1.684\,(1.03) = 17.27 < \text{mean} < 20.73$$

 40 - 1

LOS 10.k Describe
CFAI p. 530, Schweser p. 292
Sampling and Estimation

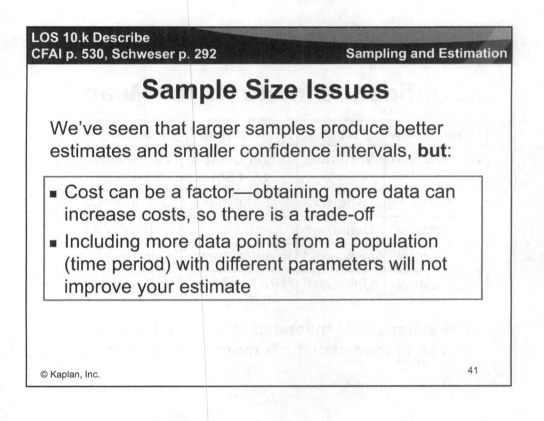

Sample Size Issues

We've seen that larger samples produce better estimates and smaller confidence intervals, **but**:

- Cost can be a factor—obtaining more data can increase costs, so there is a trade-off
- Including more data points from a population (time period) with different parameters will not improve your estimate

41

LOS 10.k Describe
CFAI p. 530, Schweser p. 292
Sampling and Estimation

Types of Bias

- **Data-mining bias** – from repeatedly doing tests on same data sample
- **Sample selection bias** – sample not really random
- **Survivorship bias** – sampling only surviving firms, mutual funds, hedge funds
- **Look-ahead bias** – using information not available at the time to construct sample
- **Time-period bias** – relationship exists only during the time period of sample data

42

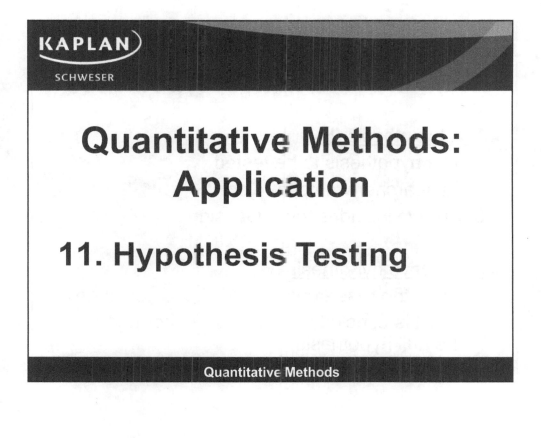

Quantitative Methods: Application

11. Hypothesis Testing

Quantitative Methods

LOS 11.a Define/Describe/Interpret/Distinguish
CFAI p. 552, Schweser p. 303 Hypothesis Testing

Steps in Hypothesis Testing

- State the hypothesis—relation to be tested
- Select a test statistic
- Specify the level of significance
- State the decision rule for the hypothesis
- Collect the sample and calculate statistics
- Make a decision about the hypothesis
- Make a decision based on the test results

 44

LOS 11.a Define/Describe/Interpret/Distinguish
CFAI p. 552, Schweser p. 303 Hypothesis Testing

Null and Alternative Hypotheses

- Null hypothesis (H_0)
  1. The hypothesis to be tested
  2. Researcher wants to reject it
  3. Always includes the equal sign

- Alternative hypothesis (H_a)
  1. What the researcher would like to conclude
  2. What is concluded if the researcher rejects the null hypothesis

 45

LOS 11.b Explain
CFAI p. 555, Schweser p. 308 Hypothesis Testing

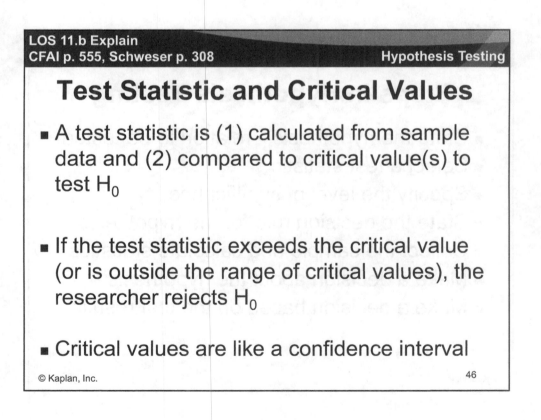

Test Statistic and Critical Values

- A test statistic is (1) calculated from sample data and (2) compared to critical value(s) to test H_0

- If the test statistic exceeds the critical value (or is outside the range of critical values), the researcher rejects H_0

- Critical values are like a confidence interval

 46

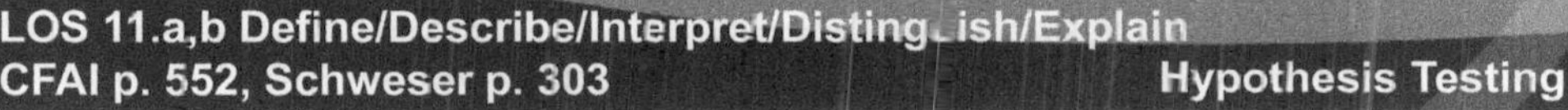

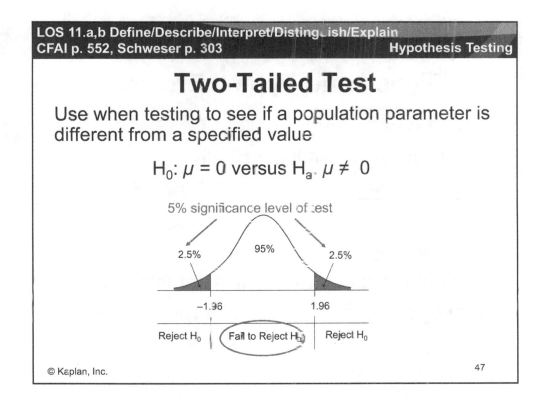

Two-Tailed Test

Use when testing to see if a population parameter is different from a specified value

H_0: $\mu = 0$ versus H_a: $\mu \neq 0$

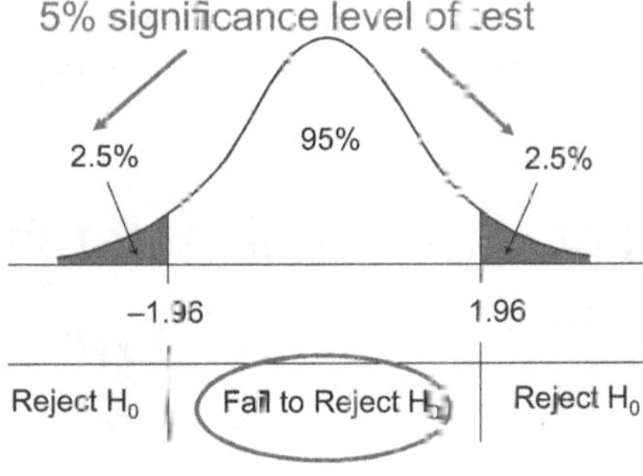

 47

LOS 11.a,b Define/Describe/Interpret/Distinguish/Explain
CFAI p. 552, Schweser p. 303 Hypothesis Testing

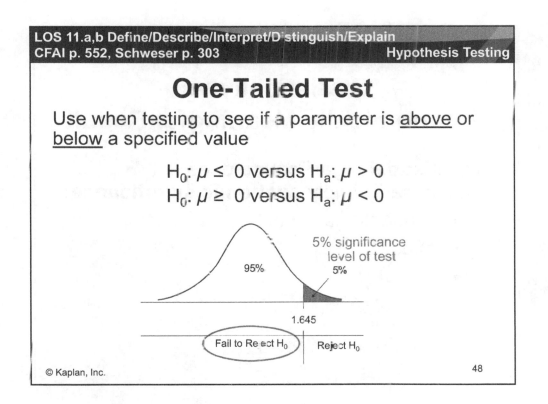

One-Tailed Test

Use when testing to see if a parameter is above or below a specified value

H_0: $\mu \leq 0$ versus H_a: $\mu > 0$
H_0: $\mu \geq 0$ versus H_a: $\mu < 0$

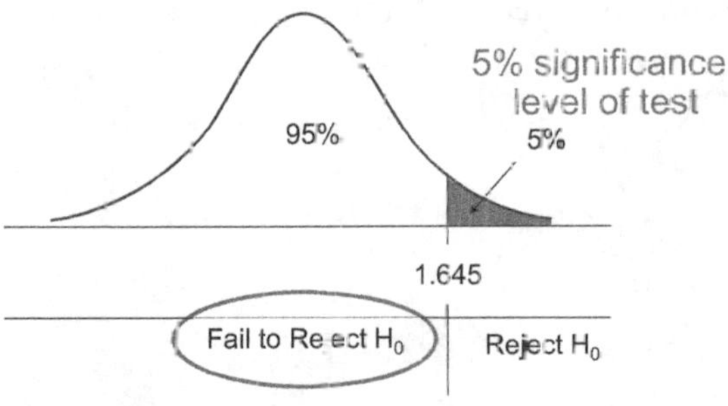

 48

LOS 11.b,c Explain
CFAI p. 555, Schweser p. 308 Hypothesis Testing

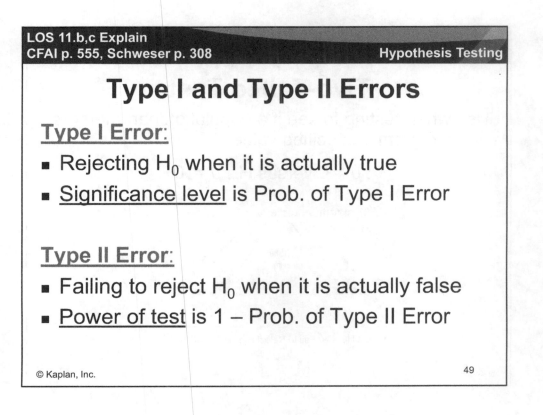

Type I and Type II Errors

Type I Error:

- Rejecting H_0 when it is actually true
- Significance level is Prob. of Type I Error

Type II Error:

- Failing to reject H_0 when it is actually false
- Power of test is 1 – Prob. of Type II Error

 49

LOS 11.d Distinguish
CFAI p. 560, Schweser p. 312 Hypothesis Testing

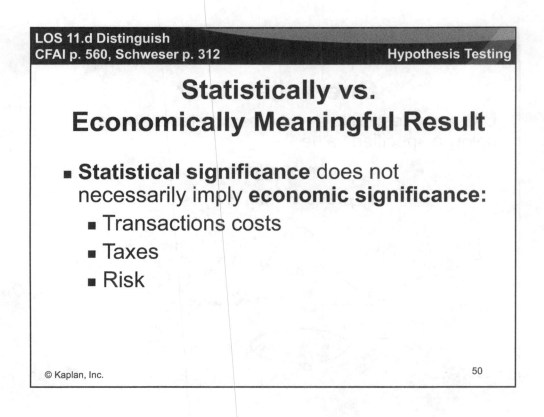

Statistically vs. Economically Meaningful Result

- **Statistical significance** does not necessarily imply **economic significance:**
  - Transactions costs
  - Taxes
  - Risk

 50

LOS 11.e Explain/Interpret
CFAI p. 560, Schweser p. 313 **Hypothesis Testing**

p-value Example

A *p*-value is the smallest level of significance at which the null can be rejected, the probability of getting the test statistic by chance if the null is true.

If the *p*-value is given as 0.0213 or 2.13%:

We **can** reject the null at 5% significance.

We **can** reject the null at 3% significance.

We **cannot** reject the null at 1% significance.

51

LOS 11.f Identify/Interpret
CFAI p. 561, Schweser p. 314 **Hypothesis Testing**

Test Statistics

Test of **mean** of normal population when population variance is **unknown**, use a ***t*-statistic**

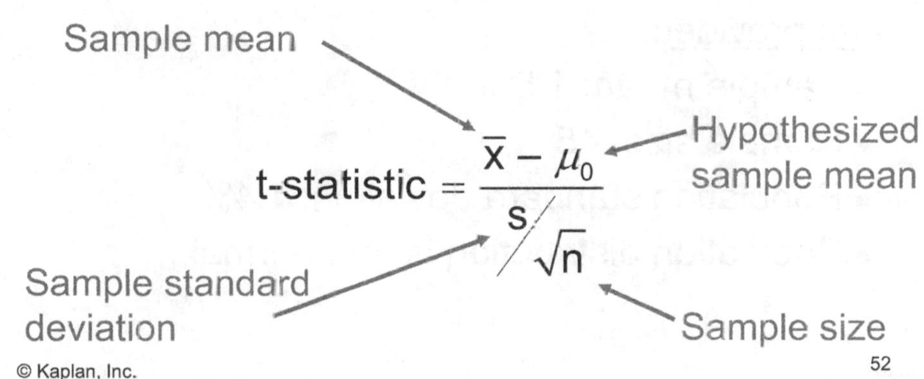

52

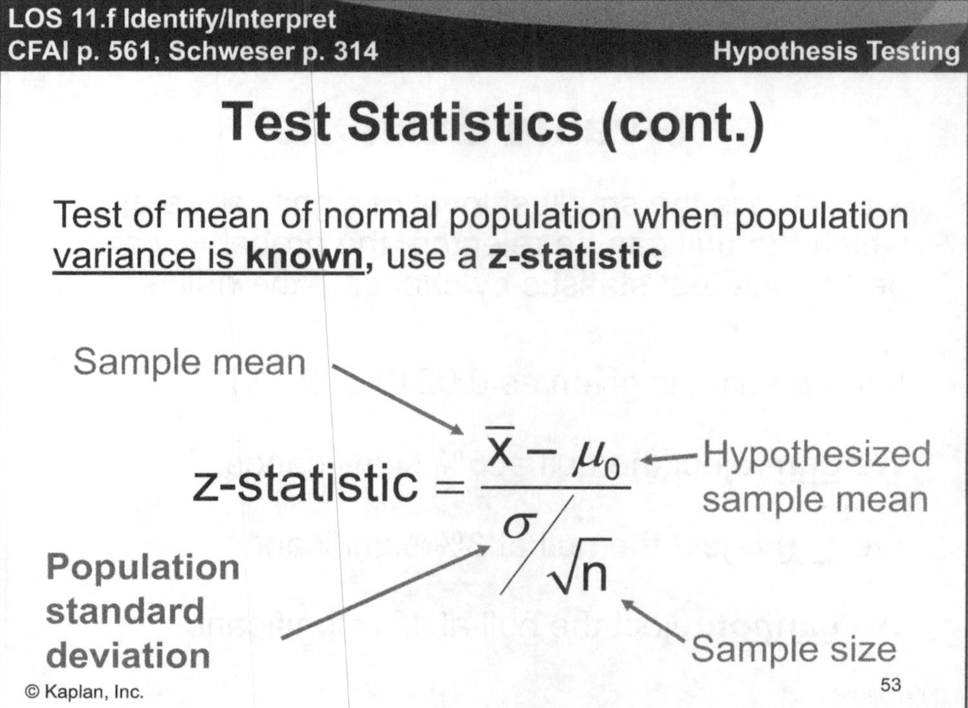
LOS 11.f Identify/Interpret
CFAI p. 561, Schweser p. 314
Hypothesis Testing
Test Statistics (cont.)
Test of mean of normal population when population variance is known, use a z-statistic
Sample mean
z-statistic = $\frac{\bar{x} - \mu_0}{\sigma / \sqrt{n}}$
Hypothesized sample mean
Population standard deviation
Sample size
© Kaplan, Inc.
53

LOS 11.f Identify/Interpret
CFAI p. 561, Schweser p. 314
Hypothesis Testing

Hypothesis Testing: Example

Test the hypothesis that a fund's mean return is equal to 1% per month at the 95% confidence (5% significance) level.

Data provided:

- Sample mean: 1.5%
- Sample size: 45
- Population standard deviation: 1.4%
- Population distribution is non-normal

54

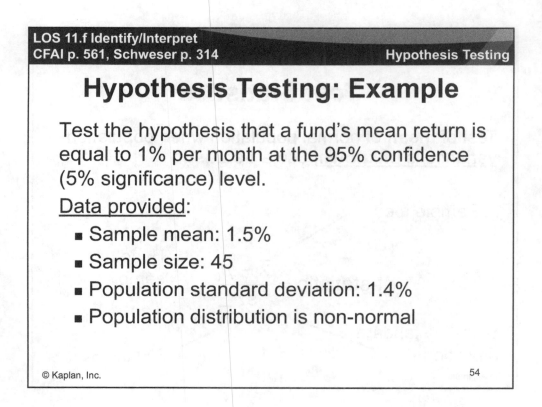

LOS 11.f Identify/Interpret
CFAI p. 561, Schweser p. 314 Hypothesis Testing

Hypothesis Testing: Example (cont.)

- With known population variance and large sample size, use *z*-test (two-tailed)
- H_0: $\mu = 0.01$ and H_a: $\mu \neq 0.01$
- The critical *z*-values for 95% confidence interval (5% significance level) are +/– 1.96
- Decision rule: If the test statistic is outside the range of critical values (–1.96 to +1.96), reject H_0

 55

LOS 11.f Identify/Interpret
CFAI p. 561, Schweser p. 314 Hypothesis Testing

Hypothesis Testing: Example (cont.)

- Calculate the test statistic:

$$\text{z-statistic} = \frac{\bar{x} - \mu_0}{\sigma / \sqrt{n}} = \frac{0.015 - 0.010}{0.014 / \sqrt{45}} = 2.396$$

Interpret results:

Reject H_0: mean return = 1%, because the *z*-stat (2.396) is outside the range of critical values (–1.96 to +1.96)

 56 - 2

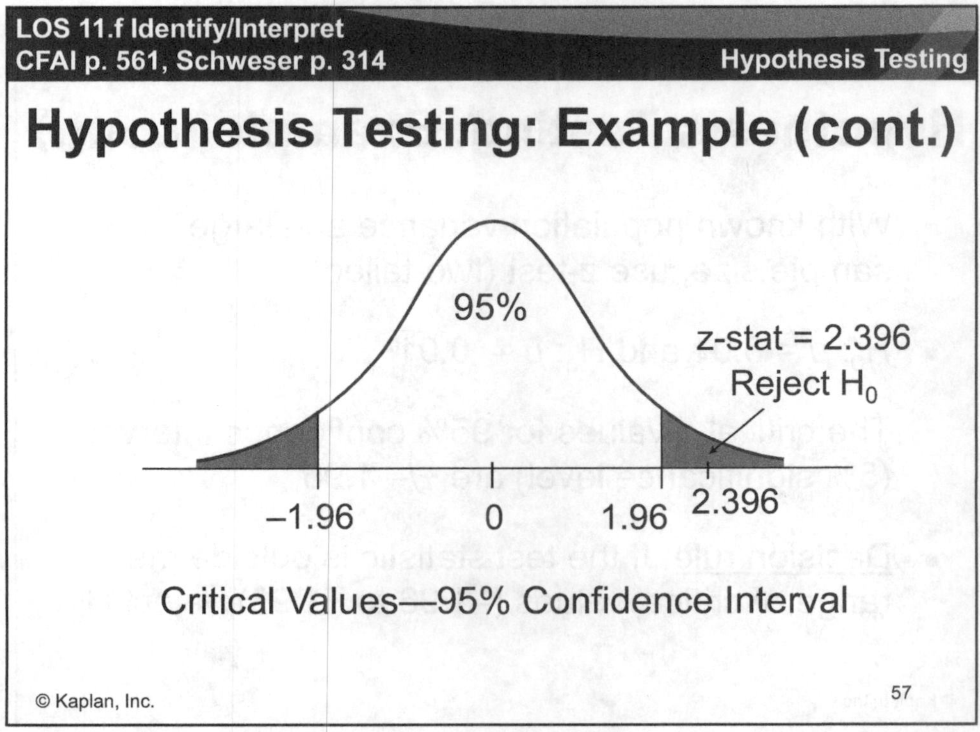

LOS 11.g Identify/Interpret
CFAI p. 568, Schweser p. 317

Hypothesis Testing

Test Statistics: Difference in Means

Test of whether the means of two normal populations are equal – **independent** samples

$$\text{t-stat} = \frac{\bar{x}_1 - \bar{x}_2}{\sqrt{\frac{S_P^2}{n_1} + \frac{S_P^2}{n_2}}}$$

When variances are assumed to be **equal** use S_P, pooled variance estimator

$$\text{t-stat} = \frac{\bar{x}_1 - \bar{x}_2}{\sqrt{\frac{S_1^2}{n_1} + \frac{S_2^2}{n_2}}}$$

When variances are assumed to be **unequal** use sum of sample variances

Reject if t-stat is greater/less than critical values

58

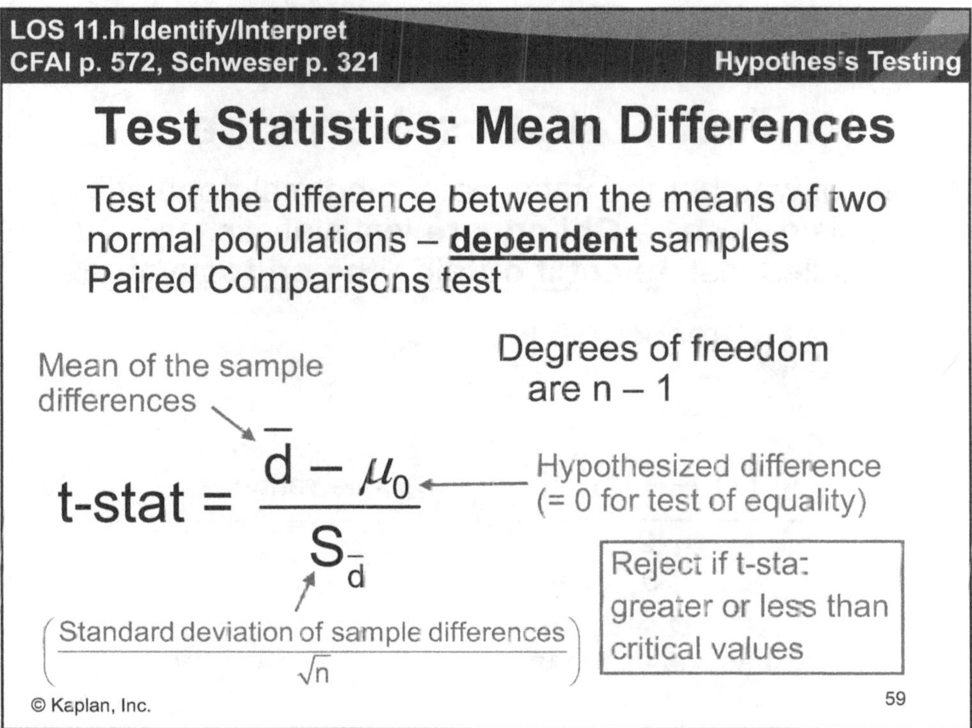

LOS 11.h Identify/Interpret
CFAI p. 572, Schweser p. 321
Hypothesis Testing
Test Statistics: Mean Differences
Test of the difference between the means of two normal populations – dependent samples
Paired Comparisons test
Mean of the sample differences
Degrees of freedom are n – 1
$$\text{t-stat} = \frac{\bar{d} - \mu_0}{S_{\bar{d}}}$$
Hypothesized difference (= 0 for test of equality)
Reject if t-stat greater or less than critical values
$\left(\frac{\text{Standard deviation of sample differences}}{\sqrt{n}}\right)$
© Kaplan, Inc.
59

LOS 11.g,h Identify/Interpret
CFAI p. 568, Schweser p. 317
Hypothesis Testing

Test Statistics

Note that the LOS only requires you to:

Identify the appropriate test statistic and interpret the results for a hypothesis test concerning:

1. The difference in means and the mean difference tests are *t*-tests, reject if t-stat is greater than critical value
2. Use **difference in means** test for samples from two independent normal populations
3. Use **mean differences** test for two dependent, equal-size, samples from normal populations.

60

LOS 11.i Identify/Interpret
CFAI p. 576, Schweser p. 325 Hypothesis Testing

Test Statistics: Variance

Test of whether the variance of a normal population equals σ_0^2 uses a **Chi-square** test statistic, two-tailed test, **reject if outside the critical values**

Degrees of freedom are n – 1

$$\chi^2_{n-1} = \frac{(n-1)S^2}{\sigma_0^2}$$

Sample variance

Hypothesized variance

 61

LOS 11.i Identify/Interpret
CFAI p. 576, Schweser p. 325 Hypothesis Testing

Test Statistics: Variance

Test of whether the variances of two normal populations are equal is an **F-test**

Putting the larger sample variance in the numerator allows us to **consider only upper critical value** – although F-test is a two-tailed test

$$F = \frac{S_1^2}{S_2^2}$$

Larger sample variance

Smaller sample variance

Degrees of freedom are $n_1 - 1$ and $n_2 - 1$

 62

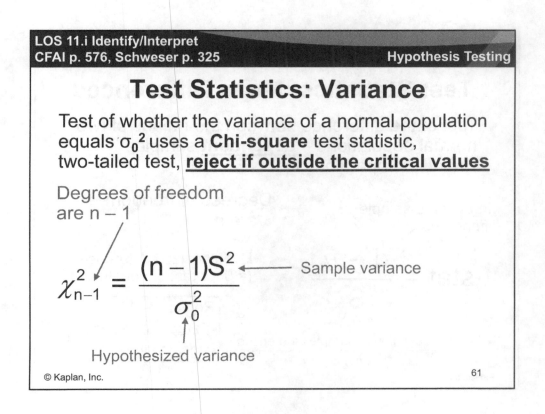

LOS 11.j Distinguish/Describe
CFAI p. 578, Schweser p. 332

Hypothesis Testing

Parametric and Nonparametric Tests

- **Parametric tests** are based on assumptions about population distributions and population parameters (e.g., *t*-test, *z*-test, F-test)
- **Nonparametric tests** make few if any assumptions about the population distribution and test things other than parameter values (e.g., runs tests, rank correlation tests)

63

Quantitative Methods: Application

12. Technical Analysis

Quantitative Methods

LOS 12.a Explain
CFAI p. 602, Schweser p. 343

Technical Analysis

Principles and Assumptions of Technical Analysis

- Stock values determined by **supply and demand which** are **driven by both rational and irrational behavior**
- Technical analysts use prices and trading volume to analyze changes in supply and demand
- Security **prices move in trends** that persist for long periods and repeat themselves in predictable ways

65

LOS 12.a Explain
CFAI p. 602, Schweser p. 343 Technical Analysis

Technical Analysis vs. Fundamental Analysis

- **Fundamental analysts** look for changes in intrinsic values (what prices **should** be) based primarily on anticipated financial results and estimates of future cash flows
- **Technical analysts** try to predict price change though analysis of past trades

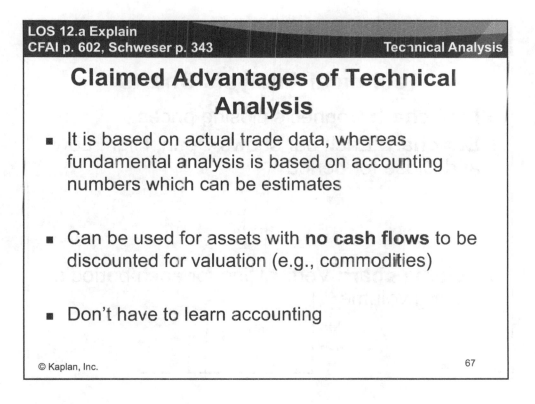

 66

LOS 12.a Explain
CFAI p. 602, Schweser p. 343 Technical Analysis

Claimed Advantages of Technical Analysis

- It is based on actual trade data, whereas fundamental analysis is based on accounting numbers which can be estimates
- Can be used for assets with **no cash flows** to be discounted for valuation (e.g., commodities)
- Don't have to learn accounting

 67

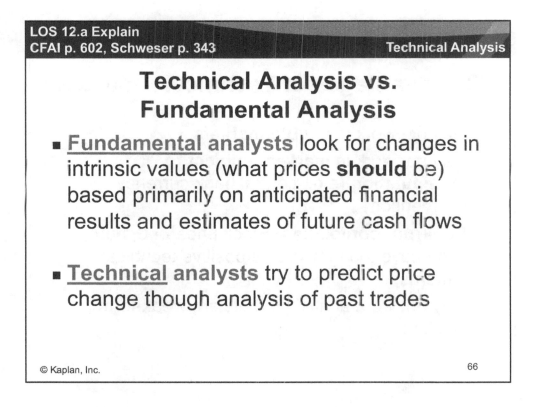

LOS 12.a Explain
CFAI p. 602, Schweser p. 343
Technical Analysis

Disadvantages of Technical Analysis

- May not work in **illiquid markets**
- May not work in **markets subject to manipulation** (e.g., central bank currency intervention)
- **Bankrupt companies:** Stock price → 0, but short covering may create positive technical patterns
- May not work at all if markets are weak-form efficient

68

LOS 12.b Describe/Interpret
CFAI p. 606, Schweser p. 344
Technical Analysis

Technical Analysis Charts

- **Line chart:** Connects closing prices
- **Bar chart:** Each bar shows Open, High, Low, and Close for period

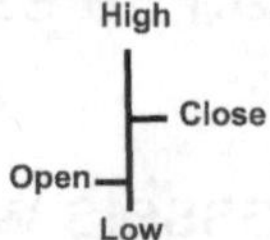

- **Volume chart:** Vertical line for each period's trading volume

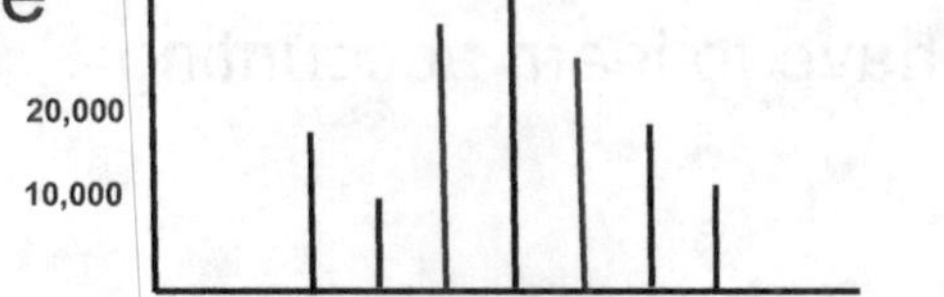

69

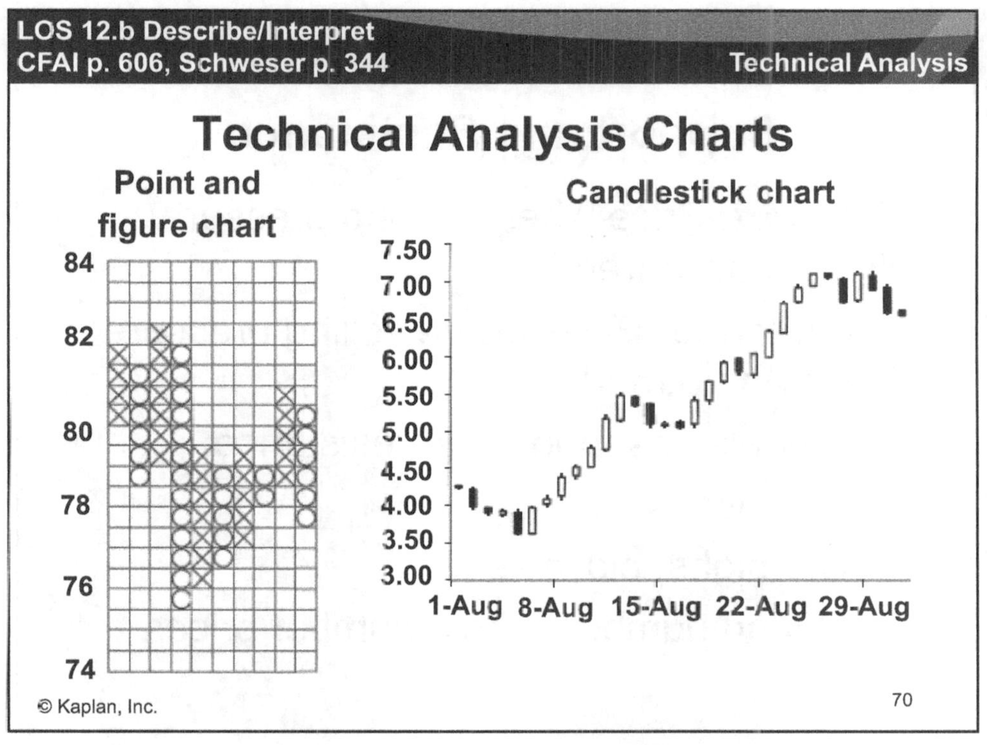
LOS 12.b Describe/Interpret
CFAI p. 606, Schweser p. 344
Technical Analysis
Technical Analysis Charts
Point and figure chart
Candlestick chart
84
82
80
78
76
74
7.50
7.00
6.50
6.00
5.50
5.00
4.50
4.00
3.50
3.00
1-Aug 8-Aug 15-Aug 22-Aug 29-Aug
© Kaplan, Inc.
70

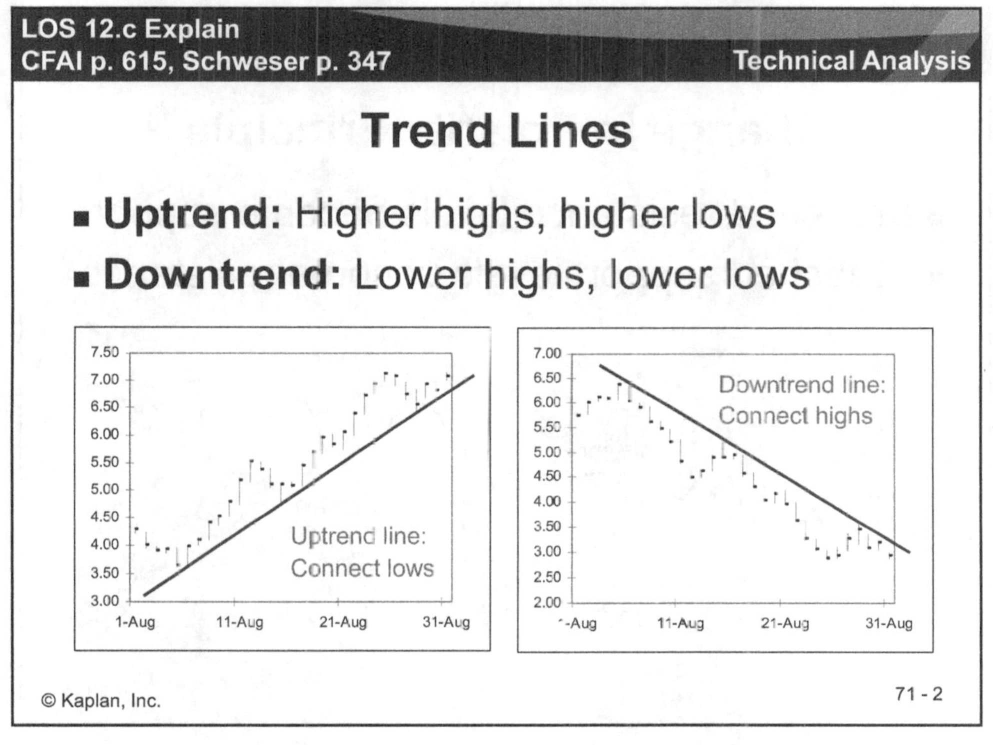
LOS 12.c Explain
CFAI p. 615, Schweser p. 347
Technical Analysis
Trend Lines
Uptrend: Higher highs, higher lows
Downtrend: Lower highs, lower lows
Uptrend line: Connect lows
Downtrend line: Connect highs
1-Aug 11-Aug 21-Aug 31-Aug
© Kaplan, Inc.
71 - 2

LOS 12.c Explain
CFAI p. 615, Schweser p. 347 Technical Analysis

Support and Resistance

- **Support:** Price where buying pressure limits a downtrend
- **Resistance:** Price where selling pressure limits an uptrend
- Examples of support and resistance:
  - Trendlines
  - Old highs, old lows
  - Round number, whole number prices

 72

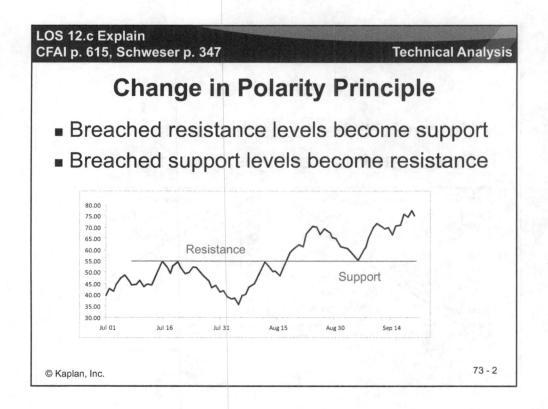

LOS 12.c Explain
CFAI p. 615, Schweser p. 347 Technical Analysis

Change in Polarity Principle

- Breached resistance levels become support
- Breached support levels become resistance

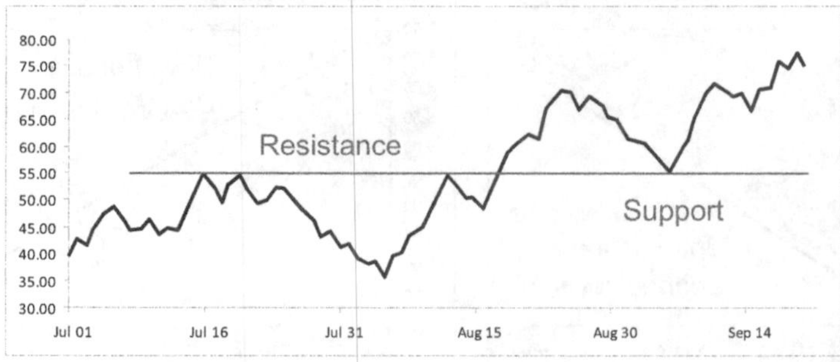

 73 - 2

LOS 12.d Identify/Interpret
CFAI p. 618, Schweser p. 348 Technical Analysis

Common Chart Patterns

Reversal patterns: Prior trend expected to reverse direction

- Head and shoulders
- Double, triple top
- Inverse head and shoulders
- Double, triple bottom

 74

LOS 12.d Identify/Interpret
CFAI p. 618, Schweser p. 348 Technical Analysis

Common Chart Patterns

Continuation patterns: Prior trend expected to continue in same direction

- Triangles
- Rectangles

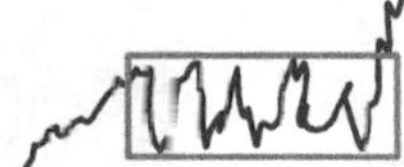

- Pennants (triangles on short-term charts)
- Flags (rectangles on short-term charts)

 75

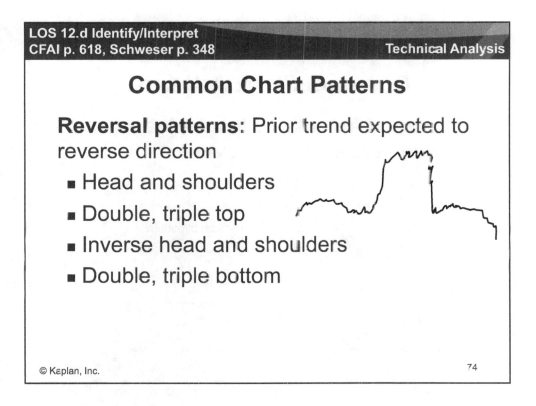

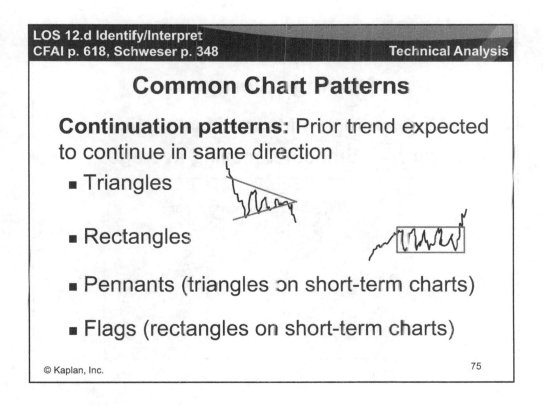

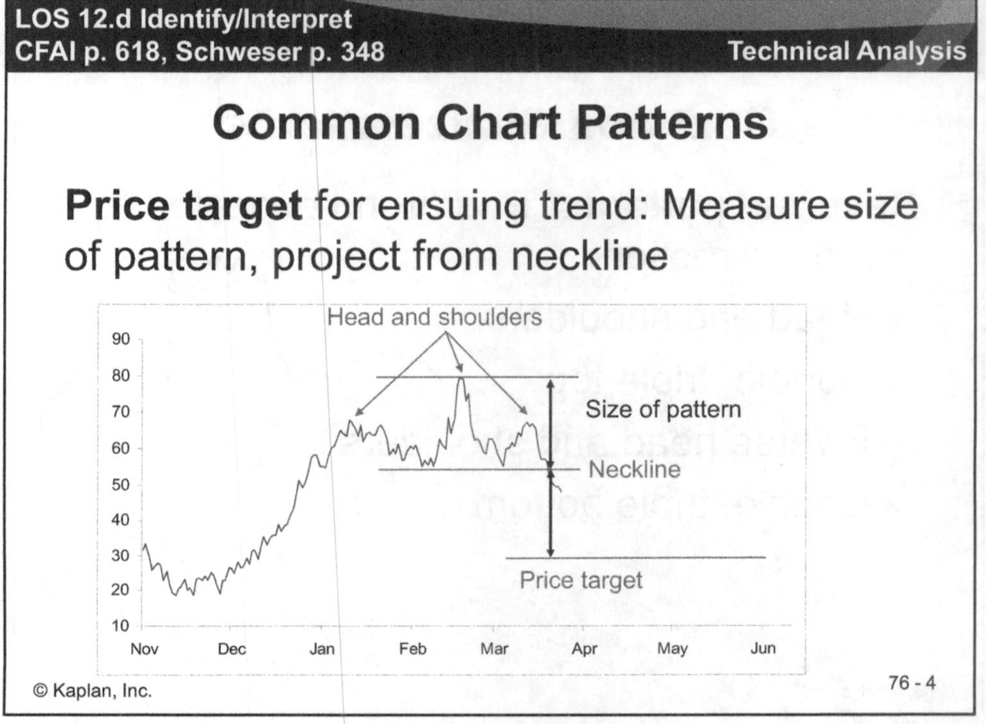
LOS 12.d Identify/Interpret
CFAI p. 618, Schweser p. 348
Technical Analysis
Common Chart Patterns
Price target for ensuing trend: Measure size of pattern, project from neckline
Head and shoulders
Size of pattern
Neckline
Price target
90
80
70
60
50
40
30
20
10
Nov
Dec
Jan
Feb
Mar
Apr
May
Jun
© Kaplan, Inc.
76 - 4

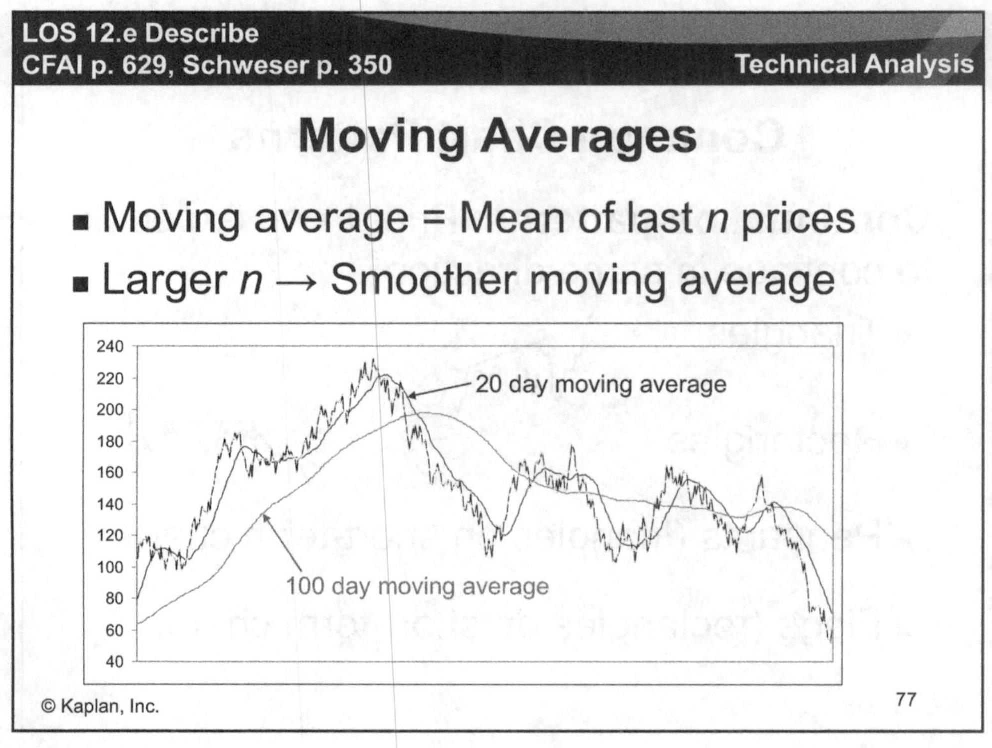
LOS 12.e Describe
CFAI p. 629, Schweser p. 350
Technical Analysis
Moving Averages
▪ Moving average = Mean of last n prices
▪ Larger n → Smoother moving average
240
220
200
180
160
140
120
100
80
60
40
20 day moving average
100 day moving average
© Kaplan, Inc.
77

LOS 12.e Describe
CFAI p. 629, Schweser p. 350

Technical Analysis

Bollinger Bands

Drawn above and below moving average by # of std. dev., # of std. dev. determined by volatility

- **Short term (contrarian)**
  - Sell at top band – security **overbought**
  - Buy at bottom band – security **oversold**
- **Longer term**
  - Buy on significant breakout above top banc
  - Sell on significant breakout below lower band

78

LOS 12.e Describe
CFAI p. 629, Schweser p. 350

Technical Analysis

Bollinger Bands

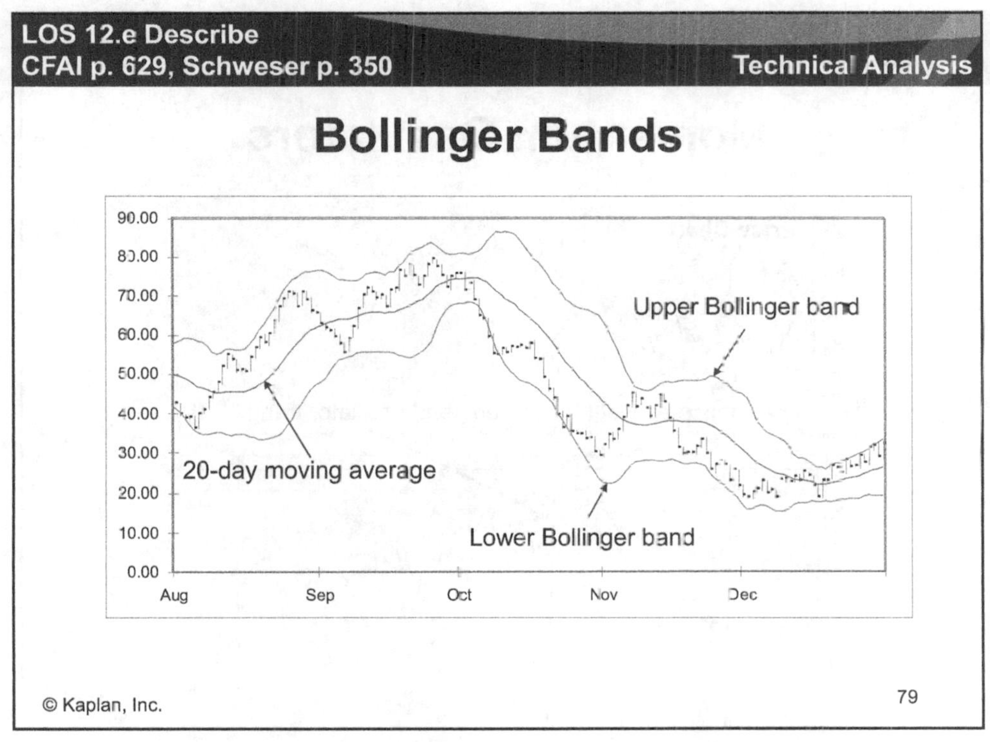

79

LOS 12.e Describe
CFAI p. 629, Schweser p. 350

Technical Analysis

Momentum Oscillators

- Scaled price-based indicators
  - Oscillate around a value (e.g., 0 or 100)
  - Oscillate between two values (e.g., 0 and 100)
- Extreme values indicate overbought or oversold markets (contrarian trading signals)
- Identify **convergence** or **divergence** of price movement and oscillator movement
  - Convergence = continuation of trend
  - Divergence = early warning of change in trend

80

LOS 12.e Describe
CFAI p. 629, Schweser p. 350

Technical Analysis

Momentum Oscillators

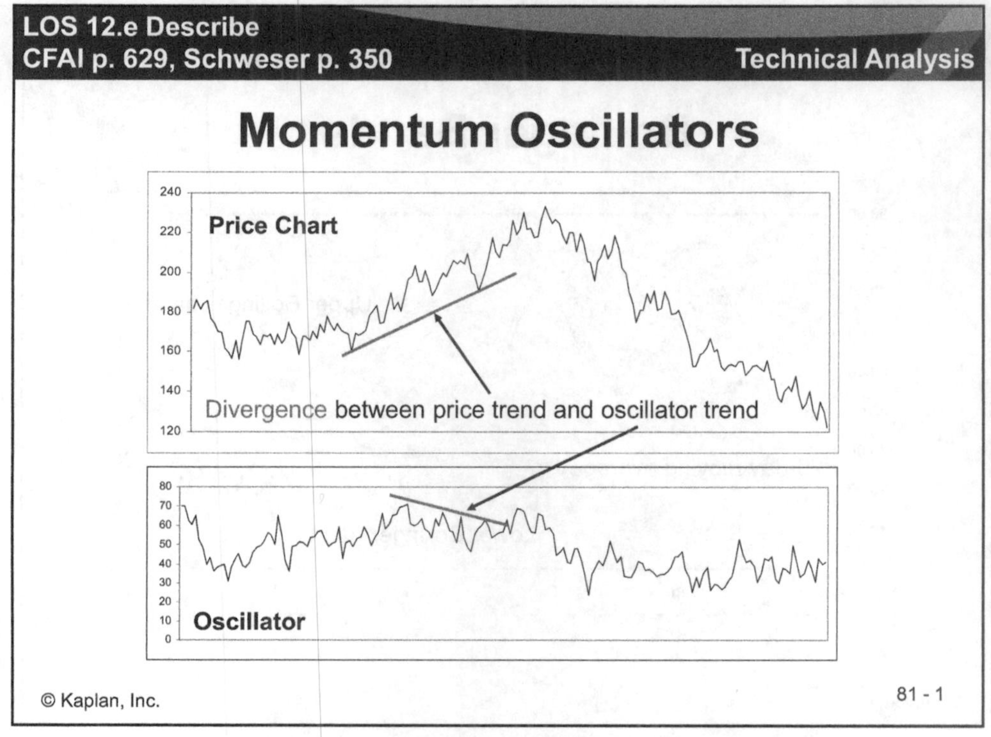

81 - 1

LOS 12.e Describe
CFAI p. 629, Schweser p. 350
Technical Analysis

Rate of Change (ROC) Oscillator

Also called a momentum oscillator

- **ROC = $(V_t - V_{t\text{-}n}) \times 100$**, oscillates around 0
- **ROC = $V_t / V_{t\text{-}n} \times 100$**, oscillates around 100

n is typically 10 days between prices

- **Buy signal:** ROC crosses above 0 (100) during uptrend
- **Sell signal:** ROC crosses below 0 (100) during downtrend

82

LOS 12.e Describe
CFAI p. 629, Schweser p. 350
Technical Analysis

Relative Strength Index (RSI)

RSI = 100 – [100 / (1 + RS)], where:

$$\textbf{RS} = \frac{\text{Sum of + changes in last } n \text{ days}}{|\text{Sum of – changes in last } n \text{ days}|}$$

- Oscillates between 0 and 100
- Overbought: RSI > 70
- Oversold: RSI < 30

83

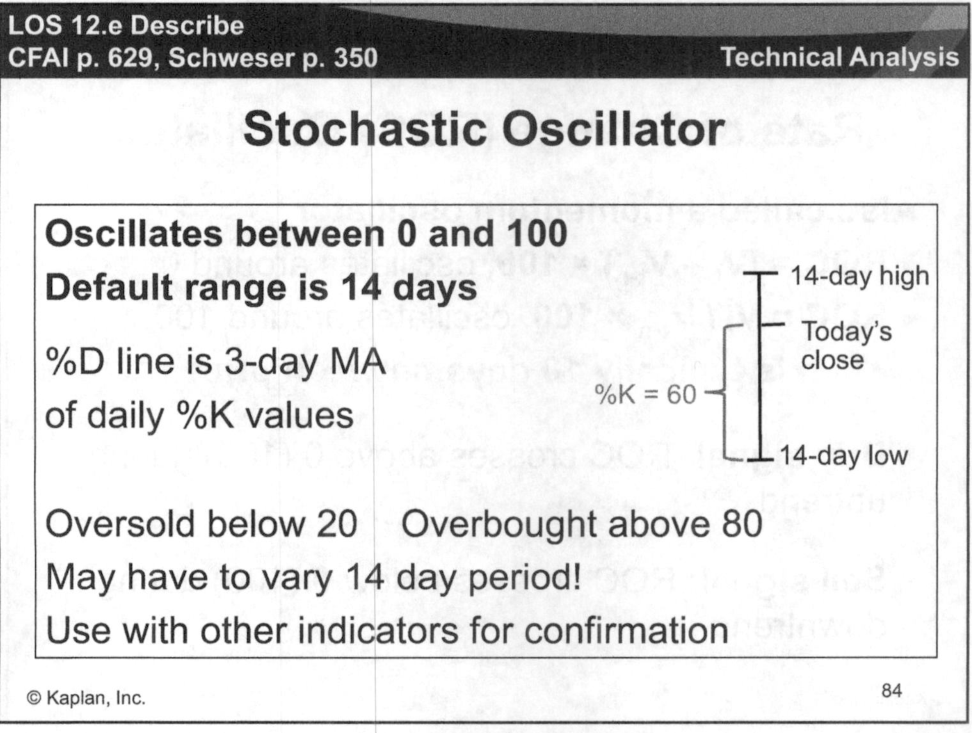

LOS 12.e Describe
CFAI p. 629, Schweser p. 350

Technical Analysis

Moving Avg. Convergence/Divergence

- Two lines: **MACD line** and **signal line**
- MACD = Difference between two exponentially smoothed moving averages typically 12-day and 26-day
- Signal line = Exponentially smoothed 9-day moving average of MACD
- Oscillates around zero

MACD crosses above signal line = Buy

MACD crosses below signal line = Sell

85

LOS 12.e Describe
CFAI p. 629, Schweser p. 350

Technical Analysis

Sentiment Indicators

- **Opinion polls**
- **Put/call ratio**
  - Put volume > call volume: Ratio > 1 → Negative sentiment
  - Call volume > put volume: Ratio < 1 → Positive sentiment
  - Contrarian indicator

86

LOS 12.e Describe
CFAI p. 629, Schweser p. 350

Technical Analysis

Sentiment Indicators

- **CBOE Volatility Index (VIX)**
  - High when investors fear market decline
  - Contrarian indicator:
    investors bearish → contrarians bullish
- **Margin debt**
- **Short interest ratio:** # shares sold short / total daily volume

87

LOS 12.e Describe
CFAI p. 629, Schweser p. 350 Technical Analysis

Flow of Funds Indicators

- **Short-term Trading Index (TRIN):** Activity in advancing stocks vs. activity in declining stocks
- **Margin debt**
- **Mutual fund cash position:**
  - Low in uptrends, high in downtrends
  - Fund cash is potential buying power → Contrarian indicator
- **New equity issuance, secondary offerings**

 88

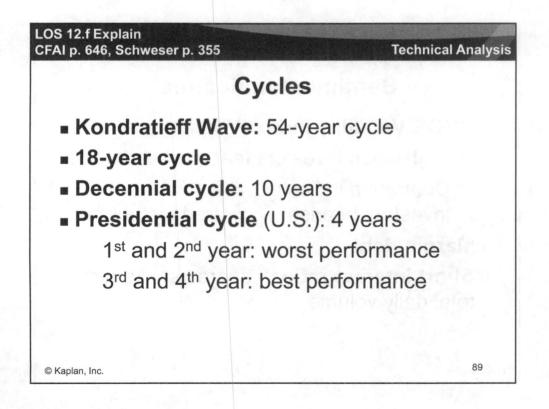

LOS 12.f Explain
CFAI p. 646, Schweser p. 355 Technical Analysis

Cycles

- **Kondratieff Wave:** 54-year cycle
- **18-year cycle**
- **Decennial cycle:** 10 years
- **Presidential cycle** (U.S.): 4 years

  1st and 2nd year: worst performance

  3rd and 4th year: best performance

 89

LOS 12.g Describe
CFAI p. 647, Schweser p. 355

Technical Analysis

Elliott Wave Theory

- Market prices move in interconnected cycles that range from very short-term to very long-term
- Uptrends: 5 waves up, 3 waves down
- Downtrends: 5 waves down, 3 waves up
- Wave sizes conform to **Fibonacci ratios**
- Fibonacci sequence:

  0, 1, 1, 2, 3, 5, 8, 13, 21, 34, …

  Add last two numbers to get next number

90

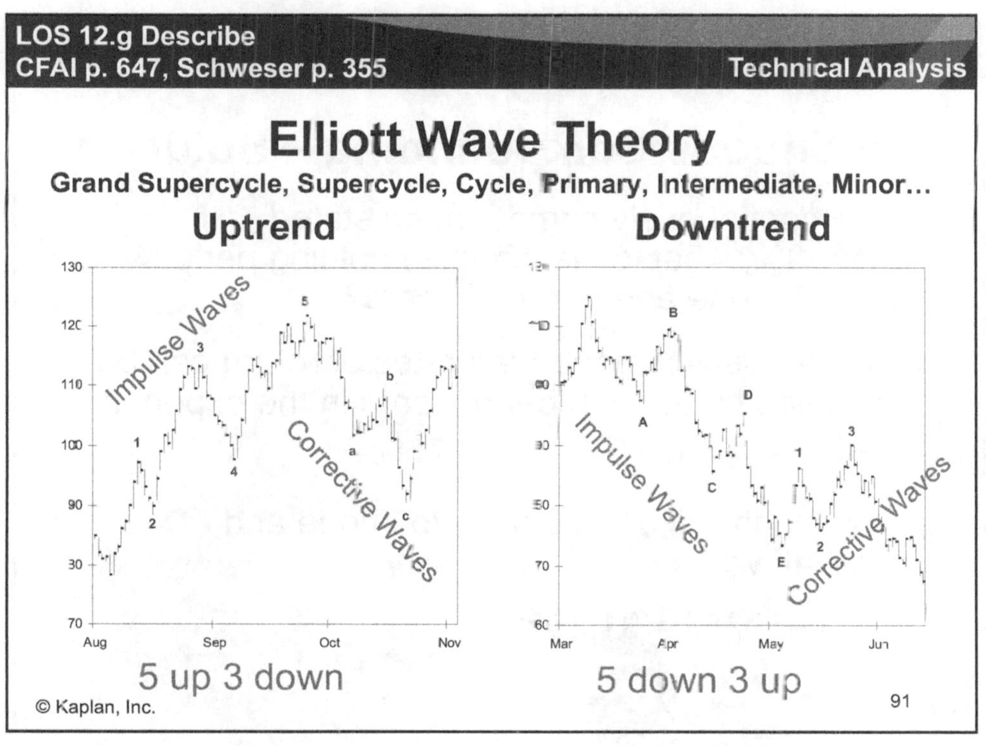

LOS 12.h Describe
CFAI p. 649, Schweser p. 356

Technical Analysis

Intermarket Analysis

All markets are interrelated, influence each other

- Equities, bonds, currencies, commodities
- Industry groups: energy, utilities, consumer staples, healthcare, financials, info tech, materials, industrials, telecom, consumer discretionary
- London, New York, Tokyo, Hong Kong, Germany

Relative strength charts show inflection points (e.g., equities/commodities, energy/S&P index, MSFT/info tech)

92

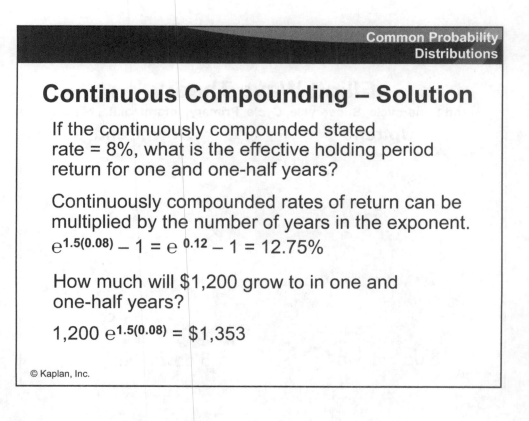

Common Probability Distributions

Continuous Compounding – Solution

If the continuously compounded stated rate = 8%, what is the effective holding period return for one and one-half years?

Continuously compounded rates of return can be multiplied by the number of years in the exponent.

$e^{1.5(0.08)} - 1 = e^{0.12} - 1 = 12.75\%$

How much will $1,200 grow to in one and one-half years?

$1{,}200\, e^{1.5(0.08)} = \$1{,}353$

Study Session 4

Economics: Microeconomic Analysis

Economics: Microeconomic Analysis

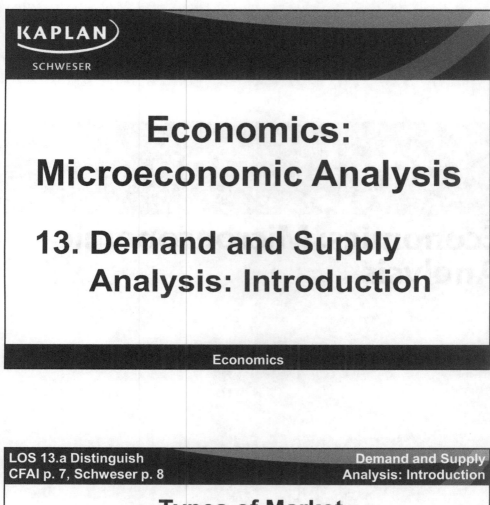

13. Demand and Supply Analysis: Introduction

Economics

LOS 13.a Distinguish
CFAI p. 7, Schweser p. 8

Demand and Supply Analysis: Introduction

Types of Market

- **Factor markets:** Factors of production
  - Raw materials, labor, etc.
  - Firms are buyers
- **Product markets:** Services and finished goods
  - Firms are sellers
  - **Intermediate markets**: One firm's finished products (components) used in the production of another firm's output

2

LOS 13.b Explain
CFAI p. 8, Schweser p. 9

Demand and Supply Analysis: Introduction

The Demand Curve

$$Q_{DX} = f(P_x, I, P_y, \ldots)$$

Quantity demanded is a function of:

- Price of good P_x
- Individuals' incomes I
- Price of related products (P_y)
- Many other factors may be added

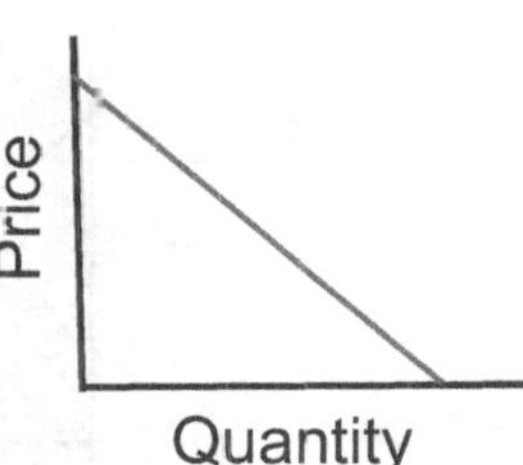

Law of Demand: Typically, quantity ↑ as price ↓

3

LOS 13.b Explain
CFAI p. 8, Schweser p. 9

Demand and Supply Analysis: Introduction

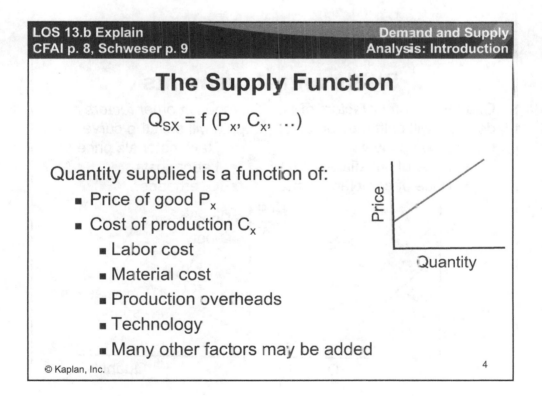

The Supply Function

$$Q_{SX} = f(P_x, C_x, \ldots)$$

Quantity supplied is a function of:

- Price of good P_x
- Cost of production C_x
  - Labor cost
  - Material cost
  - Production overheads
  - Technology
  - Many other factors may be added

Price
Quantity

4

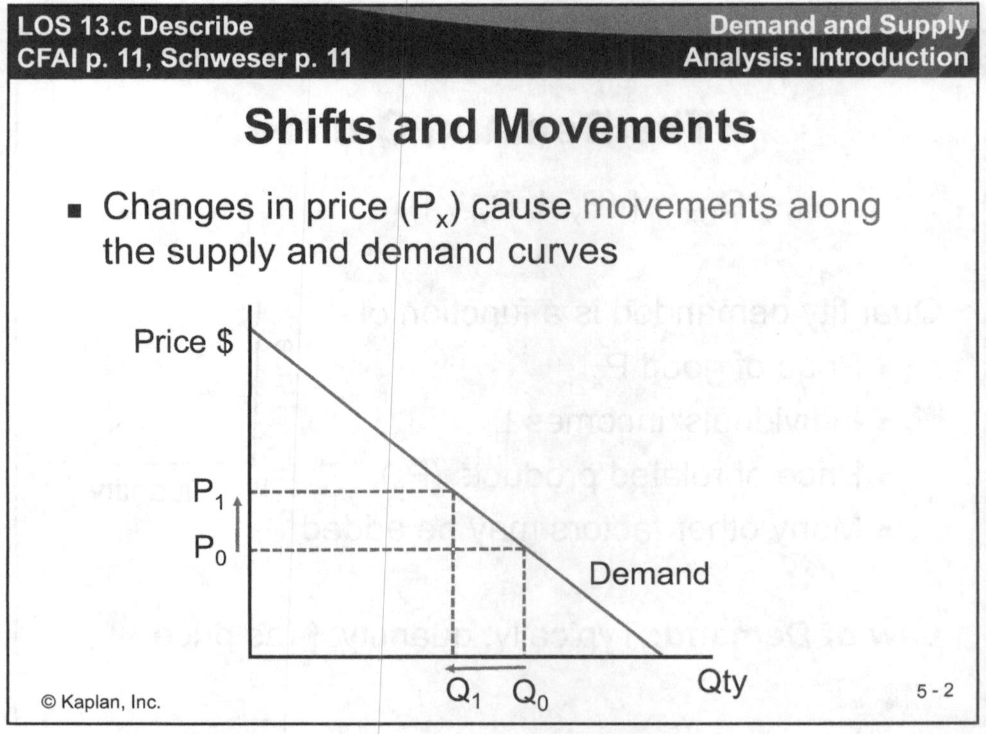
LOS 13.c Describe
CFAI p. 11, Schweser p. 11
Demand and Supply
Analysis: Introduction
Shifts and Movements
Changes in price (P_x) cause movements along the supply and demand curves
Price $
P1
P0
Demand
Q1 Q0
Qty
© Kaplan, Inc.
5 - 2

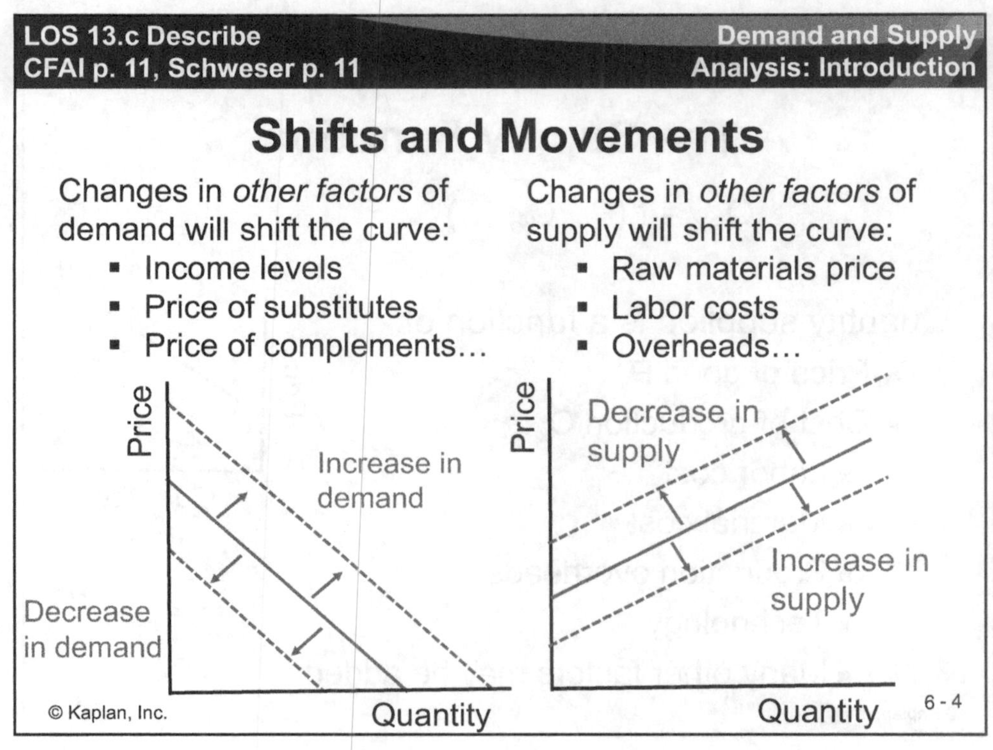
LOS 13.c Describe
CFAI p. 11, Schweser p. 11
Demand and Supply
Analysis: Introduction
Shifts and Movements
Changes in other factors of demand will shift the curve:
Income levels
Price of substitutes
Price of complements…
Changes in other factors of supply will shift the curve:
Raw materials price
Labor costs
Overheads…
Price
Increase in demand
Decrease in demand
Quantity
Price
Decrease in supply
Increase in supply
Quantity
© Kaplan, Inc.
6 - 4

LOS 13.d Describe
CFAI p. 16, Schweser p. 12

Demand and Supply Analysis: Introduction

Aggregating Demand and Supply Curves

Market supply = aggregate of the supply functions of the firms in the market

Example:

50 firms in the market

Supply function: $Q_s = -250 + 2.5P_x$

The same approach can be used to formulate market demand

Market supply: $Q_s = -(50 \times 250) + (50 \times 2.5\ P_x)$

$Q_s = -12,500 + 125\ P_x$

Invert function: $P_x = 0.008Q_s + 100$

0.008 = slope coefficient of supply curve

7 - 4

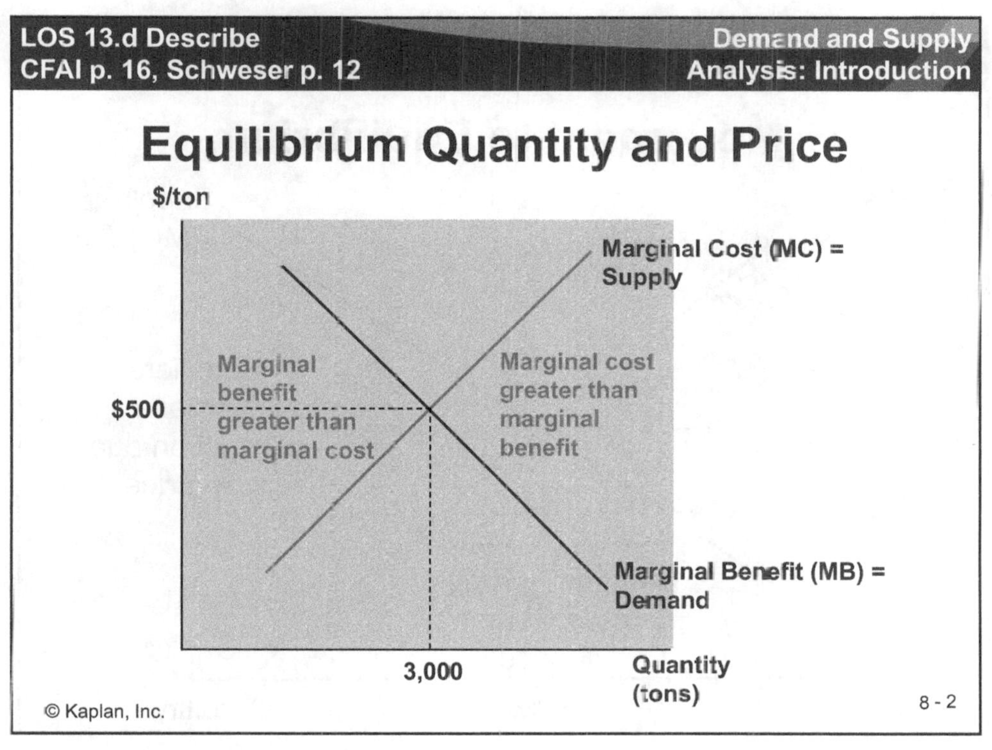

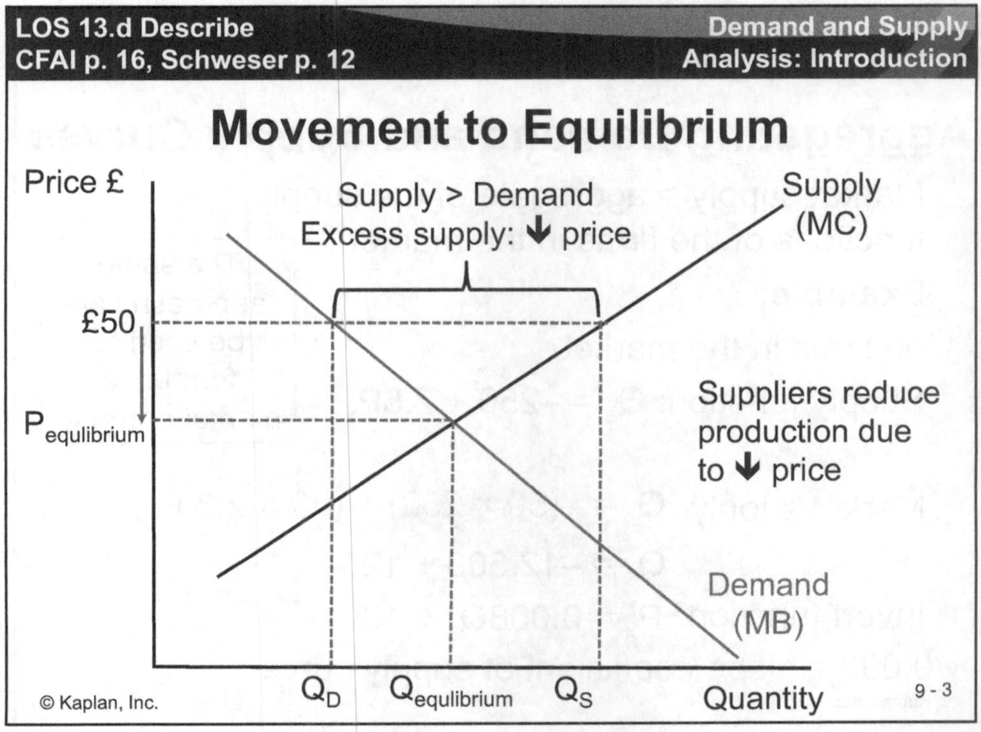
LOS 13.d Describe
CFAI p. 16, Schweser p. 12
Demand and Supply
Analysis: Introduction
Movement to Equilibrium
Price £
Supply > Demand
Excess supply: ↓ price
Supply
(MC)
£50
P equlibrium
Suppliers reduce
production due
to ↓ price
Demand
(MB)
© Kaplan, Inc.
Q D
Q equlibrium
Q S
Quantity
9 - 3

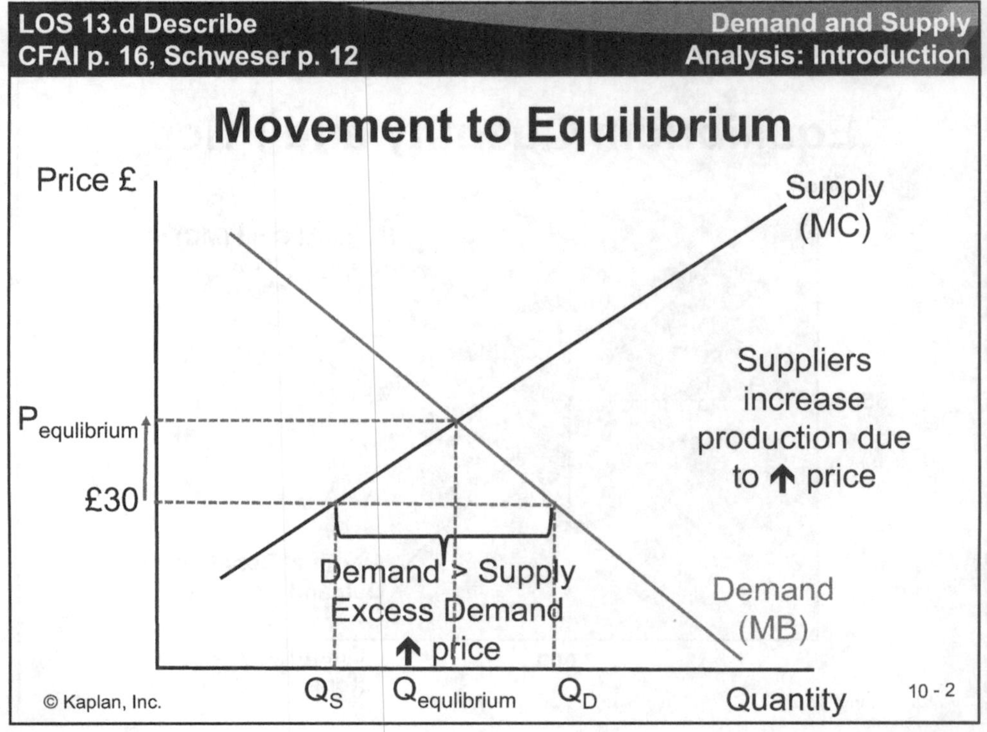
LOS 13.d Describe
CFAI p. 16, Schweser p. 12
Demand and Supply
Analysis: Introduction
Movement to Equilibrium
Price £
Supply
(MC)
Suppliers
increase
production due
to ↑ price
P equlibrium
£30
Demand > Supply
Excess Demand
↑ price
Demand
(MB)
© Kaplan, Inc.
Q S
Q equlibrium
Q D
Quantity
10 - 2

LOS 13.e Distinguish/Identify
CFAI p. 24, Schweser p. 15

Demand and Supply Analysis: Introduction

Stable and Unstable Equilibria

- **Stable:** Market forces move price and quantity back to equilibrium
- If downward sloping, supply curve must cut demand curve from above to reach stable equilibrium

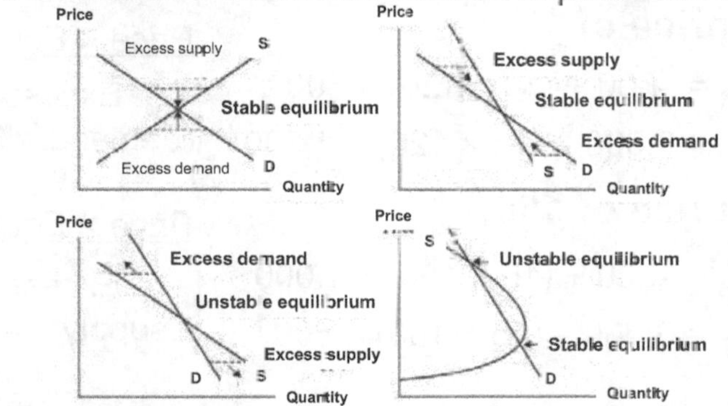

 11

LOS 13.f,g Calculate/Interpret
CFAI p. 10, Schweser p. 16

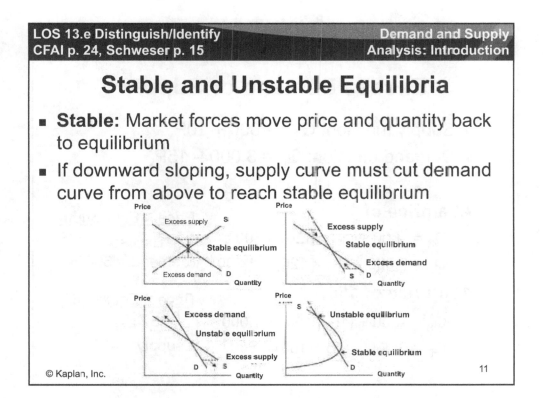

Demand and Supply Analysis: Introduction

Calculation of Equilibrium

- Supply function: $Q_S = -600 + 10P_x$
- Demand function: $Q_D = 3{,}000 - 15P_x$
- **Equilibrium:** Supply = Demand:

$$-600 + 10P_x = 3{,}000 - 15P_x$$

Solve for P_x

$3{,}600 = 25P_x$

$P_x = 144$

$Q_s = -600 + 10(144) = 840$

$Q_D = 3{,}000 - 15(144) = 840$

 12 - 5

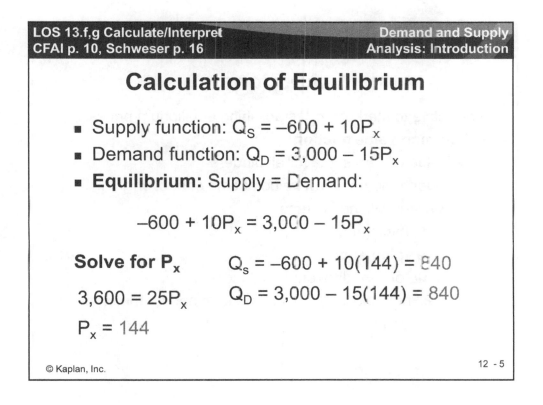

LOS 13.f,g Calculate/Interpret
CFAI p. 10, Schweser p. 16

Demand and Supply Analysis: Introduction

Excess Demand or Supply

- Supply function: $Q_S = -600 + 10P_x$
- Demand function: $Q_D = 3,000 - 15P_x$

At a price of 120:

$Q_S = -600 + (10 \times 120) = 600$
$Q_D = 3,000 - (15 \times 120) = 1,200$

Price < Equilibrium
Excess demand = 600

At a price of 160:

$Q_S = -600 + (10 \times 160) = 1,000$
$Q_D = 3,000 - (15 \times 160) = 600$

Price > Equilibrium
Excess supply = 400

13 - 6

LOS 13.h Describe/Calculate
CFAI p. 26, Schweser p. 16

Demand and Supply Analysis: Introduction

Auctions

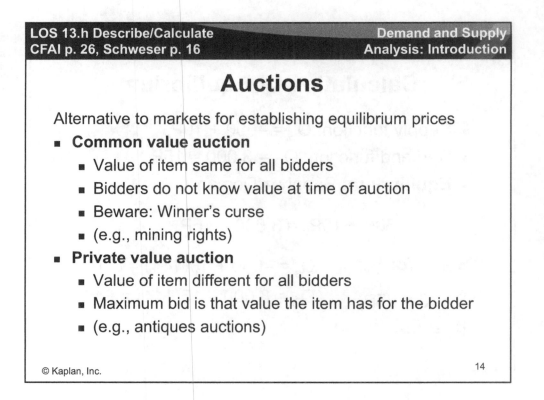

Alternative to markets for establishing equilibrium prices

- **Common value auction**
  - Value of item same for all bidders
  - Bidders do not know value at time of auction
  - Beware: Winner's curse
  - (e.g., mining rights)
- **Private value auction**
  - Value of item different for all bidders
  - Maximum bid is that value the item has for the bidder
  - (e.g., antiques auctions)

14

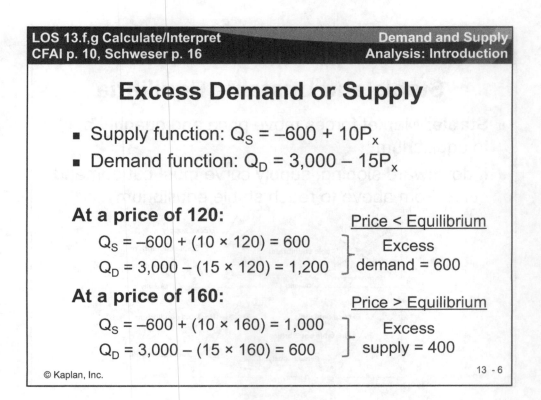

LOS 13.h Describe/Calculate
CFAI p. 26, Schweser p. 16

Demand and Supply
Analysis: Introduction

Auctions

- **Ascending price auction** (English auction)
  - Bidder must bid higher than previous bid
  - Bids publically disclosed
  - Process continues until no one is willing to bid higher
  - Highest bid wins and pays bid price (last bid made)
  - (e.g., automobile auctions)
- **Sealed bid auction**
  - Each bidder provides one bid
  - All bids remain unknown to other bidders (concealed)
  - Highest bid wins and pays price bid
  - Optimal bid < reservation price
  - (e.g., government contracts)

15

LOS 13.h Describe/Calculate
CFAI p. 26, Schweser p. 16

Demand and Supply
Analysis: Introduction

Auctions

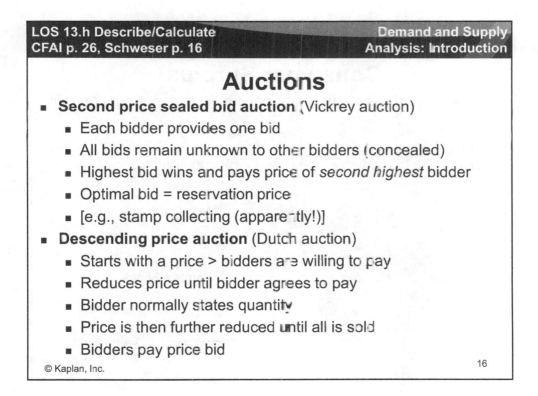

- **Second price sealed bid auction** (Vickrey auction)
  - Each bidder provides one bid
  - All bids remain unknown to other bidders (concealed)
  - Highest bid wins and pays price of *second highest* bidder
  - Optimal bid = reservation price
  - [e.g., stamp collecting (apparently!)]
- **Descending price auction** (Dutch auction)
  - Starts with a price > bidders are willing to pay
  - Reduces price until bidder agrees to pay
  - Bidder normally states quantity
  - Price is then further reduced until all is sold
  - Bidders pay price bid

16

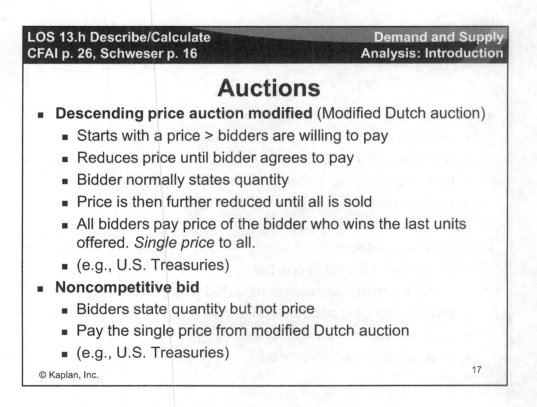

LOS 13.h Describe/Calculate
CFAI p. 26, Schweser p. 16

Demand and Supply
Analysis: Introduction

Auctions

- **Descending price auction modified** (Modified Dutch auction)
  - Starts with a price > bidders are willing to pay
  - Reduces price until bidder agrees to pay
  - Bidder normally states quantity
  - Price is then further reduced until all is sold
  - All bidders pay price of the bidder who wins the last units offered. *Single price* to all.
  - (e.g., U.S. Treasuries)
- **Noncompetitive bid**
  - Bidders state quantity but not price
  - Pay the single price from modified Dutch auction
  - (e.g., U.S. Treasuries)

 17

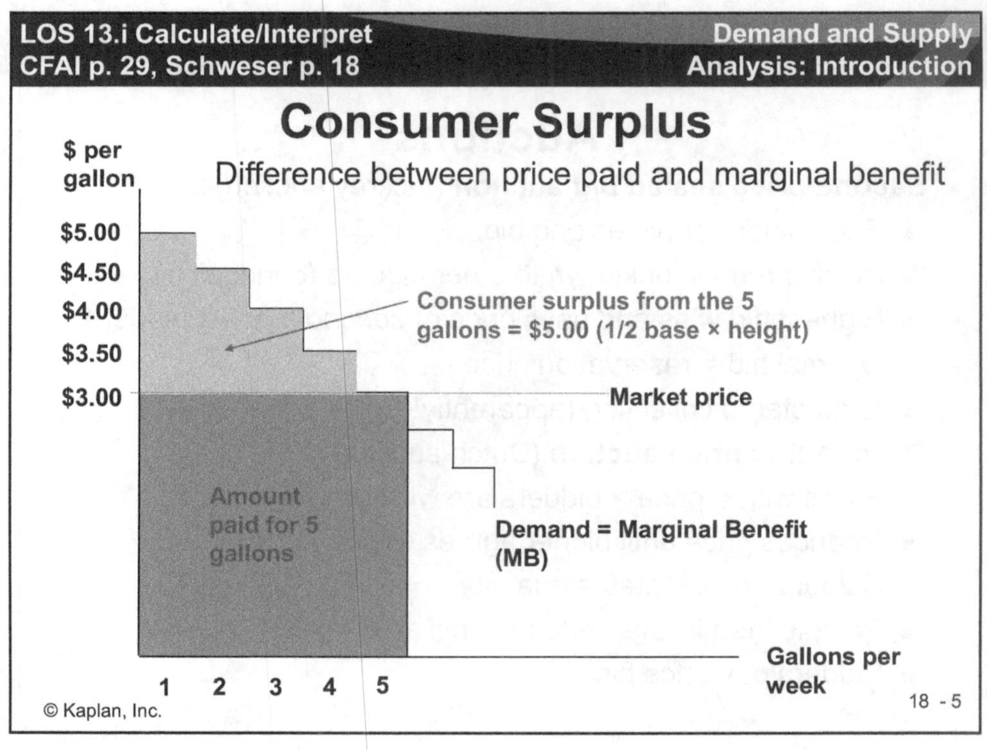

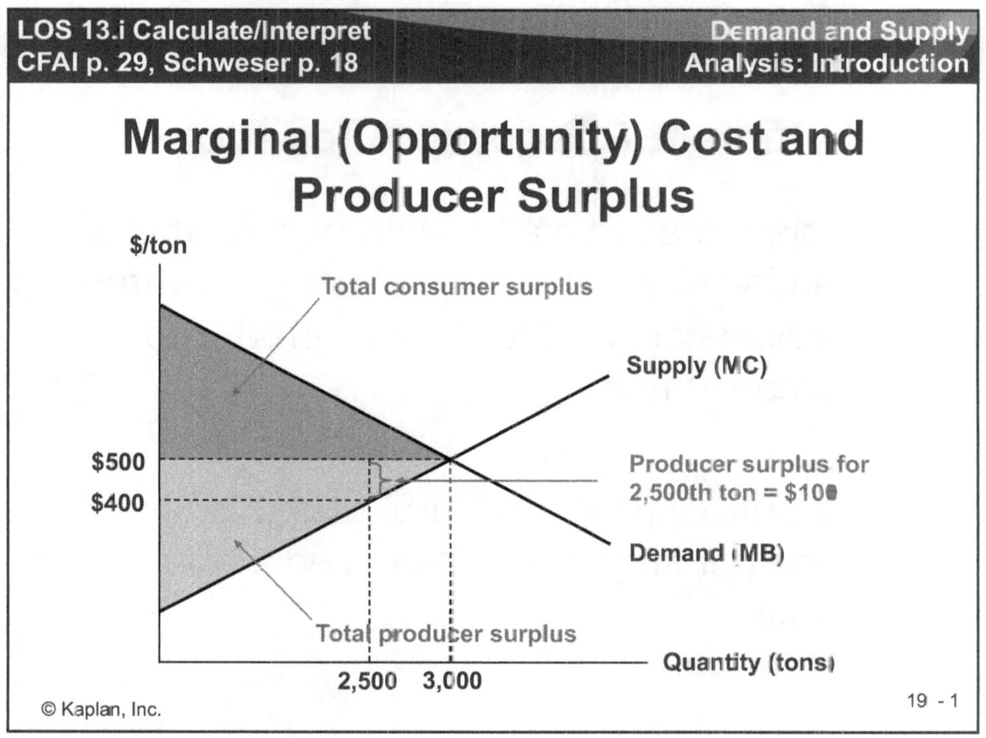

LOS 13.i Calculate/Interpret
CFAI p. 29, Schweser p. 18

Demand and Supply
Analysis: Introduction

Competitive Equilibrium

- Equilibrium in a **competitive market** occurs at the intersection of the industry supply and demand curves
- The quantity supplied at the equilibrium price equals the quantity demanded at that price

20

LOS 13.i Calculate/Interpret
CFAI p. 29, Schweser p. 18

Demand and Supply
Analysis: Introduction

Efficient Resource Allocation

- Efficient resource allocation occurs at the quantity for which marginal benefit **equals** marginal cost for the last unit produced and consumed
- The sum of producer surplus and consumer surplus is maximized at that quantity

21

LOS 13.i Calculate/Interpret
CFAI p. 29, Schweser p. 18

Demand and Supply
Analysis: Introduction

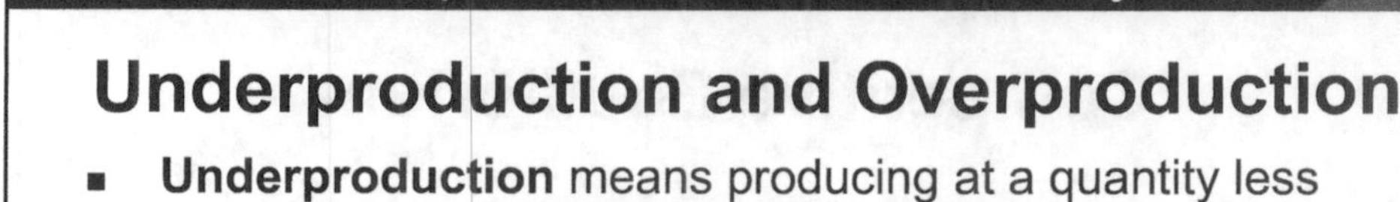

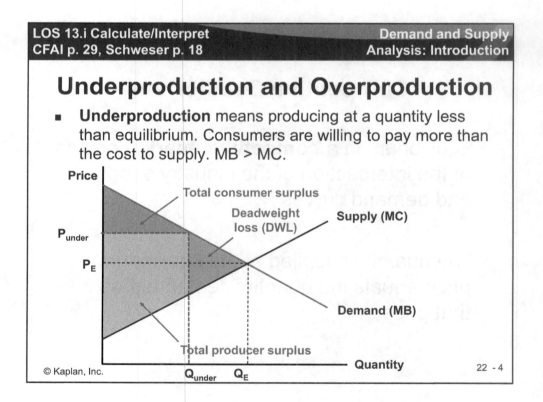

Underproduction and Overproduction

- **Underproduction** means producing at a quantity less than equilibrium. Consumers are willing to pay more than the cost to supply. MB > MC.

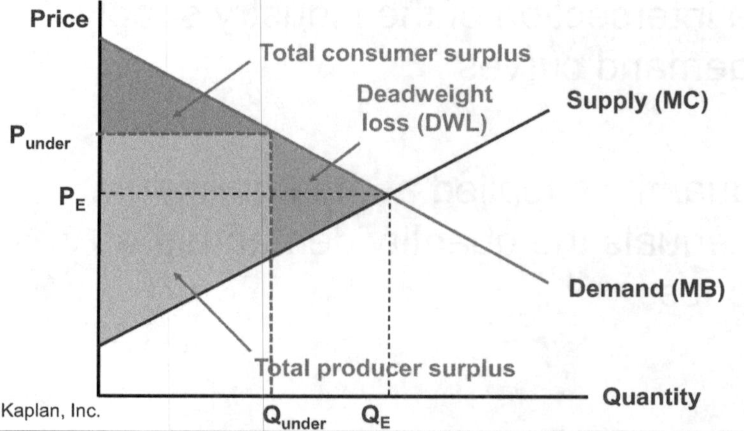

22 - 4

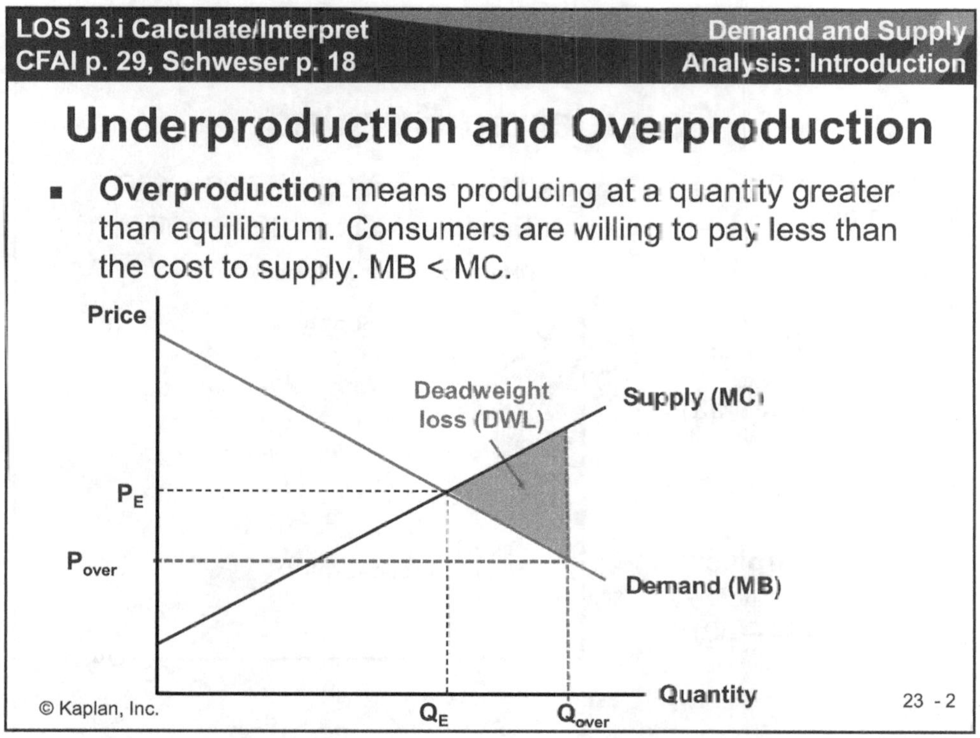

LOS 13.i Calculate/Interpret
CFAI p. 29, Schweser p. 18

Demand and Supply
Analysis: Introduction

Deadweight Loss

- Both overproduction and underproduction are examples of inefficient allocation of resources
- The scale of the inefficiency is measured by the deadweight loss
- Deadweight loss is the decrease in total surplus that results from an inefficient level of production

24

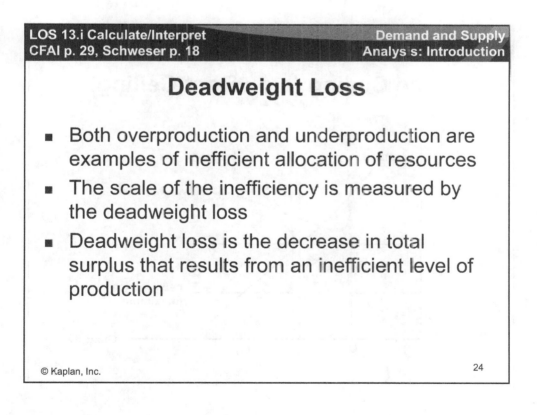

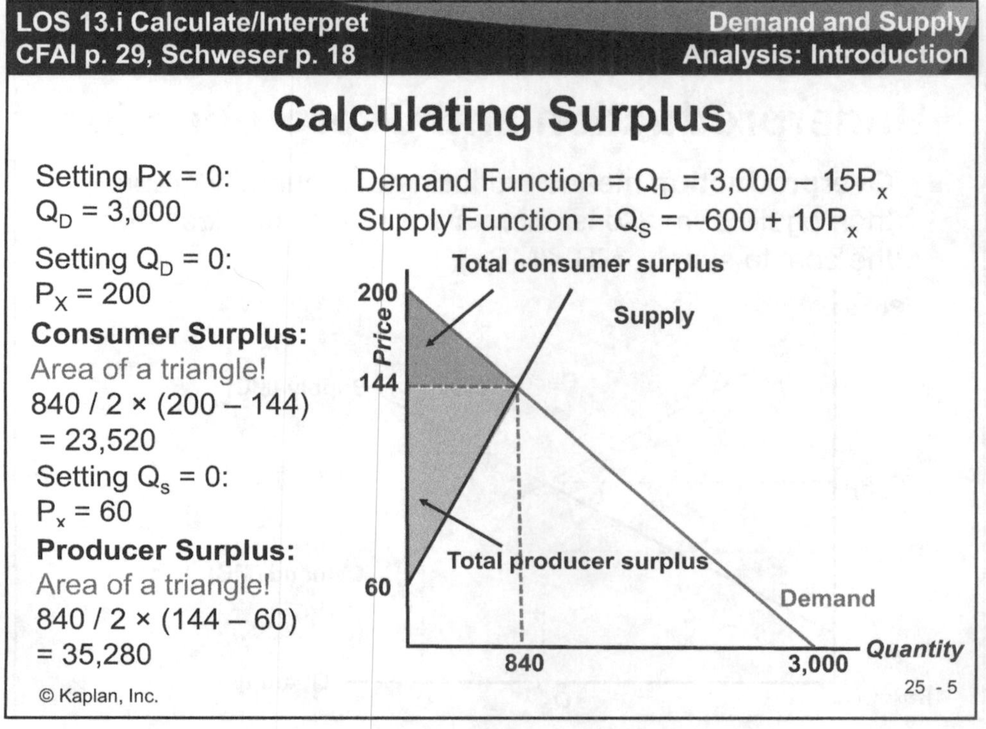
LOS 13.i Calculate/Interpret
CFAI p. 29, Schweser p. 18
Demand and Supply
Analysis: Introduction
Calculating Surplus
Setting Px = 0:
Q_D = 3,000
Setting Q_D = 0:
P_X = 200
Consumer Surplus:
Area of a triangle!
840 / 2 × (200 – 144)
= 23,520
Setting Q_s = 0:
P_x = 60
Producer Surplus:
Area of a triangle!
840 / 2 × (144 – 60)
= 35,280
Demand Function = Q_D = 3,000 – 15P_x
Supply Function = Q_S = –600 + 10P_x
Total consumer surplus
Supply
Price
200
144
60
Total producer surplus
Demand
840
3,000
Quantity
© Kaplan, Inc.
25 - 5

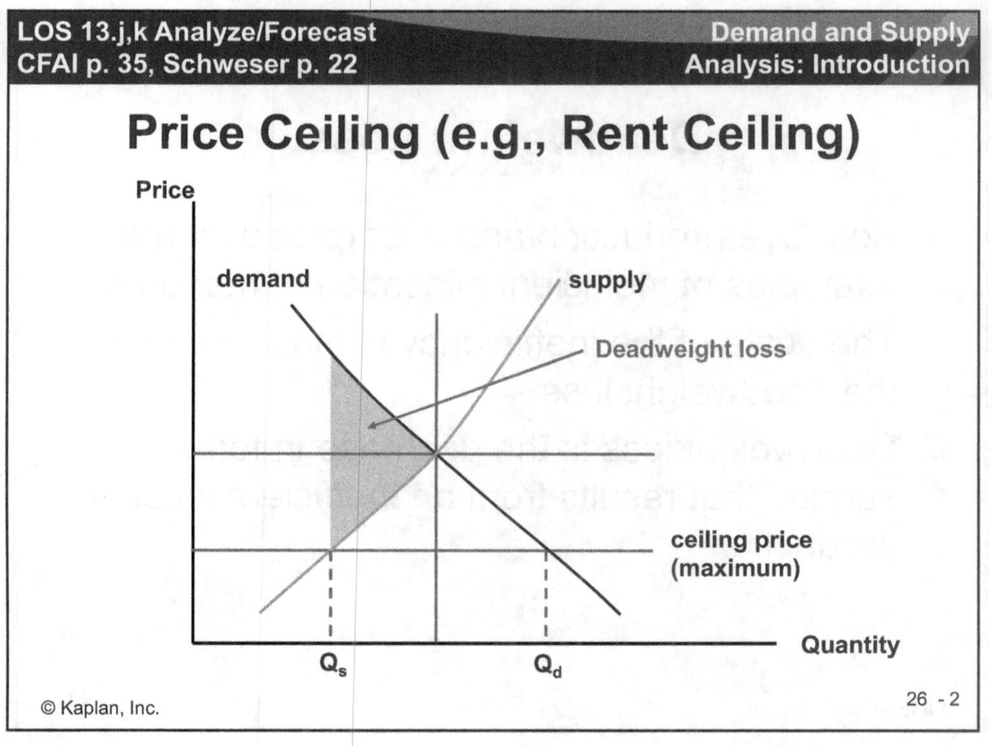
LOS 13.j,k Analyze/Forecast
CFAI p. 35, Schweser p. 22
Demand and Supply
Analysis: Introduction
Price Ceiling (e.g., Rent Ceiling)
Price
demand
supply
Deadweight loss
ceiling price
(maximum)
Q_s
Q_d
Quantity
© Kaplan, Inc.
26 - 2

LOS 13.j,k Analyze/Forecast
CFAI p. 35, Schweser p. 22

Demand and Supply Analysis: Introduction

Price Ceiling

Long-run impact:

- Long waiting period to purchase
- Sellers discriminate
- Sellers take bribes
- Sellers reduce quality
- Black markets develop (Black market prices > ceiling prices)

27

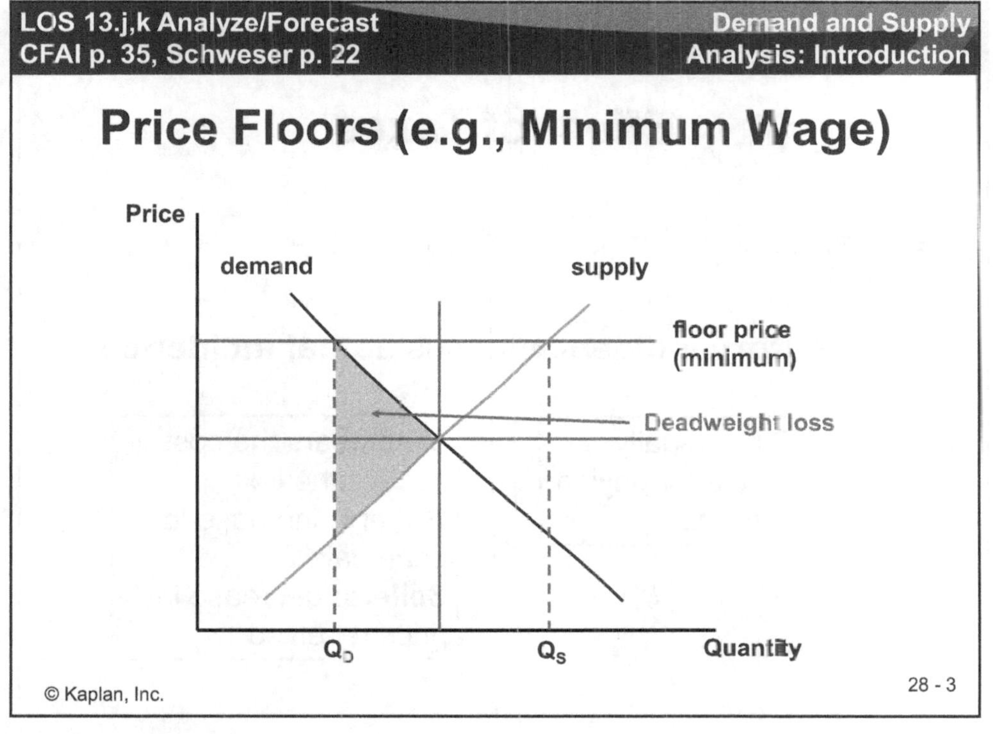

LOS 13.j,k Analyze/Forecast
CFAI p. 35, Schweser p. 22

Demand and Supply
Analysis: Introduction

Price Floor

Long-run effects

- Excess supply of the good
- Substitution in consumption away from the price controlled good

Minimum wage is an example of a price floor

- Excess supply of labor increases unemployment
- Producers substitute capital for labor
- Non-monetary benefits, working conditions, on-the-job training all decrease

29

LOS 13.j,k Analyze/Forecast
CFAI p. 35, Schweser p. 22

Demand and Supply
Analysis: Introduction

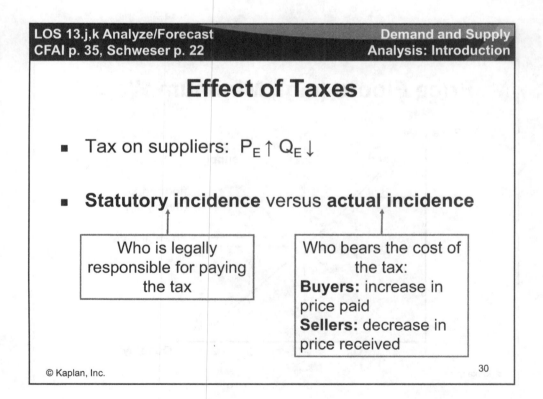

Effect of Taxes

- Tax on suppliers: $P_E \uparrow Q_E \downarrow$
- **Statutory incidence** versus **actual incidence**

Statutory incidence: Who is legally responsible for paying the tax

Actual incidence: Who bears the cost of the tax:
Buyers: increase in price paid
Sellers: decrease in price received

30

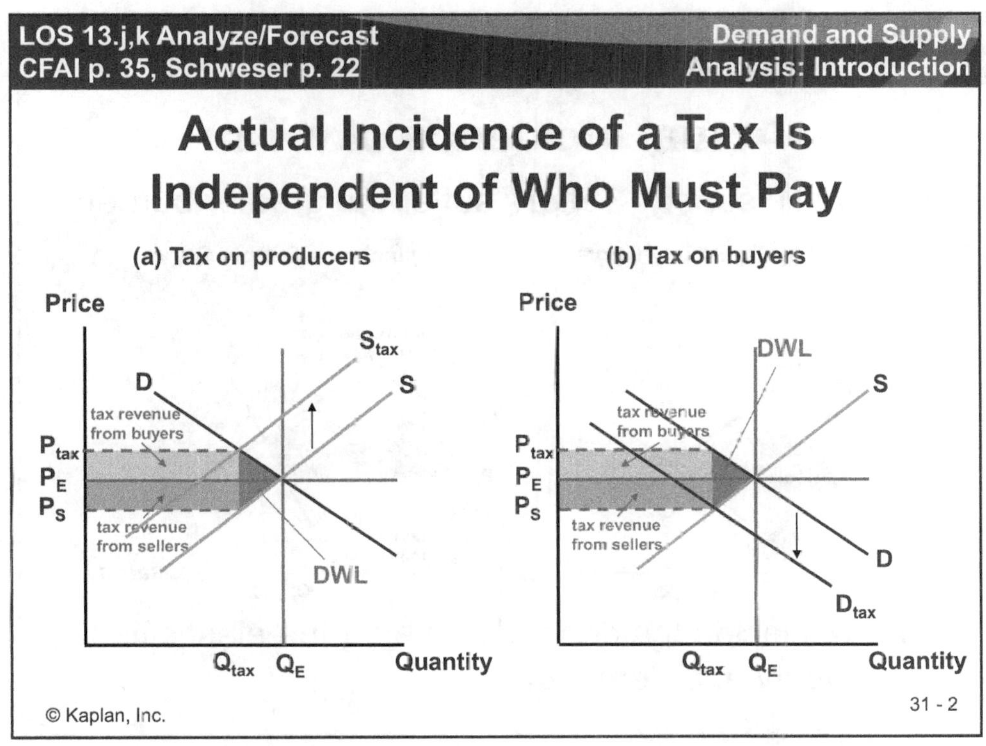
LOS 13.j,k Analyze/Forecast
CFAI p. 35, Schweser p. 22
Demand and Supply
Analysis: Introduction
Actual Incidence of a Tax Is
Independent of Who Must Pay
(a) Tax on producers
(b) Tax on buyers
Price
D
S
tax revenue from buyers
tax revenue from sellers
DWL
Quantity
D
© Kaplan, Inc.
31 - 2

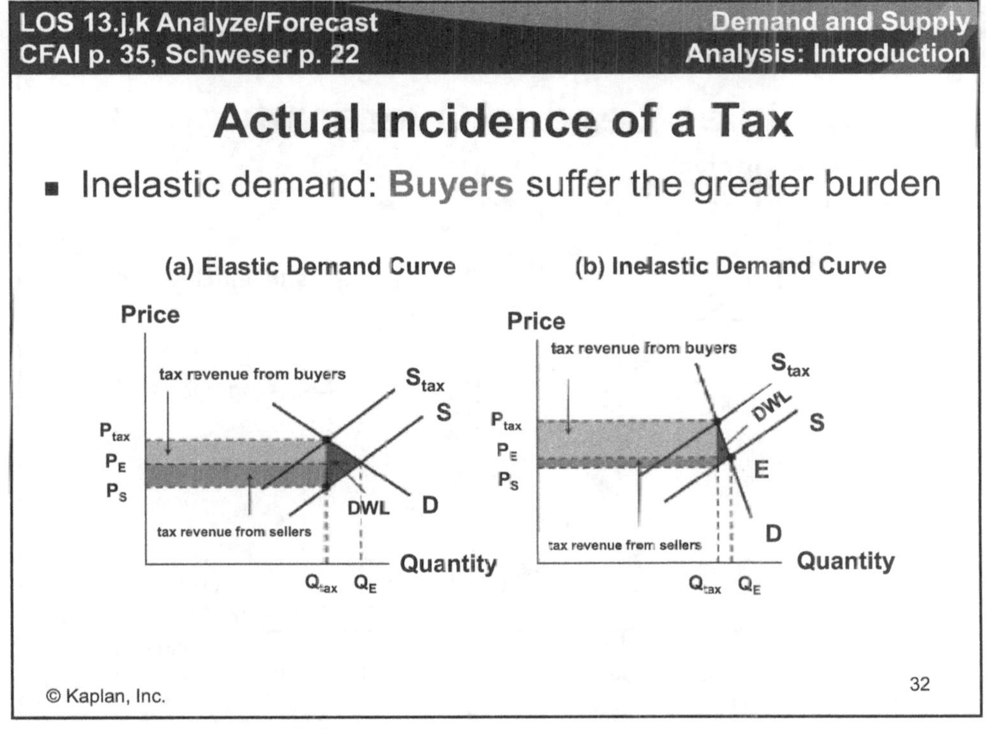
LOS 13.j,k Analyze/Forecast
CFAI p. 35, Schweser p. 22
Demand and Supply
Analysis: Introduction
Actual Incidence of a Tax
Inelastic demand: Buyers suffer the greater burden
(a) Elastic Demand Curve
(b) Inelastic Demand Curve
Price
tax revenue from buyers
S
D
DWL
E
tax revenue from sellers
Quantity
© Kaplan, Inc.
32

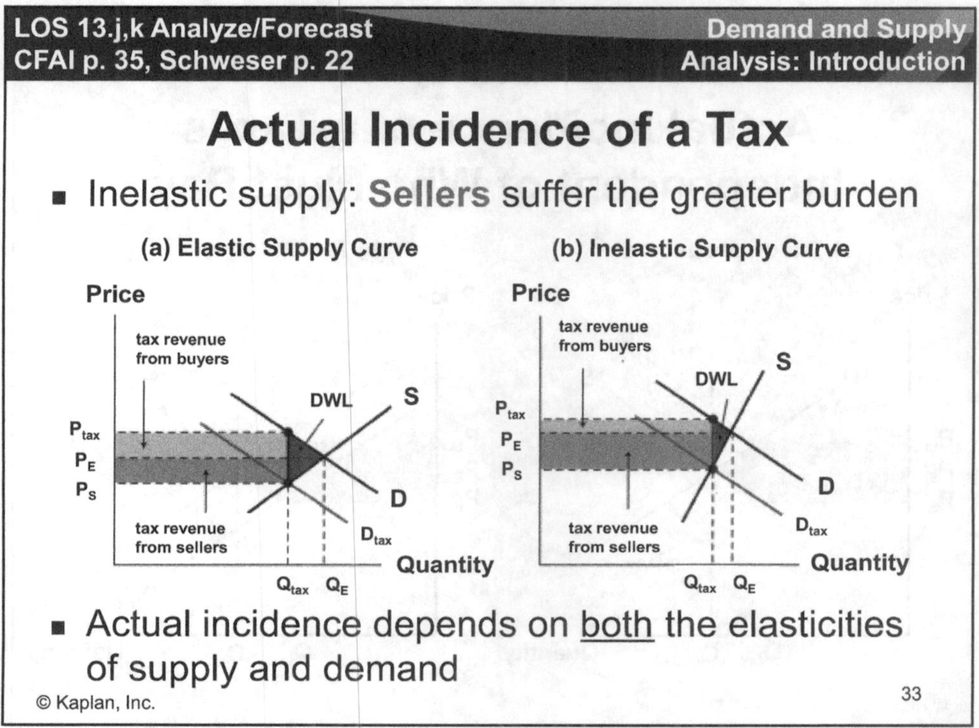
LOS 13.j,k Analyze/Forecast
CFAI p. 35, Schweser p. 22
Demand and Supply
Analysis: Introduction
Actual Incidence of a Tax
Inelastic supply: Sellers suffer the greater burden
(a) Elastic Supply Curve
(b) Inelastic Supply Curve
Price
tax revenue from buyers
DWL
S
P tax
P E
P S
D
tax revenue from sellers
D tax
Quantity
Q tax
Q E
Actual incidence depends on both the elasticities of supply and demand
© Kaplan, Inc.
33

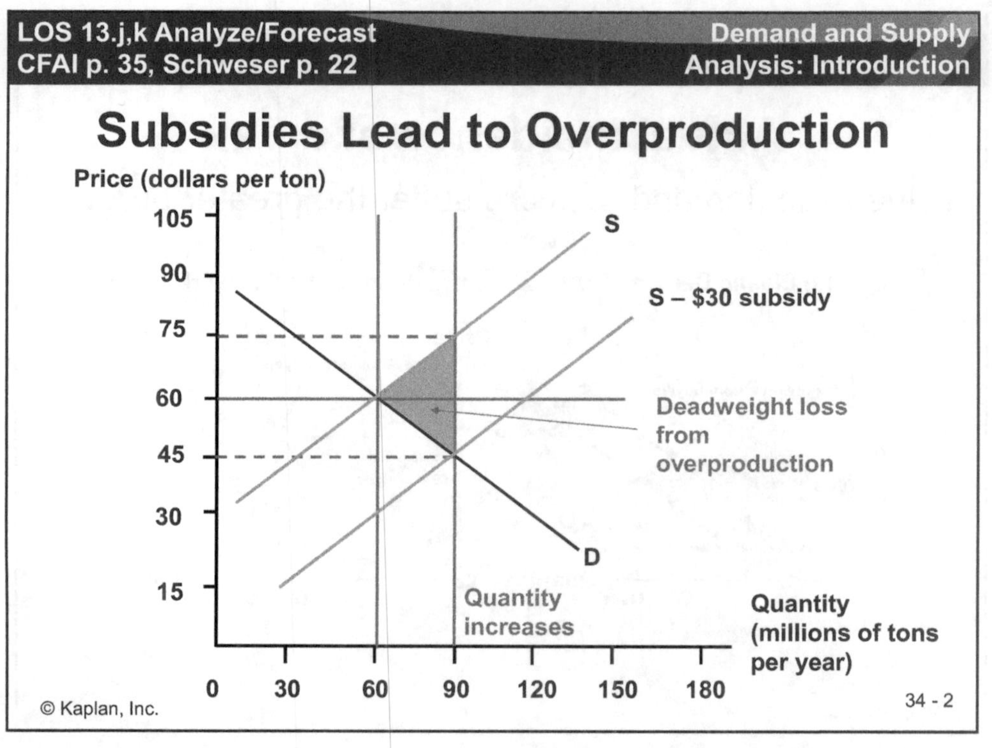
LOS 13.j,k Analyze/Forecast
CFAI p. 35, Schweser p. 22
Demand and Supply
Analysis: Introduction
Subsidies Lead to Overproduction
Price (dollars per ton)
105
90
75
60
45
30
15
S
S – $30 subsidy
Deadweight loss from overproduction
D
Quantity increases
Quantity (millions of tons per year)
0
30
60
90
120
150
180
© Kaplan, Inc.
34 - 2

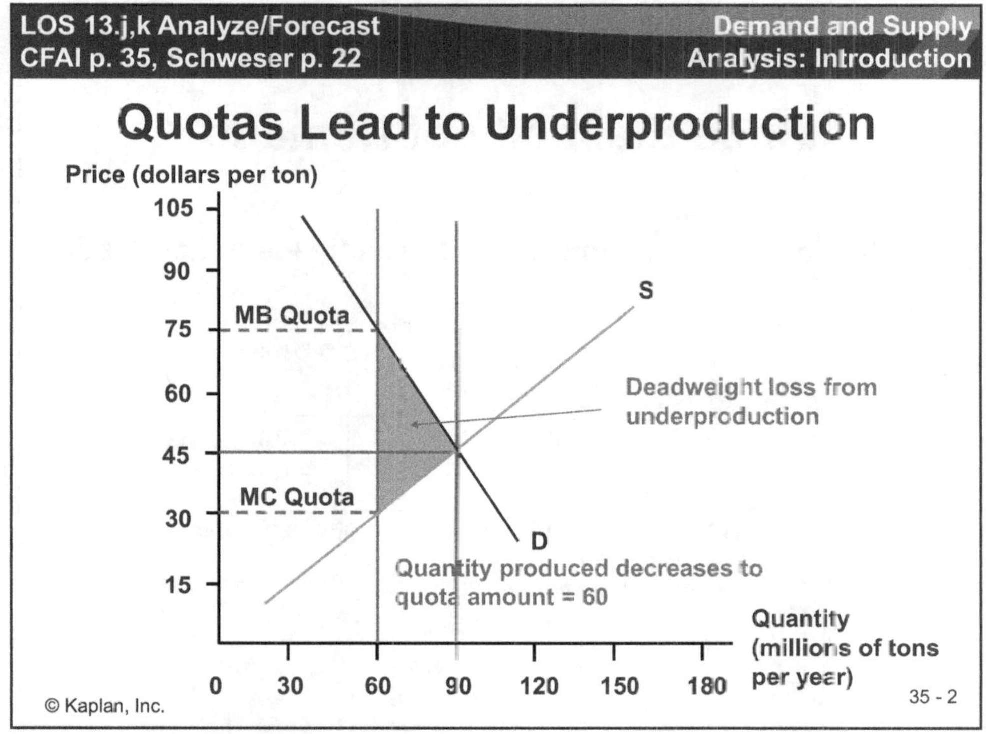

LOS 13.l Calculate/Interpret/Describe
CFAI p. 41, Schweser p. 31

Demand and Supply Analysis: Introduction

Price Elasticity of Demand

$$\text{Price Elasticity of Demand (PED)} = \frac{\%\Delta Q}{\%\Delta P_X}$$

As the price of a normal good increases, **quantity demanded** decreases

- **Elastic demand**: Percentage increase in price leads to a larger percentage decrease in quantity demanded
- **Inelastic demand**: Percentage increase in price leads to a smaller percentage decrease in quantity demanded

36

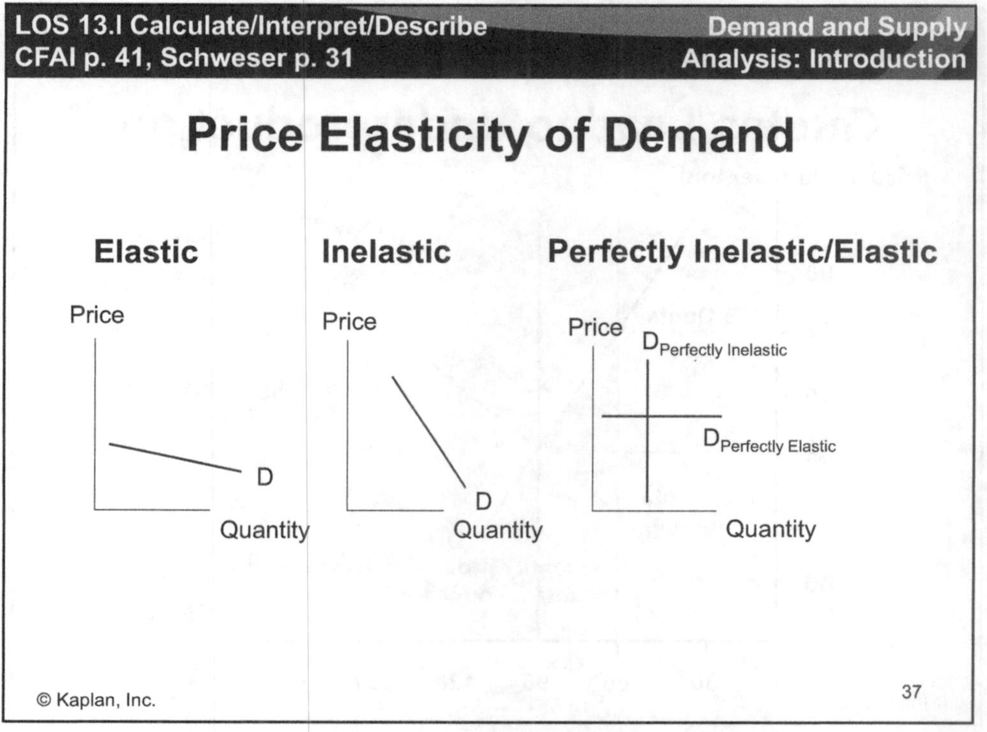

LOS 13.l Calculate/Interpret/Describe
CFAI p. 41, Schweser p. 31

Demand and Supply
Analysis: Introduction

Factors That Influence Elasticity of Demand

- Availability and closeness of **substitutes**
  - ↑ Substitutes: ↑ Elasticity
- **Proportion of income** spent on the item
  - ↑ Proportion of income: ↑ Elasticity
- **Time** elapsed since previous price change
  - ↑ Time: ↑ Elasticity

38 - 3

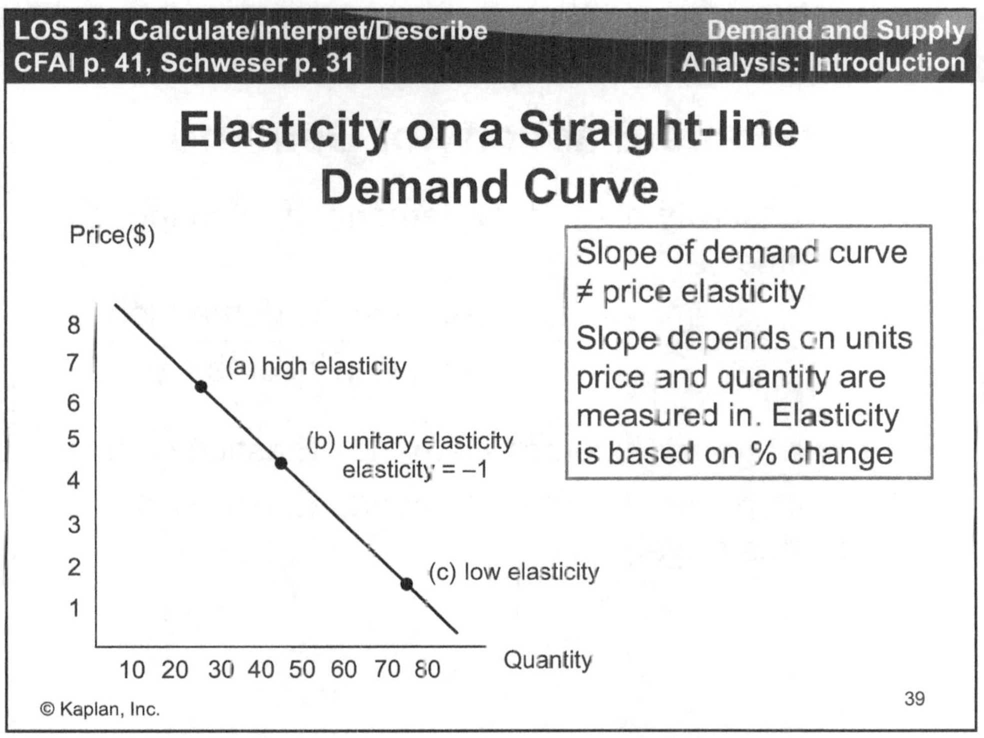

LOS 13.l Calculate/Interpret/Describe
CFAI p. 41, Schweser p. 31

Demand and Supply
Analysis: Introduction

Price Elasticity of Demand and Total Revenue

- Greatest total revenue (P × Q) at the point where elasticity = –1
- **Inelastic range:** Price increase will **increase total revenue**; percentage decrease in quantity demanded < percentage increase in price
- **Elastic range:** Price increase will **decrease total revenue;** percentage decrease in quantity demanded > percentage increase in price

40

LOS 13.l Calculate/Interpret/Describe
CFAI p. 41, Schweser p. 31

Demand and Supply Analysis: Introduction

Income Elasticity of Demand

- The sensitivity of quantity demanded to changes in income

$$\text{income elasticity} = \frac{\%\text{ change in quantity demanded}}{\%\text{ change in income}}$$

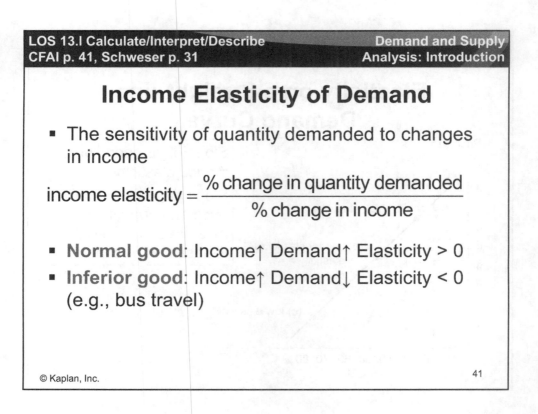

- **Normal good**: Income↑ Demand↑ Elasticity > 0
- **Inferior good**: Income↑ Demand↓ Elasticity < 0 (e.g., bus travel)

41

LOS 13.l Calculate/Interpret/Describe
CFAI p. 41, Schweser p. 31

Demand and Supply Analysis: Introduction

Cross Price Elasticity of Demand

Price of coffee increased 16.65% and demand for tea increased 11.10%

$$\text{cross price elasticity of demand} = \frac{11.10\%}{16.65\%} = 0.67$$

cross price elasticity > 0: the goods are *substitutes*

Price of pizza increased 25.0% and demand for cola decreased 10.7%

$$\text{cross price elasticity of demand} = \frac{-10.7\%}{25.0\%} = -0.43$$

cross price elasticity < 0: the goods are *complements*

42

LOS 13.l Calculate/Interpret/Describe
CFAI p. 41, Schweser p. 31

Demand and Supply Analysis: Introduction

Calculating Elasticities

$$Q_{DX} = 4{,}000 - 140\,P_X + 0.75\,I - 300\,P_Y$$

Where:

Q_{DX} = Quantity demanded of good X

P_X = Price of good X

I = Consumers' average income in € (normal good: positive coefficient)

P_Y = Price of complementary product (negative coefficient)

Assume:

I = €40,000

P_Y = €15

$Q_{DX} = 4{,}000 - 140\,P_X + 30{,}000 - 4{,}500$

$Q_{DX} = 29{,}500 - 140\,P_X$

43 - 2

LOS 13.l Calculate/Interpret/Describe
CFAI p. 41, Schweser p. 31

Demand and Supply Analysis: Introduction

Calculating Elasticities

Price elasticity of demand (PED) = $\dfrac{\%\Delta Q}{\%\Delta P_X}$

$$\frac{\%\Delta Q}{\%\Delta P_X} = \frac{\Delta Q/Q_0}{\Delta P_X/P_0} = \frac{P_0}{Q_0} \times \boxed{\frac{\Delta Q}{\Delta P_X}}$$

Slope coefficient of Price (–140)

Calculate PED at a price of €150:

$Q_{DX} = 29{,}500 - 140\,P_X$

$Q_{DX} = 29{,}500 - (140 \times €150)$

$Q_{DX} = 8{,}500$

$$\text{PED} = \left(\frac{150}{8{,}500}\right) \times (-140) = -2.47$$

44 - 2

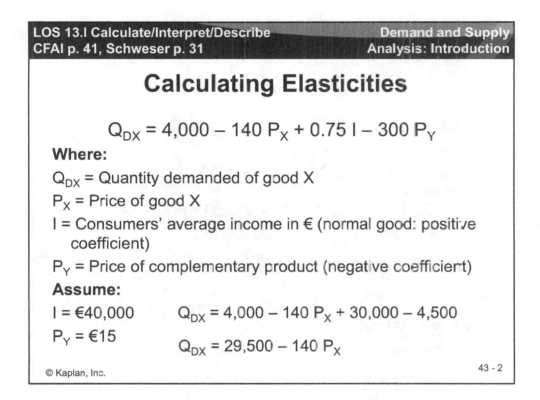

LOS 13.l Calculate/Interpret/Describe
CFAI p. 41, Schweser p. 31

Demand and Supply Analysis: Introduction

Calculating Elasticities

- Income elasticity (IE) $= \dfrac{\%\Delta Q}{\%\Delta I} = \dfrac{\Delta Q/Q_0}{\Delta I/I_0} = \dfrac{I_0}{Q_0} \times \dfrac{\Delta Q}{\Delta I}$

$Q_{DX} = 4{,}000 - 140\ P_X + 0.75\ I - 300\ P_Y$

Assume:

$P_X = €150$ $\quad Q_{DX} = 4{,}000 - 21{,}000 + 0.75\ I - 4{,}500$

$P_Y = €15$ $\quad Q_{DX} = -21{,}500 + 0.75\ I$

Calculate IE at an income of €40,000:

$Q_{DX} = -21{,}500 + 0.75\ I$

$Q_{DX} = -21{,}500 + 30{,}000$

$Q_{DX} = 8{,}500$

$$IE = \left(\frac{40{,}000}{8{,}500}\right) \times (0.75) = 3.53$$

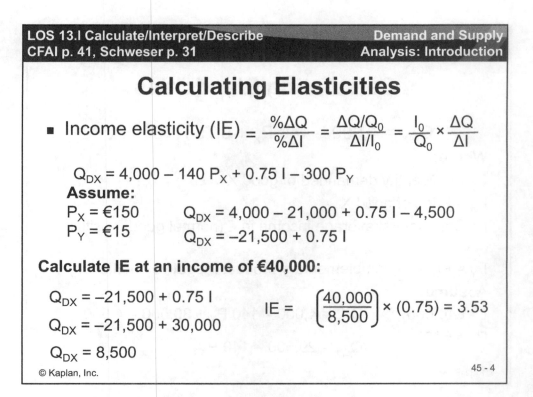

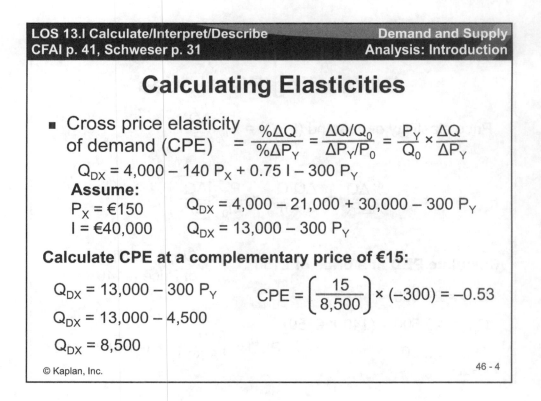

45 - 4

LOS 13.l Calculate/Interpret/Describe
CFAI p. 41, Schweser p. 31

Demand and Supply Analysis: Introduction

Calculating Elasticities

- Cross price elasticity of demand (CPE) $= \dfrac{\%\Delta Q}{\%\Delta P_Y} = \dfrac{\Delta Q/Q_0}{\Delta P_Y/P_0} = \dfrac{P_Y}{Q_0} \times \dfrac{\Delta Q}{\Delta P_Y}$

$Q_{DX} = 4{,}000 - 140\ P_X + 0.75\ I - 300\ P_Y$

Assume:

$P_X = €150$ $\quad Q_{DX} = 4{,}000 - 21{,}000 + 30{,}000 - 300\ P_Y$

$I = €40{,}000$ $\quad Q_{DX} = 13{,}000 - 300\ P_Y$

Calculate CPE at a complementary price of €15:

$Q_{DX} = 13{,}000 - 300\ P_Y$

$Q_{DX} = 13{,}000 - 4{,}500$

$Q_{DX} = 8{,}500$

$$CPE = \left(\frac{15}{8{,}500}\right) \times (-300) = -0.53$$

46 - 4

Economics: Microeconomic Analysis

14. Demand and Supply Analysis: Consumer Demand

Economics

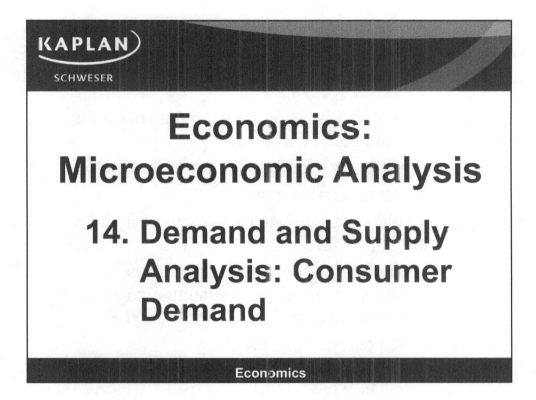

LOS 14.a Describe
CFAI p. 62, Schweser p. 45

Demand and Supply Analysis: Consumer Demand

Utility Theory

Explains consumer choice/behavior

- Preferences for combinations of goods
- Based on satisfaction
- Satisfaction measured by utility

Utility function:

$$\text{Utility} = U(Q_1, Q_2, Q_3, \ldots, Q_N)$$

- Variables are quantity consumed of goods 1 to N
- Quantity must be ≥ 0 for each good
- ↑ quantity of a good holding all others constant: ↑ utility (non-satiation)
- Utility is an ordinal measure

48

LOS 14.b Describe
CFAI p. 65, Schweser p. 46

Demand and Supply Analysis: Consumer Demand

Indifference Curves

- Consumer is indifferent among bundles of goods that lie on the same curve
- Indifference curves for 2 goods slope downwards
- Indifference curves are convex
- Higher indifference curves have more utility than lower ones (ordinal scale)
- Slope at any point is marginal rate of substitution (MRS), the rate at which the consumer is willing to exchange units of good X for units of good Y
- Indifference curves may not cross

 49

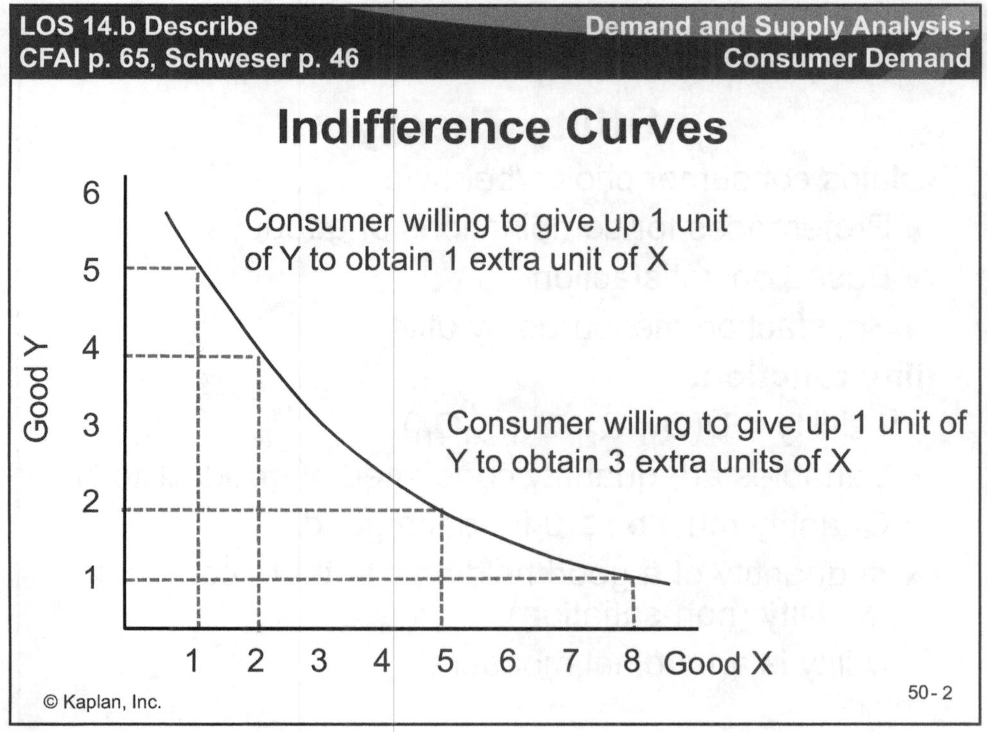
LOS 14.b Describe
CFAI p. 65, Schweser p. 46
Demand and Supply Analysis: Consumer Demand
Indifference Curves
Consumer willing to give up 1 unit of Y to obtain 1 extra unit of X
Consumer willing to give up 1 unit of Y to obtain 3 extra units of X
Good Y
6
5
4
3
2
1
1 2 3 4 5 6 7 8 Good X
© Kaplan, Inc.
50-2

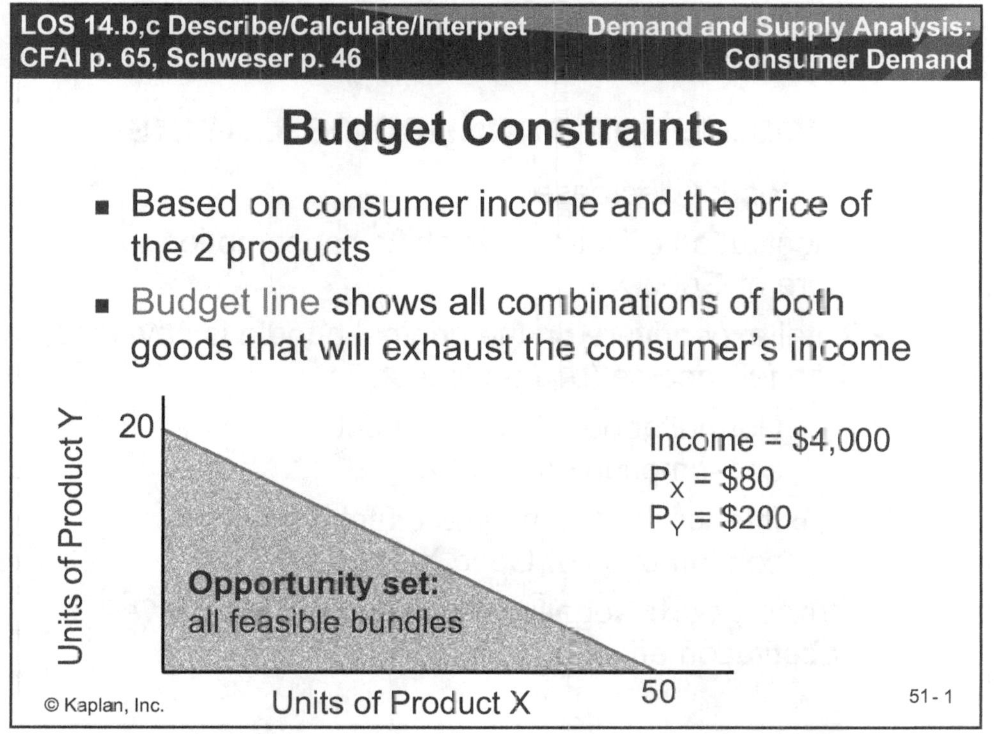
LOS 14.b,c Describe/Calculate/Interpret
CFAI p. 65, Schweser p. 46
Demand and Supply Analysis:
Consumer Demand
Budget Constraints
Based on consumer income and the price of the 2 products
Budget line shows all combinations of both goods that will exhaust the consumer's income
Income = $4,000
P_X = $80
P_Y = $200
Opportunity set:
all feasible bundles
Units of Product Y
20
Units of Product X
50
© Kaplan, Inc.
51-1

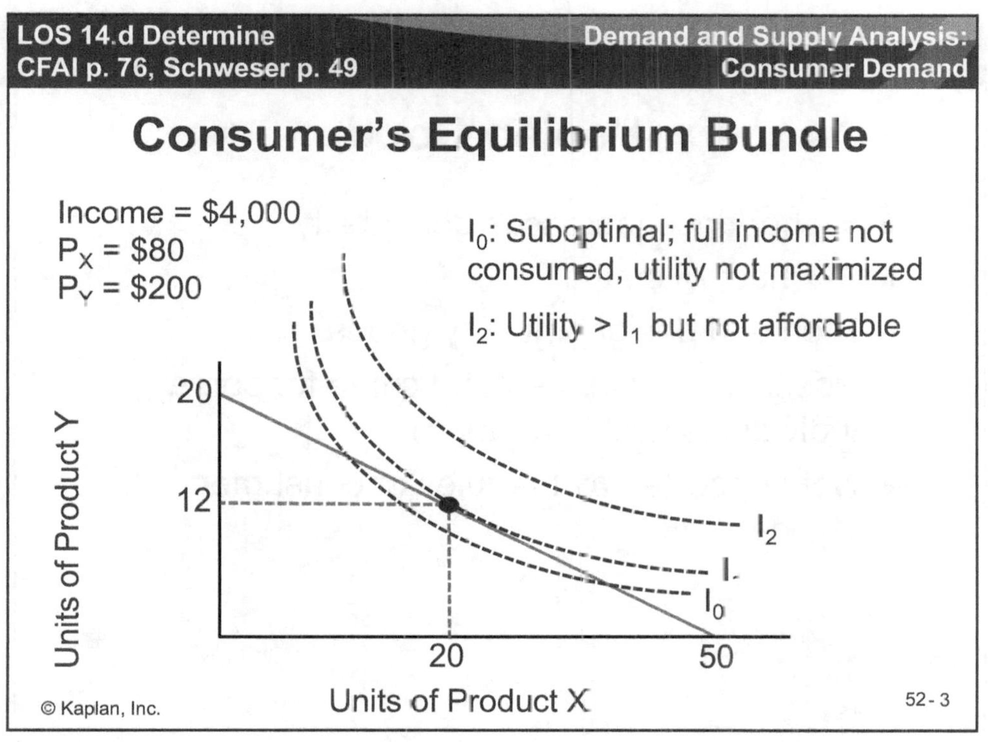
LOS 14.d Determine
CFAI p. 76, Schweser p. 49
Demand and Supply Analysis:
Consumer Demand
Consumer's Equilibrium Bundle
Income = $4,000
P_X = $80
P_Y = $200
I_0: Suboptimal; full income not consumed, utility not maximized
I_2: Utility > I_1 but not affordable
Units of Product Y
20
12
I_2
I_1
I_0
20
50
Units of Product X
© Kaplan, Inc.
52-3

LOS 14.e,f Compare/Distinguish/Explain
CFAI p. 81, Schweser p. 49

Demand and Supply Analysis: Consumer Demand

Substitution and Income Effects

Price of Good X decreases:

- Substitution effect *always* shifts consumption to more of Good X
- Total expenditure on the original bundle is now less than full income (budget line shifts)
  - Normal goods: Income effect increases consumption of Good X
  - Inferior goods: Income effect decreases consumption of Good X
- **Giffen good:** Negative income effect > positive substitution effect

53

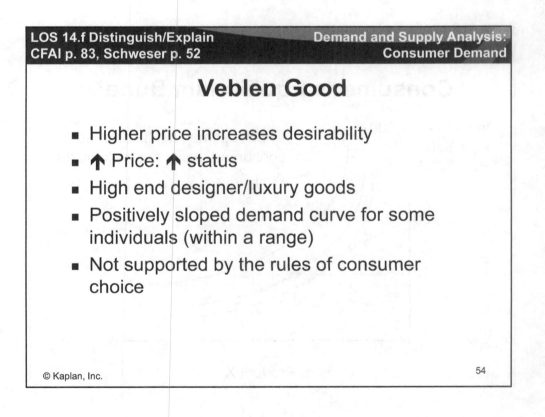

LOS 14.f Distinguish/Explain
CFAI p. 83, Schweser p. 52

Demand and Supply Analysis: Consumer Demand

Veblen Good

- Higher price increases desirability
- ↑ Price: ↑ status
- High end designer/luxury goods
- Positively sloped demand curve for some individuals (within a range)
- Not supported by the rules of consumer choice

54

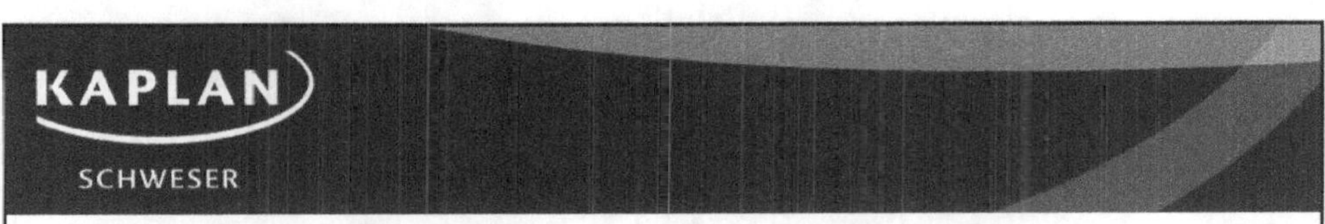

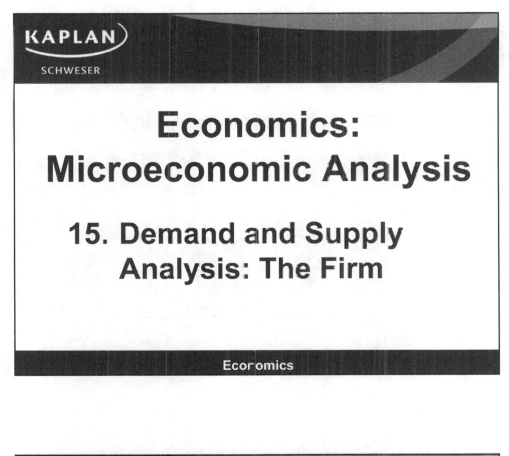

Economics: Microeconomic Analysis

15. Demand and Supply Analysis: The Firm

Economics

LOS 15.a Calculate/Interpret/Compare
CFAI p. 95, Schweser p. 57

Demand and Supply Analysis: The Firm

Economic Profit

- Accounting profit is net income
  accounting profit = revenue – explicit costs
- Economic profit = accounting profit – implicit costs
  implicit opportunity costs =
  return on owner capital
  + opportunity cost of owner's time
- Normal profit when economic profit = 0
- Effect on equity values

 56

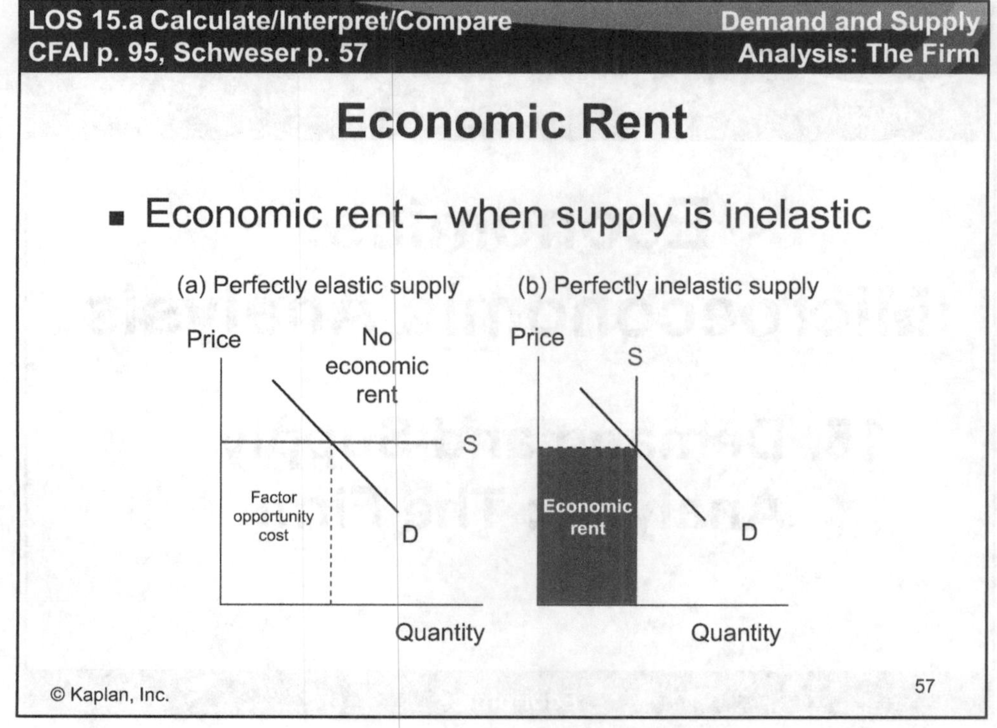
LOS 15.a Calculate/Interpret/Compare
CFAI p. 95, Schweser p. 57
Demand and Supply
Analysis: The Firm
Economic Rent
Economic rent – when supply is inelastic
(a) Perfectly elastic supply
(b) Perfectly inelastic supply
Price
No economic rent
S
Factor opportunity cost
D
Quantity
Price
S
Economic rent
D
Quantity
© Kaplan, Inc.
57

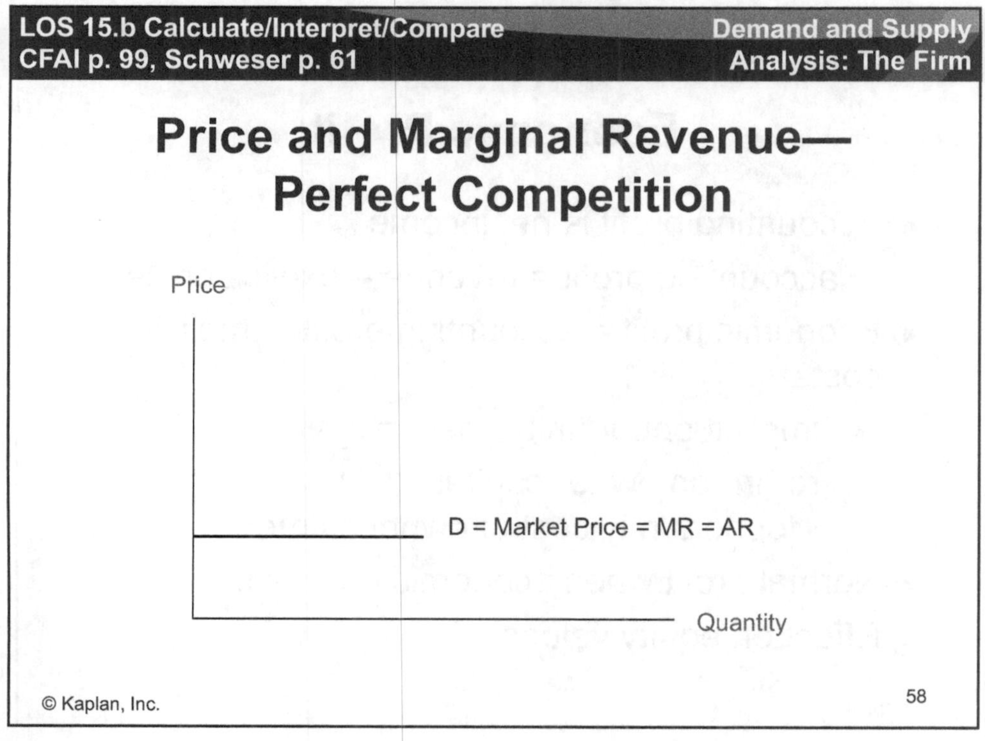
LOS 15.b Calculate/Interpret/Compare
CFAI p. 99, Schweser p. 61
Demand and Supply
Analysis: The Firm
Price and Marginal Revenue—
Perfect Competition
Price
D = Market Price = MR = AR
Quantity
© Kaplan, Inc.
58

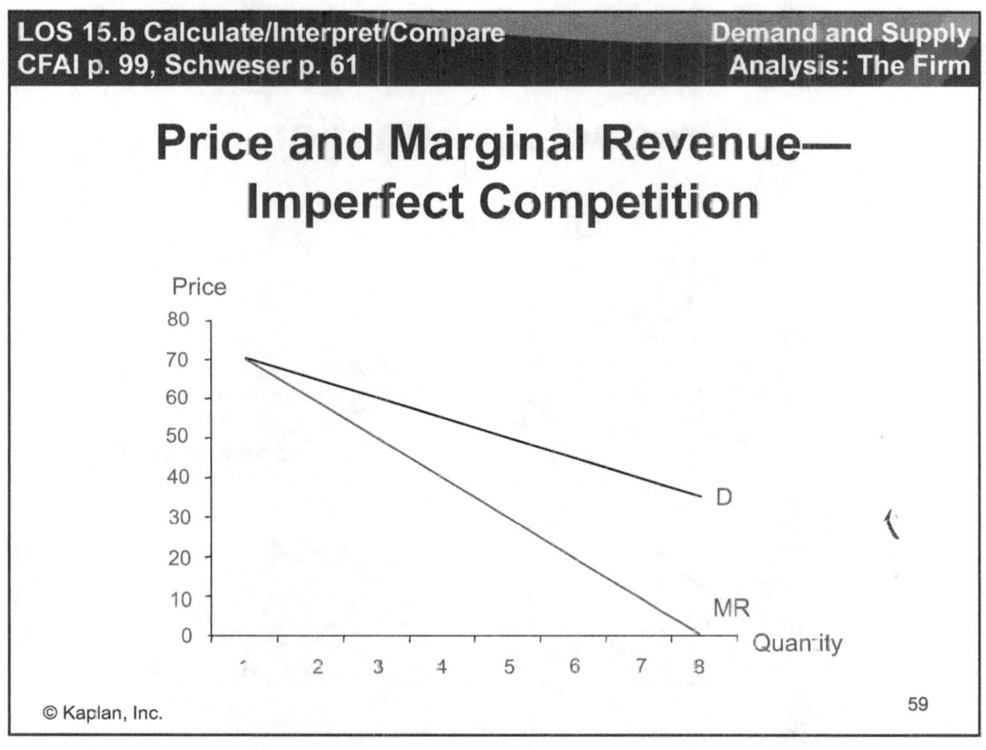

LOS 15.c Describe
CFAI p. 105, Schweser p. 63

Demand and Supply
Analysis: The Firm

Factors of Production

- Land
- Labor
- Capital
- Materials

Often we simply use Labor (L) and Capital (K)

60

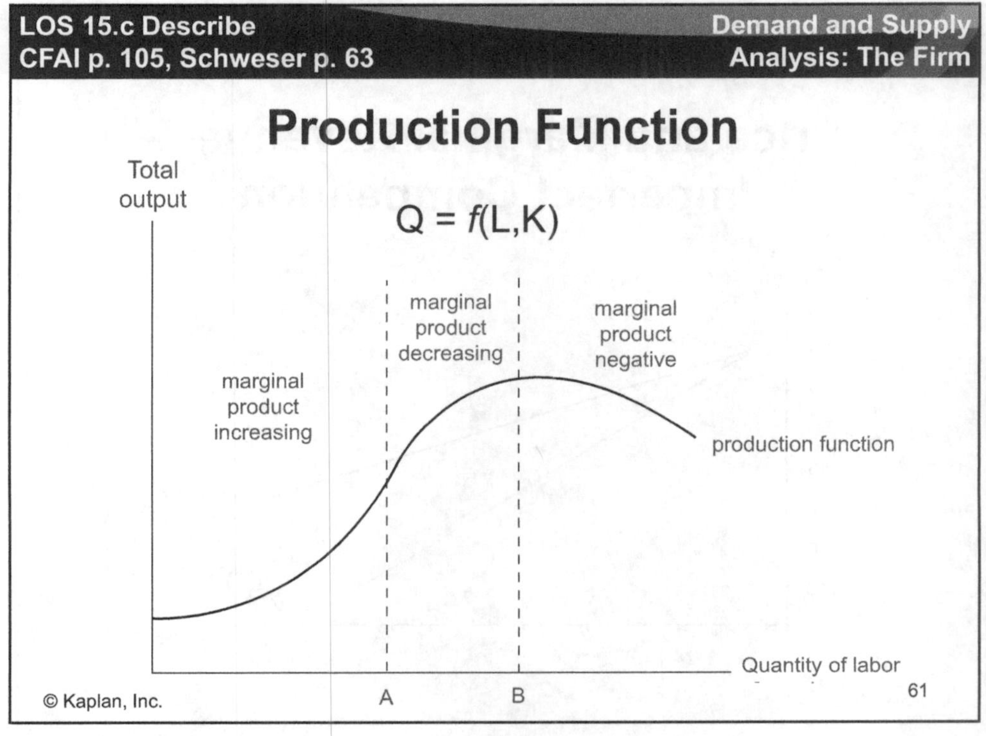
LOS 15.c Describe
CFAI p. 105, Schweser p. 63
Demand and Supply
Analysis: The Firm
Production Function
Total output
Q = f(L,K)
marginal product increasing
marginal product decreasing
marginal product negative
production function
Quantity of labor
A
B
© Kaplan, Inc.
61

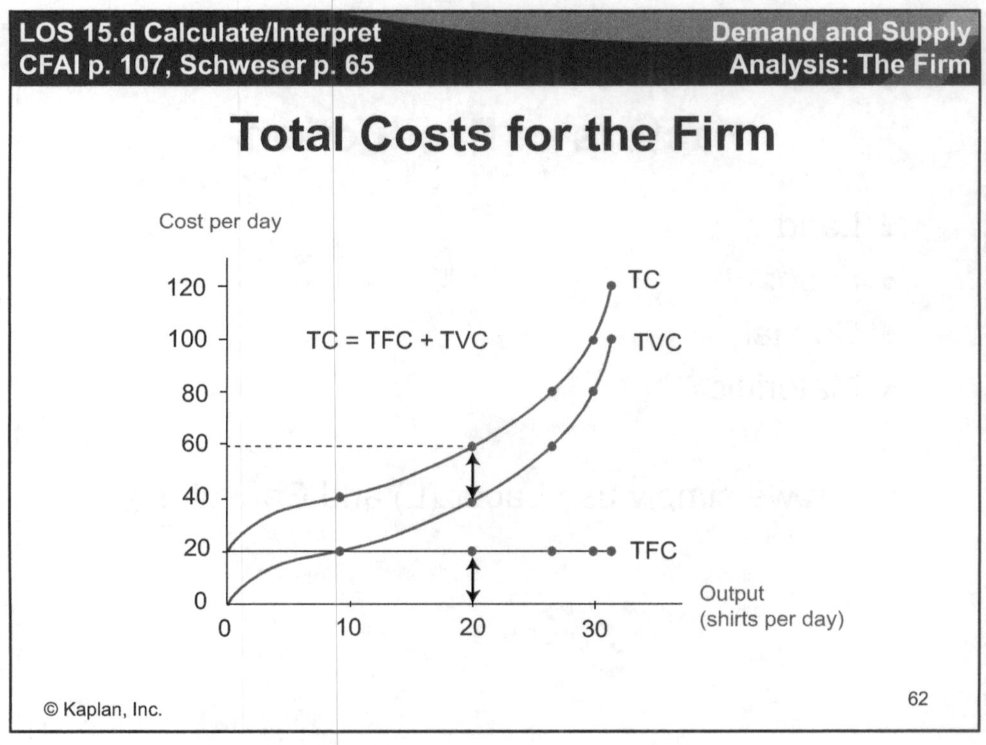
LOS 15.d Calculate/Interpret
CFAI p. 107, Schweser p. 65
Demand and Supply
Analysis: The Firm
Total Costs for the Firm
Cost per day
120
100
80
60
40
20
0
TC = TFC + TVC
TC
TVC
TFC
0
10
20
30
Output
(shirts per day)
© Kaplan, Inc.
62

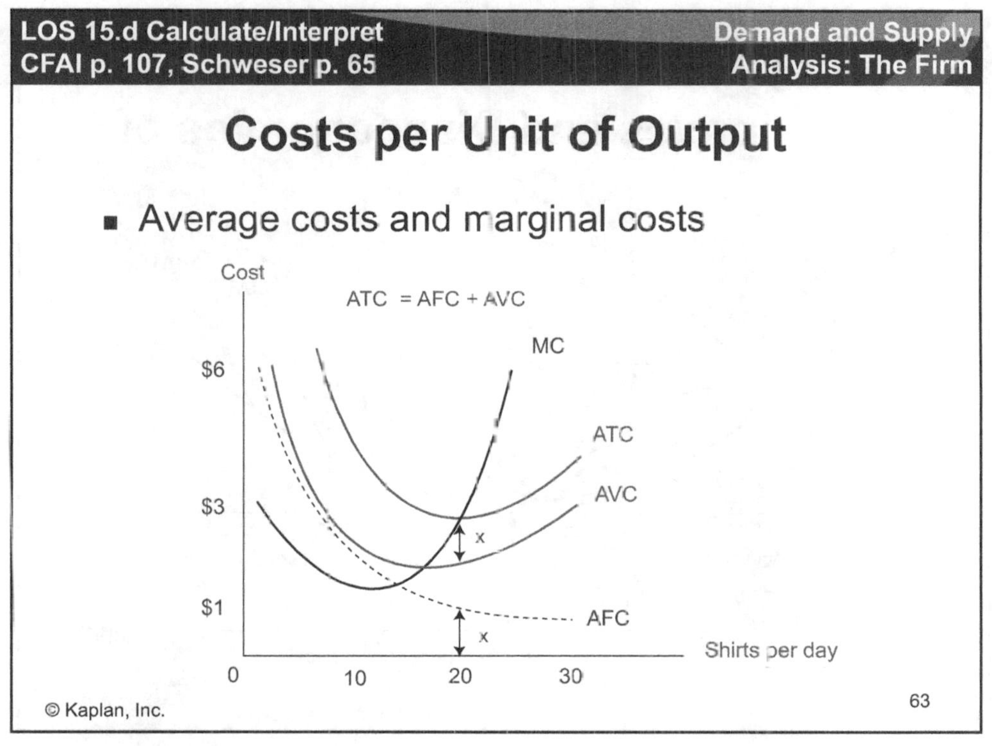
LOS 15.d Calculate/Interpret
CFAI p. 107, Schweser p. 65
Demand and Supply
Analysis: The Firm
Costs per Unit of Output
Average costs and marginal costs
Cost
ATC = AFC + AVC
MC
$6
ATC
AVC
$3
x
$1
AFC
x
Shirts per day
0
10
20
30
© Kaplan, Inc.
63

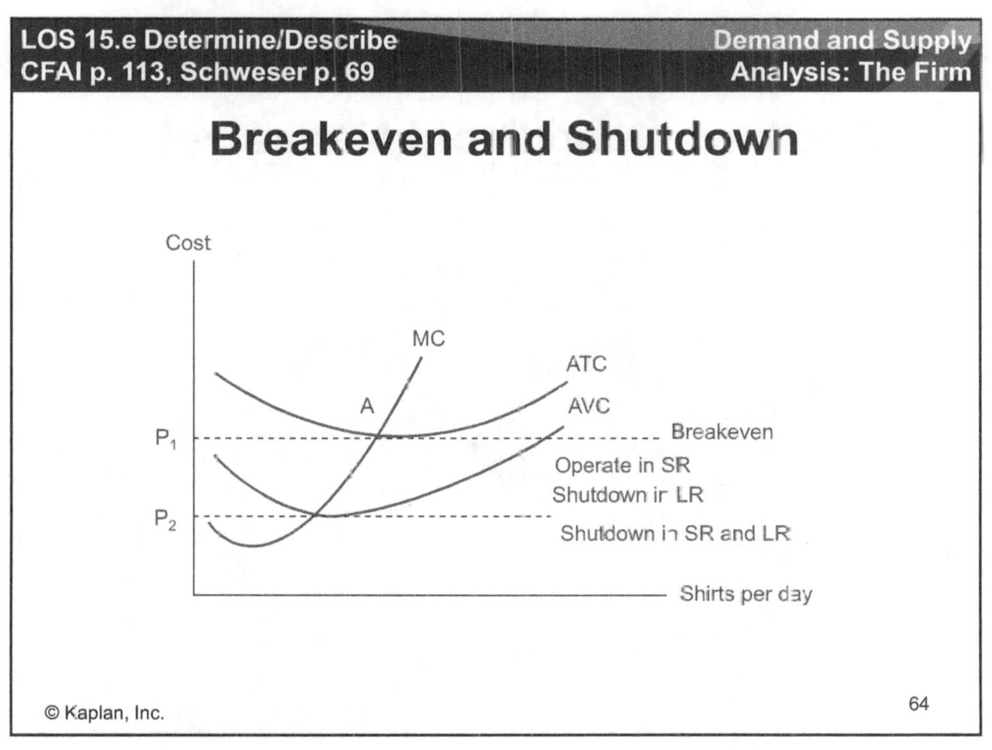
LOS 15.e Determine/Describe
CFAI p. 113, Schweser p. 69
Demand and Supply
Analysis: The Firm
Breakeven and Shutdown
Cost
MC
ATC
A
AVC
P1
Breakeven
Operate in SR
Shutdown in LR
P2
Shutdown in SR and LR
Shirts per day
© Kaplan, Inc.
64

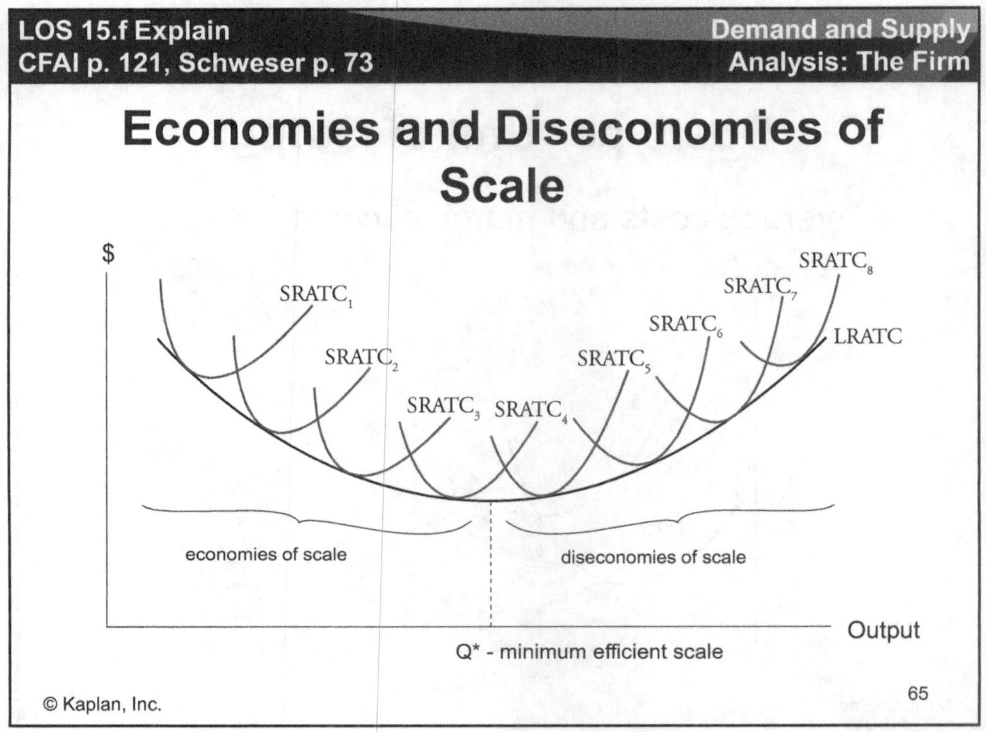
LOS 15.f Explain
CFAI p. 121, Schweser p. 73
Demand and Supply Analysis: The Firm
Economies and Diseconomies of Scale
$
SRATC1
SRATC2
SRATC3
SRATC4
SRATC5
SRATC6
SRATC7
SRATC8
LRATC
economies of scale
diseconomies of scale
Output
Q* - minimum efficient scale
© Kaplan, Inc.
65

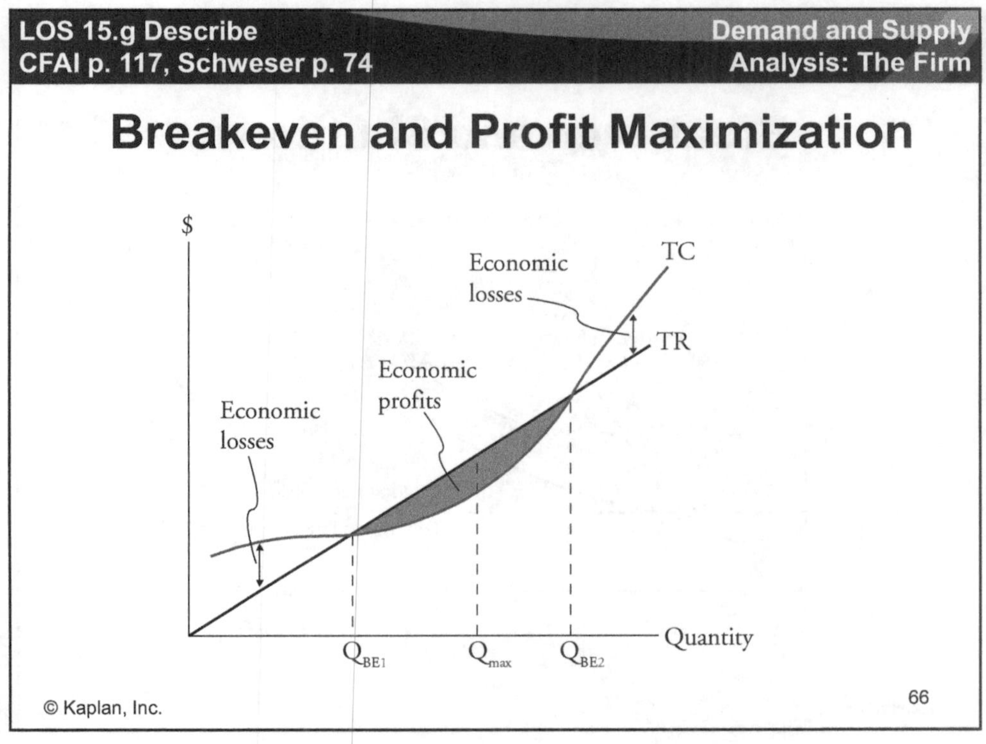
LOS 15.g Describe
CFAI p. 117, Schweser p. 74
Demand and Supply Analysis: The Firm
Breakeven and Profit Maximization
$
Economic losses
TC
TR
Economic profits
Economic losses
Quantity
QBE1
Qmax
QBE2
© Kaplan, Inc.
66

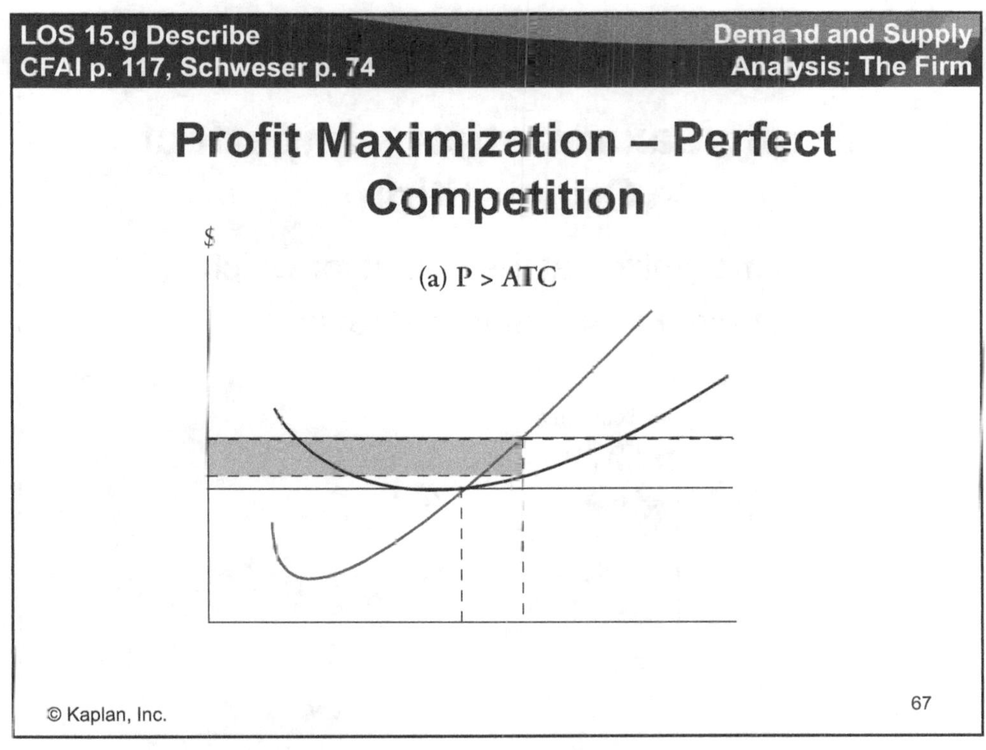
LOS 15.g Describe
CFAI p. 117, Schweser p. 74
Demand and Supply
Analysis: The Firm
Profit Maximization – Perfect Competition
$
(a) P > ATC
© Kaplan, Inc.
67

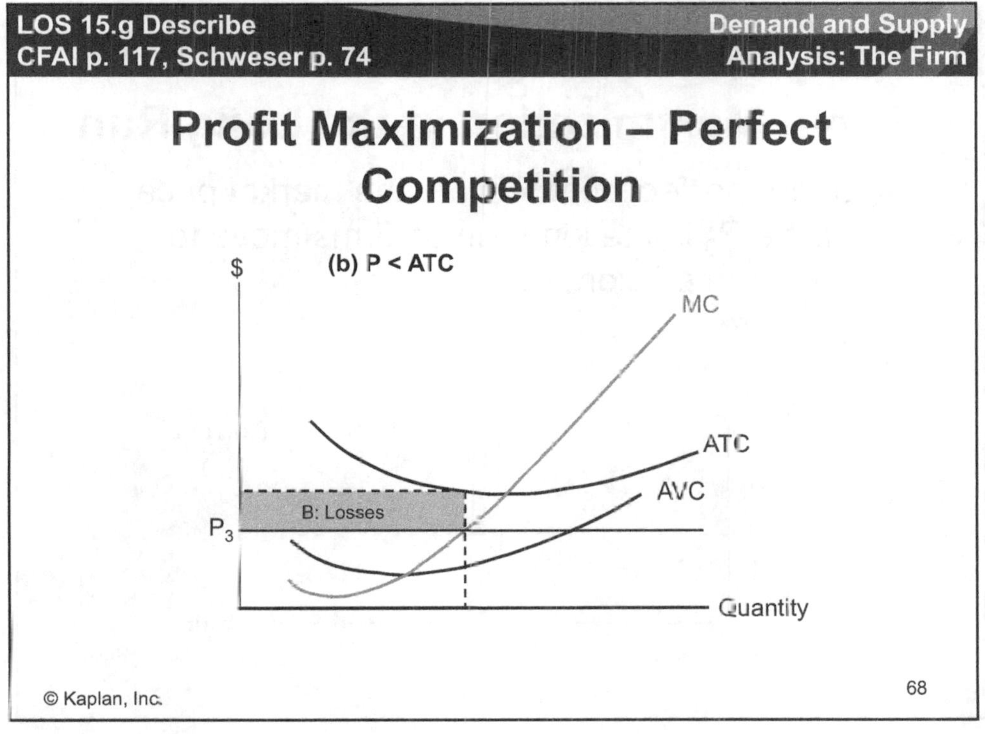
LOS 15.g Describe
CFAI p. 117, Schweser p. 74
Demand and Supply
Analysis: The Firm
Profit Maximization – Perfect Competition
$
(b) P < ATC
MC
ATC
AVC
B: Losses
P3
Quantity
© Kaplan, Inc.
68

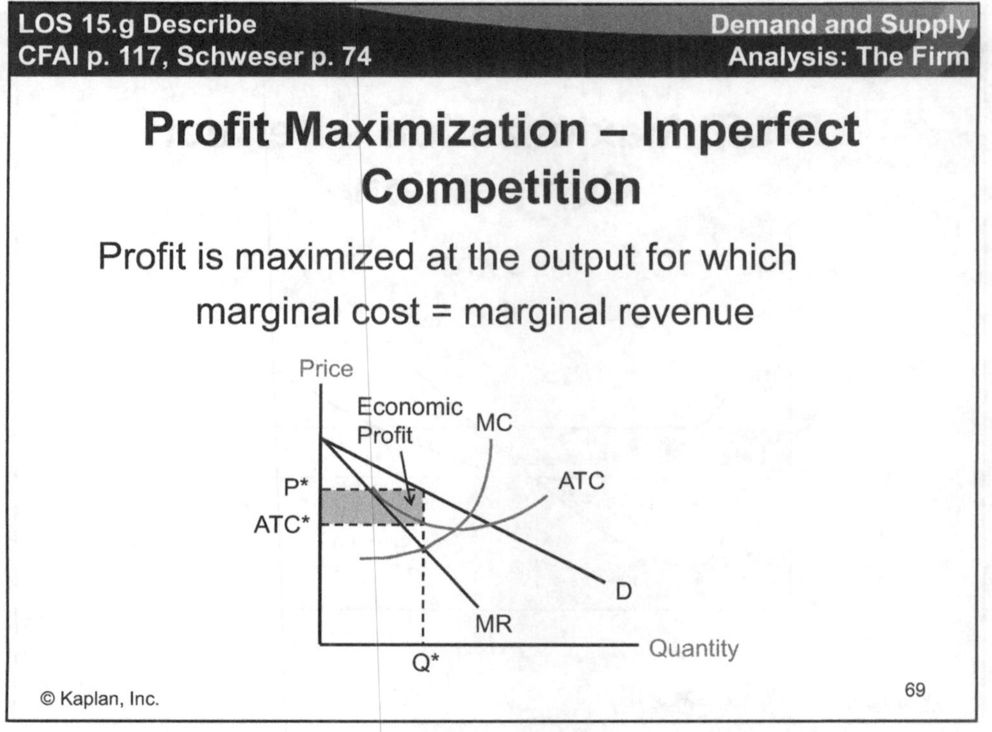

LOS 15.g Describe
CFAI p. 117, Schweser p. 74
Demand and Supply
Analysis: The Firm
Profit Maximization – Imperfect Competition
Profit is maximized at the output for which marginal cost = marginal revenue
Price
Economic Profit
MC
P*
ATC
ATC*
D
MR
Quantity
Q*
© Kaplan, Inc.
69

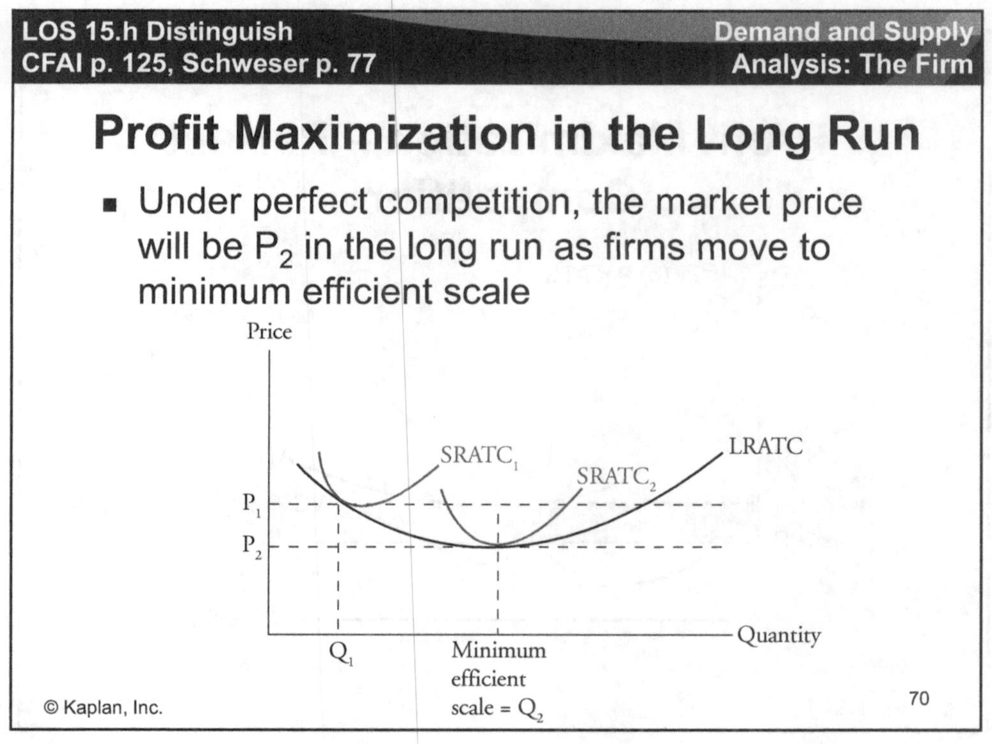

LOS 15.h Distinguish
CFAI p. 125, Schweser p. 77
Demand and Supply
Analysis: The Firm
Profit Maximization in the Long Run
Under perfect competition, the market price will be P2 in the long run as firms move to minimum efficient scale
Price
SRATC1
LRATC
SRATC2
P1
P2
Quantity
Q1
Minimum efficient scale = Q2
© Kaplan, Inc.
70

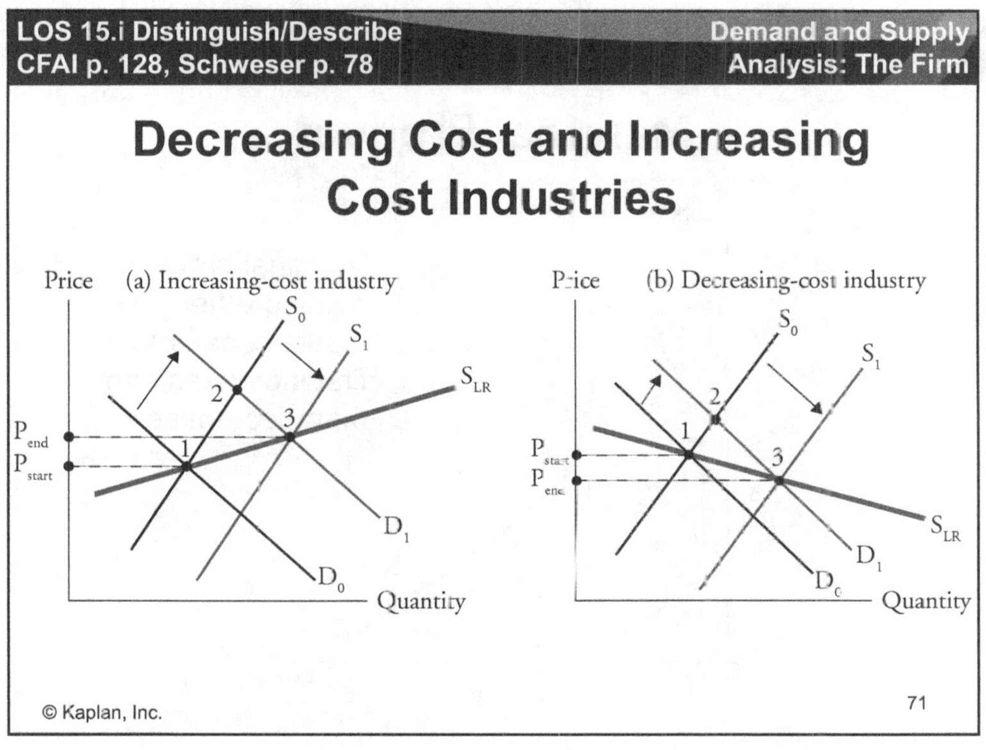

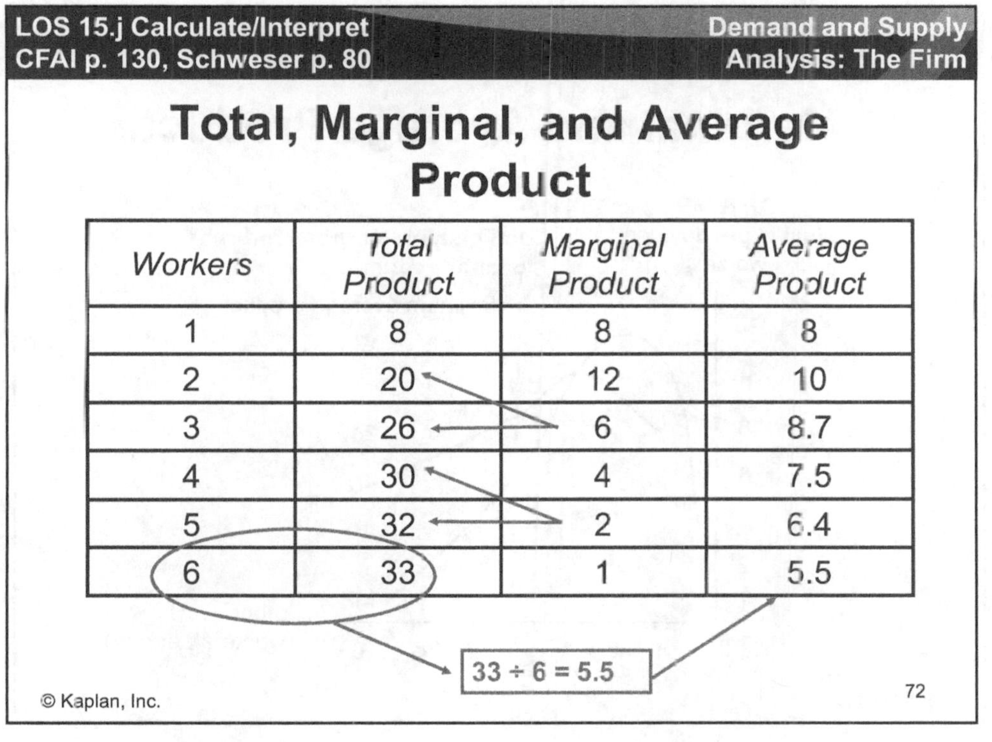

Workers	Total Product	Marginal Product	Average Product
1	8	8	8
2	20	12	10
3	26	6	8.7
4	30	4	7.5
5	32	2	6.4
6	33	1	5.5

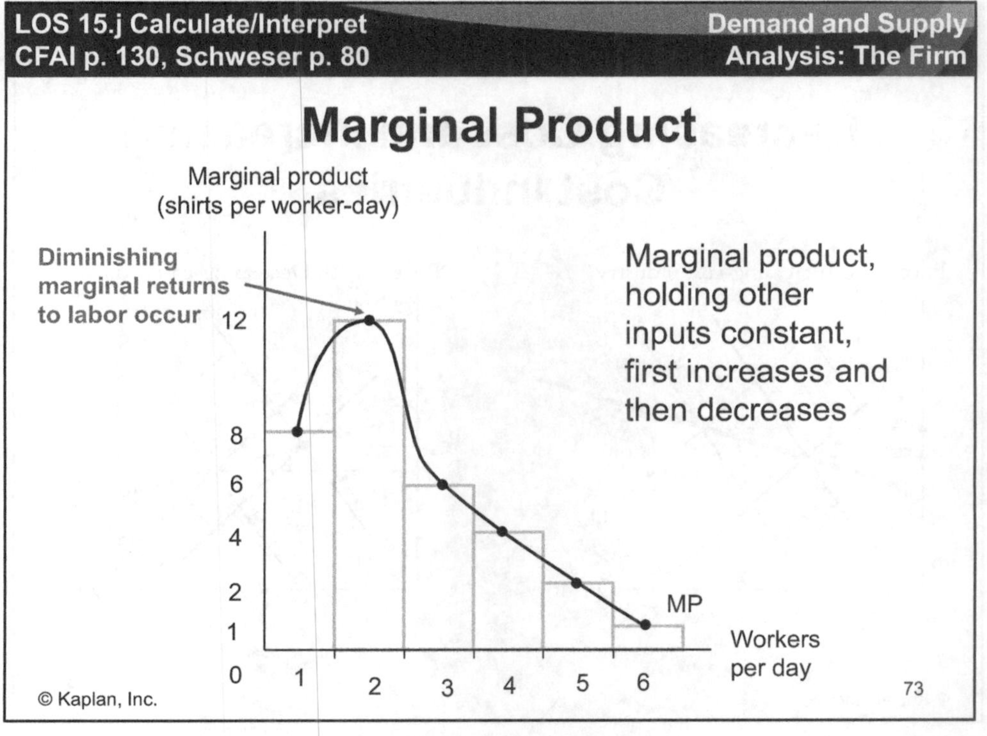
LOS 15.j Calculate/Interpret
CFAI p. 130, Schweser p. 80
Demand and Supply
Analysis: The Firm
Marginal Product
Marginal product
(shirts per worker-day)
Diminishing
marginal returns
to labor occur
12
8
6
4
2
1
0
1
2
3
4
5
6
MP
Workers
per day
Marginal product,
holding other
inputs constant,
first increases and
then decreases
© Kaplan, Inc.
73

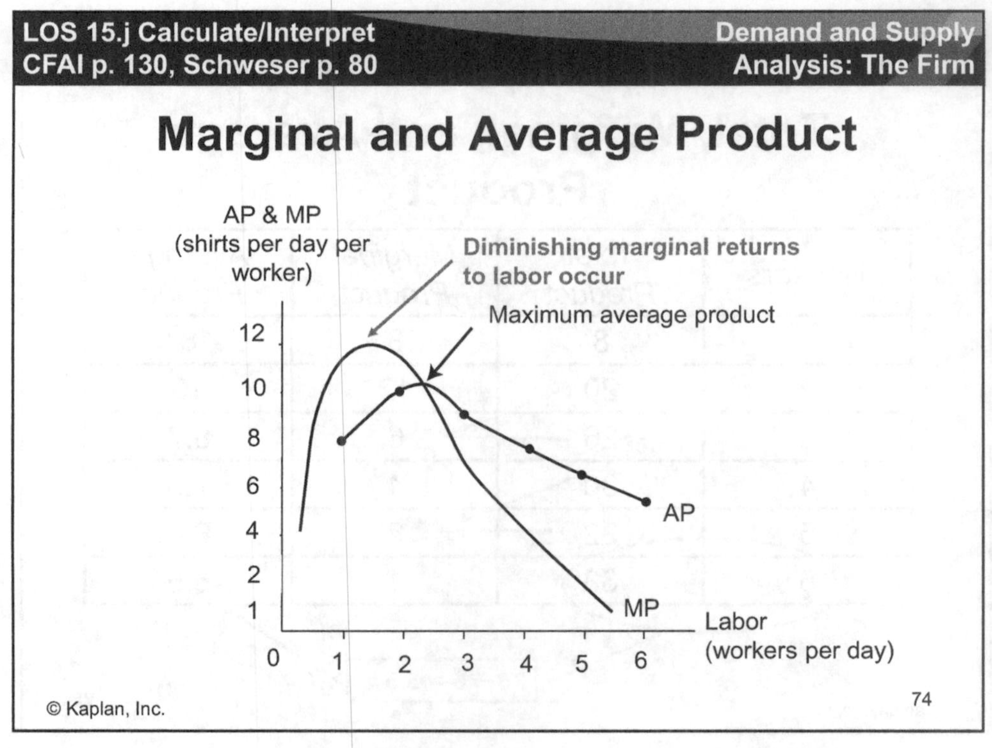
LOS 15.j Calculate/Interpret
CFAI p. 130, Schweser p. 80
Demand and Supply
Analysis: The Firm
Marginal and Average Product
AP & MP
(shirts per day per
worker)
Diminishing marginal returns
to labor occur
Maximum average product
12
10
8
6
4
2
1
0
1
2
3
4
5
6
AP
MP
Labor
(workers per day)
© Kaplan, Inc.
74

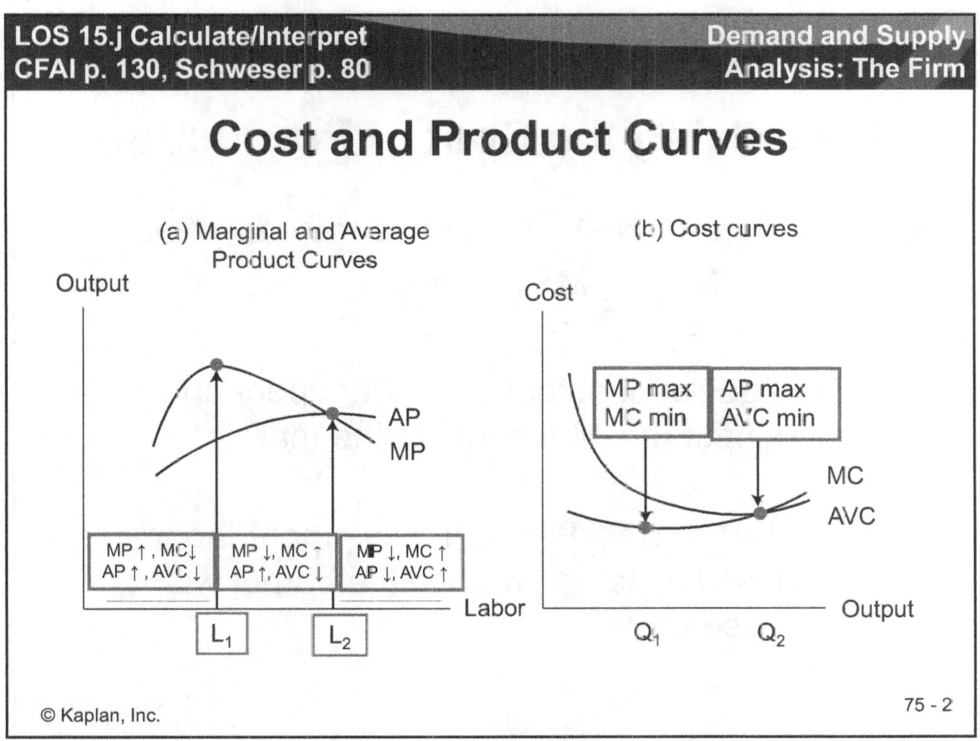

LOS 15.k Describe/Calculate/Interpret
CFAI p. 132, Schweser p. 81

Demand and Supply
Analysis: The Firm

Profit Maximizing Input Amounts

- Marginal revenue product (MRP) is the addition to total revenue from selling the additional output (MP) from employing one more unit of an input
- As each extra unit of input is added, output increases but at a decreasing rate (diminishing marginal returns)
- To maximize profits, use additional amounts of an input until MRP = unit costs
- Labor: Hire more workers until MRP_L = wage

76

LOS 15.l Determine
CFAI p. 136, Schweser p. 81

Demand and Supply Analysis: The Firm

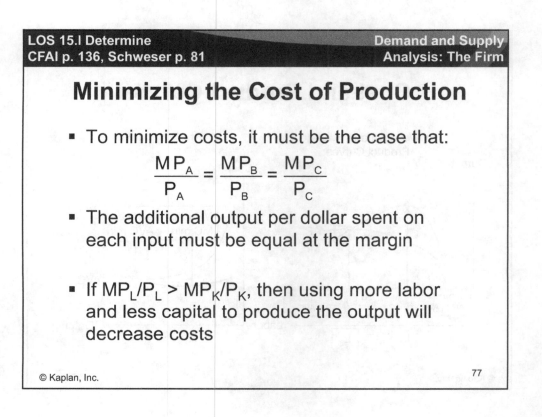

Minimizing the Cost of Production

- To minimize costs, it must be the case that:

$$\frac{MP_A}{P_A} = \frac{MP_B}{P_B} = \frac{MP_C}{P_C}$$

- The additional output per dollar spent on each input must be equal at the margin
- If $MP_L/P_L > MP_K/P_K$, then using more labor and less capital to produce the output will decrease costs

77

Economics: Microeconomic Analysis

16. The Firm and Market Structures

Economics

LOS 16.a,h Describe/Identify
CFAI p. 148, Schweser p. 92

The Firm and Market Structures

Characteristics of Market Structures

	Perfect Competition	Monopolistic Competition	Oligopoly	Monopoly
Number of sellers	Many firms	Many firms	Few firms	Single firm
Barriers to entry	Very low	Low	High	Very high
Nature of substitute products	Very good substitutes	Good substitutes but differentiated	Very good substitutes or differentiated	No good substitutes
Nature of competition	Price only	Price, marketing, features	Price, marketing, features	Advertising
Price power	None	Some	Some to significant	Significant

79

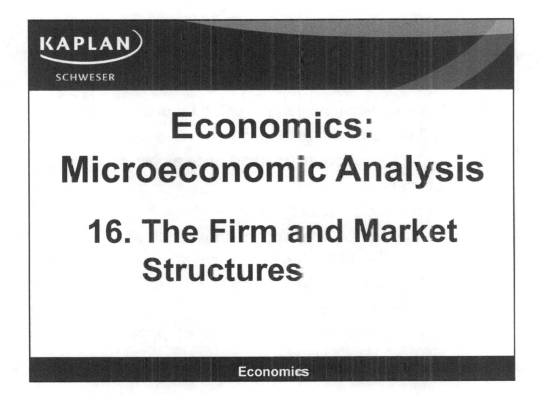

LOS 16.b,d,e Explain/Describe/Determine
CFAI p. 152, Schweser p. 94

The Firm and Market Structures

Perfect Competition

Firms in perfect competition are **price takers**

- No influence over market price
- "Take" the equilibrium (market) price as given

Characteristics:

- Homogeneous product
- Large number of independent firms; each small relative to the total market
- Perfectly elastic demand curves
- No barriers to entry or exit
- Supply and demand determine market price

80

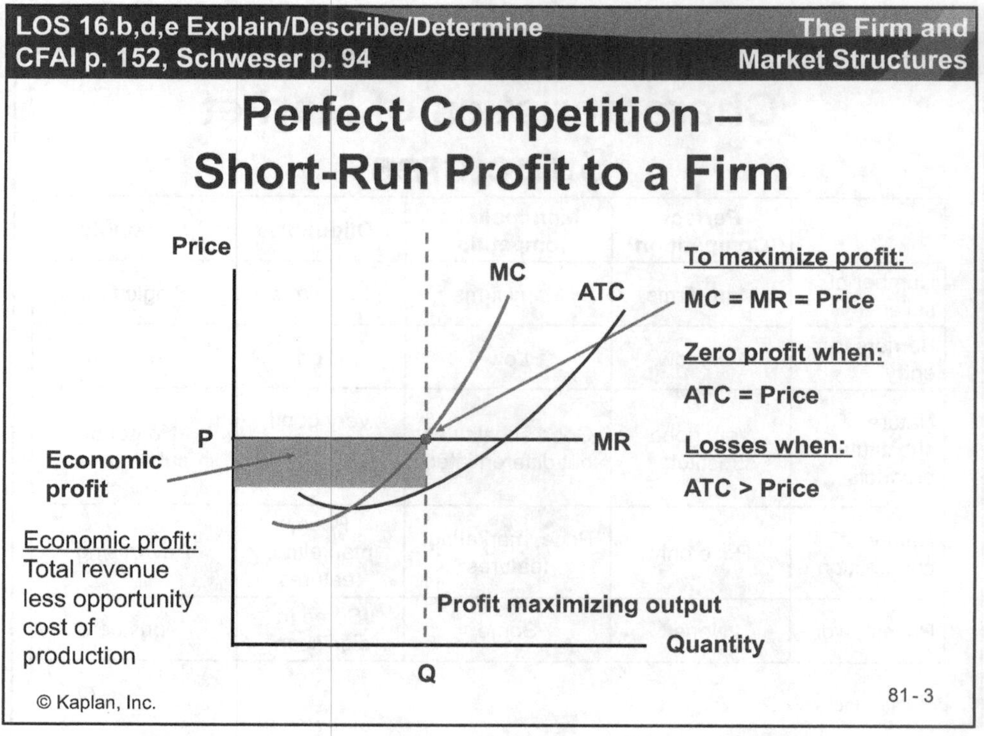

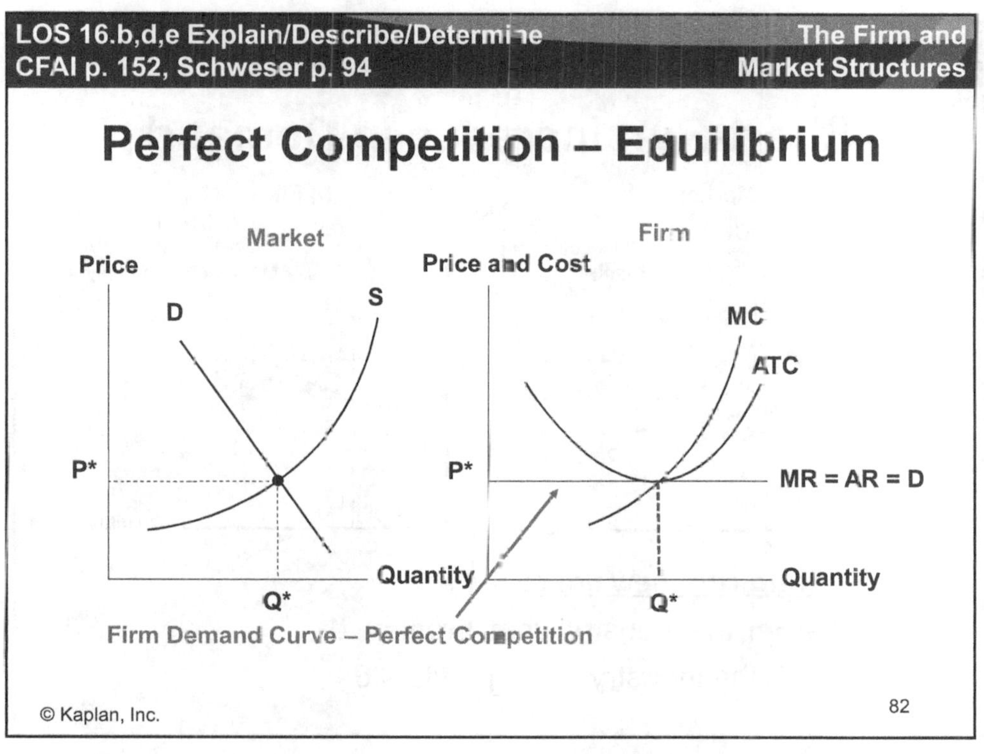
LOS 16.b,d,e Explain/Describe/Determine
CFAI p. 152, Schweser p. 94
The Firm and
Market Structures
Perfect Competition – Equilibrium
Market
Price
D
S
P*
Q*
Quantity
Firm
Price and Cost
MC
ATC
P*
MR = AR = D
Q*
Quantity
Firm Demand Curve – Perfect Competition
© Kaplan, Inc.
82

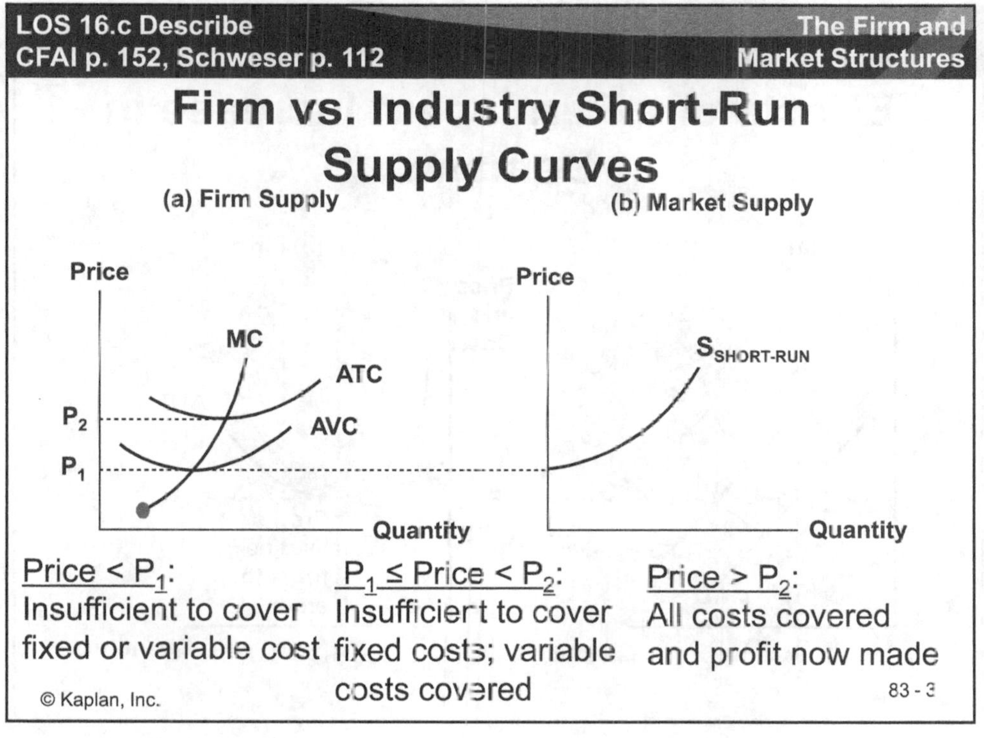
LOS 16.c Describe
CFAI p. 152, Schweser p. 112
The Firm and
Market Structures
Firm vs. Industry Short-Run
Supply Curves
(a) Firm Supply
(b) Market Supply
Price
MC
ATC
AVC
P2
P1
Quantity
Price
SSHORT-RUN
Quantity
Price < P1:
Insufficient to cover
fixed or variable cost
P1 ≤ Price < P2:
Insufficient to cover
fixed costs; variable
costs covered
Price > P2:
All costs covered
and profit now made
© Kaplan, Inc.
83 - 3

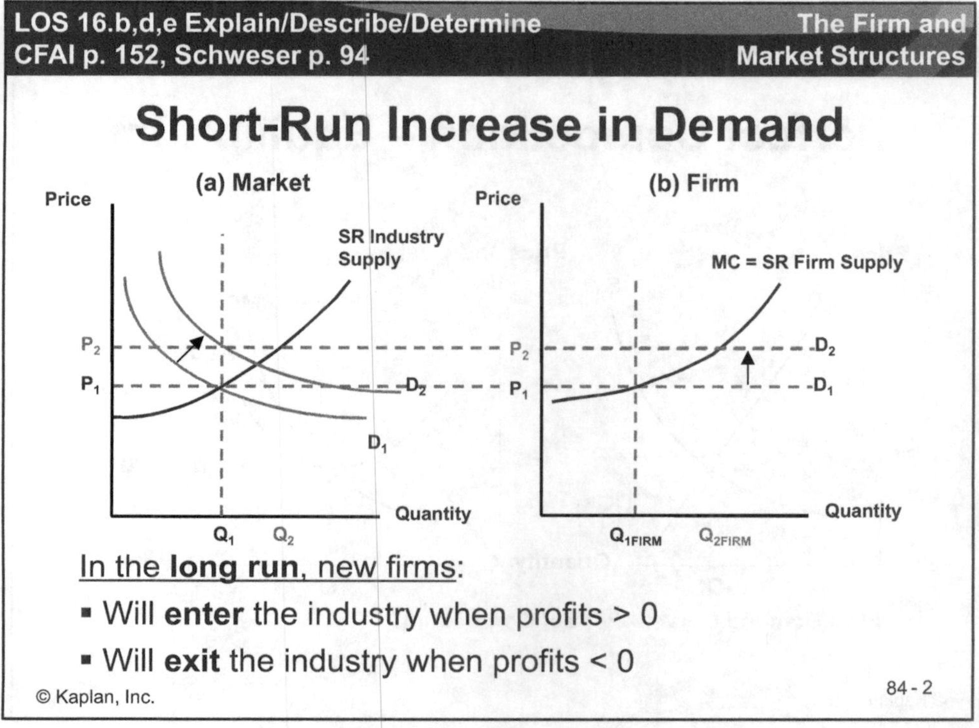
LOS 16.b,d,e Explain/Describe/Determine
CFAI p. 152, Schweser p. 94
The Firm and Market Structures
Short-Run Increase in Demand
(a) Market
Price
SR Industry Supply
P_2
P_1
D_2
D_1
Quantity
Q_1 Q_2
(b) Firm
Price
MC = SR Firm Supply
P_2
P_1
D_2
D_1
Quantity
Q_{1FIRM} Q_{2FIRM}
In the long run, new firms:
▪ Will enter the industry when profits > 0
▪ Will exit the industry when profits < 0
© Kaplan, Inc.
84 - 2

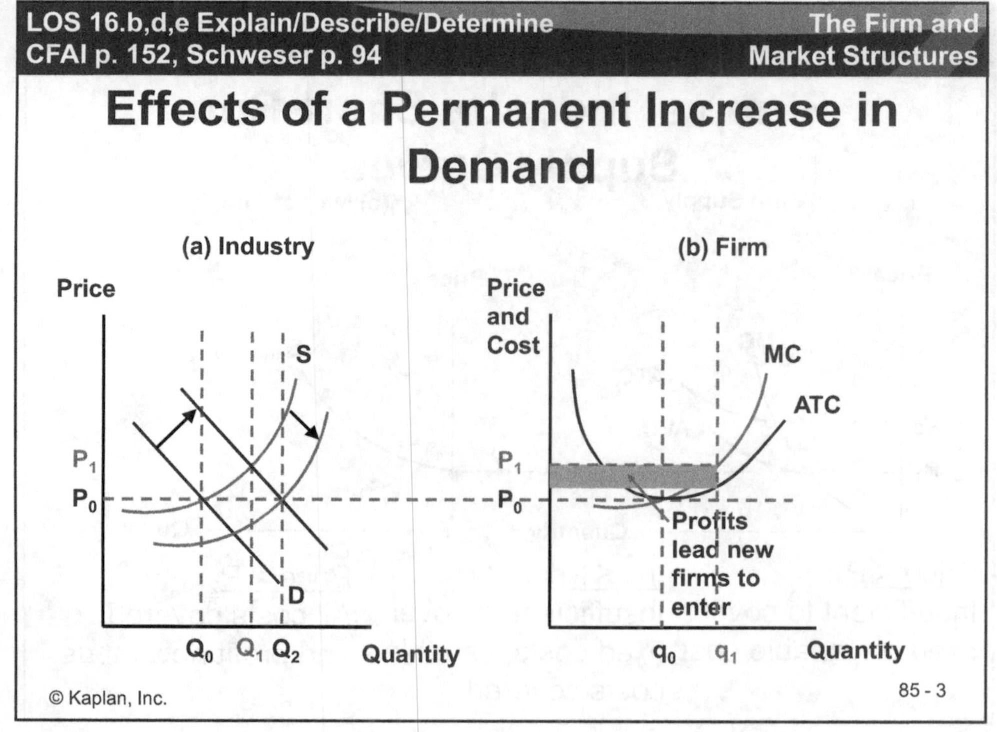
LOS 16.b,d,e Explain/Describe/Determine
CFAI p. 152, Schweser p. 94
The Firm and Market Structures
Effects of a Permanent Increase in Demand
(a) Industry
Price
S
P_1
P_0
D
Q_0 Q_1 Q_2
Quantity
(b) Firm
Price and Cost
MC
ATC
P_1
P_0
Profits lead new firms to enter
q_0 q_1
Quantity
© Kaplan, Inc.
85 - 3

The Firm and
Market Structures

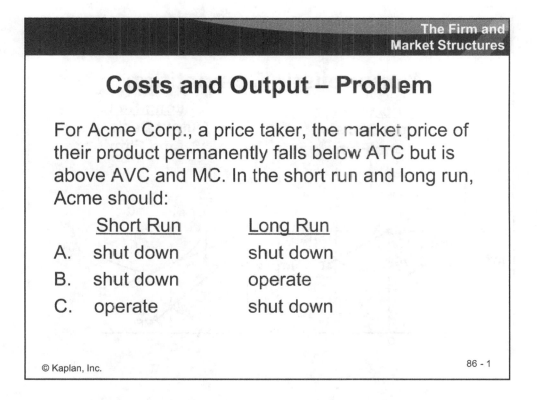

Costs and Output – Problem

For Acme Corp., a price taker, the market price of their product permanently falls below ATC but is above AVC and MC. In the short run and long run, Acme should:

	Short Run	Long Run
A.	shut down	shut down
B.	shut down	operate
C.	operate	shut down

86 - 1

LOS 16.b,d,e Explain/Describe/Determine
CFAI p. 152, Schweser p. 94

The Firm and
Market Structures

Monopolistic Competition

- A large number of firms in industry:
  - Each firm has a small market share
  - Concerned about average price
  - Collusion not possible
- Firms produce differentiated products (close but not perfect substitutes)
- Relatively elastic demand
- Firms compete on price, quality, and marketing
- Low barriers to entry

87

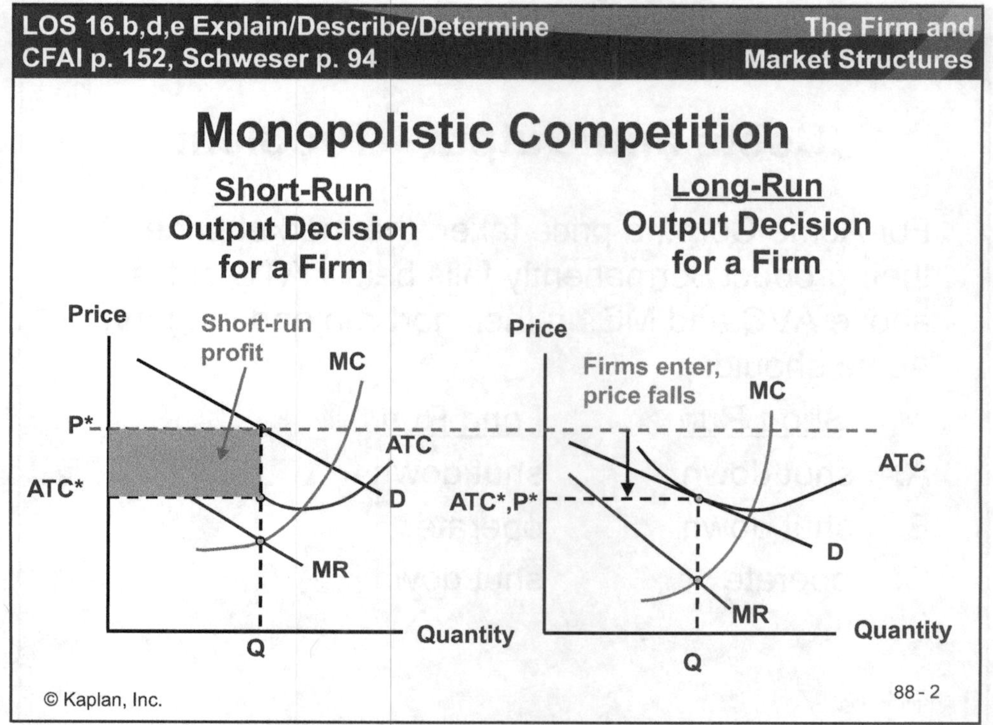

LOS 16.b,d,e Explain/Describe/Determine
CFAI p. 152, Schweser p. 94

The Firm and Market Structures

Monopolistic Competition

- Firms face downward-sloping, highly elastic (flat) demand curves
- Potential allocative efficiency is **not** clear
  - Social cost of not producing where P = MC
  - Long-run average cost is not minimized
  - Excessive advertising may take place
  - Fewer producers could be more efficient
  - However, increased product diversity has positive value to consumers

89

LOS 16.b,d,e Explain/Describe/Determine
CFAI p. 152, Schweser p. 94

The Firm and Market Structures

Efficiency of Monopolistic Competition

Brand names provide signals about quality

Product innovation and **differentiation** has value to consumers

Advertising provides valuable information to consumers

- High advertising expenditures increase fixed costs and total costs
- If advertising greatly increases sales, ATC can decline because AFC fall

90

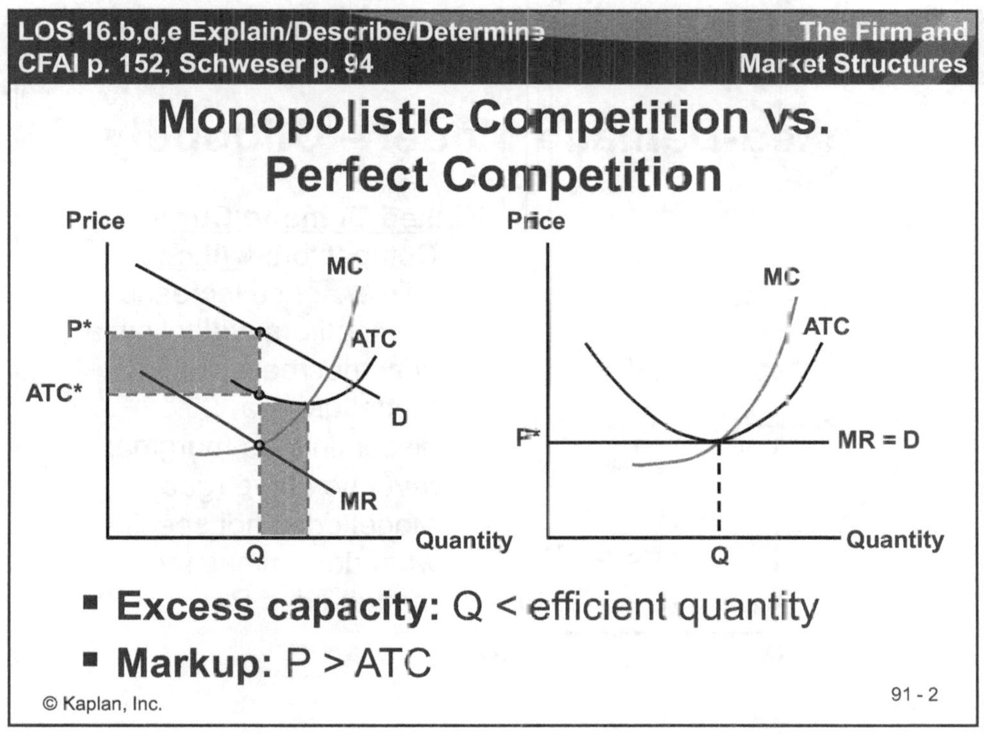

LOS 16.b,d,e Explain/Describe/Determine
CFAI p. 152, Schweser p. 94

The Firm and Market Structures

Oligopoly Characteristics

- **Small number** of sellers – downward sloping demand
- Firms' demand curve less elastic than monopolistic competition
- **Interdependence** among competitors and their demand curves
- Significant **barriers to entry** (e.g., scale of operations)
- Products may be similar *or* differentiated

92

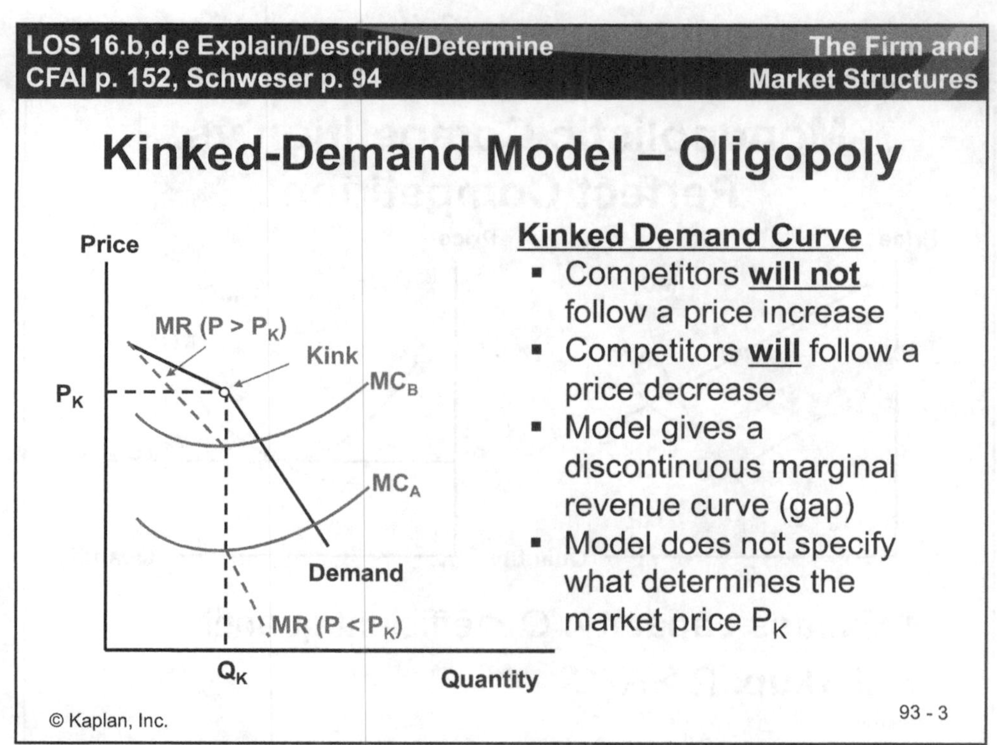

LOS 16.b,d,e Explain/Describe/Determine
CFAI p. 152, Schweser p. 94

The Firm and Market Structures

Nash Equilibrium

Choices of all firms are such that no other choice makes any firm better off (increases profits or decreases losses)

Strategic games model the best choice for a firm depending on the actions and reactions of competitors

94

LOS 16.b,d,e Explain/Describe/Determine
CFAI p. 152, Schweser p. 94

The Firm and Market Structures

Cournot Model

- Duopoly model (can be extended for more than two firms)

Assumptions:

- Homogeneous product
- Firms have market power (quantity will affect price)
- Both firms determine profit maximizing quantity assuming the other firm will not change its quantity (no retaliation)
- Firms choose quantities simultaneously
- Both firms have identical and constant marginal costs of production

95

LOS 16.b,d,e Explain/Describe/Determine
CFAI p. 152, Schweser p. 94

The Firm and Market Structures

Cournot Model

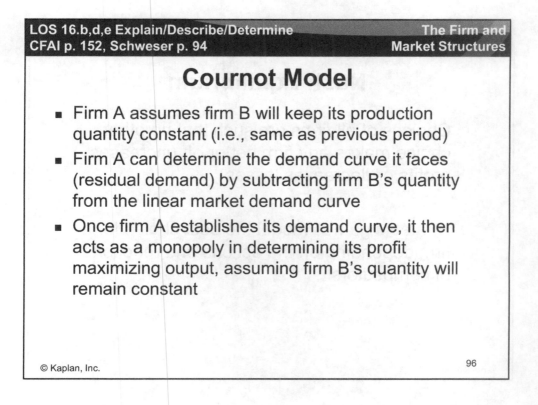

- Firm A assumes firm B will keep its production quantity constant (i.e., same as previous period)
- Firm A can determine the demand curve it faces (residual demand) by subtracting firm B's quantity from the linear market demand curve
- Once firm A establishes its demand curve, it then acts as a monopoly in determining its profit maximizing output, assuming firm B's quantity will remain constant

96

LOS 16.b,d,e Explain/Describe/Determine
CFAI p. 152, Schweser p. 94

The Firm and Market Structures

Cournot Model Conclusions

- Quantities produced by both firms change each period until they are equal (remember both firms are identical)
- Both firms will choose Nash equilibrium output levels
- Market price will be lower than monopoly
- Market price will be higher than perfect competition (marginal cost)
- As more firms are added, market price moves towards marginal cost

97

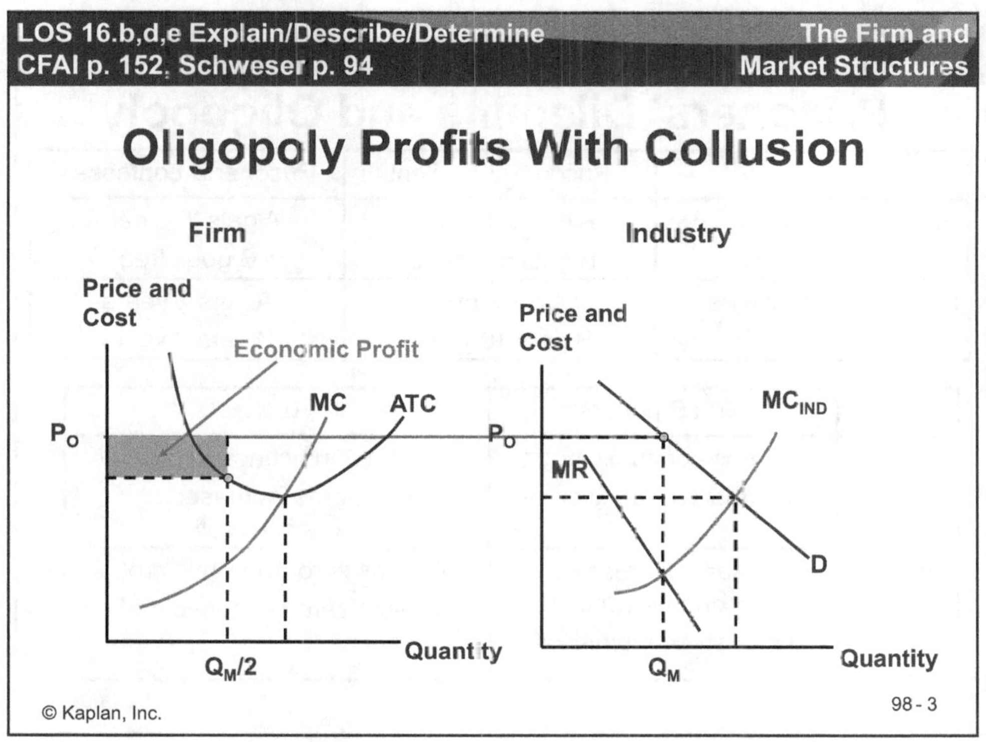

LOS 16.b,d,e Explain/Describe/Determine
CFAI p. 152, Schweser p. 94

The Firm and Market Structures

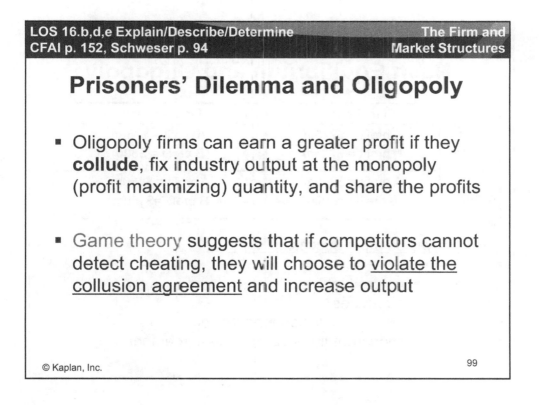

Prisoners' Dilemma and Oligopoly

- Oligopoly firms can earn a greater profit if they **collude**, fix industry output at the monopoly (profit maximizing) quantity, and share the profits
- Game theory suggests that if competitors cannot detect cheating, they will choose to violate the collusion agreement and increase output

99

LOS 16.b,d,e Explain/Describe/Determine
CFAI p. 152, Schweser p. 94

The Firm and Market Structures

Prisoners' Dilemma and Oligopoly

	Prisoner B is silent	Prisoner B confesses
Prisoner A is silent	A gets 6 months B gets 6 months	A gets 10 years B goes free
Prisoner A confesses	A goes free B gets 10 years	A gets 2 years B gets 2 years

	Firm B honors	Firm B cheats
Firm A honors	A earns economic profit B earns economic profit	A has an economic loss B earns increased economic profit
Firm A cheats	A earns increased economic profit B has an economic loss	A earns zero economic profit B earns zero economic profit

100

LOS 16.b,d,e Explain/Describe/Determine
CFAI p. 152, Schweser p. 94

The Firm and Market Structures

Nash Equilibrium and Oligopoly

	Firm B honors	Firm B cheats
Firm A honors	A profit = $225m B profit = $225m	A profit = $75m B profit = $300
Firm A cheats	A profit = $300m B profit = $75m	A profit = $150m B profit =$150m

Nash Equilibrium

Collusion will be more successful with:

- Fewer firms
- Homogeneous products
- Similar cost structures
- Certain and severe retaliation for cheating
- Little competition from firms outside the agreement

101 - 3

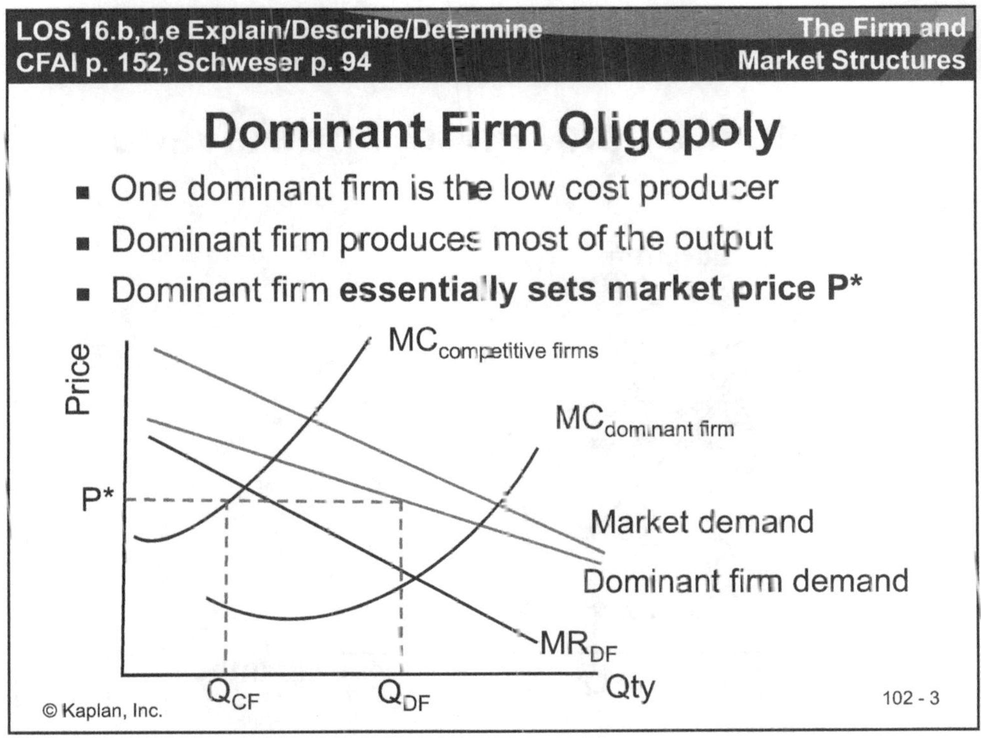

LOS 16.b,d,e Explain/Describe/Determine
CFAI p. 152, Schweser p. 94

The Firm and Market Structures

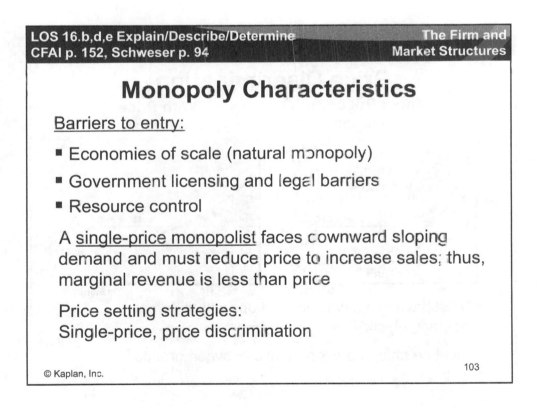

Monopoly Characteristics

Barriers to entry:

- Economies of scale (natural monopoly)
- Government licensing and legal barriers
- Resource control

A single-price monopolist faces downward sloping demand and must reduce price to increase sales; thus, marginal revenue is less than price

Price setting strategies:
Single-price, price discrimination

103

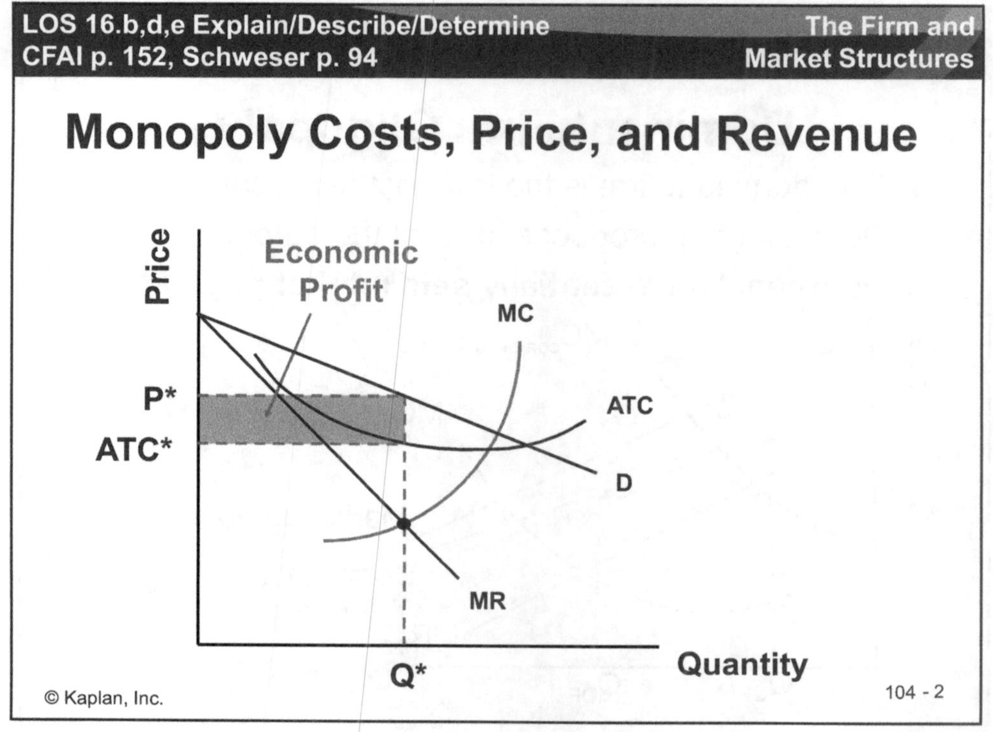
LOS 16.b,d,e Explain/Describe/Determine
CFAI p. 152, Schweser p. 94
The Firm and Market Structures
Monopoly Costs, Price, and Revenue
Price
Economic Profit
MC
P*
ATC*
ATC
D
MR
Q*
Quantity
© Kaplan, Inc.
104 - 2

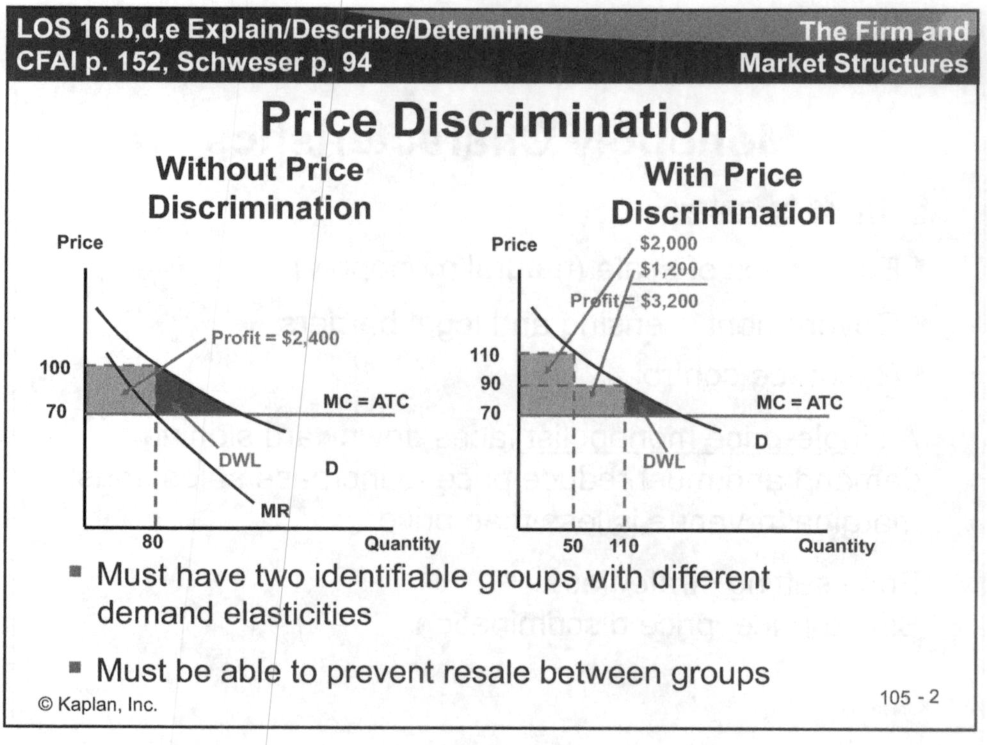
LOS 16.b,d,e Explain/Describe/Determine
CFAI p. 152, Schweser p. 94
The Firm and Market Structures
Price Discrimination
Without Price Discrimination
Price
Profit = $2,400
100
70
MC = ATC
DWL
D
MR
80
Quantity
With Price Discrimination
Price
$2,000
$1,200
Profit = $3,200
110
90
70
MC = ATC
D
DWL
50
110
Quantity
Must have two identifiable groups with different demand elasticities
Must be able to prevent resale between groups
© Kaplan, Inc.
105 - 2

LOS 16.b,d,e Explain/Describe/Determine
CFAI p. 152, Schweser p. 94

The Firm and Market Structures

Perfect Price Discrimination is Efficient

- Charge each consumer the maximum the consumer is willing to pay for each unit
- No deadweight loss
- Produce same quantity as perfect competition
- No consumer surplus; entire surplus goes to producer

 106

LOS 16.b,d,e Explain/Describe/Determine
CFAI p. 152, Schweser p. 94

The Firm and Market Structures

Monopoly vs. Perfect Competition

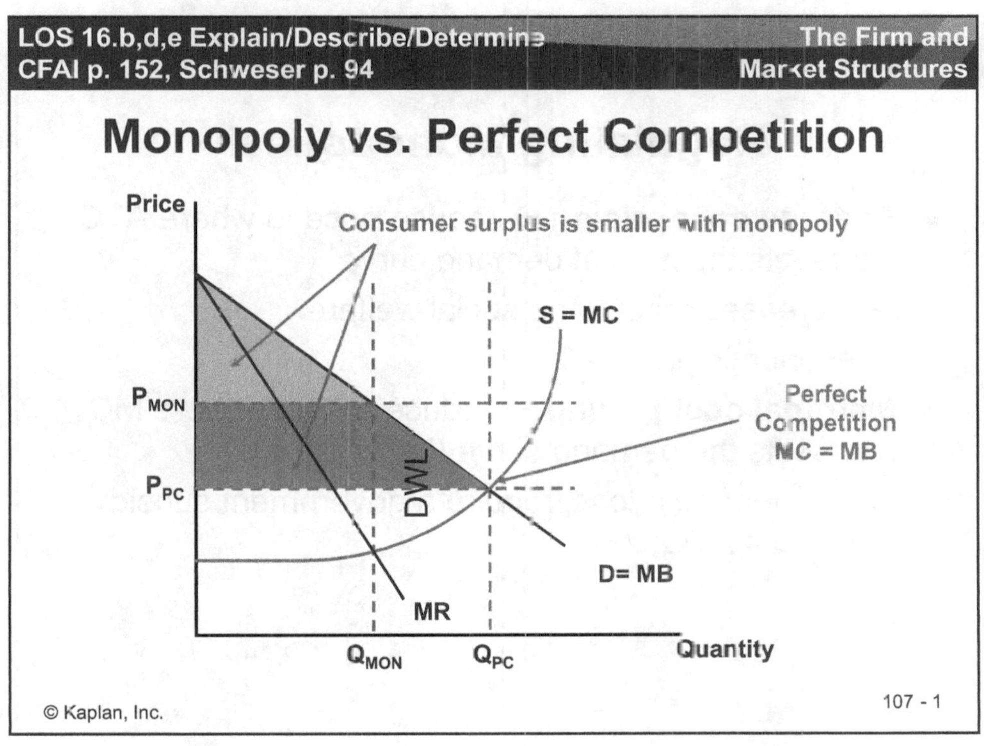

 107 - 1

LOS 16.b,d,e Explain/Describe/Determine
CFAI p. 152, Schweser p. 94

The Firm and Market Structures

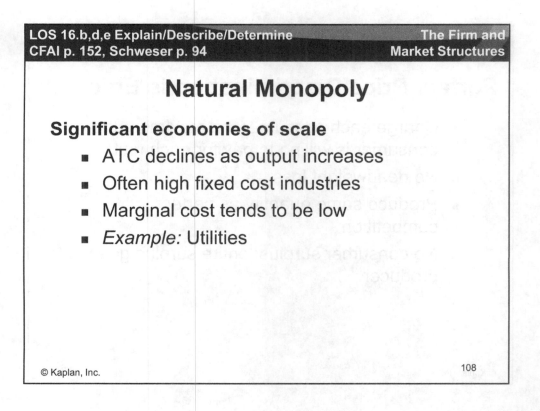

Natural Monopoly

Significant economies of scale

- ATC declines as output increases
- Often high fixed cost industries
- Marginal cost tends to be low
- *Example:* Utilities

108

LOS 16.b,d,e Explain/Describe/Determine
CFAI p. 152, Schweser p. 94

The Firm and Market Structures

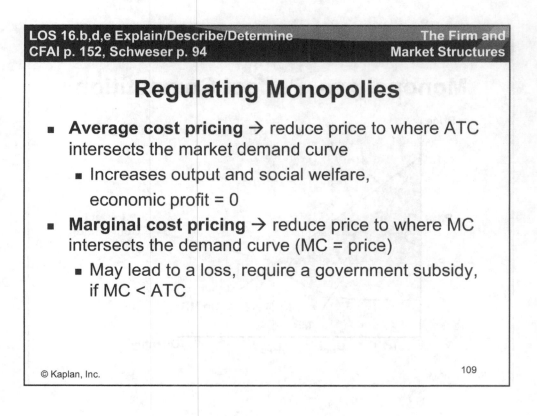

Regulating Monopolies

- **Average cost pricing** → reduce price to where ATC intersects the market demand curve
  - Increases output and social welfare, economic profit = 0
- **Marginal cost pricing** → reduce price to where MC intersects the demand curve (MC = price)
  - May lead to a loss, require a government subsidy, if MC < ATC

109

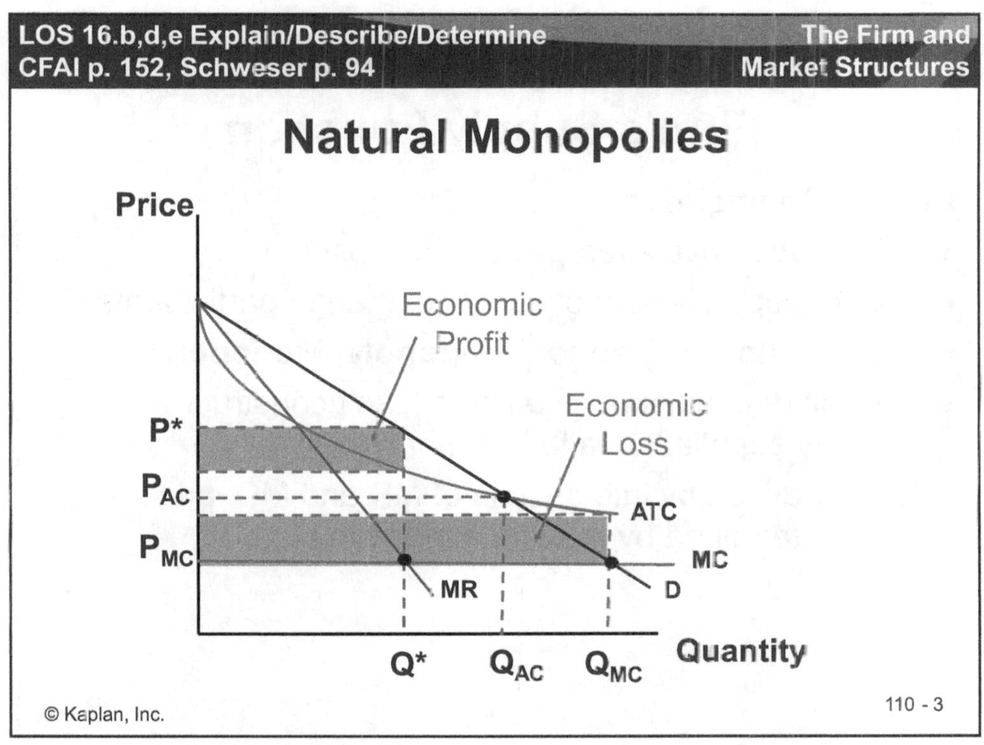

The Firm and Market Structures

Monopoly Market – Problem

What will be the effect on output and economic efficiency if a monopolist is able to employ price discrimination instead of charging a single price?

	Output	Economic Efficiency
A.	Increase	Decrease
B.	Increase	Increase
C.	Decrease	Decrease

111 - 1

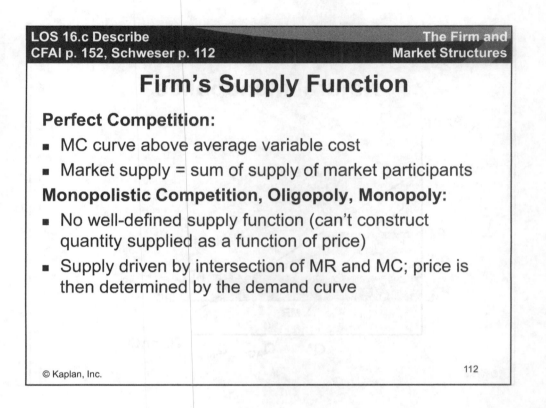

LOS 16.c Describe
CFAI p. 152, Schweser p. 112

The Firm and Market Structures

Firm's Supply Function

Perfect Competition:

- MC curve above average variable cost
- Market supply = sum of supply of market participants

Monopolistic Competition, Oligopoly, Monopoly:

- No well-defined supply function (can't construct quantity supplied as a function of price)
- Supply driven by intersection of MR and MC; price is then determined by the demand curve

LOS 16.f Describe
CFAI p. 152, Schweser p. 112

The Firm and Market Structures

Pricing Strategy

- **Perfect Competition:** Price = MR = MC at profit maximizing output quantity
- **Monopoly, Monopolistic Competition:** MR = MC at profit maximizing output quantity; price determined by downward-sloping demand curve; P > MR
- **Oligopoly:** Optimal pricing strategy depends on how other firms are expected to react
    - Kinked demand curve
    - Dominant firm
    - Game theory
    - Collusion

LOS 16.g,h Describe/Identify
CFAI p. 188, Schweser p. 113

The Firm and Market Structures

Identifying Market Structure

Price Elasticity of Demand

- Inelastic may indicate market power (monopoly)
- Analyst must estimate both demand and supply functions

Estimating Price Elasticity

- Regression analysis: Time series
- Requires a large number of observations
- Market structure may have changed significantly over the period (coefficient instability)

114

LOS 16.g,h Describe/Identify
CFAI p. 188, Schweser p. 113

The Firm and Market Structures

Identifying Market Structure

- Regression analysis: Cross sectional
- Requires substantial data gathering
- Using slightly different measures of the independent variables yields dramatically differing results

115

LOS 16.g,h Describe/Identify
CFAI p. 188, Schweser p. 113

The Firm and Market Structures

N-Firm Concentration Ratio

Sum of the percentage market shares of the *N* largest firms in an industry. **Advantage:** Simple

Market share = firms sales/total market sales

- *N*-firm ratio near 0% **perfect competition**
- Lower ratios indicate competitive market; higher ratios indicate oligopoly
- *N*-firm ratio = 100% for **monopoly**

Disadvantages

- Ignores barriers to entry
- Largely unaffected by mergers

116

LOS 16.g,h Describe/Identify
CFAI p. 188, Schweser p. 113

The Firm and Market Structures

Herfindahl-Hirschman Index (HHI)

HHI = sum of squared market shares of *N* largest firms in a market

- Very low in a market with perfect competition
- ≈ 0.1 to 0.18 → moderately competitive; 0.18+ → uncompetitive market
- 1 = 100% for a monopoly

Advantages:

- More sensitive to mergers than *N*-firm ratio
- Widely used by regulators

Disadvantages:

- Ignores barriers to entry
- Ignores demand elasticity

117

Types of Markets – Problem

A market where individual producers face downward sloping demand, barriers to entry are low, and producer pricing decisions are not directly affected by decisions of other producers is referred to as:

A. an oligopoly.

B. perfect competition.

C. monopolistic competition.

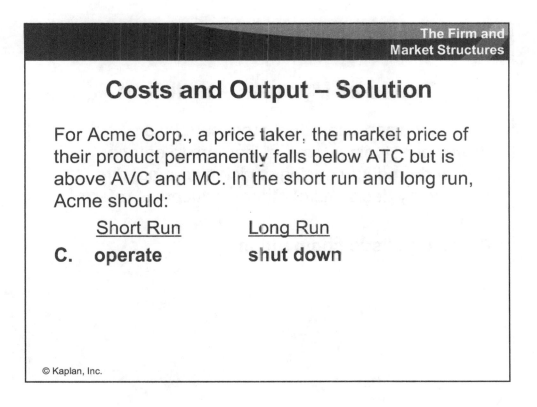

The Firm and Market Structures

Costs and Output – Solution

For Acme Corp., a price taker, the market price of their product permanently falls below ATC but is above AVC and MC. In the short run and long run, Acme should:

	Short Run	Long Run
C.	**operate**	**shut down**

© Kaplan, Inc.

The Firm and Market Structures

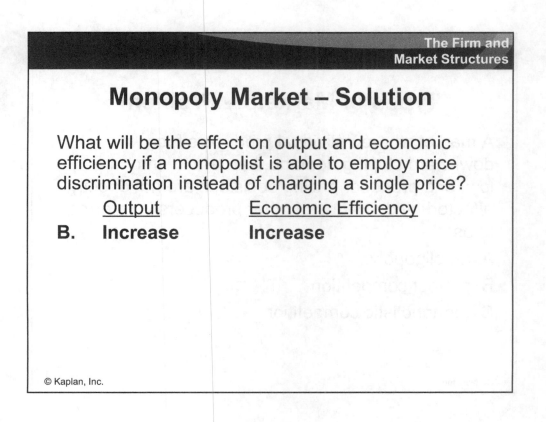

Monopoly Market – Solution

What will be the effect on output and economic efficiency if a monopolist is able to employ price discrimination instead of charging a single price?

	Output	Economic Efficiency
B.	**Increase**	**Increase**

The Firm and Market Structures

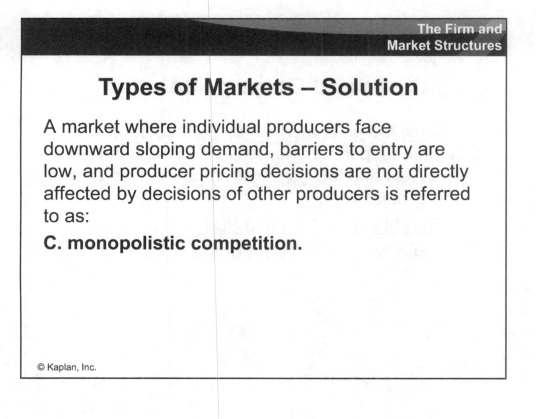

Types of Markets – Solution

A market where individual producers face downward sloping demand, barriers to entry are low, and producer pricing decisions are not directly affected by decisions of other producers is referred to as:

C. monopolistic competition.

Study Session 5

Economics: Macroeconomic Analysis

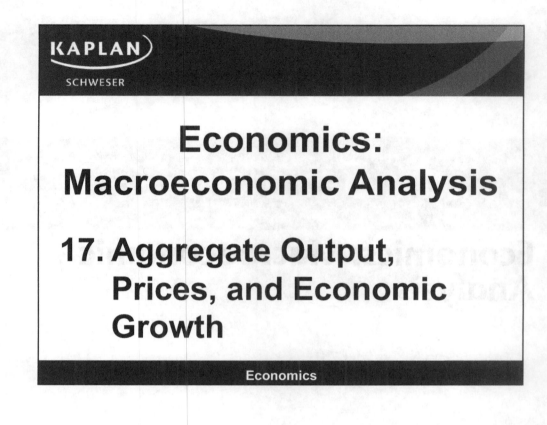

Economics: Macroeconomic Analysis

17. Aggregate Output, Prices, and Economic Growth

Economics

LOS 17.a Calculate/Explain
CFAI p. 204, Schweser p. 124

Aggregate Output, Prices, and Economic Growth

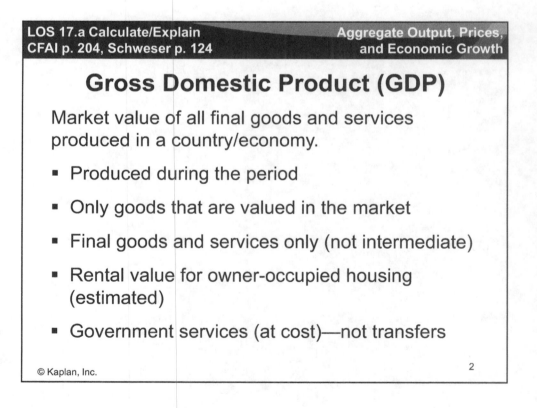

Gross Domestic Product (GDP)

Market value of all final goods and services produced in a country/economy.

- Produced during the period
- Only goods that are valued in the market
- Final goods and services only (not intermediate)
- Rental value for owner-occupied housing (estimated)
- Government services (at cost)—not transfers

2

LOS 17.a Calculate/Explain
CFAI p. 204, Schweser p. 124

Aggregate Output, Prices, and Economic Growth

Calculating GDP

Income Approach

Earnings of all households + businesses + government

Expenditures Approach

Sum the market values of all final goods and services produced in the economy

OR

Sum all the increases in value at each stage of the production process

LOS 17.a Calculate/Explain
CFAI p. 204, Schweser p. 124

Aggregate Output, Prices, and Economic Growth

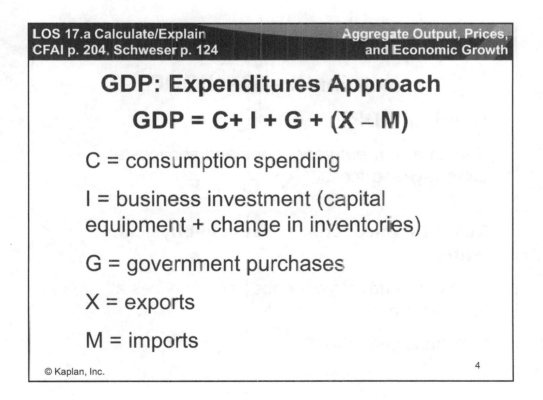

GDP: Expenditures Approach

$$GDP = C + I + G + (X - M)$$

C = consumption spending

I = business investment (capital equipment + change in inventories)

G = government purchases

X = exports

M = imports

LOS 17.b Compare
CFAI p. 205, Schweser p. 125

Aggregate Output, Prices, and Economic Growth

Final Values and Value Added

	£ Received at each stage	£ Value Added
Materials	1.21	1.21
Fabrication	2.18	0.97
Assembly	3.38	1.20
Sale to Consumer	5.14	1.76
Total		5.14

5 - 1

LOS 17.c Compare/Calculate/Interpret
CFAI p. 208, Schweser p. 125

Aggregate Output, Prices, and Economic Growth

Nominal vs. Real GDP

Nominal GDP

Sum of all current-year goods and services at current-year prices. $\sum Q_t \times P_t$

Real GDP (measures increase in physical output)

Sum of all current year goods and services at base-year prices.

With base year = t – 5: $\sum Q_t \times P_{t-5}$

6

LOS 17.c Compare/Calculate/Interpret
CFAI p. 208, Schweser p. 125

Aggregate Output, Prices, and Economic Growth

GDP Deflator

$$\text{GDP Deflator} = \frac{\text{Nominal GDP}}{\text{Real GDP}} \times 100$$

With base year t – 5, a GDP deflator of 112.3 means prices have gone up by 12.3% over 5 years—a measure of inflation

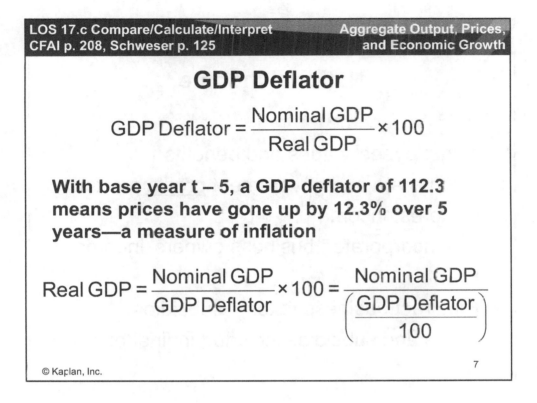

$$\text{Real GDP} = \frac{\text{Nominal GDP}}{\text{GDP Deflator}} \times 100 = \frac{\text{Nominal GDP}}{\left(\frac{\text{GDP Deflator}}{100}\right)}$$

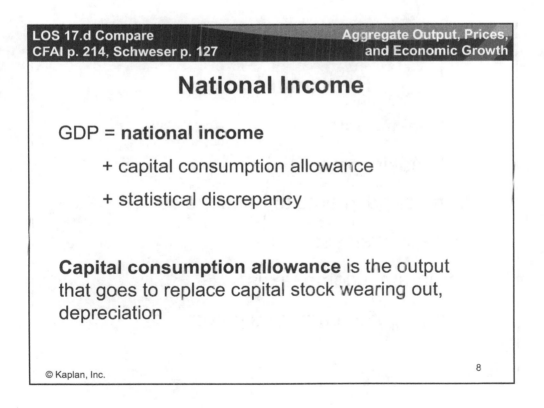

7

LOS 17.d Compare
CFAI p. 214, Schweser p. 127

Aggregate Output, Prices, and Economic Growth

National Income

GDP = **national income**

+ capital consumption allowance

+ statistical discrepancy

Capital consumption allowance is the output that goes to replace capital stock wearing out, depreciation

8

LOS 17.d Compare
CFAI p. 214, Schweser p. 127

Aggregate Output, Prices, and Economic Growth

National Income

National income
= employees' wages and benefits
+ corporate and government profits pre-tax
+ interest income
+ unincorporated business owners' income
+ rent
+ indirect business taxes – subsidies
(taxes and subsidies included in final prices)

 9

LOS 17.d Compare
CFAI p. 214, Schweser p. 127

Aggregate Output, Prices, and Economic Growth

Personal Income

Personal income
= national income
+ transfer payments to households
– indirect business taxes
– corporate income taxes
– undistributed corporate profits

 10

LOS 17.d Compare
CFAI p. 214, Schweser p. 127

Aggregate Output, Prices, and Economic Growth

Personal Disposable Income

Personal disposable income

= personal income – personal taxes

= **after-tax income**

Each period, individuals decide whether to consume or save disposable income

11

LOS 17.e Explain
CFAI p. 220, Schweser p. 128

Aggregate Output, Prices, and Economic Growth

Deriving the Fundamental Relationship

GDP = C + I + G + (X – M) Total Expenditures

GDP = C + S + T Total Income

$$\not{C} + S + T = \not{C} + I + G + (X - M)$$

$$S + T = I + G + (X - M)$$

$$S = I + (G - T) + (X - M)$$

12 - 3

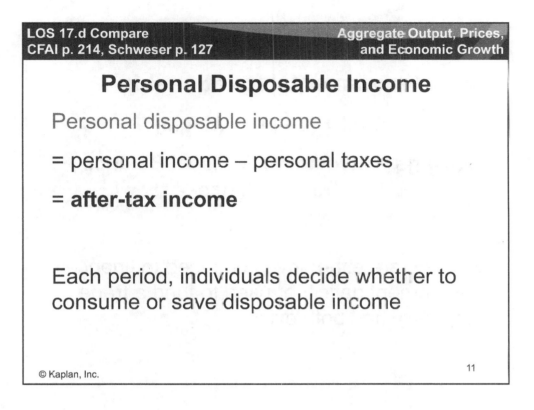

LOS 17.e Explain
CFAI p. 220, Schweser p. 128

Aggregate Output, Prices, and Economic Growth

Fundamental Relationship

S = I + (G – T) + (X – M)

Savings = Investment + Fiscal Balance + Trade Balance

Savings are either invested, used to finance government deficit, or used to fund a trade surplus, when both exist

13

LOS 17.f Explain
CFAI p. 220, Schweser p. 129

Aggregate Output, Prices, and Economic Growth

The Income = Savings (IS) Curve

When income = planned expenditure:
(S – I) = (G – T) + (X – M)

- Increase in income increases savings more than investment → **(S – I)** is an <u>increasing function</u> of income
- Increase in income decreases fiscal deficit, increases imports → **(G – T) + (X – M)** is a <u>decreasing function</u> of income

14

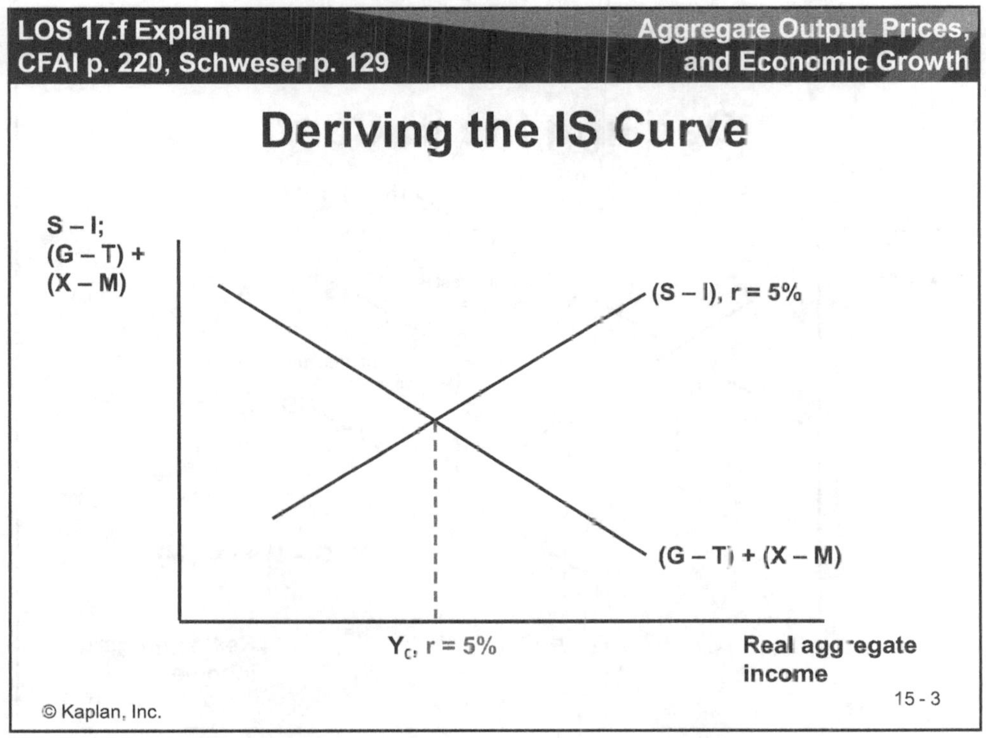

LOS 17.f Explain
CFAI p. 220, Schweser p. 129

Aggregate Output, Prices, and Economic Growth

The Income = Savings (IS) Curve

When income = planned expenditure:
(S – I) = (G – T) + (X – M)

Increase in **real interest rate**, holding (G – T) + (X – M) and (S – I) constant:

- Investment decreases
- Savings must also decrease
- Decrease in savings must result from <u>decrease in income</u>

16

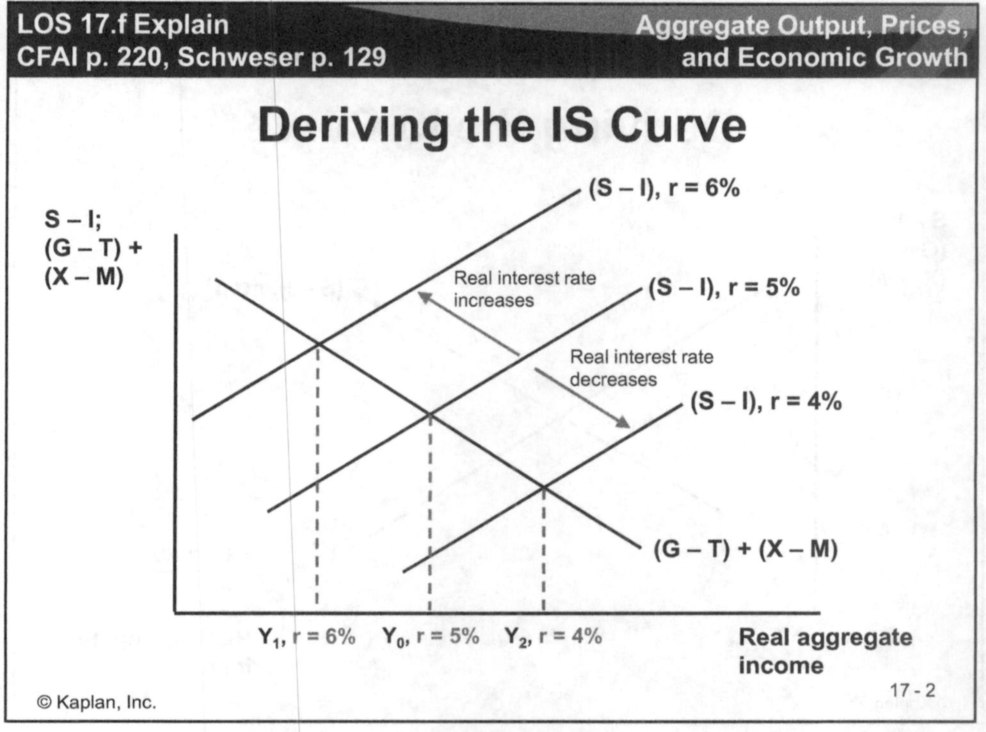
LOS 17.f Explain
CFAI p. 220, Schweser p. 129
Aggregate Output, Prices, and Economic Growth
Deriving the IS Curve
S – I;
(G – T) +
(X – M)
(S – I), r = 6%
(S – I), r = 5%
(S – I), r = 4%
Real interest rate increases
Real interest rate decreases
(G – T) + (X – M)
Y1, r = 6%
Y0, r = 5%
Y2, r = 4%
Real aggregate income
© Kaplan, Inc.
17 - 2

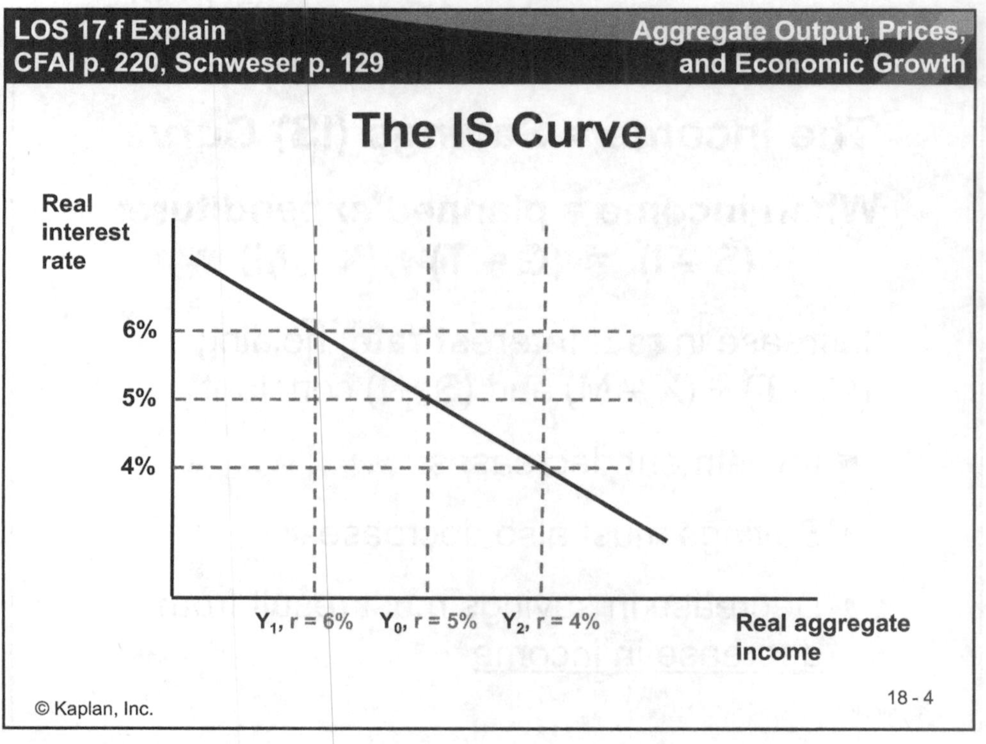
LOS 17.f Explain
CFAI p. 220, Schweser p. 129
Aggregate Output, Prices, and Economic Growth
The IS Curve
Real interest rate
6%
5%
4%
Y1, r = 6%
Y0, r = 5%
Y2, r = 4%
Real aggregate income
© Kaplan, Inc.
18 - 4

LOS 17.f Explain
CFAI p. 220, Schweser p. 129

Aggregate Output, Prices, and Economic Growth

Equilibrium in the Money Market

Real money supply (M/P)
Money demand = *f* (real rates, income)

$$M/P = MD\,(r, Y)$$

Real rates up → quantity demanded ↓
Income up → quantity demanded ↑

Higher real interest rates → higher income

19

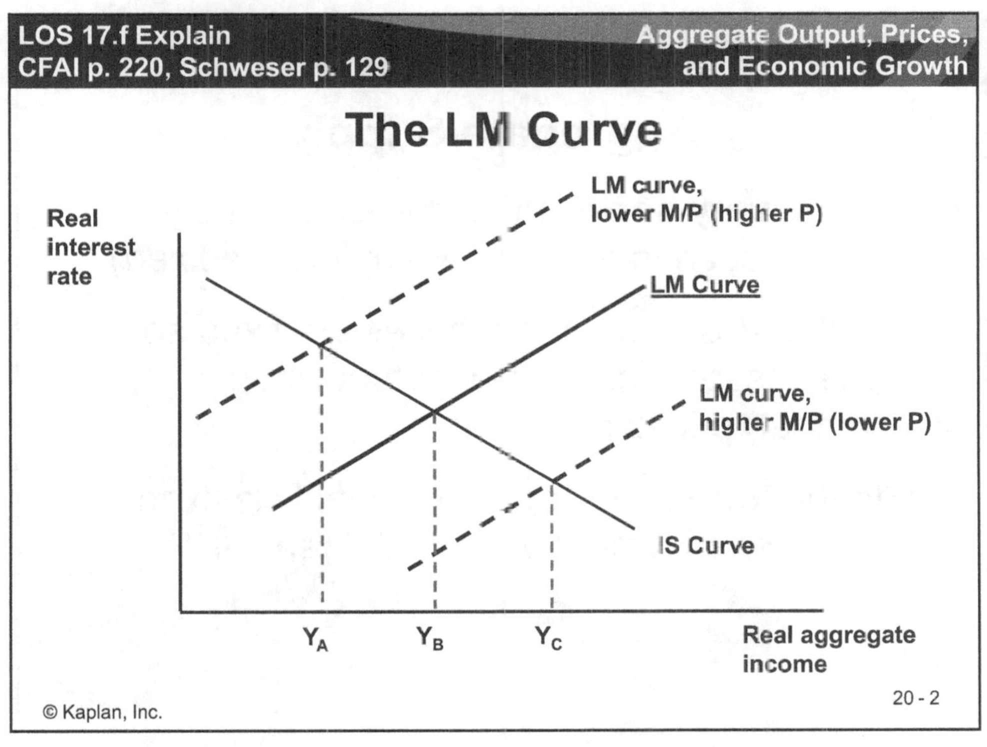

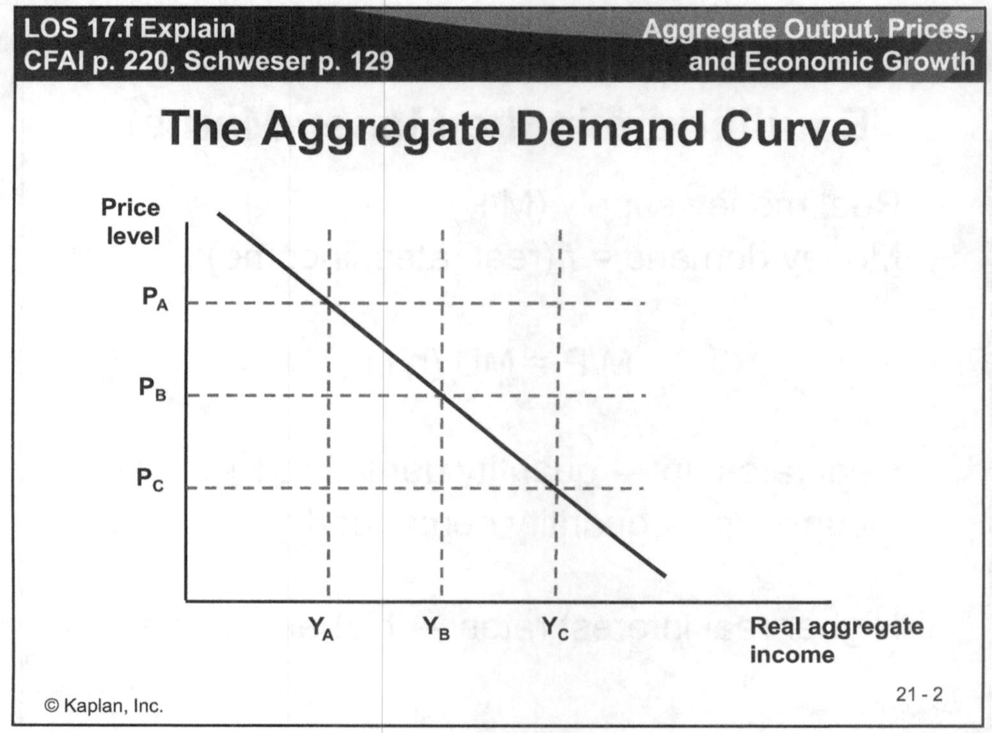

LOS 17.g Explain
CFAI p. 231, Schweser p. 134

Aggregate Output, Prices, and Economic Growth

Aggregate Supply

- In the **very short run**: Aggregate supply does not change (input quantities are fixed)
- In the **short run**: Input prices are fixed so businesses expand real output when (output) prices increase
- In the **long run**: Aggregate supply is fixed at full-employment or potential real GDP

22

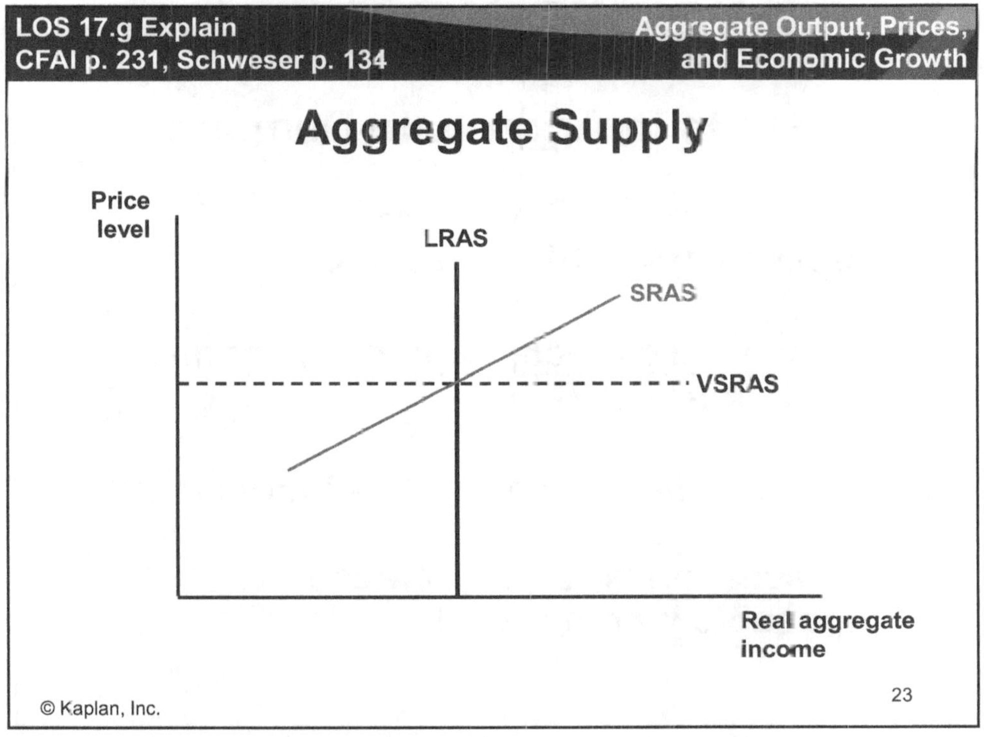

LOS 17.h Explain
CFAI p. 233, Schweser p. 135

Aggregate Output, Prices, and Economic Growth

Aggregate Demand

- The **aggregate demand curve** (AD) shows the relation between the price level and the real quantity of final goods and services (real GDP) demanded
- Components of aggregate demand
  - Consumption (C)
  - Investment (I)
  - Government spending (G)
  - Net exports (X), exports minus imports

Aggregate demand = C + I + G + $_{net}$X

24

LOS 17.h Explain
CFAI p. 233, Schweser p. 135

Aggregate Output, Prices, and Economic Growth

Shifts in Aggregate Demand

C + I + G + netX

- Increases in wealth increase C
- Increases in expectations for economic growth increase C, I
- Capacity utilization > ~85%→ increase I
- Increases in tax rates decrease disposable income and C

25

LOS 17.h Explain
CFAI p. 233, Schweser p. 135

Aggregate Output, Prices, and Economic Growth

Shifts in Aggregate Demand

C + I + G + netX

- Increases in government spending, G
- Increases in the money supply reduce real rates and increase I, C
- Depreciation of currency increases netX—imports prices up, export prices down
- Growth of foreign GDP increases netX

26

LOS 17.h Explain
CFAI p. 233, Schweser p. 135

Aggregate Output, Prices, and Economic Growth

Shifts in SR Aggregate Supply

Factors that Increase SRAS

- Decreases in input prices
- Improved expectations about future
- Decreases in business taxes
- Increases in business subsidies
- Currency appreciation that reduces the cost of imported inputs

27

LOS 17.h Explain
CFAI p. 233, Schweser p. 135

Aggregate Output, Prices, and Economic Growth

Shifts in LR Aggregate Supply

Factors that Increase LRAS

- Increase in labor supply
- Increased availability of natural resources
- Increased stock of physical capital
- Increased human capital (labor quality)
- Advances in technology/labor productivity

28

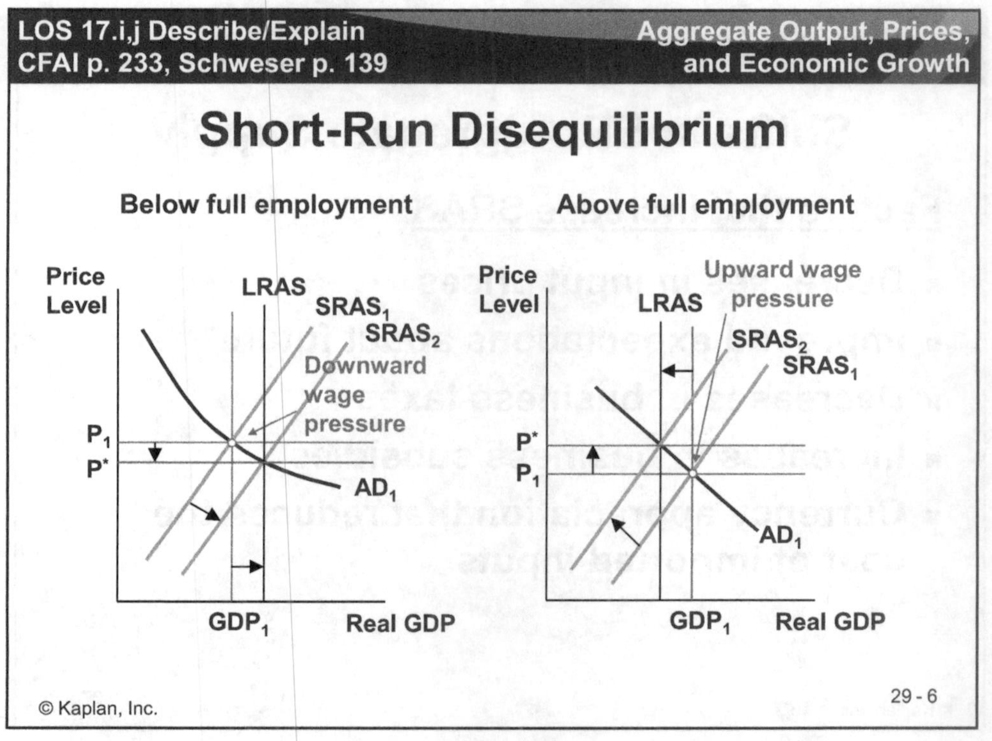
LOS 17.i,j Describe/Explain
CFAI p. 233, Schweser p. 139
Aggregate Output, Prices, and Economic Growth
Short-Run Disequilibrium
Below full employment
Above full employment
Price Level
LRAS
SRAS1
SRAS2
Downward wage pressure
P1
P*
AD1
GDP1
Real GDP
Upward wage pressure
© Kaplan, Inc.
29 - 6

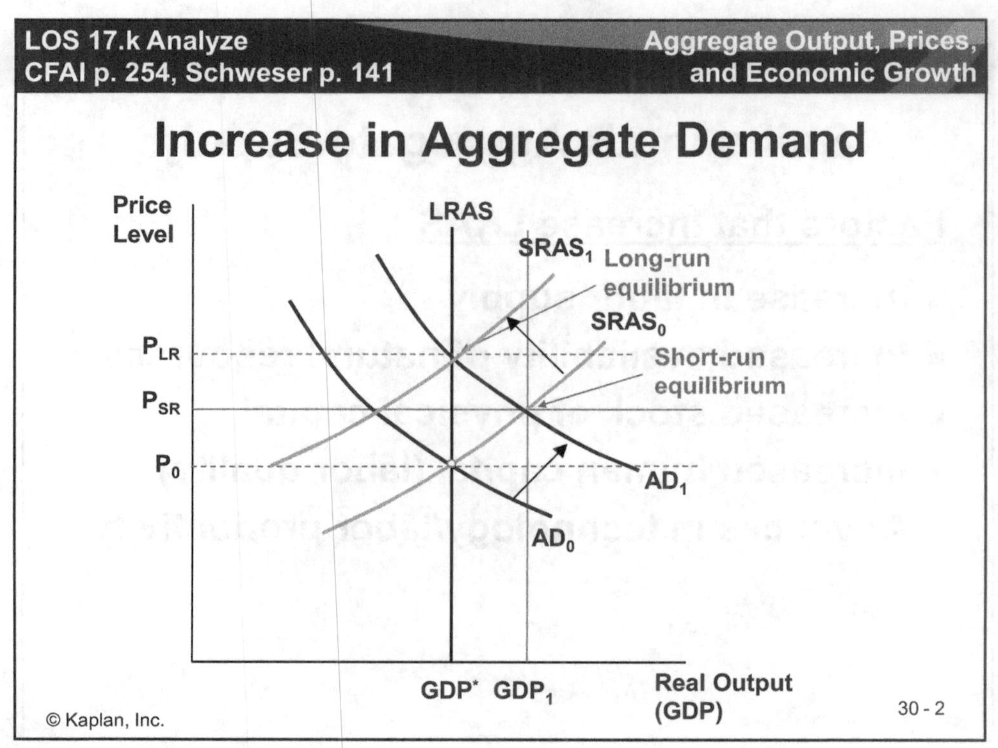
LOS 17.k Analyze
CFAI p. 254, Schweser p. 141
Aggregate Output, Prices, and Economic Growth
Increase in Aggregate Demand
Price Level
LRAS
SRAS1
Long-run equilibrium
SRAS0
Short-run equilibrium
PLR
PSR
P0
AD1
AD0
GDP* GDP1
Real Output (GDP)
© Kaplan, Inc.
30 - 2

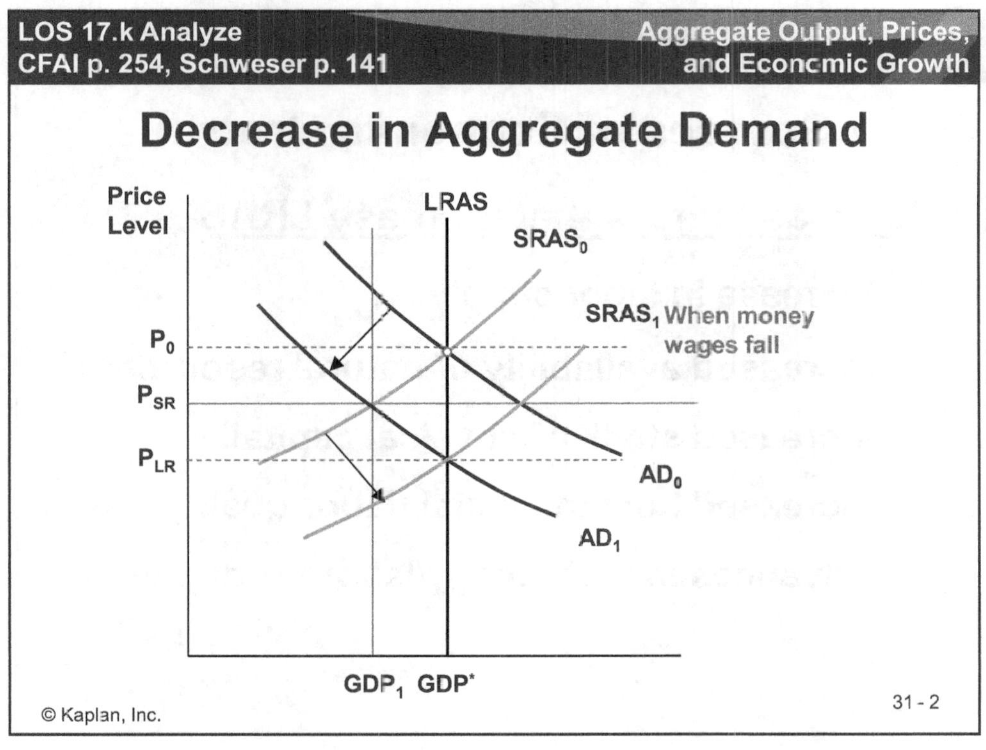

LOS 17.k Analyze
CFAI p. 254, Schweser p. 141
Aggregate Output, Prices, and Economic Growth
Decrease in Aggregate Demand
Price Level
LRAS
$SRAS_0$
$SRAS_1$ When money wages fall
P_0
P_{SR}
P_{LR}
AD_0
AD_1
GDP_1 GDP^*
© Kaplan, Inc.
31 - 2

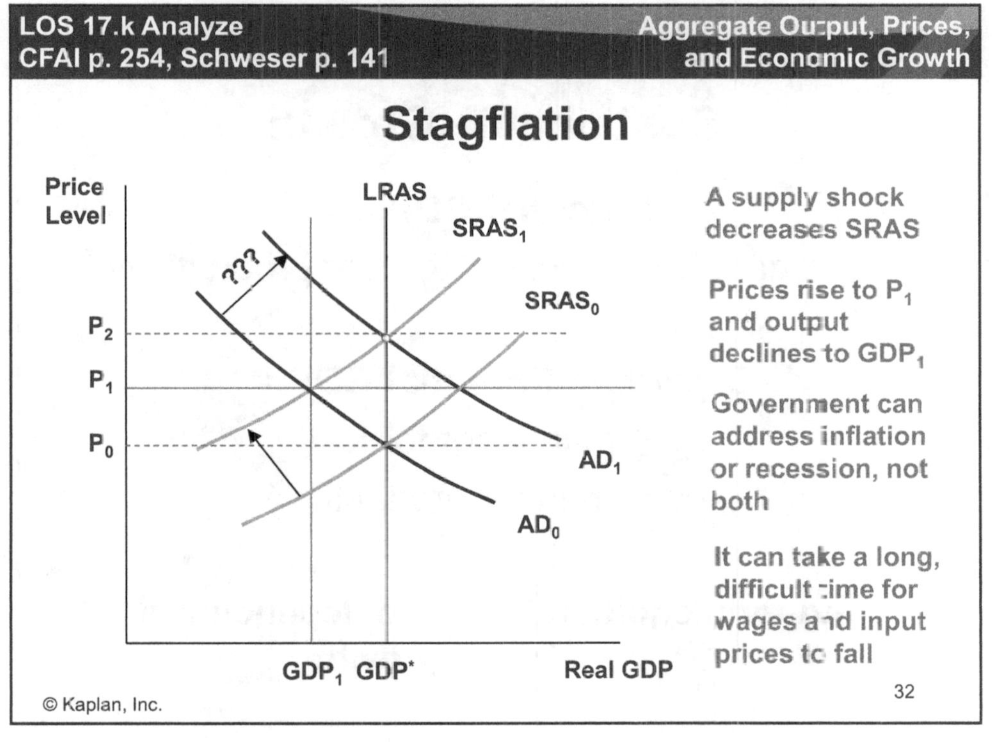

LOS 17.k Analyze
CFAI p. 254, Schweser p. 141
Aggregate Output, Prices, and Economic Growth
Stagflation
Price Level
LRAS
$SRAS_1$
$SRAS_0$
???
P_2
P_1
P_0
AD_1
AD_0
GDP_1 GDP^*
Real GDP
A supply shock decreases SRAS
Prices rise to P_1 and output declines to GDP_1
Government can address inflation or recession, not both
It can take a long, difficult time for wages and input prices to fall
© Kaplan, Inc.
32

LOS 17.l Describe
CFAI p. 256, Schweser p. 144

Aggregate Output, Prices, and Economic Growth

Sources of Economic Growth

Same as factors that increase LRAS

1. Increase in labor supply
2. Increased availability of natural resources
3. Increased stock of physical capital
4. Increased human capital (labor quality)
5. Advances in technology/labor productivity

33

LOS 17.l Describe
CFAI p. 256, Schweser p. 144

Aggregate Output, Prices, and Economic Growth

Sustainable Growth

Potential GDP =
Aggregate hours worked × labor productivity

Growth in Potential GDP =
growth in labor force +
growth in labor productivity

Long-term equity returns are dependent on sustainable growth

34

LOS 17.m Describe
CFAI p. 256, Schweser p. 145

Aggregate Output, Prices, and Economic Growth

Production Function Approach

$$Y = A \times f(L, K)$$

where:

Y = aggregate economic output

L = size of labor force

K = amount of capital available

A = total factor productivity, the increase in output not from increases in labor and capital, closely related to advances in technology

35

LOS 17.m Describe
CFAI p. 256, Schweser p. 145

Aggregate Output, Prices, and Economic Growth

Production Function Approach

One measure of economic progress is **output per worker**

$$Y/L = A \times f(K/L)$$

Because of the diminishing marginal productivity of capital, progress in developed countries relies on technology

36

LOS 17.n Distinguish
CFAI p. 261, Schweser p. 146

Aggregate Output, Prices, and Economic Growth

Components of Economic Growth

Growth in potential GDP =

growth in total factor productivity +

W_C (growth in capital) +

W_L (growth in labor)

Where the weights are each factor's share of national income

37

LOS 17.n Distinguish
CFAI p. 261, Schweser p. 146

Aggregate Output, Prices, and Economic Growth

Per Capita Growth

Growth in per-capita potential GDP =

growth in technology +

W_C(growth in the capital-to-labor ratio)

In developed countries, K/L is high and growth in per capital GDP must come from technological advancement.

38

LOS 17.n Distinguish
CFAI p. 261, Schweser p. 146

Aggregate Output, Prices, and Economic Growth

Example: Total Productivity

Growth of potential GDP has been 7% and labor's share of national income is 70%. The increase in the labor force has been 6% and the increase in the capital stock has been 5%. What is the increase in total factor productivity over the period?

$7\% = \Delta TFP + 0.7(6\%) + 0.3(5\%)$

$\Delta TFP = 1.3\%$

39 - 2

Aggregate Output, Prices, and Economic Growth

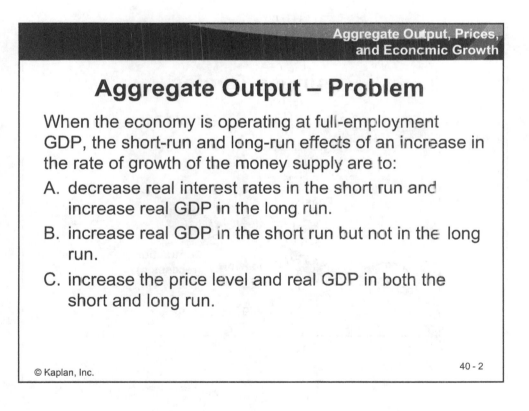

Aggregate Output – Problem

When the economy is operating at full-employment GDP, the short-run and long-run effects of an increase in the rate of growth of the money supply are to:

A. decrease real interest rates in the short run and increase real GDP in the long run.

B. increase real GDP in the short run but not in the long run.

C. increase the price level and real GDP in both the short and long run.

40 - 2

Economics: Macroeconomic Analysis

18. Understanding Business Cycles

Economics

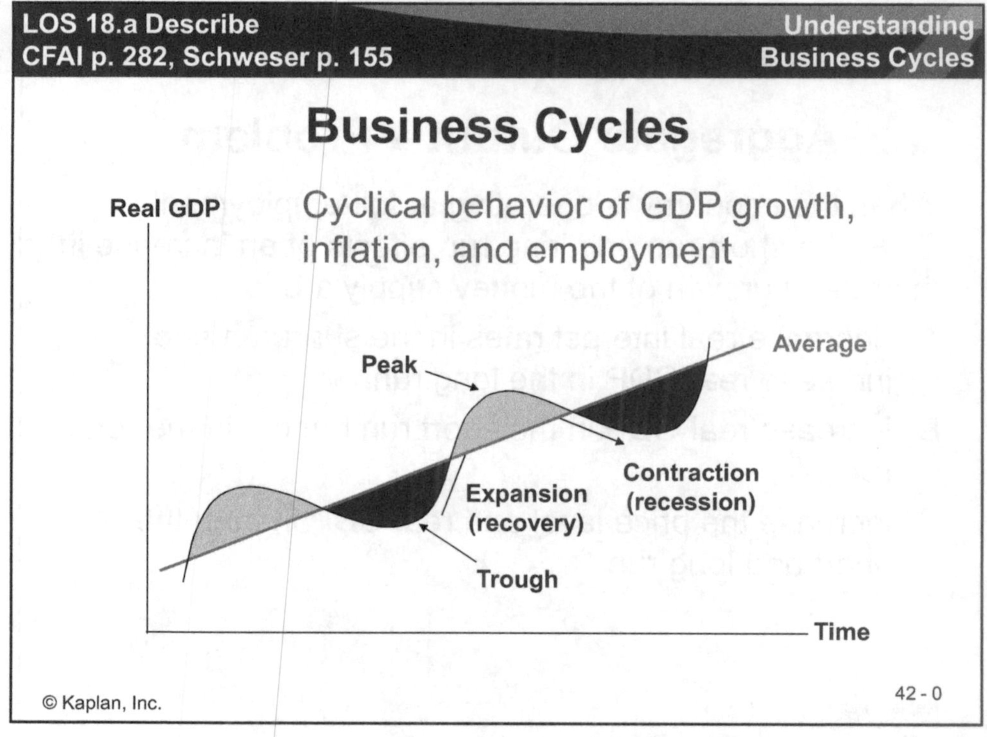

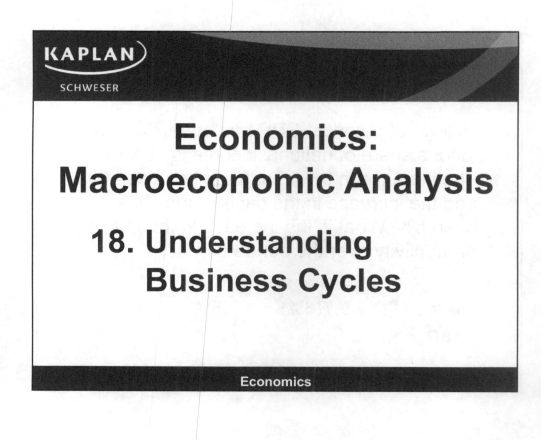

LOS 18.b Explain
CFAI p. 286, Schweser p. 156

Understanding Business Cycles

Inventory/Sales Ratios

- Early in a **contraction**, sales slow unexpectedly, causing unplanned increase in inventories; inventory/sales ratios increase to above-normal levels
- Early in an **expansion**, sales increase unexpectedly, causing unplanned decrease in inventories; inventory/sales ratios decrease to below-normal levels

43

LOS 18.b Explain
CFAI p. 286, Schweser p. 156

Understanding Business Cycles

Labor and Capital Utilization

- Firms are slow to hire/lay off employees or increase/decrease physical capital because frequent adjustments are costly
- At the beginning of a contraction, sales fall and both **labor and capital are used less intensively**
- At the beginning of an expansion, sales increase and both **labor and capital are used more intensively**
- When sales trends persist, firms adjust labor and physical capital over time

44

LOS 18.b Explain
CFAI p. 286, Schweser p. 156

Understanding Business Cycles

Housing Sector

- Highly cyclical sector of the economy
- Activity determined by:
  - **Mortgage rates**: Rates ↑, housing ↓
  - **Income / housing costs**: Income ↑, housing ↑
  - **Speculation**: Home purchases based on expected price increases (e.g., 2007-08)
  - **Demographics**: Household formations, geographic shifts in population density

45

LOS 18.b Explain
CFAI p. 286, Schweser p. 156

Understanding Business Cycles

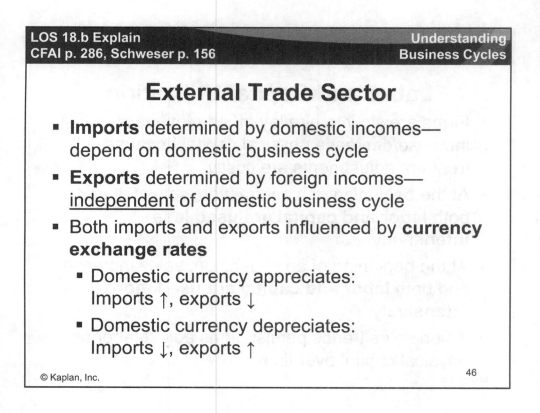

External Trade Sector

- **Imports** determined by domestic incomes—depend on domestic business cycle
- **Exports** determined by foreign incomes—independent of domestic business cycle
- Both imports and exports influenced by **currency exchange rates**
  - Domestic currency appreciates: Imports ↑, exports ↓
  - Domestic currency depreciates: Imports ↓, exports ↑

46

LOS 18.c Describe
CFAI p. 296, Schweser p. 159

Understanding Business Cycles

Business Cycle Theories

School of Thought	*Cause of Business Cycles*	*Recommended Policy*
Neoclassical	Technology changes	Allow wages, prices to adjust
Keynesian	AD shifts with changes in business expectations; contractions persist due to downward sticky wages	Use fiscal and/or monetary policy to restore full employment
New Keynesian	Same as Keynesian; but other input prices also downward sticky	Same as Keynesian

47

LOS 18.c Describe
CFAI p. 296, Schweser p. 159

Understanding Business Cycles

Business Cycle Theories

School of Thought	*Cause of Business Cycles*	*Recommended Policy*
Monetarist	Inappropriate changes in money supply growth rate	Steady, predictable growth rate of money supply
Austrian	Government intervention in economy	Don't force interest rates to artificially low levels
New Classical (Real Business Cycle theory)	Rational responses to external shocks, technology changes	Don't intervene to counteract business cycles

48

LOS 18.d Describe
CFAI p. 305, Schweser p. 160

Understanding
Business Cycles

Types of Unemployment

- **Frictional** unemployment results from time it takes employers and employees to find each other
- **Structural** unemployment results from long-term changes in the economy that require workers to gain new skills to fill new jobs
- **Cyclical** unemployment results from changes in economic growth; = 0 at full employment

49

LOS 18.d Describe
CFAI p. 305, Schweser p. 160

Understanding
Business Cycles

Unemployment Rate

- To be counted as **unemployed**, a person must be available for work and actively looking for work
- **Labor force** consists of those who are employed and those who are unemployed
- **Unemployment rate** = $\frac{\text{Number of unemployed}}{\text{Labor force}}$

50

LOS 18.d Describe
CFAI p. 305, Schweser p. 160

Understanding Business Cycles

Unemployment Measures

- **Participation ratio** =

$$\frac{\text{Labor force}}{\text{Working-age population } (>16)}$$

- **Discouraged workers** are those who are available for work but not employed or seeking employment; considered not in labor force and not counted as unemployed

LOS 18.e Explain
CFAI p. 308, Schweser p. 161

Understanding Business Cycles

Inflation, Disinflation, and Deflation

- **Inflation**: Persistent increase in price level over time
- **Inflation rate**: Percent increase in price level over a period (usually one year)
- **Disinflation**: Decrease in positive inflation rate over time
- **Deflation**: Persistent decrease in price level over time; negative inflation rate
- **Hyperinflation**: Out-of-control high inflation

LOS 18.f Explain
CFAI p. 310, Schweser p. 162

Understanding Business Cycles

Inflation Indexes

- A **price index** is a weighted average of goods and services prices compared to a base period used as a proxy for the overall or average price level
- The **consumer price index** (CPI) measures the cost of a fixed "basket" of goods and services compared to the cost in a base period

53

LOS 18.f Explain
CFAI p. 310, Schweser p. 162

Understanding Business Cycles

Calculating the CPI

- Find the cost of the CPI basket in the base period
- Find the cost of the CPI basket in the current period
- Calculate the price index:

$$\text{CPI} = \frac{\text{cost of basket at current prices}}{\text{cost of basket at base year prices}} \times 100$$

- Example:

$$\text{CPI} = \frac{\$2,900}{\$2,500} \times 100 = 116$$

Prices up 16% over the period

54

LOS 18.f,g Explain/Compare
CFAI p. 310, Schweser p. 162

Understanding Business Cycles

Other Inflation Indexes

- **Price index for personal consumption expenditures**: Surveys businesses instead of consumers
- **GDP deflator**
- **Producer price index**: Crude materials, intermediate goods, finished goods prices

55

LOS 18.f,g Explain/Compare
CFAI p. 310, Schweser p. 162

Understanding Business Cycles

Headline and Core Inflation

- Price indexes that include all goods and services measure **headline inflation**
- **Core inflation** refers to prices of all goods excluding food and energy
- Food and energy prices are subject to large short-term fluctuations that can magnify or mask the true inflation rate

56

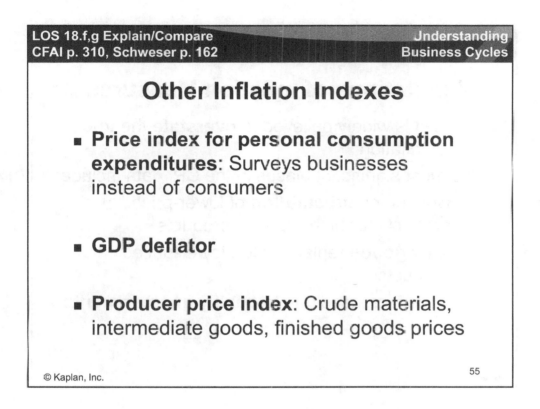

LOS 18.g Compare
CFAI p. 310, Schweser p. 165

Understanding Business Cycles

Limitations of Inflation Measures

- The CPI is widely believed to **overstate** the true rate of inflation
- The most significant biases in the CPI data include:
  - Consumer **substitution** of lower-priced products for higher-priced products
  - **New goods** replace older, lower-priced products
  - Price increases due to **quality improvements**

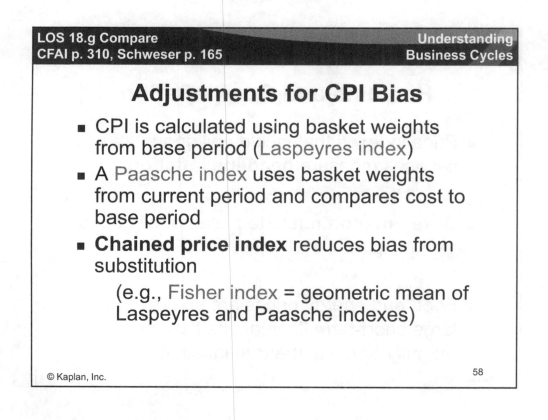

57

LOS 18.g Compare
CFAI p. 310, Schweser p. 165

Understanding Business Cycles

Adjustments for CPI Bias

- CPI is calculated using basket weights from base period (Laspeyres index)
- A Paasche index uses basket weights from current period and compares cost to base period
- **Chained price index** reduces bias from substitution

  (e.g., Fisher index = geometric mean of Laspeyres and Paasche indexes)

58

LOS 18.h Distinguish
CFAI p. 314, Schweser p. 167

Understanding Business Cycles

Factors That Affect Price Levels

- Cost-push (or wage-push) inflation: Increases in wages or other producer input prices decrease short-run aggregate supply, increase price level
- Demand-pull inflation: Increase in aggregate demand above full employment increases price level

59

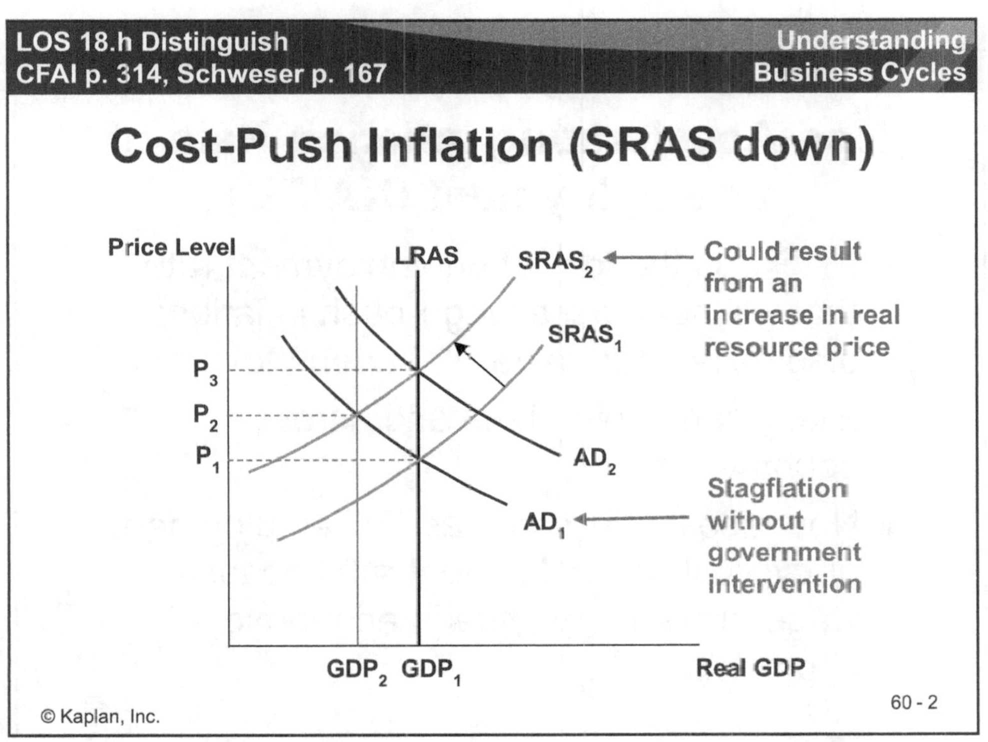

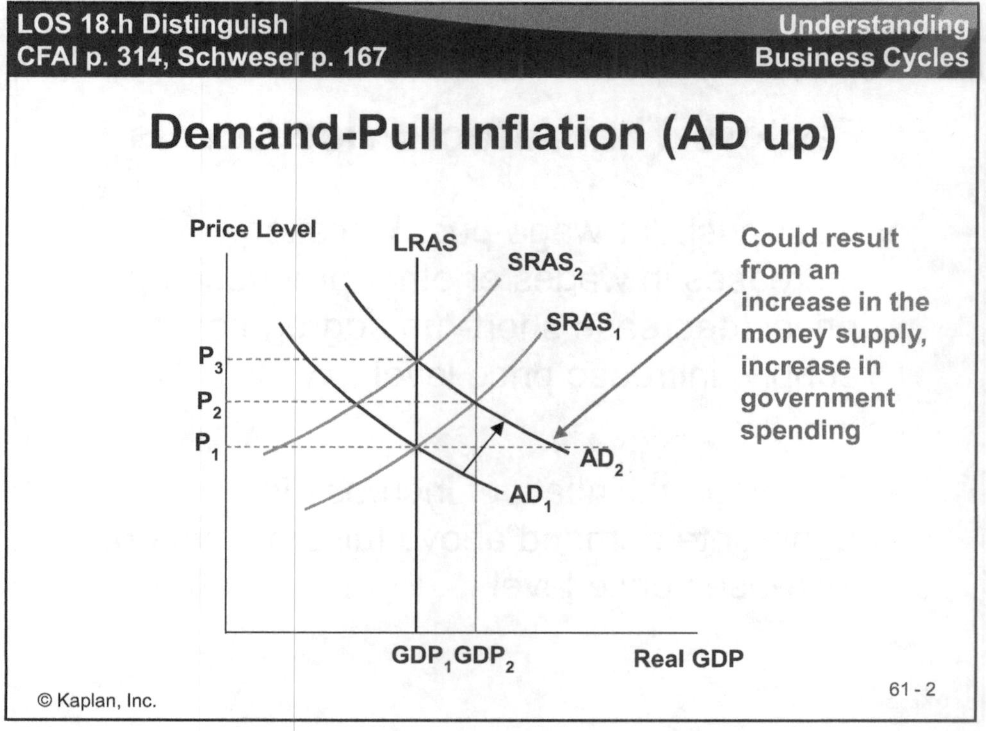

LOS 18.h Distinguish
CFAI p. 314, Schweser p. 167

Understanding Business Cycles

Non-Accelerating Inflation Rate of Unemployment (NAIRU)

- NAIRU is the lowest unemployment rate that will not induce wage-push inflation; also called natural rate of unemployment
- Likely varies over time and across countries
- Not necessarily same as "full employment" or cyclical unemployment = 0 because wage pressure may be in economic segments

62

LOS 18.i Describe
CFAI p. 319, Schweser p. 169

Understanding Business Cycles

Leading Indicators

- Turning points in these tend to precede business cycle peaks and troughs
- Leading Economic Index (U.S.):

Weekly hours, manufacturing	**Unemployment insurance claims**
Manufacturers' new orders, consumer goods	**Manufacturers' new orders, nondefense capital goods**
Vendor performance	**Building permits**
Stock prices	**Money supply**
Yield curve	**Consumer expectations**

63

LOS 18.i Describe
CFAI p. 319, Schweser p. 169

Understanding Business Cycles

Coincident Indicators

- Turning points in these tend to coincide with business cycle peaks and troughs
- Coincident Economic Index (U.S.):

Employees on nonfarm payrolls	**Personal income less transfer payments**
Industrial production	**Manufacturing and trade sales**

Source: **The Conference Board** for indexes of leading, coincident, and lagging indicators

64

LOS 18.i Describe
CFAI p. 319, Schweser p. 169

Understanding Business Cycles

Lagging Indicators

- Turning points in these tend to follow business cycle peaks and troughs
- **Unemployment rate** is a lagging indicator
- Lagging Economic Index (U.S.):

Duration of unemployment	**Prime rate**
Inventory/sales ratio, manufacturing and trade	**Manufacturing labor cost per unit of input**
Commercial and industrial loans	**Consumer credit / personal income ratio**
CPI for services	

65

LOS 18.j Identify
CFAI p. 319, Schweser p. 170

Understanding Business Cycles

Example: Phase of Business Cycle

Given the following economic indicators:

- Payroll employment is increasing
- Manufacturers' new orders are decreasing
- The average prime rate is increasing
- The yield curve is flattening
- Inventory/sales ratios are increasing

Which phase of the business cycle is the economy *most likely* in?

66

LOS 18.j Identify
CFAI p. 319, Schweser p. 170

Understanding
Business Cycles

Example: Phase of Business Cycle

- Payroll employment increasing Coincident
- New orders decreasing Leading
- Prime rate increasing Lagging
- Yield curve flattening Leading
- Inventory/sales ratios increasing Lagging

Likeliest business cycle phase: **Peak**

67 - 4

Economics: Macroeconomic Analysis

19. Monetary and Fiscal Policy

Economics

LOS 19.a Compare
CFAI p. 337, Schweser p. 178 Monetary and Fiscal Policy

Monetary Policy

- **Management of the supply of money and credit**
- **Expansionary:** Increase the money supply, decrease interest rates, increase aggregate demand
- **Contractionary:** Decease the money supply, increase interest rates, slow economic growth and inflation

 69

LOS 19.a Compare
CFAI p. 337, Schweser p. 178
Monetary and Fiscal Policy

Fiscal Policy

- **Government decisions on taxing and spending**
- **Expansionary:** Increase spending and/or decrease taxes; increase the budget deficit, increase aggregate demand
- **Contractionary:** Decease spending and/or increase taxes; decrease the budget deficit, reduce aggregate demand

70

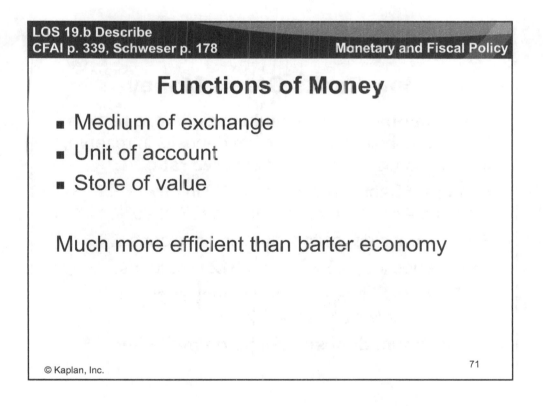

LOS 19.b Describe
CFAI p. 339, Schweser p. 178
Monetary and Fiscal Policy

Functions of Money

- Medium of exchange
- Unit of account
- Store of value

Much more efficient than barter economy

71

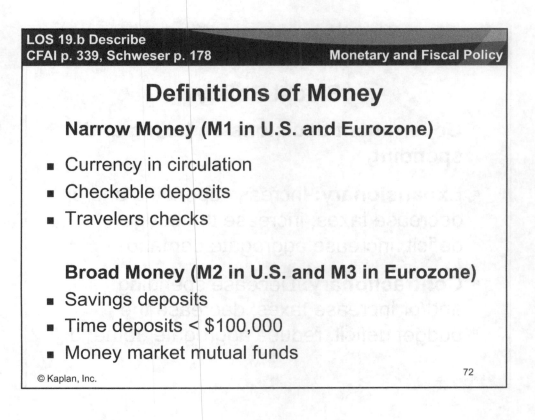

LOS 19.b Describe
CFAI p. 339, Schweser p. 178 Monetary and Fiscal Policy

Definitions of Money

Narrow Money (M1 in U.S. and Eurozone)

- Currency in circulation
- Checkable deposits
- Travelers checks

Broad Money (M2 in U.S. and M3 in Eurozone)

- Savings deposits
- Time deposits < $100,000
- Money market mutual funds

 72

LOS 19.c Explain
CFAI p. 340, Schweser p. 179 Monetary and Fiscal Policy

How Banks Create Money

In a **fractional reserve banking** system, a bank is required to hold a fraction of its deposits in reserve; this fraction is the **required reserve ratio**

Example: Bank 1 receives $1,000 in new reserves—can loan out $800 with RR of 20%...

$800 in loans deposited, $640 in new loans…

$640 deposited, 0.8 × 640 = $512 new loans…

- **Potential** increase in the money supply is 1 / 0.2 or 5 × $1,000 = $5,000
- **Maximum deposit expansion multiplier** = 5

 73

LOS 19.d Describe
CFAI p. 344, Schweser p. 181 Monetary and Fiscal Policy

Demand for Money

- **Transactions demand**: Increases with GDP
- **Precautionary demand**: Money held for unforeseen future needs, increases with GDP
- **Speculative demand**: Money held to take advantage of future investment opportunities, smaller when current returns are high, greater when risk is perceived to be high
- Supply of money is set by the monetary authority, central bank

 74

LOS 19.d Describe
CFAI p. 344, Schweser p. 181 Monetary and Fiscal Policy

Equilibrium in the Money Market

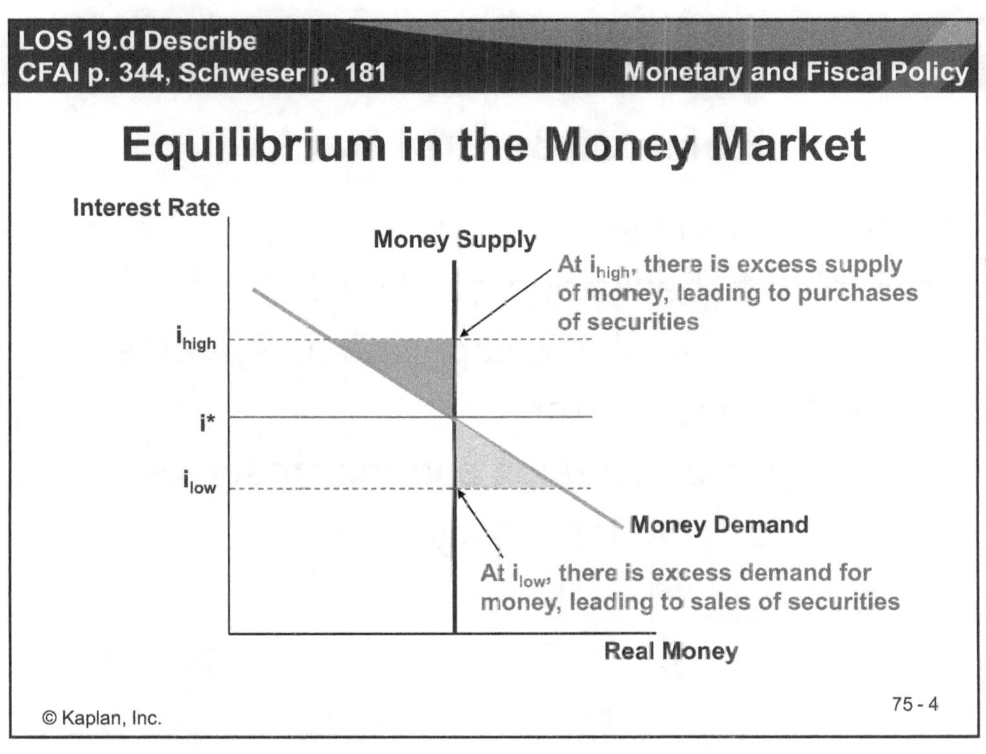
Interest Rate
Money Supply
At i_{high}, there is excess supply of money, leading to purchases of securities
i_{high}
i^*
i_{low}
Money Demand
At i_{low}, there is excess demand for money, leading to sales of securities
Real Money

 75 - 4

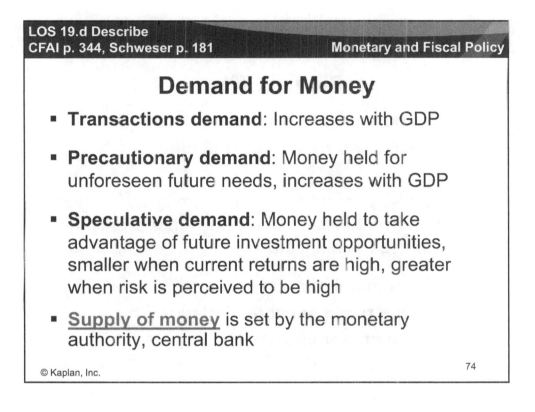

LOS 19.e Describe
CFAI p. 348, Schweser p. 183 Monetary and Fiscal Policy

Fisher Effect

Riskless nominal interest rate =
real riskless rate + expected inflation

There is also uncertainty about future inflation rates and other economic variables, and a risk premium that increases with uncertainty

Riskless nominal interest rate =
real riskless rate + expected inflation
+ risk premium for uncertainty

76

LOS 19.f Describe
CFAI p. 351, Schweser p. 183 Monetary and Fiscal Policy

Roles of Central Banks

- Issue currency
- Banker to banks and government
- Regulate banking and payments systems
- Lender of last resort
- Hold gold and foreign currency reserves
- Conduct monetary policy

77

LOS 19.f Describe
CFAI p. 351, Schweser p. 183 Monetary and Fiscal Policy

Objectives of Central Banks

All central banks have price stability (low inflation rates) as an objective. Many (except U.S. and Japan) have explicit target rates, usually 2% to 3%.

Some central banks also attempt to:

- Maintain full employment
- Promote economic growth
- Keep exchange rates stable
- Keep long-term interest rates moderate

 78

LOS 19.g Contrast
CFAI p. 355, Schweser p. 184 Monetary and Fiscal Policy

Expected and Unexpected Inflation

- **Expected inflation** increases cost of holding money, adds cost of frequently changing advertised prices
- Additional costs of **unexpected inflation**:
  - Shifts wealth from lenders to borrowers
  - Less reliable supply/demand information in price changes
    → Incorrect production decisions by firms
    → Less stable business cycles

 79

LOS 19.h Describe
CFAI p. 357, Schweser p. 186 Monetary and Fiscal Policy

Monetary Policy Tools

Policy rate: Interest rate central banks charge banks for borrowed reserves

- By raising the policy rate, Fed discourages banks from borrowing reserves; thus, they reduce their lending
- Decreasing the discount rate tends to increase the amount of lending and the money supply
- The U.S. Fed sets a target for the fed funds rate, the rate at which banks lend short-term to each other

 80

LOS 19.h Describe
CFAI p. 357, Schweser p. 186 Monetary and Fiscal Policy

Monetary Policy Tools

Open market operations: *Most often used*

- Central bank buys government securities for cash, reserves increase, money supply increases
- Selling securities decreases the money supply

Required reserve ratio: *Seldom changed*

- Reducing required reserve percentage increases excess reserves and increases the money supply
- Increasing required reserve ratio decreases the money supply

 81

LOS 19.i Describe
CFAI p. 361, Schweser p. 187
Monetary and Fiscal Policy

Central Bank Characteristics

To be effective, central banks should be:

1. **Independent**—free from political interference
   - Operational independence: Free to set policy rate
   - Target independence (ECB): Sets inflation target, measures inflation, determines horizon to meet target

Not absolute; viewed as degree of independence

82

LOS 19.i Describe
CFAI p. 361, Schweser p. 187
Monetary and Fiscal Policy

Central Bank Characteristics

To be effective, central banks should be:

2. **Credible**: Bank follows through on stated intentions and policies
3. **Transparent:** Bank discloses inflation reports, indicators they use, and how they use them

A central bank that is independent, credible, and transparent can influence expectations; policy changes are anticipated and easier to implement

83

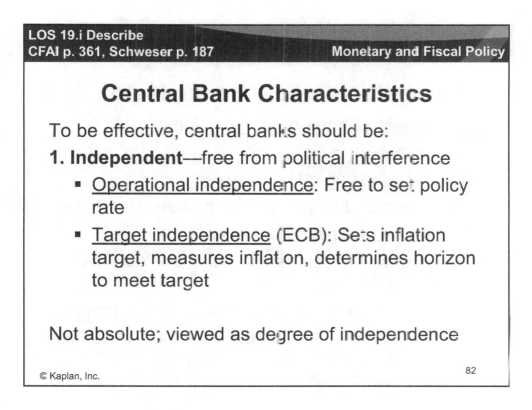

LOS 19.j Explain
CFAI p. 359, Schweser p. 188 Monetary and Fiscal Policy

Monetary Policy Transmission

When a central bank buys securities:

- Bank reserves increase
- Interbank lending rates decrease
- Short-term and long-term lending rates decrease
- Businesses increase investment
- Consumers increase house, auto, and durable goods purchases
- Domestic currency depreciates, exports increase

Overall, aggregate demand increases, increasing real GDP, employment, and inflation

 84

LOS 19.j Explain
CFAI p. 359, Schweser p. 188 Monetary and Fiscal Policy

Monetary Policy Transmission

Expansionary monetary policy affects four things:

1. Market interest rates fall, less incentive to save
2. Asset prices increase, wealth effect, consumption spending increases
3. Expectations for economic growth increase, may expect further decreases in interest rates
4. Domestic currency depreciates, import prices increase, export prices decrease

Overall, aggregate demand increases, increasing real GDP, employment, and inflation

 85

LOS 19.k Contrast
CFAI p. 361, Schweser p. 189
Monetary and Fiscal Policy

Central Bank Targets

- **Interest rate targeting**: Increase money supply growth when interest rates are above targets, decrease money supply growth when interest rates are below targets
- **Inflation targeting**: Target band for inflation rate (typically 1% to 3%)
  - Increase money supply growth when inflation is below target band, decrease money supply growth when inflation is above target band
  - Target inflation band > 0 to prevent deflation

86

LOS 19.k Contrast
CFAI p. 361, Schweser p. 189
Monetary and Fiscal Policy

Central Bank Targets

- **Exchange rate targeting**: Target band for currency exchange rate with developed country
  - Sell domestic currency when above target
  - Buy domestic currency when below target (limited by available foreign reserves)
  - Central bank does not react to domestic economic conditions
  - Result of successful exchange rate targeting is <u>same inflation rate</u> in domestic economy as in targeted developed country

87

LOS 19.l Determine
CFAI p. 369, Schweser p. 190

Monetary and Fiscal Policy

The Neutral Interest Rate

Neutral interest rate =
trend growth rate of real GDP +
target inflation rate

Policy rate > neutral rate: Contractionary

Policy rate < neutral rate: Expansionary

88

LOS 19.m Describe
CFAI p. 371, Schweser p. 190

Monetary and Fiscal Policy

Limitations of Monetary Policy

1. Long-term rates may move oppositely to short-term rates because inflation expectations change

2. If monetary tightening is extreme, expectations of recession may make long-term bonds more attractive, decreasing long-term rates

3. If demand for money is very elastic, people will hold currency even as money supply increases, referred to as a **liquidity trap**

89

LOS 19.m Describe
CFAI p. 371, Schweser p. 190 Monetary and Fiscal Policy

Limitations of Monetary Policy

4. Banks may desire to increase capital and not increase lending in response to expansionary monetary policy

5. Short-term rates cannot be below zero—limits a central bank's ability to act against deflation

   Recently, central banks have employed **"quantitative easing" (QE),** buying longer-dated government securities, mortgage securities, and risky bonds

 90

LOS 19.n Describe
CFAI p. 376, Schweser p. 192 Monetary and Fiscal Policy

Fiscal Policy

Expansionary Fiscal Policy

Increase government spending, decrease taxes, or both—increasing aggregate demand and the budget deficit

Contractionary Fiscal Policy

Decrease government spending, increase taxes, or both—decreasing aggregate demand and the budget deficit

 91

LOS 19.n Describe
CFAI p. 376, Schweser p. 192

Monetary and Fiscal Policy

Fiscal Policy

- Keynesian economists believe **discretionary fiscal policy** can stabilize the economy, increasing aggregate demand to combat recessions and decreasing aggregate demand to combat inflation
- Monetarists believe that such effects are temporary and that appropriate monetary policy will dampen economic cycles
- Automatic stabilizers (taxes and transfer payments) tend to increase deficits during recessions and decrease deficits during expansions

92

LOS 19.n Describe
CFAI p. 376, Schweser p. 192

Monetary and Fiscal Policy

Fiscal Policy Objectives

Governments use fiscal policy to:

1. Influence aggregate demand and economic growth
2. Redistribute wealth
3. Affect the allocation of resources to different sectors of the economy

93

LOS 19.o Describe
CFAI p. 383, Schweser p. 193

Monetary and Fiscal Policy

Fiscal Tools: Spending

1. **Transfer payments**: Cash payments by government to redistribute wealth
2. **Current spending**: Purchases of goods and services
3. **Capital spending**: To increase future productivity; on infrastructure, or to support research on and development of new technologies

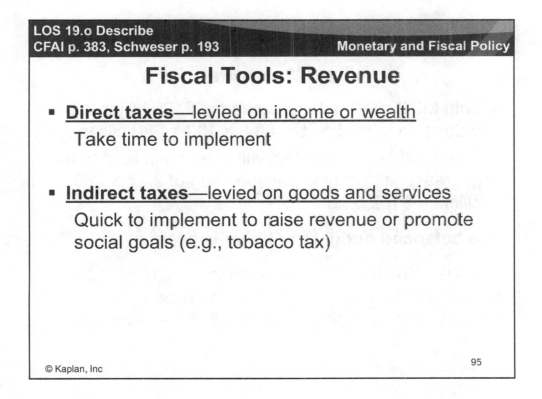

94

LOS 19.o Describe
CFAI p. 383, Schweser p. 193

Monetary and Fiscal Policy

Fiscal Tools: Revenue

- **Direct taxes**—levied on income or wealth
  Take time to implement
- **Indirect taxes**—levied on goods and services
  Quick to implement to raise revenue or promote social goals (e.g., tobacco tax)

95

LOS 19.o Describe
CFAI p. 383, Schweser p. 193
Monetary and Fiscal Policy

Fiscal Multiplier

- Initial government spending has a multiplied effect as it creates more spending

$$= \frac{1}{1 - MPC(1 - t)}$$

- ↑savings and ↑taxes reduce the multiplier
- For MPC = 0.8 and t = 0.3, a \$100 billion spending increase, over time, can increase consumption by 1 / [1 – 0.8(1 – 0.3)] × \$100 = \$227 billion

96

LOS 19.o Describe
CFAI p. 383, Schweser p. 193
Monetary and Fiscal Policy

Tax Multiplier

- With MPC = 0.8, a tax increase of \$100 billion will reduce consumption by = 0.8 × 100 = \$80 billion
- The fiscal multiplier effect will, over time, lead to a <u>decrease</u> in consumption spending of 2.27 × \$80 billion = \$182 billion

The **balanced budget multiplier** is positive

A \$100 billion increase in spending + a \$100 billion increase in taxes can, over time, increase consumption spending by \$227 – \$182 = \$45 billion

97

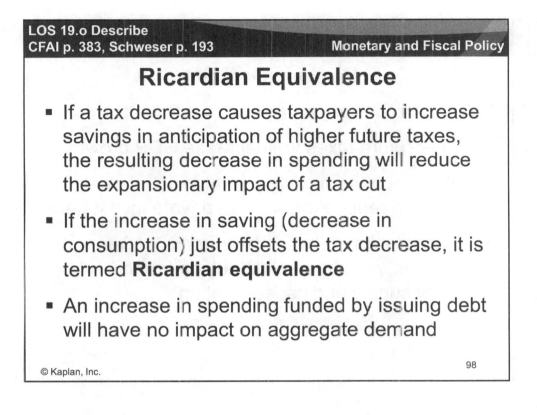

LOS 19.o Describe
CFAI p. 383, Schweser p. 193

Monetary and Fiscal Policy

Ricardian Equivalence

- If a tax decrease causes taxpayers to increase savings in anticipation of higher future taxes, the resulting decrease in spending will reduce the expansionary impact of a tax cut
- If the increase in saving (decrease in consumption) just offsets the tax decrease, it is termed **Ricardian equivalence**
- An increase in spending funded by issuing debt will have no impact on aggregate demand

98

LOS 19.p Describe
CFAI p. 382, Schweser p. 195

Monetary and Fiscal Policy

Government Debt

$$\text{Debt ratio} = \frac{\text{government debt}}{\text{GDP}}$$

If the real interest rate on government debt is less (greater) than the real rate of growth, debt ratio will decrease (increase) over time

99

LOS 19.p Describe
CFAI p. 382, Schweser p. 195 Monetary and Fiscal Policy

Budget Deficits

Reasons to be concerned about deficits

- Higher future taxes will decrease GDP growth
- Government borrowing can drive up interest rates and reduce (crowd out) private investment
- At some point, debt can become risky, interest rate rises, country may default or expand money supply and cause inflation

 100

LOS 19.p Describe
CFAI p. 382, Schweser p. 195 Monetary and Fiscal Policy

Budget Deficits

Arguments that deficits are **not** concerning

- If deficit is to finance capital investment, future GDP will be higher
- Deficits don't matter if Ricardian equivalence holds
- If the economy is operating below capacity, government borrowing will not displace capital investment

 101

LOS 19.q Explain
CFAI p. 389, Schweser p. 196 Monetary and Fiscal Policy

Fiscal Policy Lags

- Recognition lag: To identify the need for fiscal policy change
- Action lag: To enact legislation
- Impact lag: For the policy change to have the intended effect

Lags can cause fiscal policy changes to be destabilizing rather than stabilizing

 102

LOS 19.q Explain
CFAI p. 389, Schweser p. 196 Monetary and Fiscal Policy

Fiscal Policy Limitations

- If economy is at full employment, fiscal stimulus will result in higher inflation
- If economy is below full employment due to supply shortages, fiscal stimulus will lead to inflation rather than GDP growth
- If the economy has high unemployment and high inflation (stagflation), fiscal policy cannot address both

 103

LOS 19.r Determine
CFAI p. 377, Schweser p. 197 Monetary and Fiscal Policy

Analysis of Fiscal Policy

- Whether fiscal policy is expansionary or contractionary depends on the business cycle stage
- An adjusted, or full-employment, deficit amount can be used to adjust for the business cycle stage

In general:

Spending increases, tax decreases—**expansionary**

Spending decreases, tax increases—**contractionary**

 104

LOS 19.s Explain
CFAI p. 393, Schweser p. 198 Monetary and Fiscal Policy

Policy Interaction

- **Monetary ↑ and Fiscal ↑:** Strong expansionary effect, public and private sectors grow
- **Monetary ↓ and Fiscal ↓:** Decreased GDP growth, higher interest rates, public and private sectors decline
- **Monetary ↑ and Fiscal ↓:** Interest rates fall, consumption, output, and private sector expand
- **Monetary ↓ and Fiscal ↑:** Interest rates rise, aggregate demand likely higher, public sector portion of spending grows

 105

Monetary and Fiscal Policy

Fiscal Policy – Problem

The balanced budget multiplier is positive because:

A. the tax multiplier effect is stronger than the government purchases multiplier effect.

B. the government purchases multiplier effect is stronger than the tax multiplier effect.

C. The negative effect of the government purchases multiplier is less than the positive effect of the tax multiplier.

106 - 2

Aggregate Output, Prices, and Economic Growth

Aggregate Output – Solution

When the economy is operating at full-employment GDP, the short-run and long-run effects of an increase in the rate of growth of the money supply are to:

B. increase real GDP in the short run but not in the long run.

AD ↑, but over-full employment increases wage pressure, SRAS ↓

Monetary and Fiscal Policy

Fiscal Policy – Solution

The balanced budget multiplier is positive because:

B. the government purchases multiplier effect is stronger than the tax multiplier effect.

Tax multiplier is negative but smaller than purchases multiplier, which is positive

Study Session 6

Economics: Economics in a Global Context

Economics: Economics in a Global Context

20. International Trade and Capital Flows

LOS 20.a Compare
CFAI p. 410, Schweser p. 210

International Trade and Capital Flows

Gross National Product (GNP) and Gross Domestic Product (GDP)

- **GDP**: Value of goods and services produced in a country
- **GNP**: Value of goods and services produced by a country's citizens
- Differences:
  - Income of citizens working abroad, non-citizens working in country
  - Income to capital owned by foreigners, foreign capital owned by citizens

GDP is better for measuring domestic activity

2 - 1

LOS 20.b Describe
CFAI p. 417, Schweser p. 210

International Trade and Capital Flows

Benefits/Costs of International Trade

Benefits:

- Lower cost to consumers of imports
- Higher employment, wages, and profits in export industries

Costs:

Displacement of workers and lost profits in industries competing with imported goods

Economists: Benefits outweigh costs

3

LOS 20.c Distinguish
CFAI p. 421, Schweser p. 211

International Trade and Capital Flows

Absolute vs. Comparative Advantage

Absolute advantage refers to lower cost in terms of resources used

Comparative advantage refers to the lowest *opportunity cost* to produce a product

Law of comparative advantage:

- Trade makes **all countries better off**
- Each country specializes in goods they produce most efficiently and trades for other goods
- **Outcome:** Increased worldwide output and wealth with no country being worse off

4

LOS 20.c Distinguish
CFAI p. 421, Schweser p. 211

International Trade and Capital Flows

Absolute vs. Comparative Advantage

Labor/ unit	Cloth	Wine
England	100	110
Portugal	90	80

- Portugal has absolute advantage in both wine and cloth
- England has comparative advantage in cloth, opportunity cost of 100/110 in terms of wine compared to 90/80 opportunity cost in Portugal
- Portugal has comparative advantage in wine, opportunity cost of 80/90 units of cloth compared to 110/100 units of cloth in England

5

LOS 20.c Distinguish
CFAI p. 421, Schweser p. 211

International Trade and Capital Flows

Absolute vs. Comparative Advantage

Labor/ unit	Cloth	Wine
England	100	110
Portugal	90	80

- If Portugal specializes in wine production and England specializes in cloth production, both can be better off
- Trade can also produce benefits from economies of scale and efficiencies resulting from cross-border competition

6

LOS 20.d Explain
CFAI p. 427, Schweser p. 214

International Trade and Capital Flows

Models of Trade

Ricardian model

- Labor is the only factor of production
- Comparative advantage depends on relative labor productivity for different goods

Heckscher-Ohlin model

- Two factors of production: capital and labor
- Comparative advantage depends on relative amount of each factor possessed by a country

7

LOS 20.d Explain
CFAI p. 427, Schweser p. 214

International Trade and Capital Flows

Heckscher-Ohlin Model

- Under Heckscher-Ohlin model, there is a redistribution of wealth between the two factors of production due to international trade
- The price of more abundant resource will increase
- Results in a wealth transfer within a country from scarce resource to abundant resource

8

LOS 20.e Compare
CFAI p. 429, Schweser p. 215

International Trade and Capital Flows

Trade Restrictions

Tariff is a tax imposed on imported goods

Quota is a limitation on the quantity of goods imported

Export subsidies are payments by government to domestic exporters

Minimum domestic content specifies required proportion of product content to be sourced domestically

Voluntary export restraints (VERs) are agreements by exporting countries to limit the quantity of goods they will export to an importing country

9

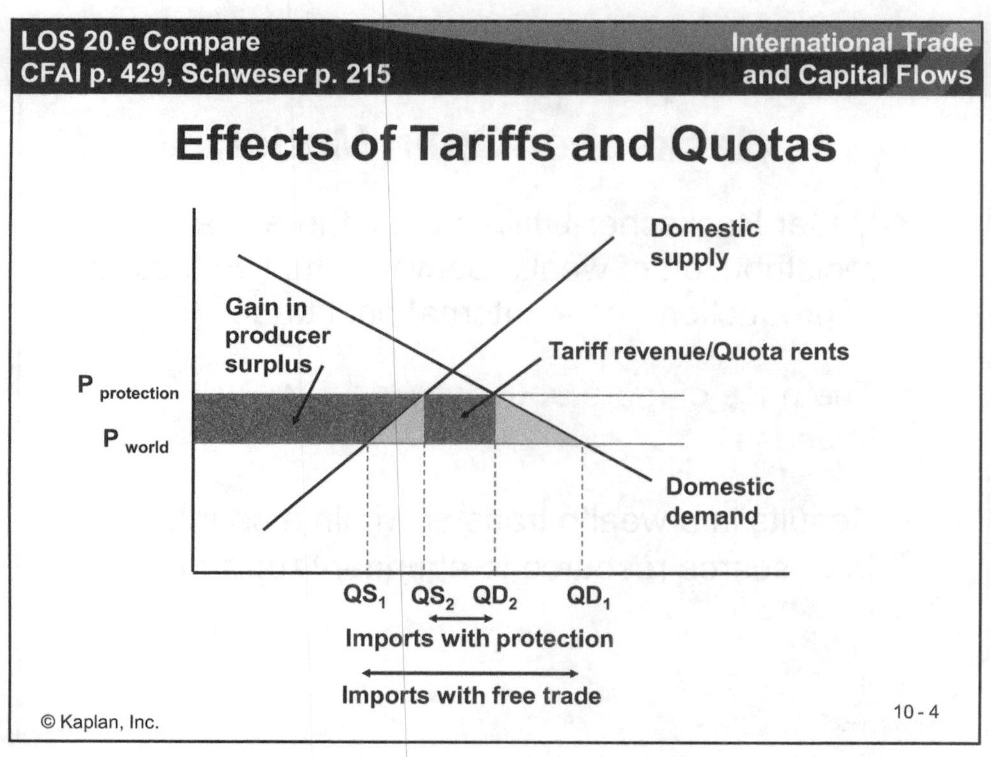

LOS 20.e Compare
CFAI p. 429, Schweser p. 215

International Trade and Capital Flows

Reasons for Trade Restrictions

Two primary goals:

1. Protecting domestic jobs
2. Protecting domestic producers

- Other reasons include countering foreign trade restrictions and export subsidies, anti-dumping, and revenues from tariff for domestic government
- A large country could actually decrease the world price by imposing a quota or tariff

11

LOS 20.e Compare
CFAI p. 429, Schweser p. 215

International Trade and Capital Flows

Trade Restrictions

Trade Restriction	Domestic Consumer	Domestic Producer	Domestic Government	Foreign Exporter
Tariff	Loses	Gains	Gains	Loses
Quota	Loses	Gains	Gains[1]	Gains[1]
VER	Loses	Gains	None	Gains
Export Subsidy	Loses	Gains	Loses	NA

1. In case of quotas, the distribution of gains between the domestic government and foreign exporter depends on the amount of **quota rent** collected by the domestic government

12

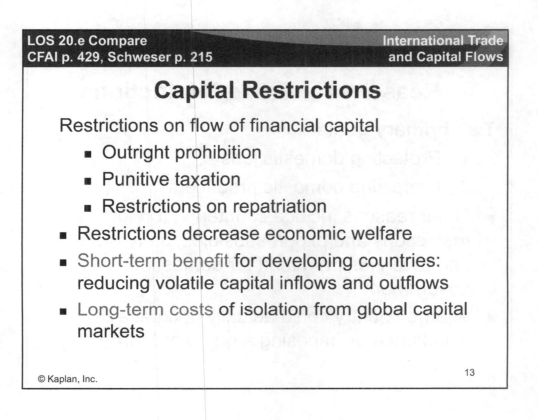

LOS 20.e Compare
CFAI p. 429, Schweser p. 215

International Trade and Capital Flows

Capital Restrictions

Restrictions on flow of financial capital

- Outright prohibition
- Punitive taxation
- Restrictions on repatriation

- Restrictions decrease economic welfare
- Short-term benefit for developing countries: reducing volatile capital inflows and outflows
- Long-term costs of isolation from global capital markets

13

LOS 20.f Explain
CFAI p. 434, Schweser p. 218

International Trade and Capital Flows

Trading Blocs, Common Markets, and Economic Unions

- **Economic welfare** is improved by reducing trade restrictions
- Gains from reducing trade restrictions between member countries are **offset** by losses if bloc increases restrictions on non-member countries

14

LOS 20.f Explain
CFAI p. 434, Schweser p. 218

International Trade and Capital Flows

Trading Blocs

Free trade area (FTA):

- Removes all barriers to trade between member countries
- Example: NAFTA

Customs Union (CU):

- FTA + common trade restrictions with non-members

Common Market (CM):

- CU + removes barriers to movement of labor and capital among members

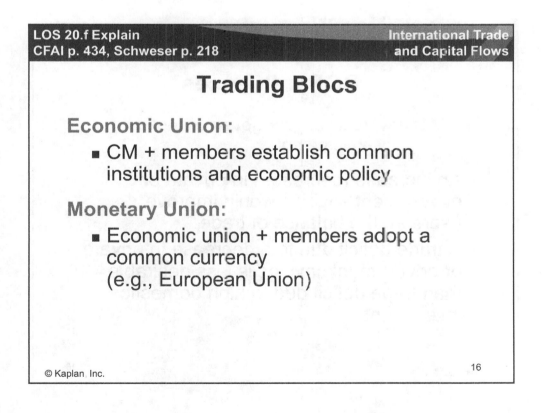

15

LOS 20.f Explain
CFAI p. 434, Schweser p. 218

International Trade and Capital Flows

Trading Blocs

Economic Union:

- CM + members establish common institutions and economic policy

Monetary Union:

- Economic union + members adopt a common currency (e.g., European Union)

16

LOS 20.g Describe
CFAI p. 442, Schweser p. 220

International Trade and Capital Flows

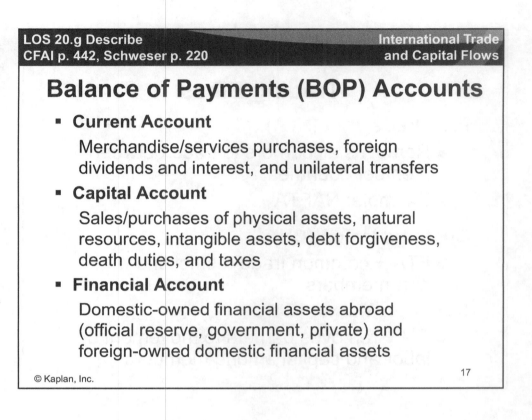

Balance of Payments (BOP) Accounts

- **Current Account**

  Merchandise/services purchases, foreign dividends and interest, and unilateral transfers

- **Capital Account**

  Sales/purchases of physical assets, natural resources, intangible assets, debt forgiveness, death duties, and taxes

- **Financial Account**

  Domestic-owned financial assets abroad (official reserve, government, private) and foreign-owned domestic financial assets

17

LOS 20.h Explain
CFAI p. 446, Schweser p. 221

International Trade and Capital Flows

BOP Influences

X – M = private savings + government savings – investment

- An increase (decrease) in private or government savings would improve (worsen) the balance of trade
- A trade deficit due to a decrease in private or government savings is less desirable than trade deficit due to high domestic investment

18

LOS 20.i Describe
CFAI p. 453, Schweser p. 222

International Trade and Capital Flows

International Organizations

International Monetary Fund (IMF)

- Monetary cooperation
- Growth of trade
- Exchange stability
- Multilateral system of payments
- Overcome temporary BOP difficulties

World Bank

- Fight poverty
- Development and assistance

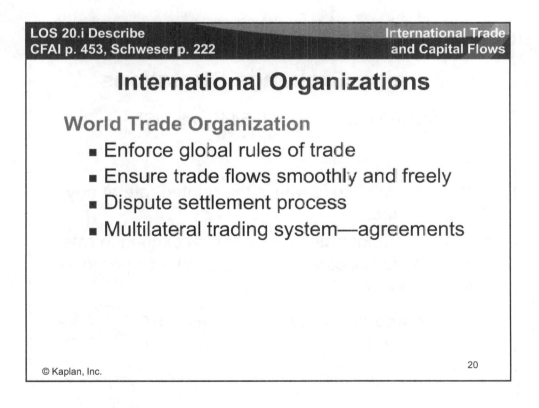

19

LOS 20.i Describe
CFAI p. 453, Schweser p. 222

International Trade and Capital Flows

International Organizations

World Trade Organization

- Enforce global rules of trade
- Ensure trade flows smoothly and freely
- Dispute settlement process
- Multilateral trading system—agreements

20

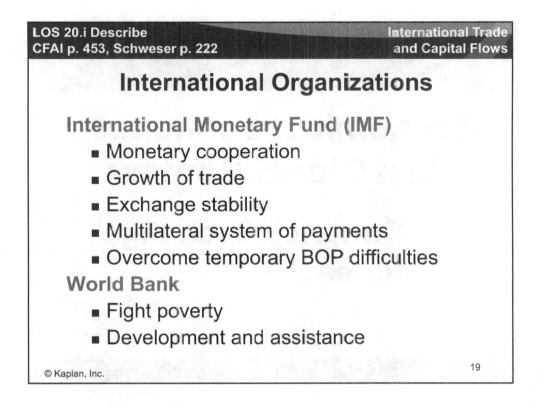

Economics: Economics in a Global Context

21. Currency Exchange Rates

LOS 21.a Define/Distinguish
CFAI p. 472, Schweser p. 230

Currency Exchange Rates

Foreign Exchange Quotations

0.5440 GBP/USD means £0.5440 **per** USD

Price currency — Base currency

- **Nominal** exchange rate is the quoted rate at any point in time
- **Real** exchange rate is the nominal exchange rate adjusted for inflation in each country compared to a base period

$$\text{real exchange rate (d / f)} = \text{nominal exchange rate (d / f)} \times \left(\frac{CPI_{foreign}}{CPI_{domestic}}\right)$$

22

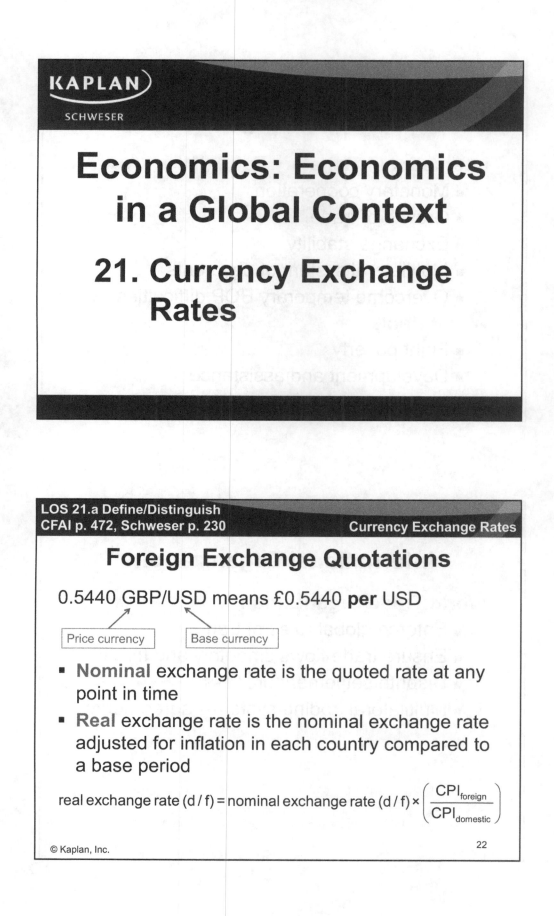

LOS 21.a Define/Distinguish
CFAI p. 472, Schweser p. 230
Currency Exchange Rates

Example: Real Exchange Rate

Base period: 1/1/X1 exchange rate = 1.20 \$/€

1/1/X3 exchange rate = 1.30 \$/€

Base period: 1/1/X1 CPI_{USD} = 100; CPI_{euro} = 100

On 1/1/X3, CPI_{USD} = 114; CPI_{euro} = 109

Calculate the real exchange rate on 1/1/X3.

$$\text{real exchange rate } (d/f) = \text{nominal exchange rate } (d/f) \times \left(\frac{CPI_{foreign}}{CPI_{domestic}}\right)$$

$= 1.30 \times 109 / 114 = 1.243$ \$/€

The real cost of euro zone goods to a U.S. citizen has gone up by 1.243 / 1.20 – 1 = 3.6%; which is less than the nominal rate has gone up (8.3%) because U.S. inflation was higher.

23 - 3

LOS 21.a Define/Distinguish
CFAI p. 472, Schweser p. 230
Currency Exchange Rates

Spot Market vs. Forward Market

Spot exchange rates: Exchange rates for immediate delivery

Forward contract: An agreement to buy or sell a specific amount of a foreign currency at a future date at the quoted forward exchange rate (e.g., 30, 60, or 90 days in the future)

24

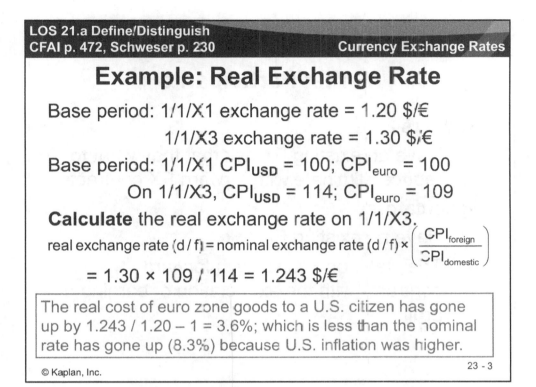

LOS 21.b Describe
CFAI p. 478, Schweser p. 232 Currency Exchange Rates

Market Participants

Hedgers

Have an existing FX risk that they want to reduce/eliminate with forward FX contracts

Speculators

Have no existing FX risk

They take on FX risk with forward contracts with the expectation of earning a profit

 25

LOS 21.b Describe
CFAI p. 478, Schweser p. 232 Currency Exchange Rates

Market Participants

Sell side

Market makers: Large multinational banks

Buy side

- Corporations
- Investment accounts: Real money and leveraged
- Governments, sovereign wealth funds, pension plans, central banks
- Retail market: Households (e.g., tourism)

 26

LOS 21.c Calculate/Interpret
CFAI p. 492, Schweser p. 233
Currency Exchange Rates

Currency Appreciation or Depreciation

Consider a USD/GBP exchange rate that has gone **down** from 1.61 to 1.59.

The USD price of a British pound has gone **down** 1.59 / 1.61 – 1 = –1.24%, and we say the pound has **depreciated** relative to the USD by 1.24%

The GBP/USD exchange rate has gone **up** from 1 / 1.61 = 0.6211 to 1 / 1.59 = 0.6289

The GBP price of a USD has gone **up** by 0.6289 / 0.6211 – 1 = 1.26%, and we say the USD has **appreciated** relative to the GBP by 1.26%

 27

LOS 21.d Calculate/Interpret
CFAI p. 493, Schweser p. 233
Currency Exchange Rates

Cross Rates Example

Given the following FX rates:

1.5600 USD/GBP and **1.4860 CHF/USD**

Calculate the CHF/GBP cross rate

Just algebra: Set up the quotes so the common currency cancels

$$\frac{\not{USD}}{GBP} \times \frac{CHF}{\not{USD}} = \frac{CHF}{GBP}$$

$$1.5600\frac{USD}{GBP} \times 1.4860\frac{CHF}{USD} = 2.3182\frac{CHF}{GBP}$$

 28 - 3

LOS 21.e Convert
CFAI p. 496, Schweser p. 234 Currency Exchange Rates

Forward Quotes—Point Basis

- Forward quote is points above (below) spot
- Point is last digit of the spot rate quote

Last digit is 0.0001

Spot 1.4320 $/€, Forward quote + 22.1 points

Forward = 1.4320 + 22.1(0.0001) = 1.43421 $/ €

 29

LOS 21.e Convert
CFAI p. 496, Schweser p. 234 Currency Exchange Rates

Forward Quotes—Percentage Basis

Spot 1.6135 $/£

90-day forward quote is –0.29%

Forward = 1.6135 (1 – 0.0029) = $1.6088 $/£

We say the U.S. dollar is **trading at a forward premium** relative to the British pound

If the forward quote is –47 points, **percentage forward quote** is –0.0047 / 1.6135 = –0.0029 = –0.29%

 30

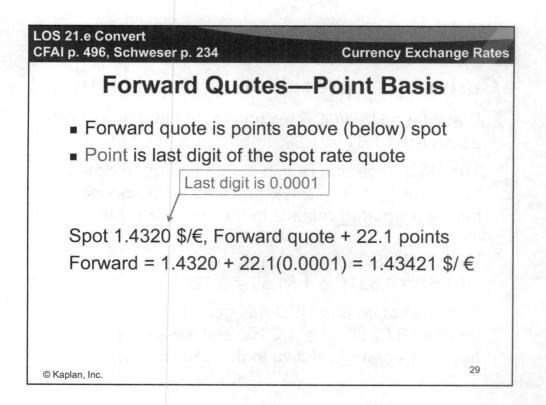

LOS 21.f,g Explain/Calculate/Interpret
CFAI p. 498, Schweser p. 235 Currency Exchange Rates

No-Arbitrage Forward Exchange Rate

$$\frac{\text{Forward}(A/B)}{\text{Spot}(A/B)} = \frac{1+\text{Interest Rate}_A}{1+\text{Interest Rate}_B}$$

- Follow the Numerator-Denominator rule: Given a quote A/B, use A's interest rate in numerator and B's interest rate in the denominator

 31

LOS 21.f,g Explain/Calculate/Interpret
CFAI p. 498, Schweser p. 235 Currency Exchange Rates

Example: No-Arbitrage Forward Rate

Spot rate = 1.50 \$/£; riskless \$ interest rate is 2%; riskless £ interest rate 2.5%. **Calculate** the arbitrage-free 1-year forward rate.

$$\text{Forward}(\$/£) = \left[\frac{1+\text{Interest Rate}_{\$}}{1+\text{Interest Rate}_{£}}\right] \times \text{Spot}(\$/£)$$

$$= \left[\frac{1+0.02}{1+0.025}\right] \times 1.50 = 1.4927\ \$/£$$

U.K. interest rate is higher, so forward \$ / £ is less than spot \$ / £

 32

Currency Exchange Rates

Forward Exchange Rate – Problem

The euro interest rate is 3% and the and the AUD interest rate is 4%. The spot EUR/AUD rate is 0.7276. The 90-day forward AUD/EUR no-arbitrage rate is *closest* to:

A. 1.3877.

B. 1.3778.

C. 1.3710.

33 - 3

LOS 21.h Describe
CFAI p. 503, Schweser p. 237

Currency Exchange Rates

Exchange Rate Regimes

Countries without sovereign currency

Formal dollarization: Uses other country's currency

Monetary union: Several countries use a common currency

Country cannot have its own monetary policy

34

LOS 21.h Describe
CFAI p. 503, Schweser p. 237

Currency Exchange Rates

Exchange Rate Regimes

Countries with sovereign currency

Currency board: Commits to a fixed rate of exchange of domestic for a foreign currency

Conventional fixed peg: Maintain at pegged rate (+/– 1%) via direct intervention in the FX markets or indirectly via monetary policy changes

Target zone: Gives flexibility to maintain the exchange rate within a wider range (e.g., +/– 2%)

35

LOS 21.h Describe
CFAI p. 503, Schweser p. 237

Currency Exchange Rates

Exchange Rate Regimes

Countries with sovereign currency (cont.)

Crawling peg: Allows exchange rate to move slowly with changes in fundamentals

- Active: Announced and implemented
- Passive: Managed but market driven

Managed floating: Does not have a target exchange rate; influences exchange rate through direct intervention or monetary policy

Independently floating: Market determined

36

LOS 21.i Explain
CFAI p. 514, Schweser p. 238 Currency Exchange Rates

Exchange Rates, Trade, and Capital

(X – M) = (Private savings – investment) + (tax revenue – government spending)

Same as before

- (X – M) > 0, trade surplus when private savings + government surplus exceeds domestic investment
- (X – M) < 0, trade deficit when private savings – domestic investment is less than budget deficit

 37

LOS 21.i Explain
CFAI p. 514, Schweser p. 238 Currency Exchange Rates

Exchange Rates and Trade Deficit

Elasticities Approach

$$W_M = \frac{\text{Imports}}{\text{Imports} + \text{Exports}} \qquad W_X = \frac{\text{Exports}}{\text{Imports} + \text{Exports}}$$

ε_X and ε_M are demand elasticities of exports and imports

Generalized Marshall-Lerner condition

If $W_X\varepsilon_X + W_M(\varepsilon_M - 1) > 0$, then depreciation of domestic currency will decrease trade deficit

 38

LOS 21.i Explain
CFAI p. 514, Schweser p. 238 Currency Exchange Rates

Exchange Rates and Trade Deficit

Note that when $W_X = W_M = 0.5$ we get the

Classic Marshall-Lerner condition

$$\varepsilon_X + \varepsilon_M > 1$$

This is a sufficient condition, not a necessary condition, for a currency depreciation to reduce the trade deficit

39

LOS 21.i Explain
CFAI p. 514, Schweser p. 238 Currency Exchange Rates

Exchange Rates and Trade Deficit

J-Curve Effect

In the short run, due to existing contracts, export and import demand are relatively inelastic

- Currency depreciation initially leads to a larger trade deficit

In the long run, elasticities increase

- Currency depreciation leads to a reduction in the trade deficit

40

LOS 21.i Explain
CFAI p. 514, Schweser p. 238

Currency Exchange Rates

Exchange Rates and Trade Deficit

The **absorption approach** includes the effect of currency depreciation on capital flows as well as trade flows

Exports – Imports = National Income – Expenditures

For depreciation to improve the balance of trade:

- National income must increase relative to expenditures
- National saving (private + government) must increase relative to domestic investment in physical capital

41

Currency Exchange Rates

Currency Depreciation Effect – Problem

Sylvania's currency, S$ has depreciated relative to their trading partners' currencies. Given the following information, Sylvania's balance of trade would *most likely*:

Item	S$	Elasticity
Exports	4,000,000	0.60
Imports	6,000,000	0.75
Total Trade	10,000,000	

A. worsen.
B. improve.
C. remain the same.

42 - 4

Currency Exchange Rates

Forward Exchange Rate – Solution

The euro interest rate is 3% and the and the AUD interest rate is 4%. The spot EUR/AUD rate is 0.7276. The 90-day forward AUD/EUR no-arbitrage rate is *closest* to:

B. 1.3778.

$$\text{Spot } {}^{AUD}\!/_{EUR} = {}^{1}\!/_{0.7276} = 1.3744$$

$$90\text{-day forward} = 1.3744\left[\frac{1+0.04\left(\frac{90}{360}\right)}{1+0.03\left(\frac{90}{360}\right)}\right] = 1.3778$$

Currency Exchange Rates

Currency Depreciation Effect – Solution

Sylvania's currency, S$ has depreciated relative to their trading partners' currencies. Given the following information, Sylvania's balance of trade would *most likely*:

Item	S$	Elasticity
Exports	4,000,000	0.60
Imports	6,000,000	0.75
Total Trade	10,000,000	$W_X = 0.4$; $W_M = 0.6$

B. improve.

$$W_X\varepsilon_X + W_M(\varepsilon_M - 1)$$
$$= 0.4 \times 0.60 + 0.6 \times (0.75 - 1)$$
$$= 0.09 > 0$$

Sylvania has a trade deficit of S$2,000,000. According to generalized Marshall-Lerner condition, depreciation of S$ will decrease trade deficit (improve balance of trade).

Study Session 7

Financial Reporting and Analysis: An Introduction

Financial Reporting and Analysis: An Introduction

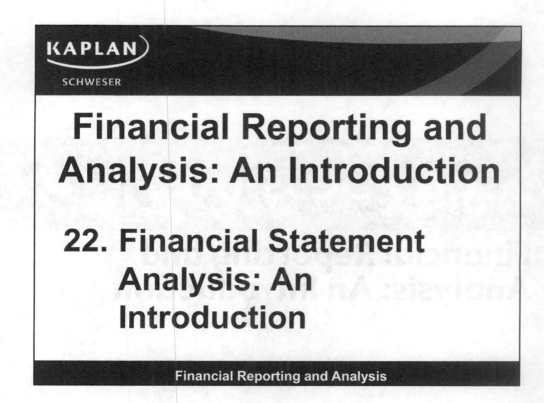

22. Financial Statement Analysis: An Introduction

Financial Reporting and Analysis

LOS 22.a Describe
CFAI p. 6, Schweser p. 10

Financial Statement Analysis: An Introduction

Role of Financial Reporting

"The objective of general purpose financial reporting is to provide financial information about the reporting entity that is useful to existing and potential investors, lenders, and other creditors in making decisions about providing resources to the entity. Those decisions involve buying, selling or holding equity and debt instruments, and providing or settling loans and other forms of credit."

IASB Conceptual Framework

2

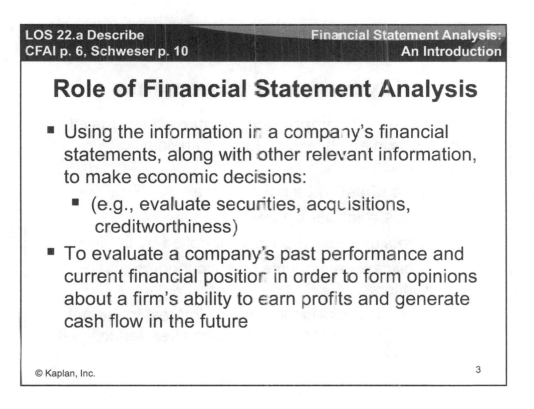

LOS 22.a Describe
CFAI p. 6, Schweser p. 10

Financial Statement Analysis: An Introduction

Role of Financial Statement Analysis

- Using the information in a company's financial statements, along with other relevant information, to make economic decisions:
  - (e.g., evaluate securities, acquisitions, creditworthiness)
- To evaluate a company's past performance and current financial position in order to form opinions about a firm's ability to earn profits and generate cash flow in the future

 3

LOS 22.b Describe
CFAI p. 11, Schweser p. 11

Financial Statement Analysis: An Introduction

Key Financial Statements

1. **Income statement** (statement of operations or the profit and loss statement)

   Summarizes events over a period:

   - *Revenues* are inflows from delivering or producing goods, rendering services, or other activities that constitute the entity's ongoing major or central operations
   - *Expenses* are outflows from delivering or producing goods or services that constitute the entity's ongoing major or central operations
   - *Other income* includes gains and losses which may or may not arise in ordinary course of business

 4

LOS 22.b Describe
CFAI p. 11, Schweser p. 11

Financial Statement Analysis: An Introduction

Key Financial Statements

2. **Statement of comprehensive income** reports all changes in equity except for shareholder transactions
3. **Balance sheet**—at a point in time
   - Assets = liabilities + owners' equity
   - *Assets* are the resources controlled by the firm
   - *Liabilities* are amounts owed to lenders and other creditors
   - *Owners' equity* is the residual interest in the net assets of an entity that remains after deducting its liabilities

 5

LOS 22.b Describe
CFAI p. 11, Schweser p. 11

Financial Statement Analysis: An Introduction

Key Financial Statements

4. **Cash flow statement** reconciles beginning and ending cash balance, splitting changes into three categories:
   - *Operating cash flows (CFO)*
   - *Investing cash flows (CFI)*
   - *Financing cash flows (CFF)*
5. **Statement of changes in owners' equity**—amounts and sources of changes in shareholders' equity over the period

 6

LOS 22.c Describe
CFAI p. 23, Schweser p. 12

Financial Statement Analysis: An Introduction

Footnotes and Supplementary Schedules

- Basis of presentation
- Accounting methods and assumptions
- Further information on amounts in primary statements
- Business acquisitions/disposals
- Contingencies
- Legal proceedings
- Stock options and benefit plans
- Significant customers
- Segment data
- Quarterly data
- Related-party transactions

7

LOS 22.c Describe
CFAI p. 23, Schweser p. 12

Financial Statement Analysis: An Introduction

Management Discussion and Analysis

- Nature of the business
- Results from operations, business overview
- Trends in sales and expenses
- Capital resources and liquidity
- Cash flow trends
- Discussion of critical accounting choices
- Effects of inflation, price changes, and uncertainties on future results

8

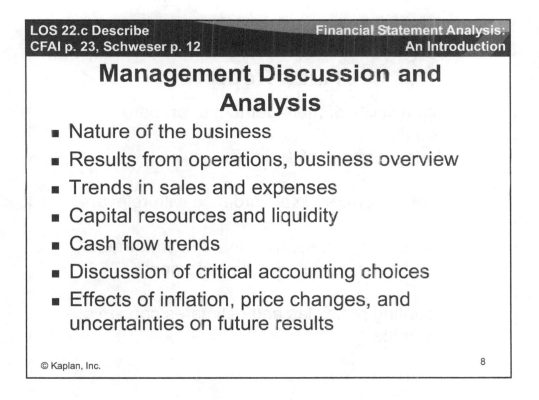

LOS 22.d Describe
CFAI p. 26, Schweser p. 12

Financial Statement Analysis: An Introduction

The Audit Report

- **Audit:** *Independent review* of company's financial statements
- **Reasonable assurance** that financial statements are free of material errors
- **Audit opinion:**

  Unqualified: "Clean" opinion

  Qualified: Exceptions to accounting principles

  Adverse: Statements not presented fairly

  Disclaimer of opinion: Unable to form an opinion
- Must provide opinion on company's **internal controls** under U.S. GAAP

 9

LOS 22.d Describe
CFAI p. 26, Schweser p. 12

Financial Statement Analysis: An Introduction

Audit Report

1. Responsibility of management to prepare accounts
   - Independence of auditors
2. Properly prepared in accordance with relevant GAAP
   - Reasonable assurance that the statements are free from material misstatement
3. Accounting principles and estimates chosen are reasonable

 10

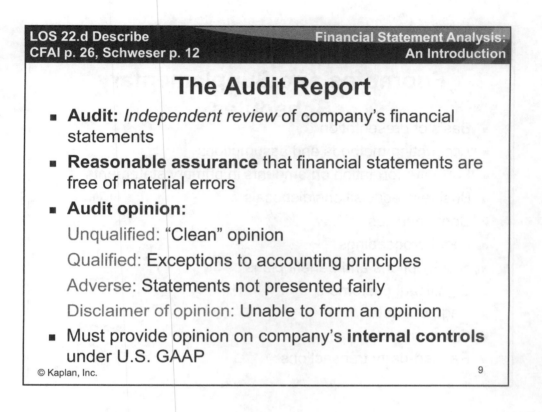

LOS 22.e Identify/Explain
CFAI p. 29, Schweser p. 13

Financial Statement Analysis: An Introduction

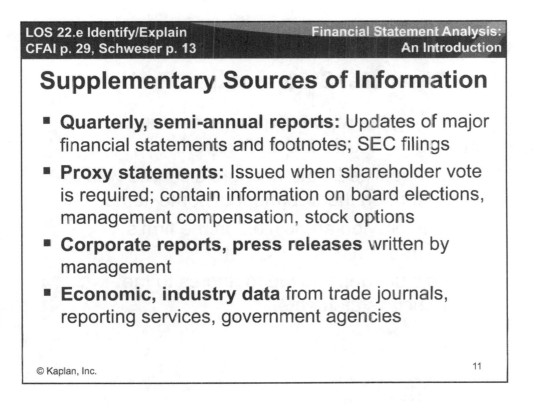

Supplementary Sources of Information

- **Quarterly, semi-annual reports:** Updates of major financial statements and footnotes; SEC filings
- **Proxy statements:** Issued when shareholder vote is required; contain information on board elections, management compensation, stock options
- **Corporate reports, press releases** written by management
- **Economic, industry data** from trade journals, reporting services, government agencies

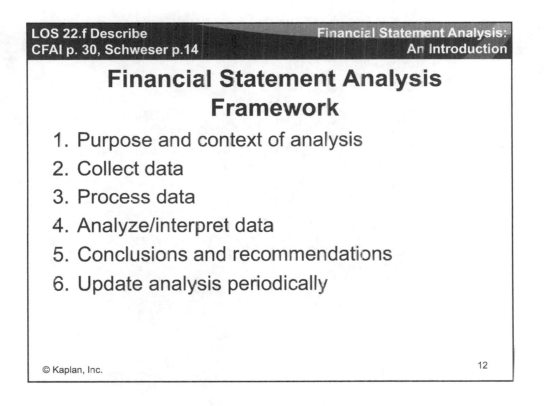

11

LOS 22.f Describe
CFAI p. 30, Schweser p.14

Financial Statement Analysis: An Introduction

Financial Statement Analysis Framework

1. Purpose and context of analysis
2. Collect data
3. Process data
4. Analyze/interpret data
5. Conclusions and recommendations
6. Update analysis periodically

12

Financial Statement Analysis:
An Introduction

Financial Statements – Problem

Regarding the report of independent auditors under U.S. GAAP, the audit report:

A. is unqualified if the auditors disagree with the firm on the treatment of some items.

B. must provide an opinion on the firm's internal controls.

C. does not apply to the footnotes to the financial statements.

13 - 1

Financial Reporting and Analysis: An Introduction

23. Financial Reporting Mechanics

Financial Reporting and Analysis

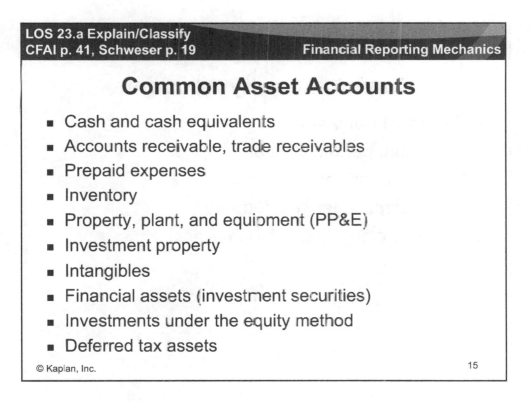

LOS 23.a Explain/Classify
CFAI p. 41, Schweser p. 19

Financial Reporting Mechanics

Common Asset Accounts

- Cash and cash equivalents
- Accounts receivable, trade receivables
- Prepaid expenses
- Inventory
- Property, plant, and equipment (PP&E)
- Investment property
- Intangibles
- Financial assets (investment securities)
- Investments under the equity method
- Deferred tax assets

15

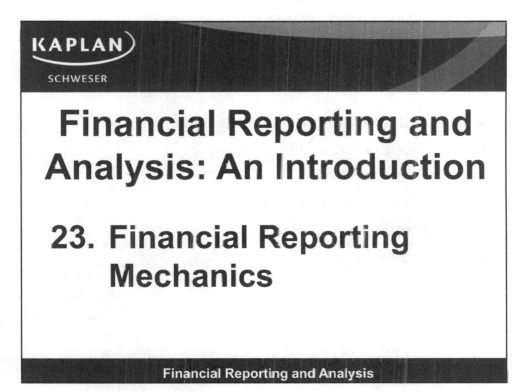

LOS 23.a Explain/Classify
CFAI p. 41, Schweser p. 19

Financial Reporting Mechanics

Common Liability Accounts

- Accounts payable, trade payables
- Provisions/accrued liabilities
- Financial liabilities
- Current and deferred tax
- Unearned revenue
- Debt payable
- Bonds

16

LOS 23.a Explain/Classify
CFAI p. 41, Schweser p. 19

Financial Reporting Mechanics

Common Equity Accounts

- Capital at par value
- Additional paid-in capital
- Retained earnings
- Other comprehensive income
- Noncontrolling (minority) interest

17

LOS 23.a Explain/Classify
CFAI p. 41, Schweser p. 19 Financial Reporting Mechanics

Common Income Statement Items

- Revenue
  - Sales
  - Gains
  - Investment income
- Expense
  - Cost of goods sold
  - SG&A (selling, general, and admin)
  - Depreciation/amortization
  - Interest
  - Tax expense
  - Losses

 18

LOS 23.b Explain
CFAI p. 44, Schweser p. 20 Financial Reporting Mechanics

Accounting Equations

Revenue – Expenses = Net income

Assets = Liabilities + Owners' equity

Assets – Liabilities = Owners' equity

Owners' equity = Contributed capital + Retained earnings

 19

LOS 23.b Explain
CFAI p. 44, Schweser p. 20 Financial Reporting Mechanics

Accounting Equations

	$m
Beginning retained earnings	X
Net income (loss)	X
Dividends	(X)
Ending retained earnings	X

 20

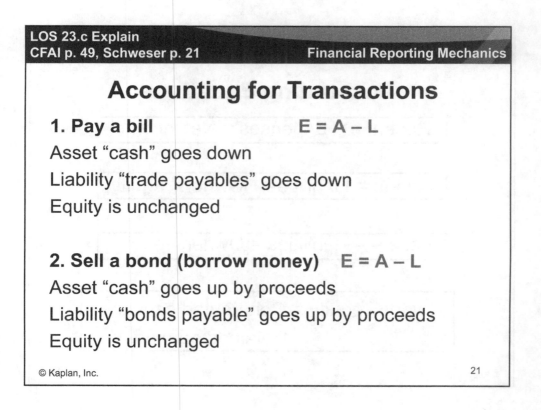

LOS 23.c Explain
CFAI p. 49, Schweser p. 21 Financial Reporting Mechanics

Accounting for Transactions

1. Pay a bill **E = A – L**
Asset "cash" goes down
Liability "trade payables" goes down
Equity is unchanged

2. Sell a bond (borrow money) **E = A – L**
Asset "cash" goes up by proceeds
Liability "bonds payable" goes up by proceeds
Equity is unchanged

 21

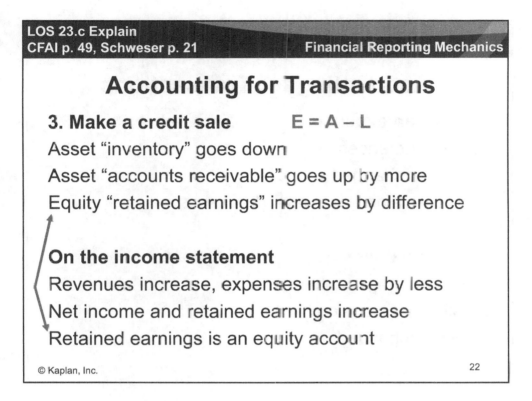

LOS 23.c Explain
CFAI p. 49, Schweser p. 21

Financial Reporting Mechanics

Accounting for Transactions

3. Make a credit sale E = A – L

Asset "inventory" goes down

Asset "accounts receivable" goes up by more

Equity "retained earnings" increases by difference

On the income statement

Revenues increase, expenses increase by less

Net income and retained earnings increase

Retained earnings is an equity account

22

LOS 23.c Explain
CFAI p. 49, Schweser p. 21

Financial Reporting Mechanics

Accounting for Transactions

4. Buy materials on credit E = A – L

Asset "inventory" increases

Liability "accounts payable" increases

Equity is unchanged

5. Issue stock E = A – L

Asset "cash" goes up

Liabilities unchanged

Equity "common stock" increases

23

LOS 23.c Explain
CFAI p. 49, Schweser p. 21
Financial Reporting Mechanics

Accounting for Transactions

6. Incur an expense E = A – L

Liability increases

Assets unchanged

Equity "retained earnings" decreases

7. Pay a liability E = A – L

Asset "cash" goes down

Liability goes down

Equity unchanged

24

LOS 23.c Explain
CFAI p. 49, Schweser p. 21
Financial Reporting Mechanics

Accounting for Transactions

8. Declare dividend E = A – L

Liability "dividends payable" increases

Assets unchanged

Equity "retained earnings" decreases

9. Pay dividend E = A – L

Asset "cash" goes down

Liability "dividends payable" goes down

Equity unchanged

25

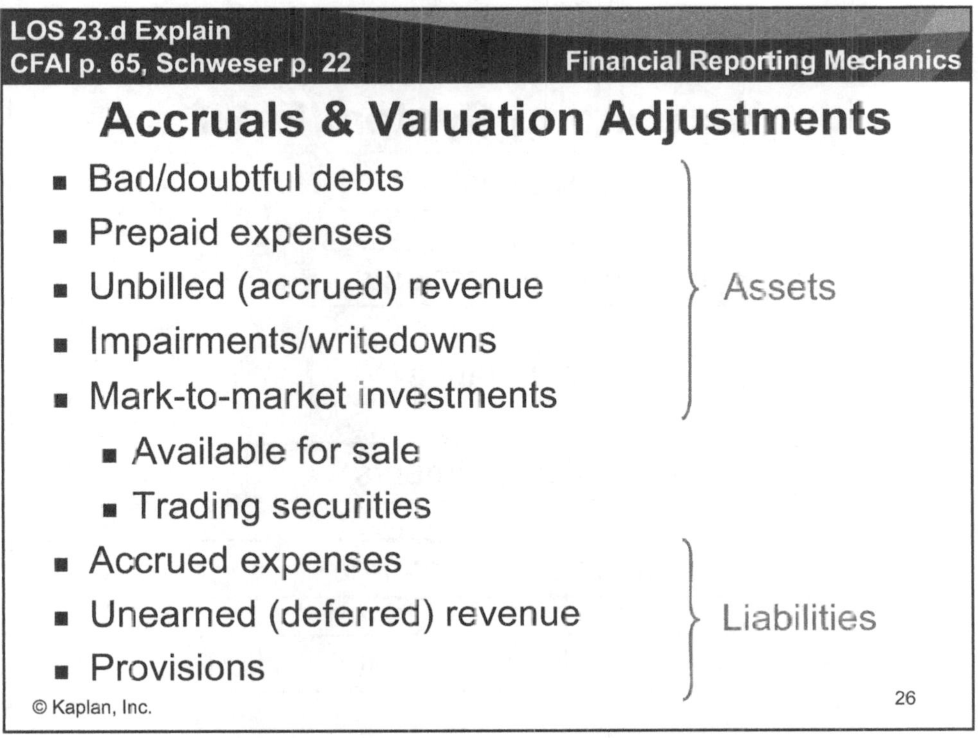
LOS 23.d Explain
CFAI p. 65, Schweser p. 22
Financial Reporting Mechanics
Accruals & Valuation Adjustments
Bad/doubtful debts
Prepaid expenses
Unbilled (accrued) revenue
Impairments/writedowns
Mark-to-market investments
Available for sale
Trading securities
Assets
Accrued expenses
Unearned (deferred) revenue
Provisions
Liabilities
© Kaplan, Inc.
26

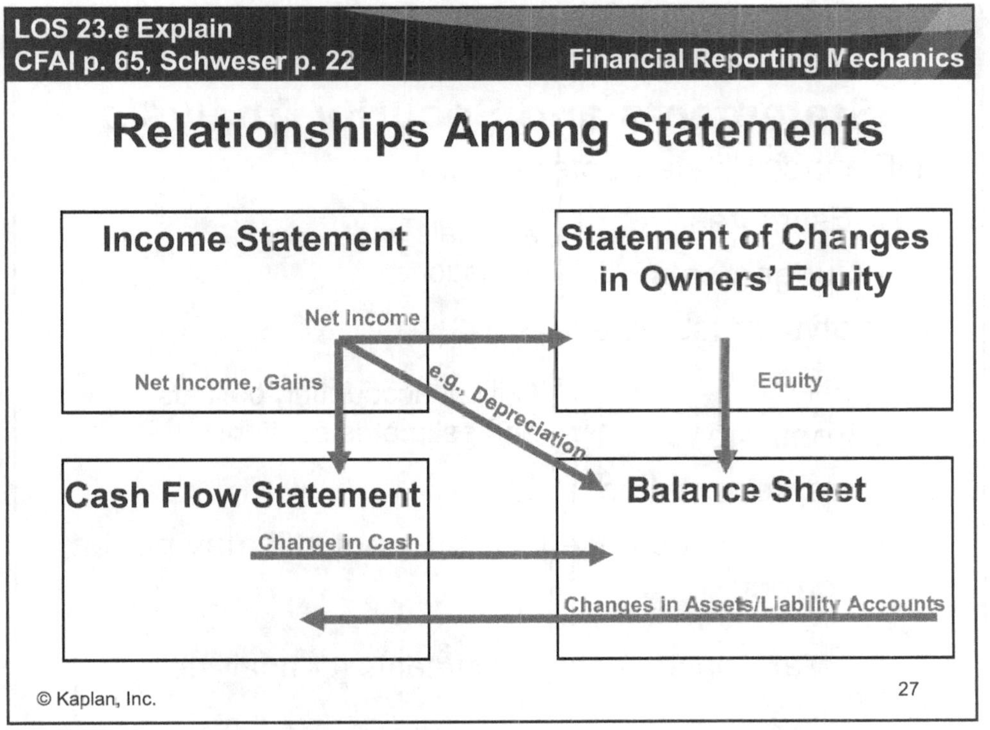
LOS 23.e Explain
CFAI p. 65, Schweser p. 22
Financial Reporting Mechanics
Relationships Among Statements
Income Statement
Net Income
Net Income, Gains
Statement of Changes in Owners' Equity
Equity
e.g., Depreciation
Cash Flow Statement
Change in Cash
Balance Sheet
Changes in Assets/Liability Accounts
© Kaplan, Inc.
27

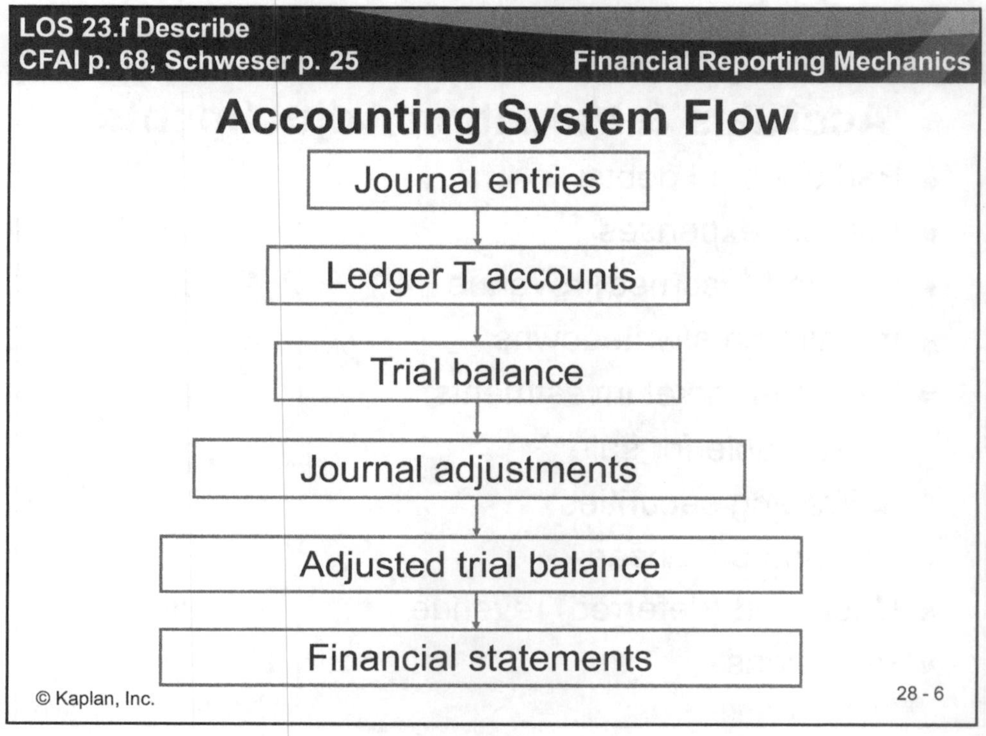
LOS 23.f Describe
CFAI p. 68, Schweser p. 25
Financial Reporting Mechanics
Accounting System Flow
Journal entries
Ledger T accounts
Trial balance
Journal adjustments
Adjusted trial balance
Financial statements
© Kaplan, Inc.
28 - 6

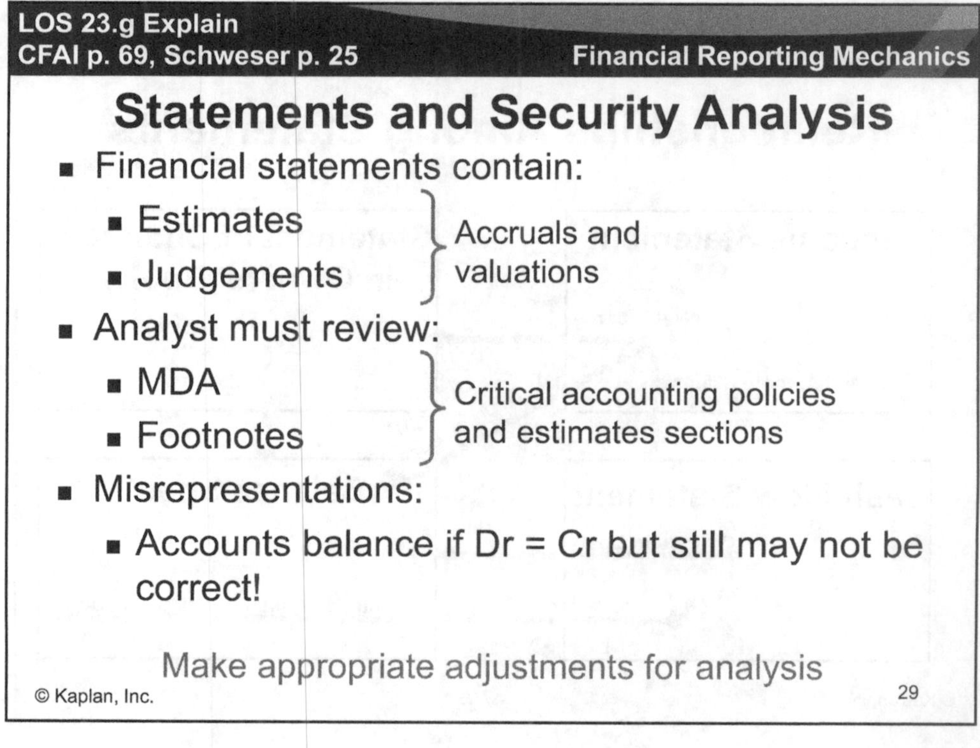
LOS 23.g Explain
CFAI p. 69, Schweser p. 25
Financial Reporting Mechanics
Statements and Security Analysis
Financial statements contain:
Estimates
Judgements
Accruals and valuations
Analyst must review:
MDA
Footnotes
Critical accounting policies and estimates sections
Misrepresentations:
Accounts balance if Dr = Cr but still may not be correct!
Make appropriate adjustments for analysis
© Kaplan, Inc.
29

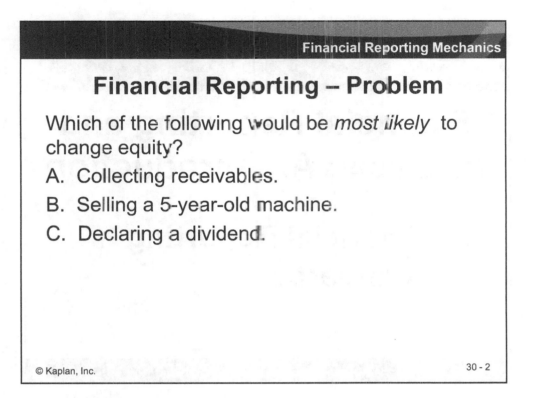

Financial Reporting Mechanics

Financial Reporting – Problem

Which of the following would be *most likely* to change equity?

A. Collecting receivables.

B. Selling a 5-year-old machine.

C. Declaring a dividend.

30 - 2

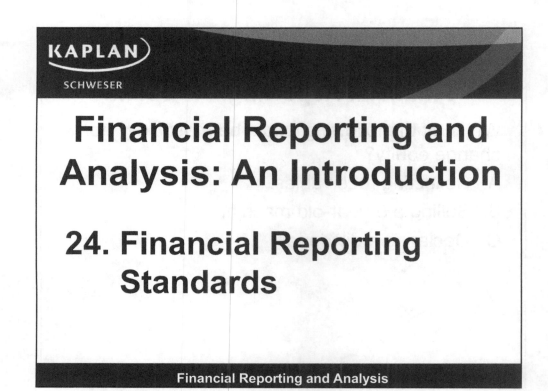

Financial Reporting and Analysis: An Introduction

24. Financial Reporting Standards

Financial Reporting and Analysis

LOS 24.a Describe
CFAI p. 94, Schweser p. 33

Financial Reporting Standards

Objective of Financial Statements

"The objective of general purpose financial is to provide financial information about the reporting entity that is useful to existing and potential investors, lenders, and other creditors in making decisions about providing resources to the entity.

Those decisions involve buying, selling or holding equity and debt instruments, and providing or settling loans and other forms of credit."

IASB Conceptual Framework (2010)

32

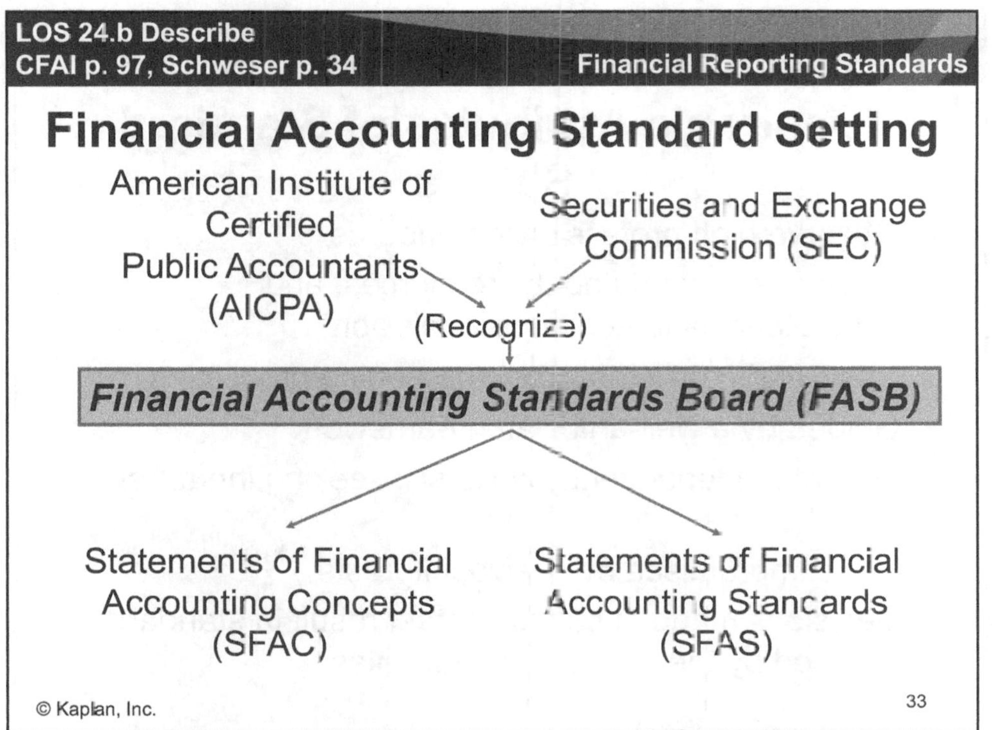

LOS 24.b Describe
CFAI p. 97, Schweser p. 34

Financial Reporting Standards

Accounting Standards

- Financial Accounting Standards Board (FASB) U.S.
- International Accounting Standards Board (IASB) most other countries

34

LOS 24.b Describe
CFAI p. 97, Schweser p. 34
Financial Reporting Standards

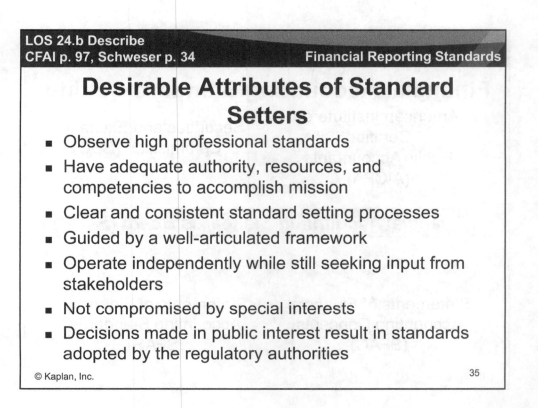

Desirable Attributes of Standard Setters

- Observe high professional standards
- Have adequate authority, resources, and competencies to accomplish mission
- Clear and consistent standard setting processes
- Guided by a well-articulated framework
- Operate independently while still seeking input from stakeholders
- Not compromised by special interests
- Decisions made in public interest result in standards adopted by the regulatory authorities

35

LOS 24.b Describe
CFAI p. 97, Schweser p. 34
Financial Reporting Standards

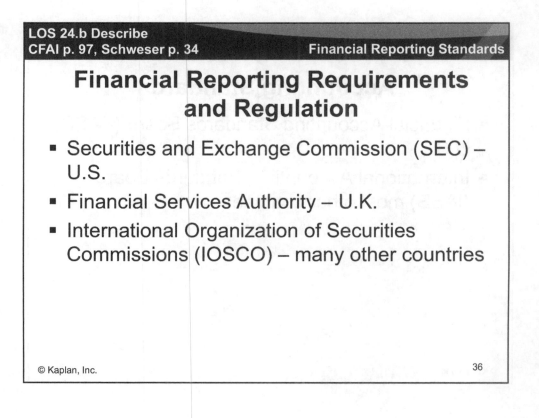

Financial Reporting Requirements and Regulation

- Securities and Exchange Commission (SEC) – U.S.
- Financial Services Authority – U.K.
- International Organization of Securities Commissions (IOSCO) – many other countries

36

LOS 24.b Describe
CFAI p. 97, Schweser p. 34
Financial Reporting Standards

International Organization of Securities Commissions (IOSCO)

- 181 members regulating 90% of the world's capital markets (SEC & FSA)
- 1998 Core Objectives of Securities Regulation:
  1. Protecting investors
  2. Ensuring fair, transparent, and efficient markets
  3. Reducing systematic risk
- Goal = uniform regulation

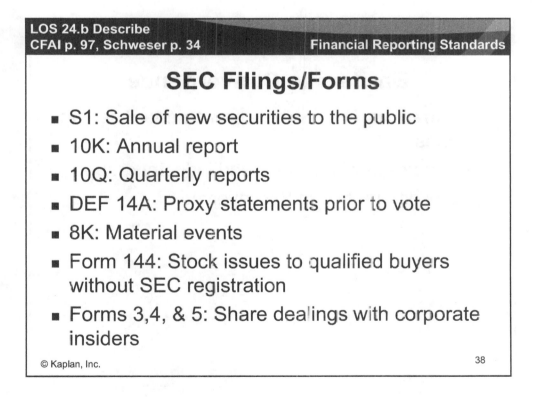

 37

LOS 24.b Describe
CFAI p. 97, Schweser p. 34
Financial Reporting Standards

SEC Filings/Forms

- S1: Sale of new securities to the public
- 10K: Annual report
- 10Q: Quarterly reports
- DEF 14A: Proxy statements prior to vote
- 8K: Material events
- Form 144: Stock issues to qualified buyers without SEC registration
- Forms 3,4, & 5: Share dealings with corporate insiders

 38

LOS 24.c Describe
CFAI p. 105, Schweser p. 35

Financial Reporting Standards

Global Convergence of Accounting Standards

Convergence refers to reducing differences in worldwide accounting standards

1. Increase comparability
2. Decrease problems and expenses of raising capital in foreign markets
3. Decrease problems and expenses of preparing consolidated financial statements for foreign subsidiaries

Accounting standards in most major countries are converging over time with IFRS

39

LOS 24.c Describe
CFAI p. 105, Schweser p. 35

Financial Reporting Standards

Barriers to Convergence

- **Differences in view** between standard setting bodies
- **Pressure** from business and industry groups
- Many different countries involved

40

LOS 24.d Describe
CFAI p. 109, Schweser p. 36

Financial Reporting Standards

IFRS Conceptual Framework

Two qualitative characteristics:

1. **Relevance**
   - The information can influence users' economic decisions or affect users' evaluations of past events or forecasts of future events
   - Information should have predictive value, confirmatory value (confirm prior expectations), or both. **Materiality** is an aspect of relevance.

41

LOS 24.d Describe
CFAI p. 109, Schweser p. 36

Financial Reporting Standards

IFRS Conceptual Framework

2. **Faithful representation**
   - Information that is faithfully representative is complete, neutral (absence of bias), and free from error

   Characteristics:
   - Comparability
   - Verifiability
   - Timeliness
   - Understandability

42

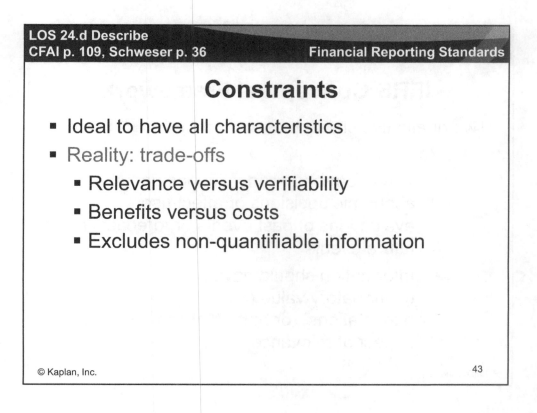

LOS 24.d Describe
CFAI p. 109, Schweser p. 36 Financial Reporting Standards

Constraints

- Ideal to have all characteristics
- Reality: trade-offs
  - Relevance versus verifiability
  - Benefits versus costs
  - Excludes non-quantifiable information

 43

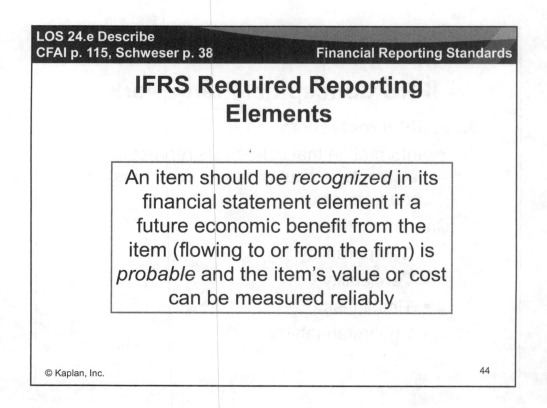

LOS 24.e Describe
CFAI p. 115, Schweser p. 38 Financial Reporting Standards

IFRS Required Reporting Elements

An item should be *recognized* in its financial statement element if a future economic benefit from the item (flowing to or from the firm) is *probable* and the item's value or cost can be measured reliably

 44

LOS 24.e Describe
CFAI p. 115, Schweser p. 38 Financial Reporting Standards

IFRS Required Reporting Elements

Assets

- Resources controlled by the entity resulting from past transactions
- Probable future economic benefits flow to enterprise

Liabilities

- Obligations resulting from past events
- Settlement results in probable resource outflow

Equity

- Shareholders' residual interest
- Assets – liabilities

 45

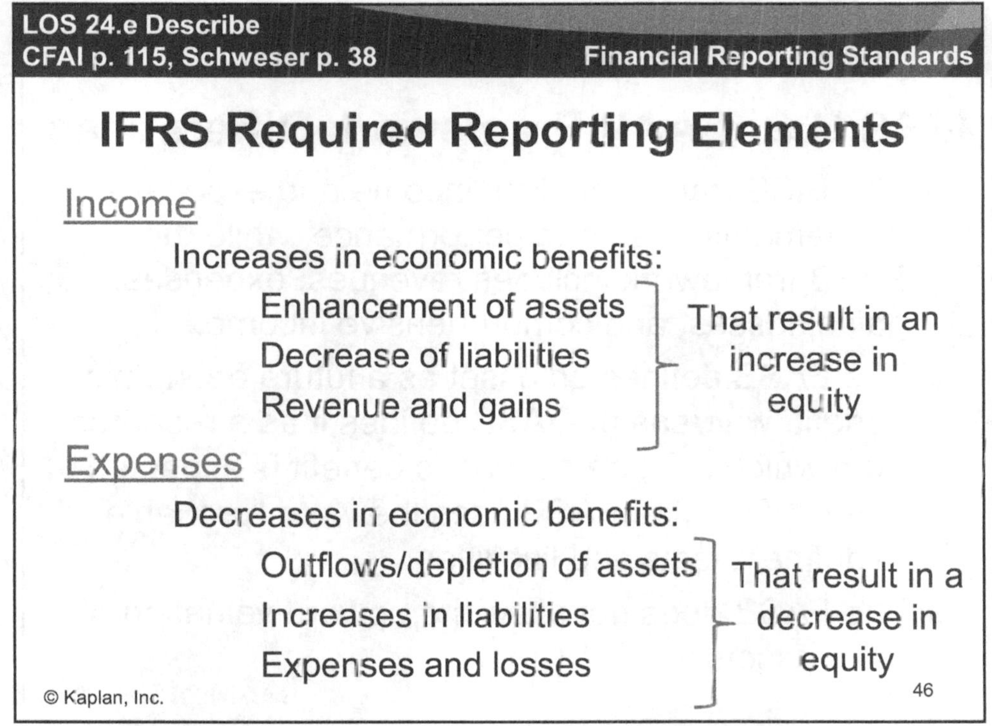

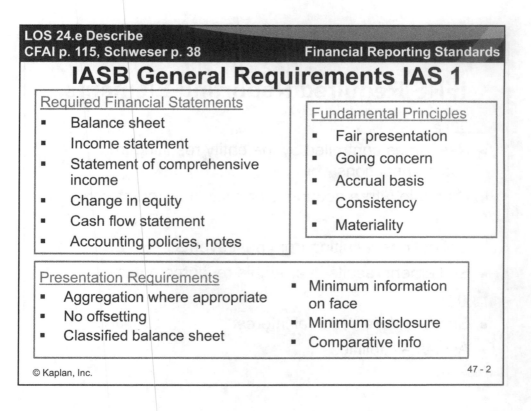

LOS 24.e Describe
CFAI p. 115, Schweser p. 38

Financial Reporting Standards

IASB General Requirements IAS 1

Required Financial Statements

- Balance sheet
- Income statement
- Statement of comprehensive income
- Change in equity
- Cash flow statement
- Accounting policies, notes

Fundamental Principles

- Fair presentation
- Going concern
- Accrual basis
- Consistency
- Materiality

Presentation Requirements

- Aggregation where appropriate
- No offsetting
- Classified balance sheet
- Minimum information on face
- Minimum disclosure
- Comparative info

47 - 2

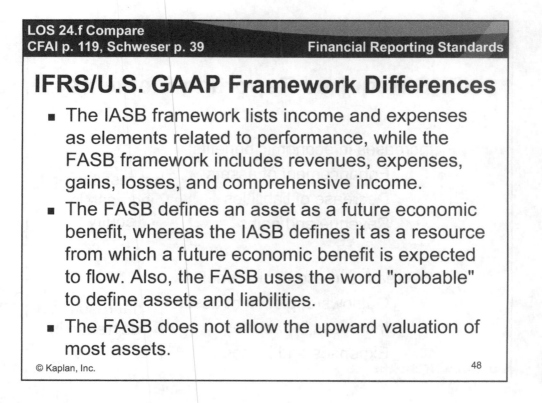

LOS 24.f Compare
CFAI p. 119, Schweser p. 39

Financial Reporting Standards

IFRS/U.S. GAAP Framework Differences

- The IASB framework lists income and expenses as elements related to performance, while the FASB framework includes revenues, expenses, gains, losses, and comprehensive income.
- The FASB defines an asset as a future economic benefit, whereas the IASB defines it as a resource from which a future economic benefit is expected to flow. Also, the FASB uses the word "probable" to define assets and liabilities.
- The FASB does not allow the upward valuation of most assets.

48

LOS 24.g Identify
CFAI p. 121, Schweser p. 39 Financial Reporting Standards

Characteristics of a Coherent Reporting Framework

- Transparency
  - Accounts reflect economic substance
  - Full disclosure and fair presentation
- Comprehensiveness
  - Full spectrum of financial transactions
  - Framework flexible enough to adapt to new transactions
- Consistency
  - Transactions measured and presented in a similar way (across companies and time)
  - Sufficient flexibility to show economic substance

 49

LOS 24.g Identify
CFAI p. 121, Schweser p. 39 Financial Reporting Standards

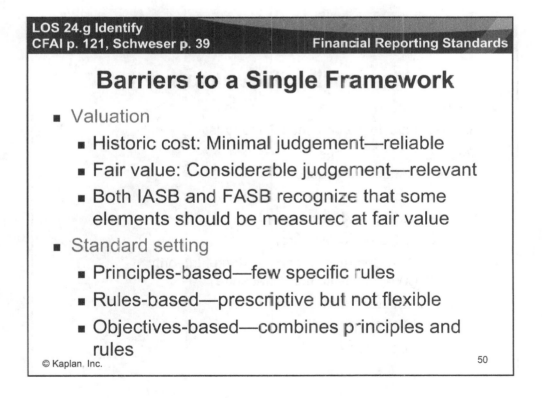

Barriers to a Single Framework

- Valuation
  - Historic cost: Minimal judgement—reliable
  - Fair value: Considerable judgement—relevant
  - Both IASB and FASB recognize that some elements should be measured at fair value
- Standard setting
  - Principles-based—few specific rules
  - Rules-based—prescriptive but not flexible
  - Objectives-based—combines principles and rules

 50

LOS 24.g Identify
CFAI p. 121, Schweser p. 39
Financial Reporting Standards

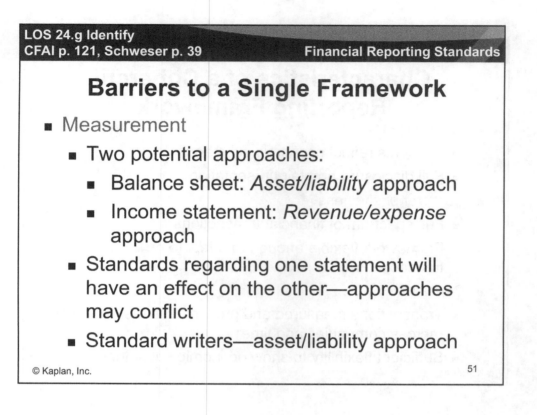

Barriers to a Single Framework

- Measurement
  - Two potential approaches:
    - Balance sheet: *Asset/liability* approach
    - Income statement: *Revenue/expense* approach
  - Standards regarding one statement will have an effect on the other—approaches may conflict
  - Standard writers—asset/liability approach

 51

LOS 24.h Explain
CFAI p. 123, Schweser p. 40
Financial Reporting Standards

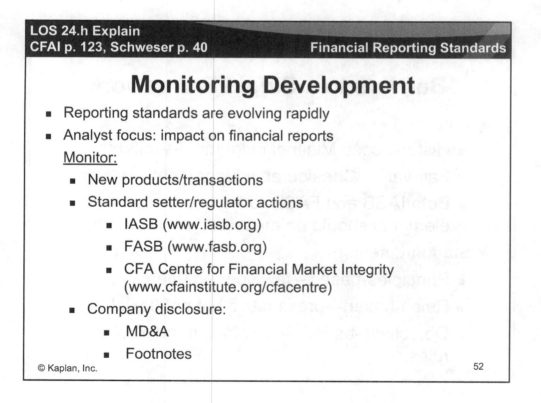

Monitoring Development

- Reporting standards are evolving rapidly
- Analyst focus: impact on financial reports

  Monitor:
  - New products/transactions
  - Standard setter/regulator actions
    - IASB (www.iasb.org)
    - FASB (www.fasb.org)
    - CFA Centre for Financial Market Integrity (www.cfainstitute.org/cfacentre)
  - Company disclosure:
    - MD&A
    - Footnotes

 52

LOS 24.i Analyze
CFAI p. 126, Schweser p. 40

Financial Reporting Standards

Company Disclosures

- Critical and significant accounting policies
- Accounting estimates
- Changes in accounting policy
- Footnote disclosure and discussion in MD&A

Analyst focus:

- What policies have been discussed?
- Do the policies cover all significant transactions?
- Which balances require significant estimation?
- Have there been changes?

53

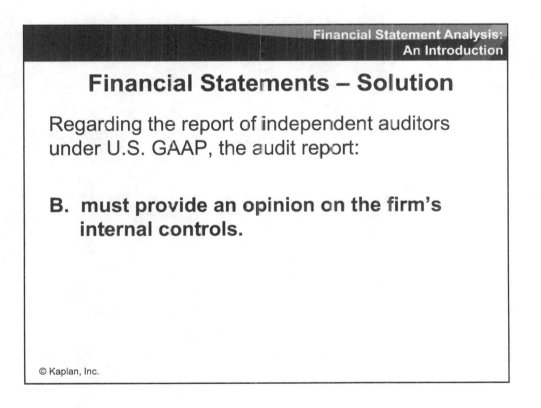

Financial Statement Analysis: An Introduction

Financial Statements – Solution

Regarding the report of independent auditors under U.S. GAAP, the audit report:

B. must provide an opinion on the firm's internal controls.

Financial Reporting Mechanics

Financial Reporting – Solution

Which of the following would be *most likely* to change equity?

C. Declaring a dividend.

Declaring a dividend will always decrease equity, as it increases a liability (dividends payable).

Study Session 8

Financial Reporting and Analysis: Income Statements, Balance Sheets, and Cash Flow Statements

Income Statements, Balance Sheets, and Cash Flow Statements

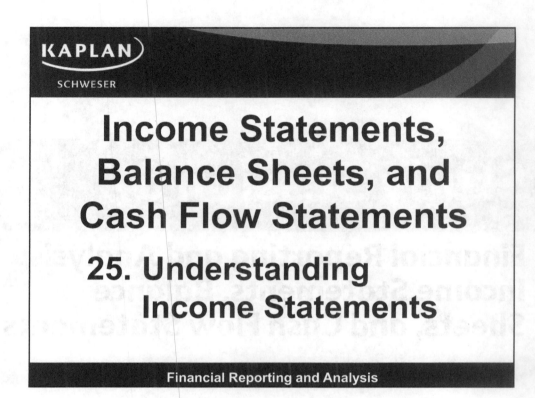

25. Understanding Income Statements

Financial Reporting and Analysis

LOS 25.a Describe
CFAI p. 140, Schweser p. 47

Understanding Income Statements

Income Statement

- Alternative names:
  - Statement of operations
  - Statement of earnings
  - Profit and loss statement

Revenue – Expenses = Net Income

- IFRS: May combine with comprehensive income items
- Two types:
  - Single step
  - Multi-step

2

LOS 25.a Describe
CFAI p. 140, Schweser p. 47
Understanding Income Statements

Income Statement

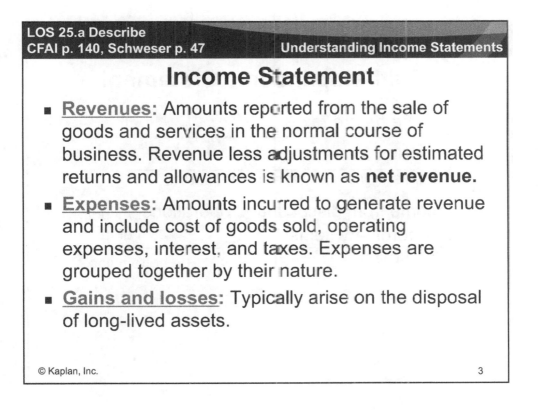

- **Revenues**: Amounts reported from the sale of goods and services in the normal course of business. Revenue less adjustments for estimated returns and allowances is known as **net revenue.**
- **Expenses**: Amounts incurred to generate revenue and include cost of goods sold, operating expenses, interest, and taxes. Expenses are grouped together by their nature.
- **Gains and losses**: Typically arise on the disposal of long-lived assets.

 3

LOS 25.a Describe
CFAI p. 140, Schweser p. 47
Understanding Income Statements

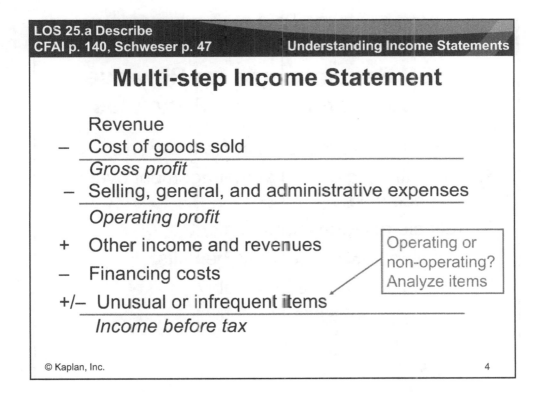

Multi-step Income Statement

	Revenue
–	Cost of goods sold
	Gross profit
–	Selling, general, and administrative expenses
	Operating profit
+	Other income and revenues
–	Financing costs
+/–	Unusual or infrequent items
	Income before tax

Operating or non-operating? Analyze items

 4

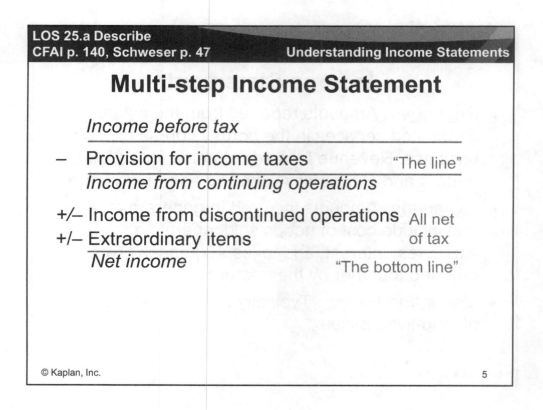

LOS 25.a Describe
CFAI p. 140, Schweser p. 47 Understanding Income Statements

Multi-step Income Statement

Income before tax

– Provision for income taxes "The line"

Income from continuing operations

+/– Income from discontinued operations All net
+/– Extraordinary items of tax

Net income "The bottom line"

 5

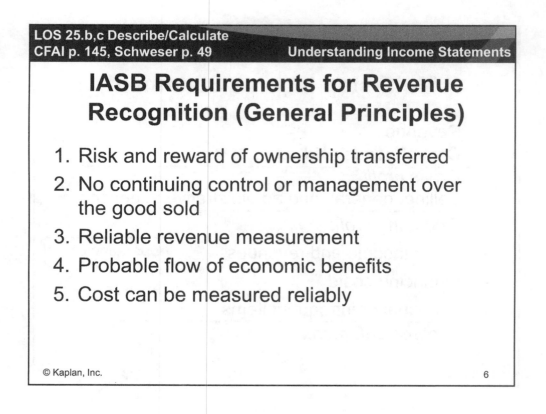

LOS 25.b,c Describe/Calculate
CFAI p. 145, Schweser p. 49 Understanding Income Statements

IASB Requirements for Revenue Recognition (General Principles)

1. Risk and reward of ownership transferred
2. No continuing control or management over the good sold
3. Reliable revenue measurement
4. Probable flow of economic benefits
5. Cost can be measured reliably

 6

LOS 25.b,c Describe/Calculate
CFAI p. 145, Schweser p. 49 Understanding Income Statements

IASB Requirements for Revenue Recognition for Services

1. When the outcome can be measured reliably, revenue will be recognized by reference to the stage of completion
2. Outcome can be measured reliably if:
   - Amount of revenue can be measured
   - Probable flow of economic benefits
   - Stage of completion can be measured
   - Cost incurred and remaining cost to complete can be measured

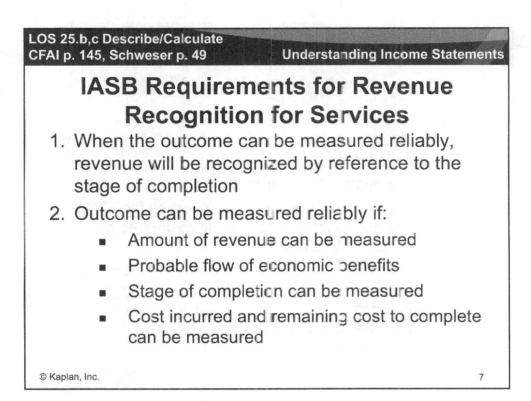

 7

LOS 25.b,c Describe/Calculate
CFAI p. 145, Schweser p. 49 Understanding Income Statements

SEC Requirements for Revenue Recognition

"Revenue should be recognized when it is realizable and earned" FASB

SEC additional guidance:

1. Evidence of an arrangement between buyer and seller
2. Completion of the earnings process, firm has delivered product or service
3. Price is determined
4. Assurance of payment, able to estimate probability of payment

 8

LOS 25.b,c Describe/Calculate
CFAI p. 145, Schweser p. 49 Understanding Income Statements

Revenue Recognition Methods

- **Sales-basis method**—used when good or service is provided at time of sale, cash, or credit with high payment probability (majority of transactions)

Exceptions (construction contracts)

1. **Percentage-of-completion method**—used for L-T projects under contract, with **reliable estimates** of revenues, costs, and completion time
2. **Completed-contract method (U.S. GAAP)**—used for L-T projects with no contract, or unreliable estimates of revenue or costs; revenue and expenses are not recognized until **project is completed** (**IFRS:** Report revenue but no profit)

 9

LOS 25.b,c Describe/Calculate
CFAI p. 145, Schweser p. 49 Understanding Income Statements

Revenue Recognition Methods

Installment sale: A firm finances a sale and payments are expected to be received over an extended period. If collectability is certain, revenue is recognized at the time of sale using the normal revenue recognition criteria.

3. **Installment sales method (U.S. GAAP)**—used when firm cannot estimate likelihood of collection, but cost of goods/services is known; revenue and profit are based on percentage of cash collected
4. **Cost recovery method (most extreme)**—used when cost of goods/services is unknown and firm cannot estimate the likelihood of collection; only recognize profit after all costs are recovered

 10

LOS 25.b,c Describe/Calculate
CFAI p. 145, Schweser p. 49 Understanding Income Statements

Percentage-of-Completion Method

Ledesma Properties Ltd. has a contract to build a hotel for $2,000,000 to be received in equal installments over 4 years. A reliable estimate of total cost of this contract is $1,600,000. During the first year, Ledesma incurred $400,000 in cost. During the second year, $500,000 of costs were incurred. The estimate of the project's total cost did not change in the second year.

Calculate the revenue and profit to be recognized in each of the first two years.

 11

LOS 25.b,c Describe/Calculate
CFAI p. 145, Schweser p. 49 Understanding Income Statements

Percentage-of-Completion Method

Cumulative revenue

$$\frac{\text{Total costs to date}}{\text{Total project cost}} \times \text{Sales price} = X$$

Revenue recognized in prior years	(X)
This period's revenue	X
Costs incurred in period	(X)
Profit recognized in period	X

 12

LOS 25.b,c Describe/Calculate
CFAI p. 145, Schweser p. 49 Understanding Income Statements

Percentage-of-Completion Method Solution

Year 1: $2,000,000 × (400,000 / 1,600,000)

Revenue = $500,000

Profit = $500,000 – $400,000 = $100,000

Year 2: $2,000,000 × (900,000 / 1,600,000) – $500,000

Revenue = $625,000

Profit = $625,000 – $500,000 = $125,000

 13 - 6

LOS 25.b,c Describe/Calculate
CFAI p. 145, Schweser p. 49 Understanding Income Statements

Completed-Contract Method

Revenue and expenses are not recognized until **project is completed**

Example: Building a hotel for $40 million, cost to build is $32 million; cost incurred in Year 1 is $6.4 million

revenue = 0; expense = 0; income = 0

On completion/final year:

revenue = $40m; expenses = $32m; income = $8m

 14

LOS 25.b,c Describe/Calculate
CFAI p. 145, Schweser p. 49 Understanding Income Statements

IFRS: Long-term Contracts With Uncertain Outcome

Revenue and expenses are recognized over the project's life; however, no profit is recorded until **project is completed**

Example: Building a hotel for €40 million, cost to build is €32 million; cost incurred in Year 1 is €6.4 million

Revenue = 6.4m; expense = 6.4m; income = 0

On completion/final year:

Income = €8m

 15

LOS 25.b,c Describe/Calculate
CFAI p. 145, Schweser p. 49 Understanding Income Statements

Percentage-of-Completion (POC) vs. Completed Contract (CC) Method

- Net income is **higher** for POC because CC does not recognize revenue until completion
  ↑ Net income → ↑ Equity (until final year)
- Income volatility is **greater** with CC method because POC recognizes some revenue and income each year instead of all at one time
- Cash flow is the **same** for both (CF is unaffected by the revenue recognition method used)

 16

LOS 25.b,c Describe/Calculate
CFAI p. 145, Schweser p. 49

Understanding Income Statements

Installment Sales Method – Example

- During 20X0, Cook, Inc. sold $20,000 of inventory on installment, with a cost of $10,000.
- During 20X0 and 20X1, Cook collected $8,000 and $12,000, respectively, of its receivables. Under the installment method, what are the sales and gross profit to be reported in each of the two years?

 17

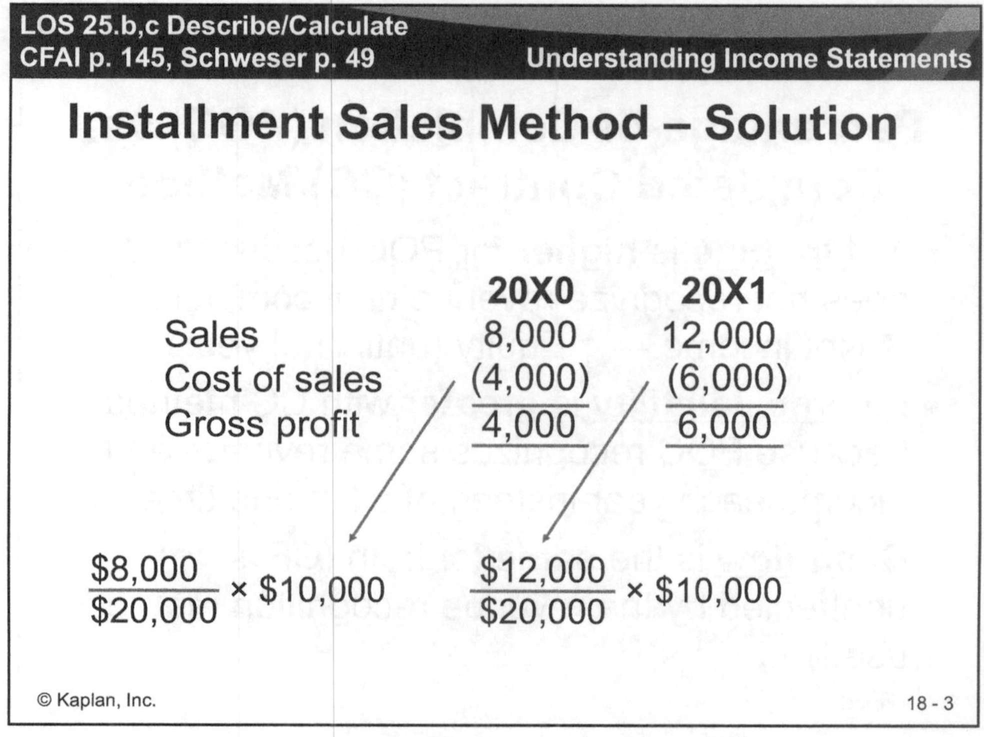

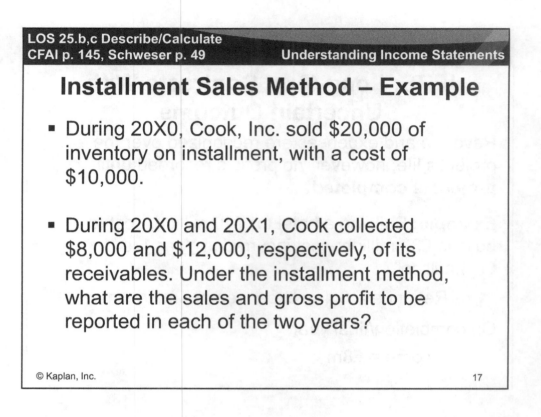

LOS 25.b,c Describe/Calculate
CFAI p. 145, Schweser p. 49 Understanding Income Statements

Cost Recovery Method – Example

During 20X0, Cook, Inc. sold $20,000 of services, but the cost of providing this service was unclear at the outset of the contract. During 20X0 and 20X1, Cook collected $8,000 and $12,000, respectively, of its receivables. The project was completed during 20X1, at which time the company had incurred total costs of $10,000.

Under the cost recovery method, what are the sales and gross profit to be reported in each of the two years?

 19

LOS 25.b,c Describe/Calculate
CFAI p. 145, Schweser p. 49 Understanding Income Statements

Cost Recovery Method – Solution

	20X0	**20X1**
Sales	8,000	12,000
Cost of sales	(8,000)	(2,000)
Gross profit	0	10,000

 20 - 3

LOS 25.b,c Describe/Calculate
CFAI p. 145, Schweser p. 49 Understanding Income Statements

Installment Sales: IFRS

- Present value of the installment payments is recognized at the time of sale
- Difference between installment payments and the discounted present value is recognized as interest over time
- If outcome of the project cannot be estimated reliably, revenue recognition under IFRS is similar to cost recovery method

 21

LOS 25.b,c Describe/Calculate
CFAI p. 145, Schweser p. 49 Understanding Income Statements

Barter

- Exchange of goods or services between two parties (no exchange of cash)
- A agrees to exchange inventory for a service provided by B
- **IFRS:** Revenue = fair value of similar non-barter transactions with unrelated parties
- **U.S. GAAP:** Revenue = fair value only if the company has received cash payments for such services historically (otherwise record sale at carrying value of asset)

 22

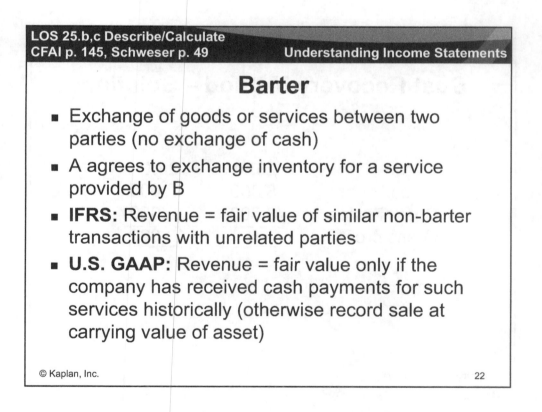

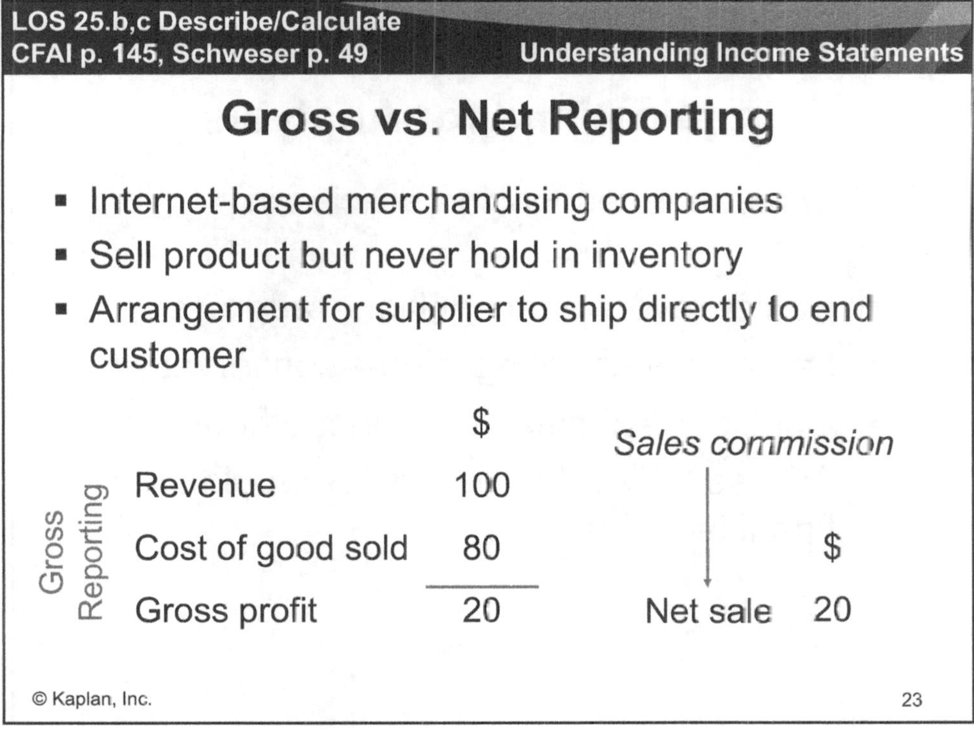

LOS 25.b,c Describe/Calculate
CFAI p. 145, Schweser p. 49 — Understanding Income Statements

Gross vs. Net Reporting

U.S. GAAP: Report gross if company:

- Is primary obligator
- Bears inventory risk
- Bears credit risk
- Can choose supplier
- Has latitude to set price

If criteria are not met, then company is acting as an agent: report net

 24

LOS 25.b,c Describe/Calculate
CFAI p. 145, Schweser p. 49

Understanding Income Statements

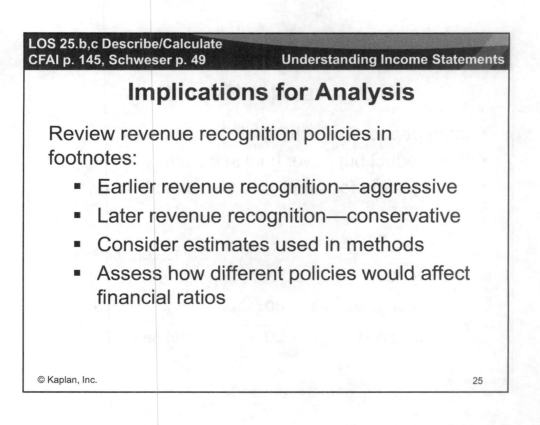

Implications for Analysis

Review revenue recognition policies in footnotes:

- Earlier revenue recognition—aggressive
- Later revenue recognition—conservative
- Consider estimates used in methods
- Assess how different policies would affect financial ratios

 25

Understanding Income Statements

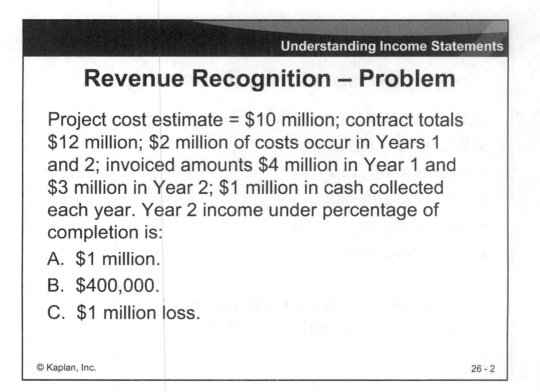

Revenue Recognition – Problem

Project cost estimate = $10 million; contract totals $12 million; $2 million of costs occur in Years 1 and 2; invoiced amounts $4 million in Year 1 and $3 million in Year 2; $1 million in cash collected each year. Year 2 income under percentage of completion is:

A. $1 million.

B. $400,000.

C. $1 million loss.

 26 - 2

LOS 25.d Describe
CFAI p. 157, Schweser p. 55
Understanding Income Statements

Expense Recognition

- Accrual basis—matching principle
  - Match costs against associated revenues
  - Examples
    - Inventory
    - Depreciation/amortization
    - Warranty expense
    - Doubtful debt expense
- Period expenses
  - Expenditures that less directly match the timing of revenues (e.g., admin costs)

 27

LOS 25.d Describe
CFAI p. 157, Schweser p. 55
Understanding Income Statements

Analysis Implications

- Inventory valuation
- Warranty expense
- Depreciation
- Amortization
- Doubtful debt provisions
- Revenue recognition

All require significant estimates and assumptions affecting net income

- Review year-on-year consistency
- Review footnotes and MD&A

 28

LOS 25.d Describe
CFAI p. 157, Schweser p. 55 Understanding Income Statements

Inventories: Matching Principle

Beginning inventory + Purchases – Ending inventory = COGS

Cost of goods sold should be matched with items sold and recorded as revenue over the period

Inventory cost flow should match goods flow

Specific identification First-in-first-out

Average cost

29

LOS 25.d Describe
CFAI p. 157, Schweser p. 55 Understanding Income Statements

Depreciation Methods

Match depreciation to asset's decrease in value over time:

- Truck cost $20,000, will run 100,000 miles—depreciate at $0.20 per mile used
- Oil tanker will last 25 years and then be sold for scrap—use straight-line depreciation
- DVDs purchased for rental decrease rapidly in value the first year—use accelerated depreciation

30

LOS 25.d Describe
CFAI p. 157, Schweser p. 55 Understanding Income Statements

Amortization

- Amortization of intangible assets (e.g., patents)
- Spreading cost over life
- If the earnings pattern cannot be established, use straight line (IAS 38)
- IFRS and U.S. GAAP firms both typically amortize straight-line with no residual value
- Goodwill not amortized—checked annually for impairment

 31

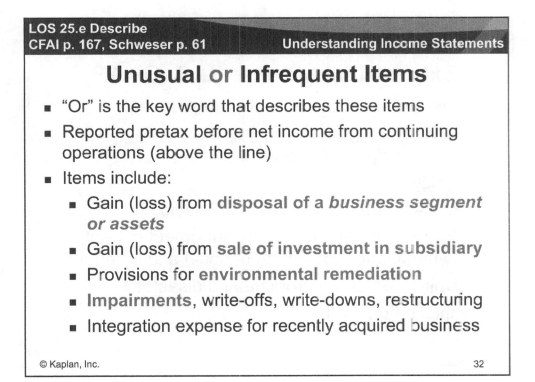

LOS 25.e Describe
CFAI p. 167, Schweser p. 61 Understanding Income Statements

Unusual or Infrequent Items

- "Or" is the key word that describes these items
- Reported pretax before net income from continuing operations (above the line)
- Items include:
  - Gain (loss) from **disposal of a *business segment or assets***
  - Gain (loss) from **sale of investment in subsidiary**
  - Provisions for **environmental remediation**
  - **Impairments**, write-offs, write-downs, restructuring
  - Integration expense for recently acquired business

 32

LOS 25.e Describe
CFAI p. 167, Schweser p. 61 Understanding Income Statements

Discontinued Operations

- Operations that management has decided to dispose of but (1) has not done so yet or (2) did so in current year after it generated profit or loss
- Reported net of taxes after net income from continuing operations (below the line)
- Assets, operations, and financing activities must be physically and operationally distinct from firm

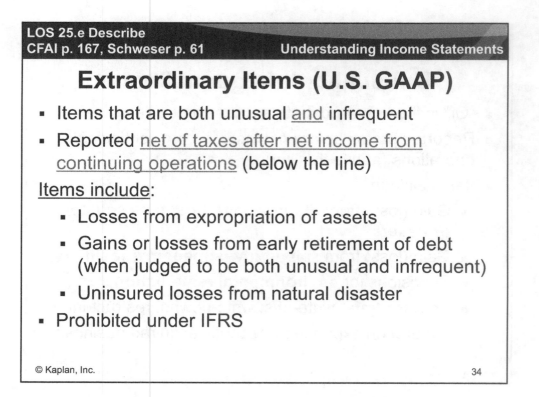

 33

LOS 25.e Describe
CFAI p. 167, Schweser p. 61 Understanding Income Statements

Extraordinary Items (U.S. GAAP)

- Items that are both unusual and infrequent
- Reported net of taxes after net income from continuing operations (below the line)

Items include:

- Losses from expropriation of assets
- Gains or losses from early retirement of debt (when judged to be both unusual and infrequent)
- Uninsured losses from natural disaster

- Prohibited under IFRS

 34

LOS 25.e Describe
CFAI p. 167, Schweser p. 61 Understanding Income Statements

Accounting Changes

- Two types of accounting changes:
  1. **Change in accounting principle** (e.g., LIFO to FIFO)
  - Retrospective application: IFRS and U.S. GAAP require prior years' data shown in the financial statements to be adjusted

 35

LOS 25.e Describe
CFAI p. 167, Schweser p. 61 Understanding Income Statements

Accounting Changes

2. **Change in accounting estimate** (e.g., change in the estimated useful life of a depreciable asset)
   - Does not require restatement of prior period earnings
   - Disclosed in footnotes
   - Typically, changes do not affect cash flow

 36

LOS 25.e Describe
CFAI p. 167, Schweser p. 61 Understanding Income Statements

Accounting Changes

Prior period adjustments

- Correcting errors or changing from an **incorrect accounting method** to one that is acceptable under GAAP
- Typically **requires restatement of prior period financial statements**
- Must **disclose** the nature of the error and its effect on net income

 37

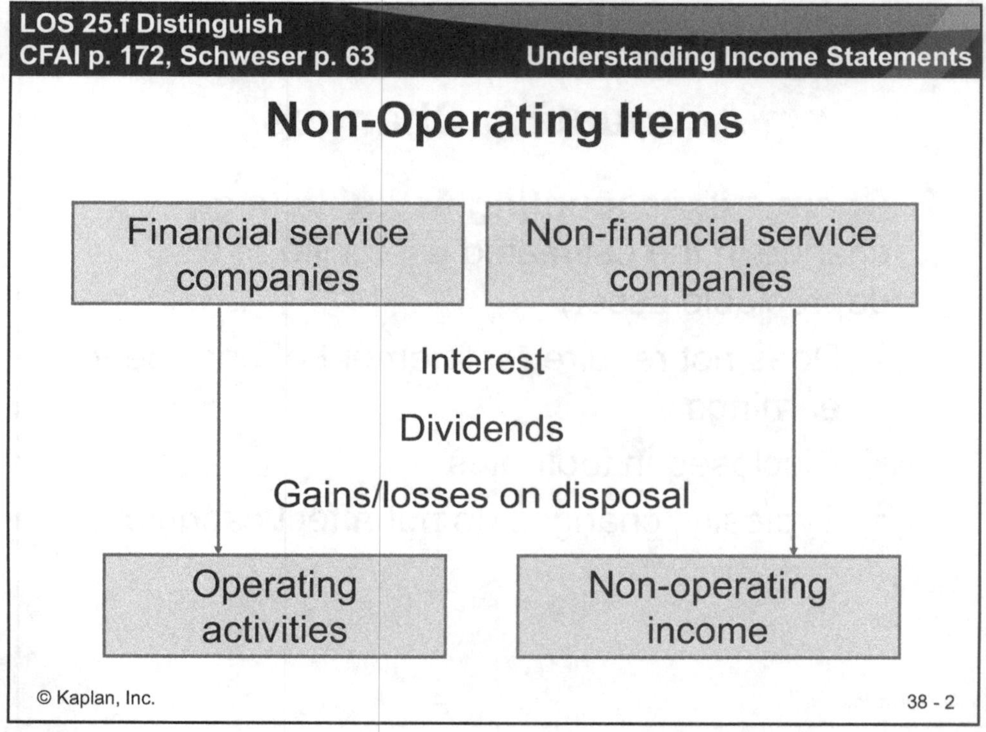

LOS 25.g,h Describe/Calculate/Interpret/Distinguish
CFAI p. 173, Schweser p. 64 Understanding Income Statements

Simple vs. Complex Capital Structures

- A simple capital structure contains no *potentially* dilutive securities
  - Firm reports only basic EPS
- A complex capital structure contains *potentially* dilutive securities
  - Firm must report both basic and diluted EPS

 39

LOS 25.g,h Describe/Calculate/Interpret/Distinguish
CFAI p. 173, Schweser p. 64 Understanding Income Statements

Dilutive vs. Antidilutive Securities

Potentially dilutive securities:

- Stock options
- Warrants
- Convertible debt
- Convertible preferred stock
- **Dilutive securities** decrease EPS if exercised or converted to common stock
- **Antidilutive securities** increase EPS if exercised or converted to common stock

 40

LOS 25.g,h Describe/Calculate/Interpret/Distinguish
CFAI p. 173, Schweser p. 64 Understanding Income Statements

Calculating Basic EPS

$$\text{Basic EPS} = \frac{\text{Net income} - \text{preferred dividends}}{\text{Weighted average \# common stock}}$$

- Net income minus preferred dividends equals earnings available to common stockholders
- Note that common stock dividends are not subtracted from net income

 41

LOS 25.g,h Describe/Calculate/Interpret/Distinguish
CFAI p. 173, Schweser p. 64 Understanding Income Statements

Stock Dividends and Stock Splits

- A 10% stock dividend increases shares outstanding by 10%
- A 2-for-1 stock split increases shares outstanding by 100%
- In calculating the weighted average shares outstanding, stock dividends and splits are applied retroactively to the beginning of the year, or the stock's issue date for new stock
- Although weighted average shares are actually based on days, the exam is likely to use months

 42

LOS 25.g,h Describe/Calculate/Interpret/Distinguish
CFAI p. 173, Schweser p. 64 Understanding Income Statements

Calculating the Weighted-Average Number of Shares Outstanding

1/1/X3	Shares outstanding	10,000
4/1/X3	Shares issued	4,000
7/1/X3	10% stock dividend	
9/1/X3	Shares repurchased	3,000

Shares adjusted for the 10% dividend:		
1/1/X3	Initial shares (× 1.1)	**11,000**
4/1/X3	Shared issued (× 1.1)	**4,400**
9/1/X3	Shares repurchased (no adj.)	**3,000**

 43 - 3

LOS 25.g,h Describe/Calculate/Interpret/Distinguish
CFAI p. 173, Schweser p. 64 Understanding Income Statements

Calculating the Weighted-Average Number of Shares Outstanding

Initial shares (11,000) (12 months)	**132,000**
Shares issued (4,400) (9 months)	**39,600**
Shares repurchased (3,000) (4 months)	**(12,000)**
Total weighted shares	**159,600**
Weighted average shares outstanding 159,600 / 12	**13,300**

 44 - 5

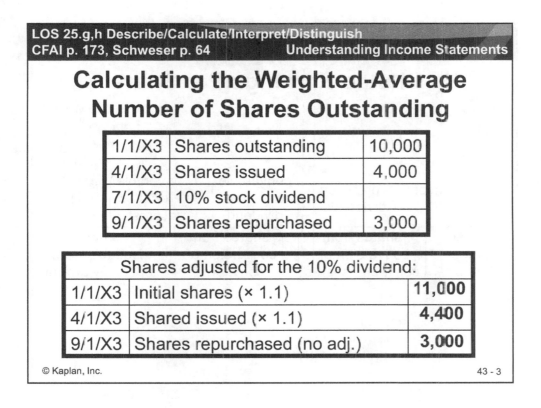

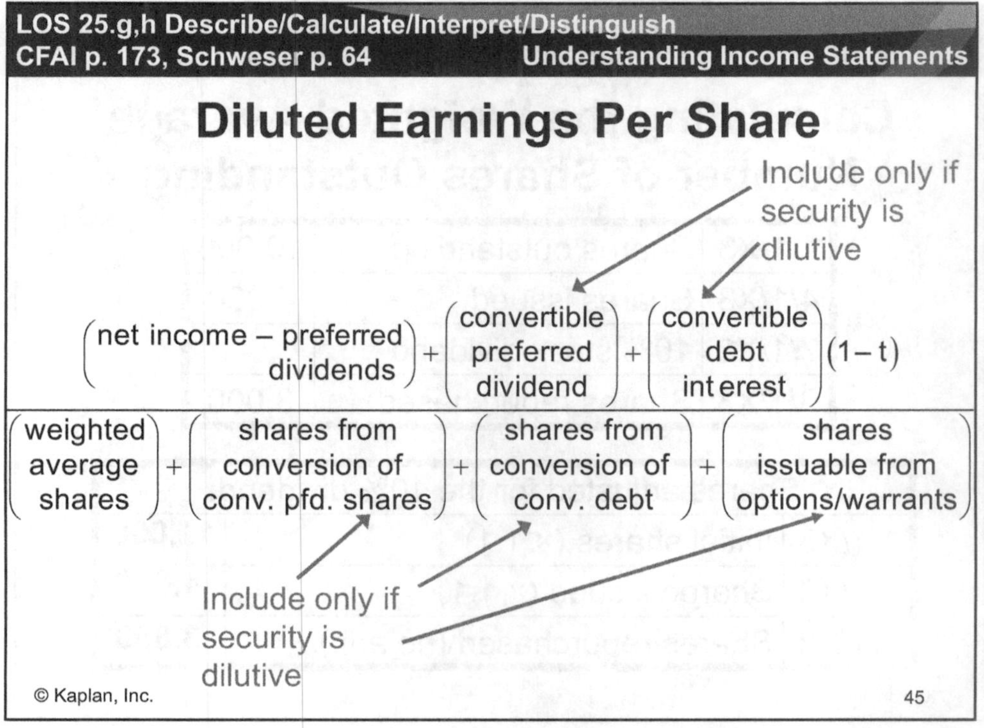

LOS 25.g,h Describe/Calculate/Interpret/Distinguish
CFAI p. 173, Schweser p. 64 Understanding Income Statements

Checking for Dilution

- Only those securities that **would reduce EPS** below basic EPS if converted are used in the calculation of diluted EPS

<u>Conv. pfd</u>: is dividends/new shares < basic?
<u>Conv. debt</u>: is interest (1 – t) / new shares < basic?
<u>Options and warrants</u>: is avg. price > ex. price?

If answer is **yes**, the security is **dilutive**

46

LOS 25.g,h Describe/Calculate/Interpret/Distinguish
CFAI p. 173, Schweser p. 64 Understanding Income Statements

Diluted EPS – Example

Earnings available to common, year to 12/31/X1	$4,000,000
Common stock	2,000,000 sh.
Basic EPS	$2.00

$5,000,000 of 7% convertible preferred stock is outstanding all year. The terms of conversion are that every $10 nominal value of preferred stock can be converted to 1.1 common shares.

Calculate fully diluted EPS for 20X1.

 47

LOS 25.g,h Describe/Calculate/Interpret/Distinguish
CFAI p. 173, Schweser p. 64 Understanding Income Statements

Convertible Preferred Stock – Example

	$
Earnings available to common	4,000,000
Add: Preferred dividend saved	350,000
	4,350,000

No. of common stock shares if preferred shares were converted:

Outstanding all year	2,000,000
On conversion $5,000,000 / 10 × 1.1	550,000
	2,550,000

 48 - 2

LOS 25.g,h Describe/Calculate/Interpret/Distinguish
CFAI p. 173, Schweser p. 64 Understanding Income Statements

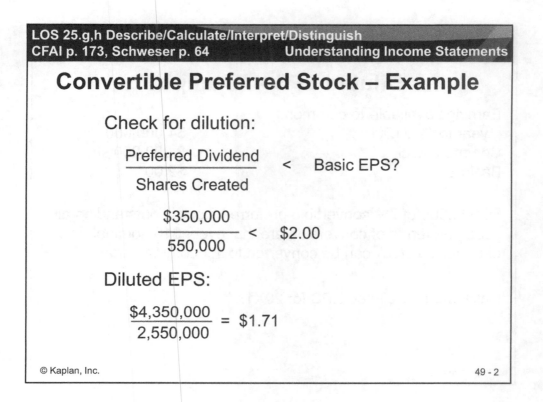

Convertible Preferred Stock – Example

Check for dilution:

$$\frac{\text{Preferred Dividend}}{\text{Shares Created}} < \text{Basic EPS?}$$

$$\frac{\$350{,}000}{550{,}000} < \$2.00$$

Diluted EPS:

$$\frac{\$4{,}350{,}000}{2{,}550{,}000} = \$1.71$$

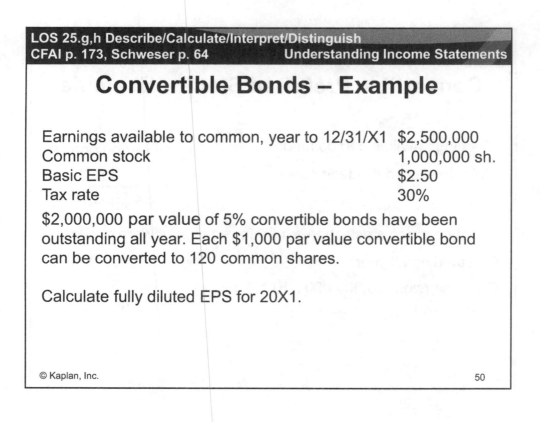

 49 - 2

LOS 25.g,h Describe/Calculate/Interpret/Distinguish
CFAI p. 173, Schweser p. 64 Understanding Income Statements

Convertible Bonds – Example

Earnings available to common, year to 12/31/X1	$2,500,000
Common stock	1,000,000 sh.
Basic EPS	$2.50
Tax rate	30%

$2,000,000 par value of 5% convertible bonds have been outstanding all year. Each $1,000 par value convertible bond can be converted to 120 common shares.

Calculate fully diluted EPS for 20X1.

 50

LOS 25.g,h Describe/Calculate/Interpret/Distinguish
CFAI p. 173, Schweser p. 64 Understanding Income Statements

Diluted EPS – Convertible Bond – Example

	$	$
Earnings available to common		2,500,000
Add: Interest saved	100,000	
Less: Tax @ 30%	(30,000)	
		70,000
		2,570,000

No. of common shares if bonds were converted:	
Outstanding	1,000,000
On conversion $2,000,000 / $1,000 × 120	240,000
	1,240,000

 51 - 3

LOS 25.g,h Describe/Calculate/Interpret/Distinguish
CFAI p. 173, Schweser p. 64 Understanding Income Statements

Diluted EPS – Convertible Bond – Solution

Check for dilution:

$$\frac{\text{Interest savings } (1-t)}{\text{Shares created}} < \text{Basic EPS?}$$

$$\frac{\$70{,}000}{240{,}000} < \$2.50$$

Diluted EPS:

$$\frac{\$2{,}570{,}000}{1{,}240{,}000} = \$2.07$$

 52 - 2

LOS 25.g,h Describe/Calculate/Interpret/Distinguish
CFAI p. 173, Schweser p. 64 Understanding Income Statements

Dilutive Stock Options – Treasury Stock Method

Dilutive only when the exercise price is less than the average market price

STEPS

1. Calculate number of common shares created if options are exercised
2. Calculate cash received from exercise
3. Calculate number of shares that can be purchased at the average market price with sale proceeds
4. Calculate net increase in common shares outstanding

 53

LOS 25.g,h Describe/Calculate/Interpret/Distinguish
CFAI p. 173, Schweser p. 64 Understanding Income Statements

Dilutive Employee Stock Options— Example

Earnings for equity in year to 31/Dec/X1	$1,200,000
Weighted average no. of common stock shares	500,000
Average price of common stock during year	$20
Exercise price	$15
Number of options outstanding in the year	100,000
Basic EPS	**$2.40**

Calculate diluted EPS for 20X1.

 54

LOS 25.g,h Describe/Calculate/Interpret/Distinguish
CFAI p. 173, Schweser p. 64 Understanding Income Statements

Dilutive Stock Options – Example

Step 1 – Assume all options are exercised

Shares issued = 100,000

Step 2 – Calculate Cash Proceeds

Proceeds if all options exercised: 100,000 × $15 = $1,500,000

Step 3 – Calculate number of shares that can be bought at average price

$$\frac{\$1,500,000}{\$20} = 75,000 \text{ shares}$$

Step 4 – Calculate Net Increase In Common Stock

Total shares needed	100,000
Shares "purchased" with proceeds	75,000
Number of new shares needed	25,000

 55 - 4

LOS 25.g,h Describe/Calculate/Interpret/Distinguish
CFAI p. 173, Schweser p. 64 Understanding Income Statements

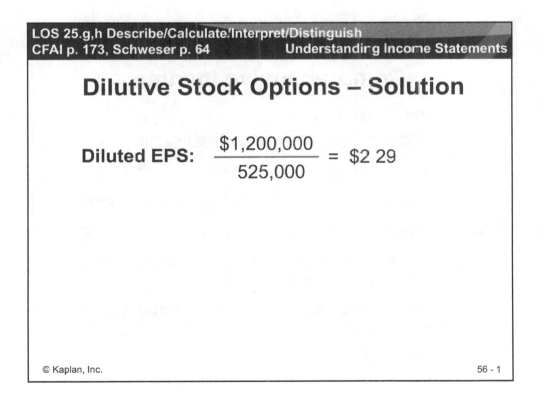

Dilutive Stock Options – Solution

Diluted EPS: $\frac{\$1,200,000}{525,000} = \$2\ 29$

 56 - 1

LOS 25.i,j Convert/Evaluate
CFAI p. 182, Schweser p. 73 Understanding Income Statements

Vertical Common-Size Income Statements

$$\frac{\text{Income statement account}}{\text{Sales}} \quad \textit{e.g.,} \quad \frac{\textit{Marketing expense}}{\textit{Sales}}$$

- Converts income statement to relative percentages
- Useful for comparing entities of differing sizes
- Compare % to strategy in MD&A
- Time series or cross-section use
- Gross and net profit margin are common-size ratios

 57

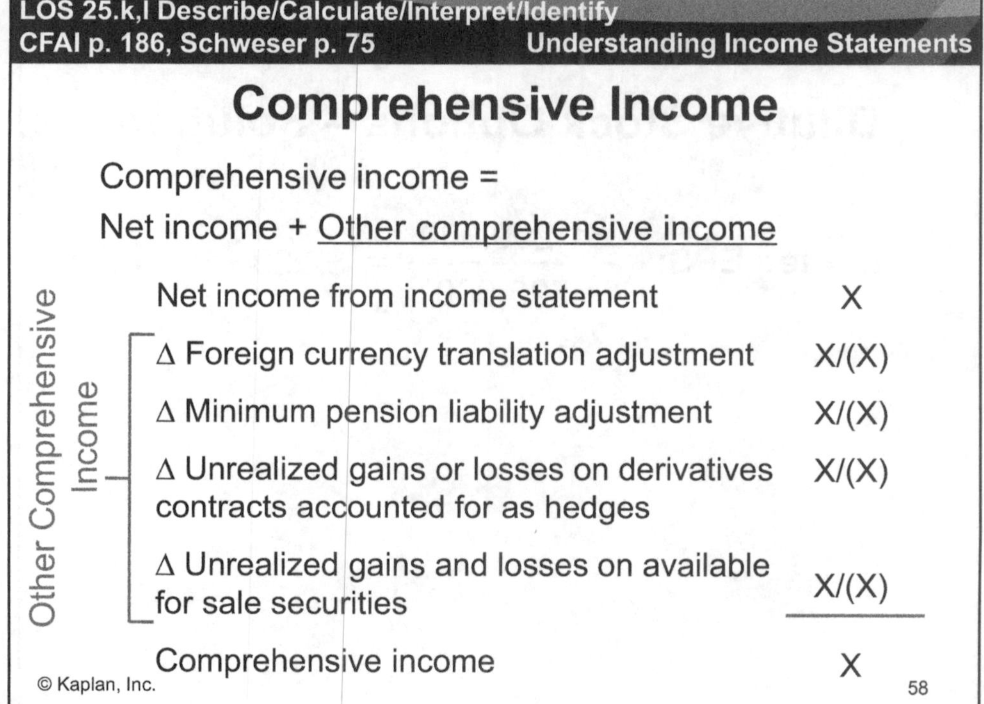

LOS 25.k,l Describe/Calculate/Interpret/Identify
CFAI p. 186, Schweser p. 75
Understanding Income Statements
Comprehensive Income
Comprehensive income =
Net income + Other comprehensive income
Net income from income statement X
Other Comprehensive Income
Δ Foreign currency translation adjustment X/(X)
Δ Minimum pension liability adjustment X/(X)
Δ Unrealized gains or losses on derivatives contracts accounted for as hedges X/(X)
Δ Unrealized gains and losses on available for sale securities X/(X)
Comprehensive income X
© Kaplan, Inc.
58

Understanding Income Statements

Weighted-Average Shares – Problem

Jan 1 10,000 shares

Mar 1 3,000 shares issued

July 1 20% stock dividend

Nov 1 3,000 shares repurchased

The weighted average number of shares outstanding over the year equals:

A. 12,000.

B. 11,300.

C. 14,500.

 59 - 2

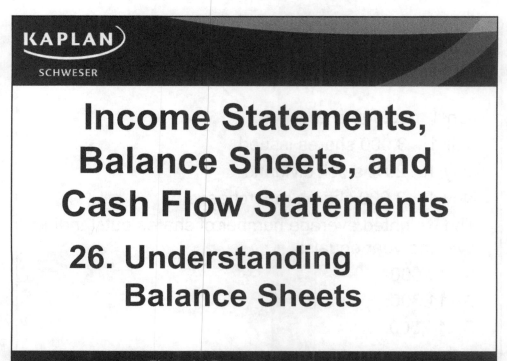

Income Statements, Balance Sheets, and Cash Flow Statements

26. Understanding Balance Sheets

Financial Reporting and Analysis

LOS 26.a Describe
CFAI p. 200, Schweser p. 86 — Understanding Balance Sheets

Components and Format of Balance Sheet

Balance Sheet	$m		$m
Current assets		**Current liabilities**	70
Cash	50	**Long-term liabilities**	180
Others	100		250
	150	**Owners' equity**	
Long-lived assets		Contributed capital	100
Investments	20	Retained earnings	70
PP&E	200		170
Intangibles	50	**Liabilities and equity**	420
Total assets	420		

 61

LOS 26.a Describe
CFAI p. 200, Schweser p. 86

Understanding Balance Sheets

Assets

Asset recognition:

- Probable future flow of future economic benefit to the entity
- Measurable with reliability

Assets Disclosed on the B/S

- Cash and equivalents
- Inventories
- Trade and other receivables
- Prepaid expenses
- Financial assets
- Deferred tax assets
- Property, plant, and equipment
- Investment property
- Intangible assets
- Equity a/c investments
- Natural resources
- Assets held for sale

62

LOS 26.a Describe
CFAI p. 200, Schweser p. 86

Understanding Balance Sheets

Liabilities

Liability recognition:

- Probable sacrifice of future economic benefit to the entity as a result of past transactions/events
- Amounts received but not reported as revenue in the income statement (deferred/unearned revenue)
- Amounts reported as expenses but which have not been paid

Liabilities Disclosed on the B/S

- Bank borrowings
- Notes payable
- Provisions
- Unearned revenues
- Accounts payable
- Financial liabilities
- Accrued liabilities
- Deferred tax liabilities

63

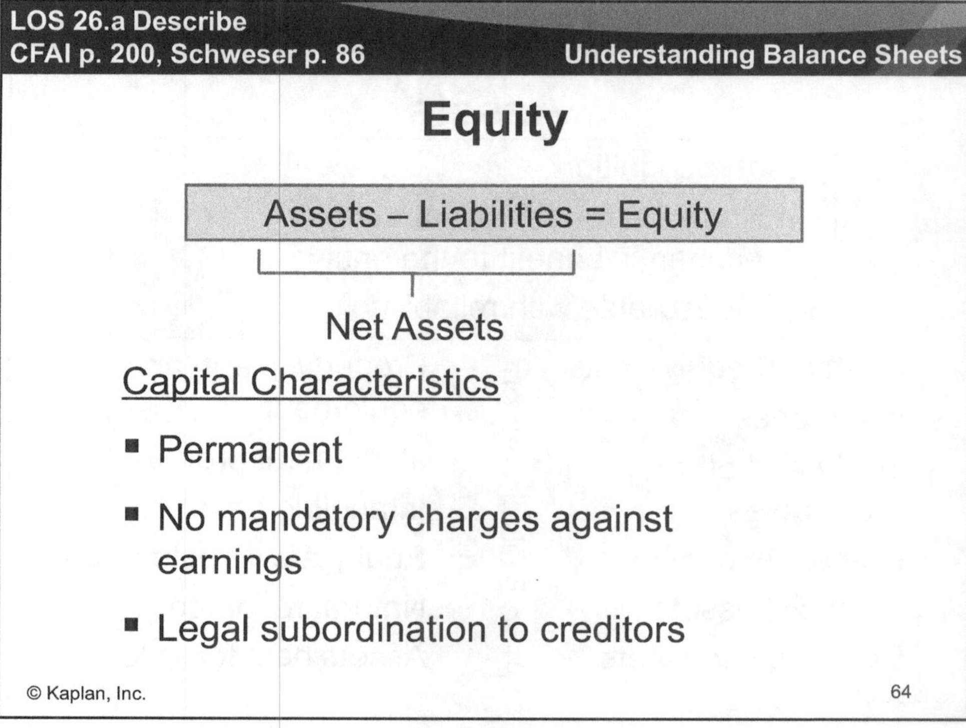

LOS 26.b Describe
CFAI p. 200, Schweser p. 87 — Understanding Balance Sheets

Balance Sheet Analysis

Uses of balance sheet analysis

- Assessing liquidity, solvency, and ability to make distributions to shareholders

Limitations

- Mixed measurement conventions:
  - Historic cost
  - Amortized cost
  - Fair value
- Fair values may change after balance sheet date
- <u>Off-balance-sheet</u> assets and liabilities

 65

LOS 26.c Describe
CFAI p. 201, Schweser p. 87
Understanding Balance Sheets

Balance Sheet Format

- Report format
  - Assets, liabilities, and equity in a single column
- Account format
  - Assets on the left
  - Liabilities and equity on the right
- Classified balance sheet
  - Grouping of accounts into sub-categories:
    - Current vs. non-current
    - Financial vs. non-financial
  - Liquidity-based presentation (financial institutions)

66

LOS 26.d,e Distinguish/Describe
CFAI p. 204, Schweser p. 87
Understanding Balance Sheets

Current Assets

- **Current assets** include cash and other assets that will likely be converted into cash or used up within one year or one operating cycle, whichever is greater
- The **operating cycle** is the time it takes to produce or purchase inventory, sell the product, and collect the cash
- Current assets presented in the order of liquidity
- Current assets reveal information about the operating activities/capacity of the firm

67

LOS 26.d,e Distinguish/Describe
CFAI p. 204, Schweser p. 87
Understanding Balance Sheets

Current Assets

- Cash and cash equivalents: amortized cost or fair value
- Marketable securities: amortized cost or fair value
- Accounts receivable/trade receivables: net realizable value
- Inventories:
  - Raw materials, work in process, finished goods
  - Manufacturing (standardized costs)
  - Cost flow methodology (FIFO, Avco, LIFO)
- Prepaid expenses: historic cost
- Deferred tax assets: net of valuation allowance

68

LOS 26.d,e Distinguish/Describe
CFAI p. 204, Schweser p. 87
Understanding Balance Sheets

Inventory—IFRS

Lower of cost or net realizable value

All standard costs of bringing the inventory to its current location and condition

Excludes:
- Abnormal amounts
- Storage costs
- Admin overheads
- Selling costs

NRV	
Estimated selling price	X
Estimated cost of completion	(X)
Selling costs	(X)
	X

U.S. GAAP: Lower of cost or market value

69

LOS 26.d,e Distinguish/Describe
CFAI p. 204, Schweser p. 87 Understanding Balance Sheets

Noncurrent Assets

- Assets held for continuing use within the business, not resale
- Assets not consumed or disposed of in the current period
- Represent the infrastructure from which the entity operates
- Provides information on the firm's investing activities

 70

LOS 26.d,e Distinguish/Describe
CFAI p. 204, Schweser p. 87 Understanding Balance Sheets

Accounting for Long-Term Assets

Long-term assets convey benefits over time

- **Tangible assets** (e.g., land, buildings, equipment, natural resources)
- **Intangible assets** (e.g., copyrights, patents, trademarks, franchises, and goodwill)
- **Investment property (IFRS only)**—generates investment income or capital appreciation

Plant, property, and equipment recorded at purchase cost including shipping and installation, or construction cost including labor, materials, overhead, and interest

 71

LOS 26.d,e Distinguish/Describe
CFAI p. 204, Schweser p. 87 Understanding Balance Sheets

Depreciation and Depletion

- **Tangible assets** have decreased value over time: **depreciation** is the allocation of the cost of tangible assets over time; land is not depreciated
- **Natural resources** are used up over time: **depletion** is the allocation of the cost (per unit) of natural resources as they are used
- Balance sheet (book) values are:

  Historical cost less accumulated depreciation or depletion, unless asset values are **impaired** (U.S. GAAP & IFRS)

  Fair value less any accumulated depreciation (IFRS)

 72

LOS 26.d,e Distinguish/Describe
CFAI p. 204, Schweser p. 87 Understanding Balance Sheets

Intangible Assets

- Identifiable intangible
  - Can be acquired singularly, linked to rights and privileges having finite benefit periods
  - Amortized over estimated useful life
- Unidentifiable intangible
  - Cannot be acquired singularly and has indefinite benefit period (e.g., goodwill)
  - Not amortized
  - Annual impairment review

 73

LOS 26.d,e Distinguish/Describe
CFAI p. 204, Schweser p. 87 Understanding Balance Sheets

Intangible Assets

- May only be recognized if they can be measured reliably
- Generally excludes internally generated intangibles—subjectivity
- Typical intangibles:
  - Purchased patents and copyrights
  - Purchased brands and trademarks
  - Purchased franchise and licence costs
  - Direct response advertising
  - Goodwill
  - Computer software development costs

 74

LOS 26.d,e Distinguish/Describe
CFAI p. 204, Schweser p. 87 Understanding Balance Sheets

Expensed Items

- Internally generated brands, mastheads, publishing titles, customer lists, etc.
- Start-up costs
- Training costs
- Administrative and general overhead
- Advertising and promotion
- Relocation and reorganization costs
- Redundancy and termination costs
- Research and development (Development may be capitalized under IFRS)

 75

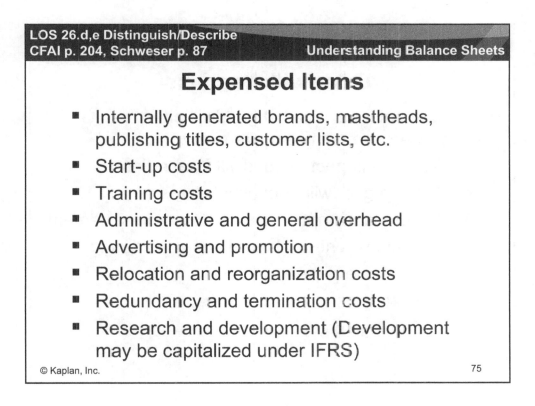

LOS 26.d,e Distinguish/Describe
CFAI p. 204, Schweser p. 87 — Understanding Balance Sheets

Goodwill

Goodwill is the difference between acquisition price and the fair market value of the acquired firm's net assets

The additional amount paid represents the amount paid for assets not recorded on the balance sheet

	$
Acquisition price	X
FMV net assets acquired	(X) ← Fair value involves management discretion—goodwill is not amortized!
Goodwill	X

 76

LOS 26.d,e Distinguish/Describe
CFAI p. 204, Schweser p. 87 — Understanding Balance Sheets

Goodwill Analysis

- Impairment indicates that goodwill often results from overpayment to acquire entity
- Remove the impact of goodwill from ratios
  - Remove goodwill from assets
  - Remove any impairment from income statement
  - Evaluate business acquisitions considering:
    - Purchase price
    - Net assets
    - Earnings prospects

 77

LOS 26.d,e Distinguish/Describe
CFAI p. 204, Schweser p. 87 Understanding Balance Sheets

Financial Assets/Liabilities

- Stocks
- Bonds
- Receivables
- Notes receivable
- Notes payable
- Loans
- Derivatives

 78

LOS 26.d,e Distinguish/Describe
CFAI p. 204, Schweser p. 87 Understanding Balance Sheets

Fair Value Assets and Liabilities

Financial assets

- Trading securities
- Available-for-sale securities
- Derivatives (standalone or embedded in a non-derivative instrument)
- Assets with fair value exposures hedged by derivatives

Financial liabilities

- Derivatives
- Non-derivative investments with fair value exposures hedged by derivatives

 79

LOS 26.d,e Distinguish/Describe
CFAI p. 204, Schweser p. 87 Understanding Balance Sheets

Cost or Amortized Cost

Financial assets

- Unlisted instruments
- Held-to-maturity investments
- Loans
- Receivables

Financial liabilities

- All other liabilities (e.g., bonds, notes payable, etc.)

 80

LOS 26.d,e Distinguish/Describe
CFAI p. 204, Schweser p. 87 Understanding Balance Sheets

Marketable Securities

Classification of securities based on company's intent with regard to eventual sale:

Held-to-maturity securities

- Debt securities which the company intends to hold to maturity
- Securities are carried at cost
- I/S income and realized gains/(losses) on disposal

Available-for-sale securities

- May be sold to satisfy company needs
- Debt or equity
- Current or non-current
- Carried on balance sheet at market value
- Income statement same as HTM method

 81

LOS 26.d,e Distinguish/Describe
CFAI p. 204, Schweser p. 87 Understanding Balance Sheets

Marketable Securities

Trading securities

- Acquired for the purpose of selling in the near term
- Carried on the balance sheet as current assets at market value
- Income statement includes dividends, realized and unrealized gains/losses

 82

LOS 26.d,e Distinguish/Describe
CFAI p. 204, Schweser p. 87 Understanding Balance Sheets

Marketable Securities Example

Ellerslie, Inc. purchased 30 5% annual-pay, $1,000 face value bonds on January 1, 20x4 at par. The market price of the bonds on December 31, 20x4 was $1,010.

Interest on the bonds of 30 × 0.05 × $1,000 = $1,500 was paid during the year.

What are the balance sheet and income statement entries for 20x4 if these bonds are classified by the firm as held-to-maturity, available-for-sale, or trading securities?

 83

LOS 26.d,e Distinguish/Describe
CFAI p. 204, Schweser p. 87 Understanding Balance Sheets

Marketable Securities Example

Treatment of interest received

- The interest received, $1,500, will be **reported as income** on the income statement for 20x4, regardless of how the securities are classified by the firm

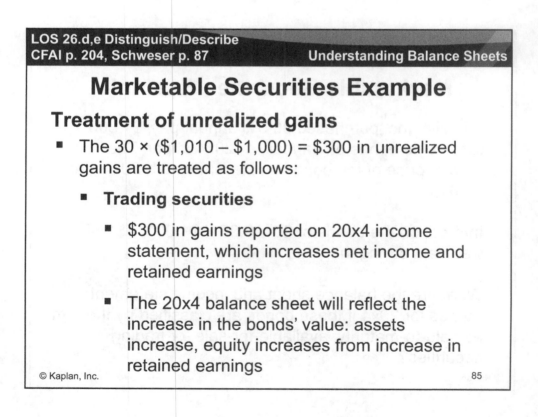

 84

LOS 26.d,e Distinguish/Describe
CFAI p. 204, Schweser p. 87 Understanding Balance Sheets

Marketable Securities Example

Treatment of unrealized gains

- The 30 × ($1,010 – $1,000) = $300 in unrealized gains are treated as follows:
  - **Trading securities**
    - $300 in gains reported on 20x4 income statement, which increases net income and retained earnings
    - The 20x4 balance sheet will reflect the increase in the bonds' value: assets increase, equity increases from increase in retained earnings

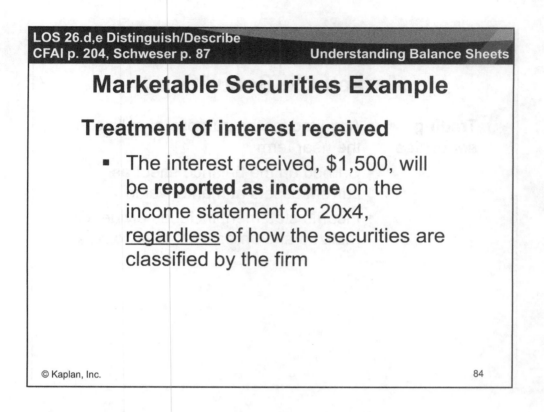

 85

LOS 26.d,e Distinguish/Describe
CFAI p. 204, Schweser p. 87 Understanding Balance Sheets

Marketable Securities Example

Treatment of unrealized gains

- **Available-for-sale securities**
  - $300 unrealized gains reported as other comprehensive income for 20x4, not reported on income statement
  - The 20x4 balance sheet will reflect the increase in the bonds' value: assets increase and equity increases from increase in other comprehensive income

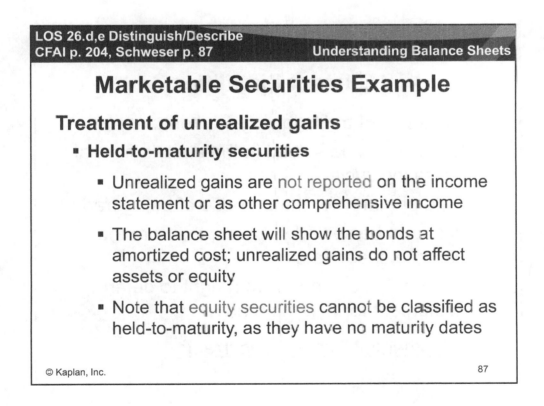

 86

LOS 26.d,e Distinguish/Describe
CFAI p. 204, Schweser p. 87 Understanding Balance Sheets

Marketable Securities Example

Treatment of unrealized gains

- **Held-to-maturity securities**
  - Unrealized gains are not reported on the income statement or as other comprehensive income
  - The balance sheet will show the bonds at amortized cost; unrealized gains do not affect assets or equity
  - Note that equity securities cannot be classified as held-to-maturity, as they have no maturity dates

 87

LOS 26.d,e Distinguish/Describe
CFAI p. 204, Schweser p. 87 Understanding Balance Sheets

Classification of Securities: Summary

- Dividends, interest, and realized gains always appear on the income statement
- Unrealized G/L only affect the income statement for trading securities
- Unrealized G/L are reflected on the balance sheet for both trading and available-for-sale securities
- Unrealized G/L on available-for-sale securities show up as other comprehensive income, not on income statement

 88

LOS 26.d,e Distinguish/Describe
CFAI p. 204, Schweser p. 87 Understanding Balance Sheets

Current Liabilities

Satisfies any of the following 4 criteria:

1. Expected to be settled in the entity's normal operating cycle
2. Held primarily for the purpose of being traded
3. Is due to be settled < 12 months from the balance sheet date
4. The entity does not have a right to defer settlement for > 12 months

All other liabilities—noncurrent

 89

LOS 26.d,e Distinguish/Describe
CFAI p. 204, Schweser p. 87

Understanding Balance Sheets

Current Liabilities

- Accounts payable/trade payables
- Notes payable
- Current portion of long-term debt
- Accrued liabilities
- Taxes payable
- Unearned revenue

90

LOS 26.f Describe
CFAI p. 204, Schweser p. 88

Understanding Balance Sheets

Components of Equity

- Capital contributed by owners
  - Issued and authorized
- Preferred stock (irredeemable)
- Treasury stock (reduces equity)
- Retained earnings
- Noncontrolling (minority) interest
- Accumulated other comprehensive income

91

LOS 26.g Analyze
CFAI p. 231, Schweser p. 97 Understanding Balance Sheets

Statement of Changes in Stockholders' Equity

	Common Stock	*Retained Earnings (in thousands)*	*Accumulated Other Comprehensive Income (loss)*	*Total*
Beginning balance	$49,234	$26,664	($406)	$75,492
Net income		6,994		6,994
Net unrealized loss on available-for-sale securities			(40)	(40)
Net unrealized loss on cash flow hedges			(56)	(56)
Adjustments to net pension liability			(26)	(26)
Cumulative translation adjustment			42	42
Comprehensive income				6,914
Issuance of common stock	1,282			1,282
Repurchases of common stock	(6,200)			(6,200)
Dividends		(2,360)		(2,360)
Ending balance	$44,316	$31,298	($486)	$75,128

 92

LOS 26.h Convert/Interpret
CFAI p. 232, Schweser p. 98 Understanding Balance Sheets

Common Size Balance Sheet

$$\frac{\text{Balance sheet account}}{\text{Total assets}} \quad \textit{e.g.,} \quad \frac{\textit{Inventory}}{\textit{Total assets}}$$

Uses:

Comparisons over time (trend analysis)

Cross-sectional comparisons

 93

LOS 26.i Calculate/Interpret
CFAI p. 239, Schweser p. 100 Understanding Balance Sheets

Liquidity Ratios

Current ratio $\frac{\text{Current assets}}{\text{Current liabilities}}$

Quick ratio $\frac{\text{Current assets} - \text{inventory}}{\text{Current liabilities}}$

Cash ratio $\frac{\text{Cash + marketable securities}}{\text{Current liabilities}}$

 94

LOS 26.i Calculate/Interpret
CFAI p. 239, Schweser p. 100 Understanding Balance Sheets

Solvency Ratios

Long-term debt to equity $\frac{\text{Total long-term debt}}{\text{Total equity}}$

Debt to equity $\frac{\text{Total debt}}{\text{Total equity}}$

Total debt $\frac{\text{Total debt}}{\text{Total assets}}$

Financial leverage $\frac{\text{Total assets}}{\text{Total equity}}$

 95

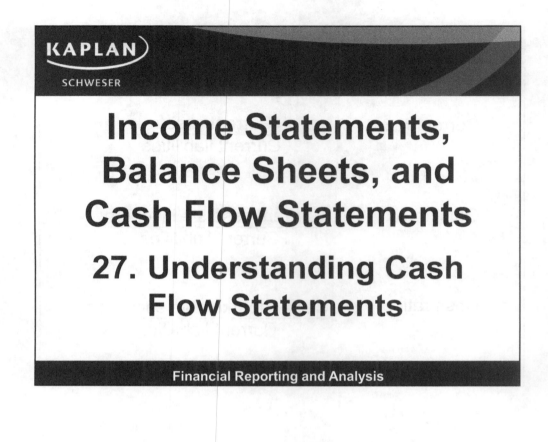

Income Statements, Balance Sheets, and Cash Flow Statements

27. Understanding Cash Flow Statements

Financial Reporting and Analysis

LOS 27.a Compare/Classify
CFAI p. 253, Schweser p. 109

Understanding Cash Flow Statements

Importance of Cash Flow Statement

Net income from accrual accounting does not tell us about the **sources and uses of cash** to meet liabilities and operating needs

The statement of cash flows has **three components** under both IFRS and U.S. GAAP:

- Cash provided or used by **operating** activities
- Cash provided or used by **investing** activities
- Cash provided or used in **financing** activities

97

LOS 27.a Compare/Classify
CFAI p. 253, Schweser p. 109

Understanding Cash Flow Statements

Operating Cash Flows (CFO)

	$
Cash received from customers	X
Cash dividends received	X
Cash interest received	X
Other cash income	X
Payments to suppliers	(X)
Cash expenses (wages, etc.)	(X)
Cash interest paid	(X)
Cash taxes paid	(X)
CFO	X/(X)

 98

LOS 27.a Compare/Classify
CFAI p. 253, Schweser p. 109

Understanding Cash Flow Statements

Investing Cash Flows (CFI)

- Purchases of property, plant, and equipment
- Proceeds from sales of assets
- Investments in joint ventures and affiliates
- Payments for businesses acquired
- Purchases and sales of intangibles
- Purchases or sales of marketable securities

  Excludes:
  - Trading securities (part of CFO)
  - Cash equivalents (part of balance sheet cash)

 99

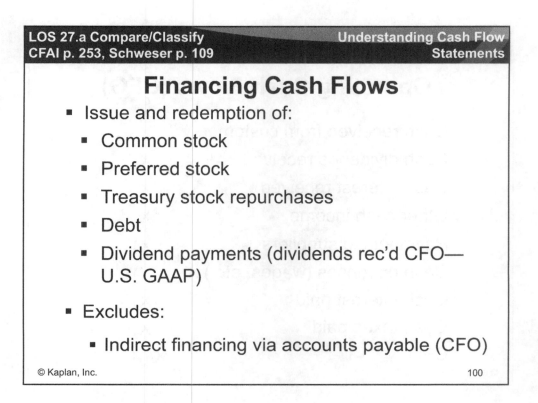

LOS 27.a Compare/Classify
CFAI p. 253, Schweser p. 109

Understanding Cash Flow Statements

Financing Cash Flows

- Issue and redemption of:
  - Common stock
  - Preferred stock
  - Treasury stock repurchases
  - Debt
  - Dividend payments (dividends rec'd CFO—U.S. GAAP)
- Excludes:
  - Indirect financing via accounts payable (CFO)

 100

LOS 27.b Describe
CFAI p. 255, Schweser p. 111

Understanding Cash Flow Statements

Non-Cash Investing and Financing Activities

- Several types of transactions do not involve the payment or receipt of cash and are not reflected in financing and investing cash flows, but are disclosed in the footnotes or other schedules

Non-cash financing and investing activities:

- Converting debt or preferred into common equity
- Assets acquired under capital leases
- Purchase of assets via issuance of debt/equity
- Exchanging one non-cash asset for another
- Stock dividends

 101

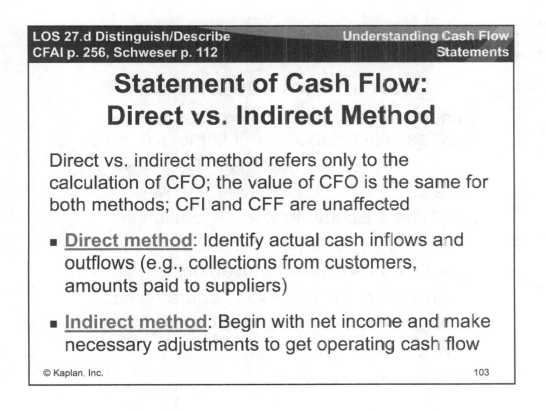

LOS 27.c Contrast
CFAI p. 255, Schweser p. 111

Understanding Cash Flow Statements

U.S. GAAP vs. IFRS

	U.S. GAAP	*IFRS*
Interest received	CFO	CFO or CFI
Interest paid	CFO	CFO or CFF
Dividends received	CFO	CFO or CFI
Dividends paid	CFF	CFO or CFF
Taxes paid	CFO	CFO or CFI & CFF
Bank overdraft	CFF	*

* Considered part of cash and cash equivalents

 102

LOS 27.d Distinguish/Describe
CFAI p. 256, Schweser p. 112

Understanding Cash Flow Statements

Statement of Cash Flow: Direct vs. Indirect Method

Direct vs. indirect method refers only to the calculation of CFO; the value of CFO is the same for both methods; CFI and CFF are unaffected

- **Direct method**: Identify actual cash inflows and outflows (e.g., collections from customers, amounts paid to suppliers)
- **Indirect method**: Begin with net income and make necessary adjustments to get operating cash flow

 103

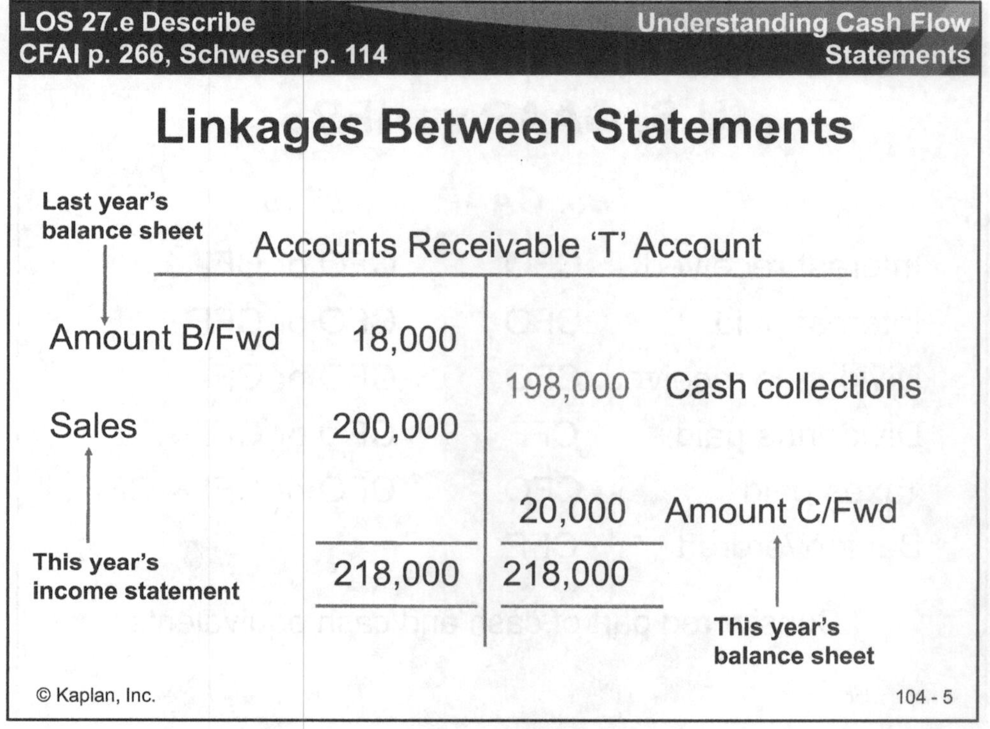

LOS 27.e Describe
CFAI p. 266, Schweser p. 114
Understanding Cash Flow Statements
Linkages Between Statements
Last year's balance sheet
Accounts Receivable 'T' Account
Amount B/Fwd 18,000
198,000 Cash collections
Sales 200,000
20,000 Amount C/Fwd
218,000 218,000
This year's income statement
This year's balance sheet
© Kaplan, Inc.
104 - 5

LOS 27.f Describe
CFAI p. 267, Schweser p. 115

Understanding Cash Flow Statements

Cash Inflows and Outflows

General rules regarding increases and decreases in balance sheet items over time:

	Increase	Decrease
Assets	outflow	inflow
Liabilities & Equity	inflow	outflow

e.g.: An increase in AR or inventory uses cash

An increase in payables generates cash

Adjust net income for these changes (indirect)

105

LOS 27.f Describe
CFAI p. 267, Schweser p. 115

Understanding Cash Flow Statements

Ecclestone Industries—Example

Ecclestone Industries has the following income statement for 20X9 and balance sheets for 20X8 and 20X9. You are to construct the statement of cash flows using the **indirect method**.

Additional information:
Equipment was purchased for $50,000
Ecclestone has a tax rate of 40%

 106

LOS 27.f Describe
CFAI p. 267, Schweser p. 115

Understanding Cash Flow Statements

Income Statement for Year to 31 December 20X9

	$	$	
Sales revenue		200,000	
Expenses:			
Cost of goods sold	80,000		
Salaries	10,000		
Depreciation	14,000		+ 14
Interest	1,000		
		105,000	
		95,000	
Gain from sale of PPE		20,000	- 20
Pre-tax income		115,000	
Provision for taxes		40,000	
Net income		75,000	*

 107

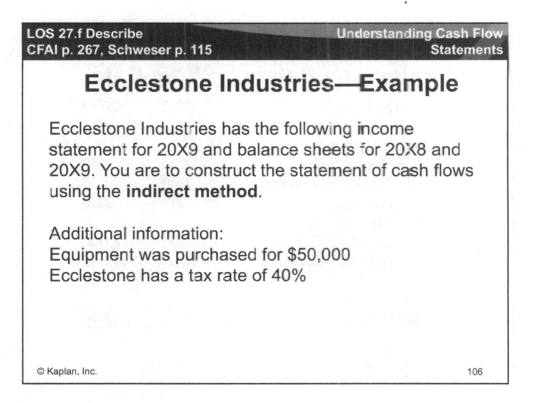

LOS 27.f Describe
CFAI p. 267, Schweser p. 115

Understanding Cash Flow Statements

Ecclestone Balance Sheet Data

Balance Sheets	**20X8 $**	**20X9 $**
Current assets		
Cash	18,000	66,000
Accounts receivable	18,000	20,000
Inventory	14,000	10,000
Non-current assets		
Gross PPE	282,000	312,000
Accum. Depr.	(80,000)	(84,000)
Total Assets	**252,000**	**324,000**

108

LOS 27.f Describe
CFAI p. 267, Schweser p. 115

Understanding Cash Flow Statements

Balance Sheets	**20X8 $**	**20X9 $**
Current liabilities		
Accounts payable	10,000	18,000
Salaries payable	16,000	9,000
Interest payable	6,000	7,000
Taxes payable	8,000	10,000
Dividends payable	2,000	12,000
Noncurrent liabilities		
Bonds	20,000	30,000
Deferred taxes	30,000	40,000
Stockholders' equity		
Common stock	100,000	80,000
Retained earnings	60,000	118,000
Total Liabilities & Equity	**252,000**	**324,000**

109

LOS 27.f Describe
CFAI p. 267, Schweser p. 115

Understanding Cash Flow Statements

Indirect Method CFO

Steps

1. Start with net income
2. Adjust net income for changes in relevant balance sheet items:

Increases in an asset: deduct
Increase in a liability: add
Decrease in an asset: add
Decrease in a liability: deduct

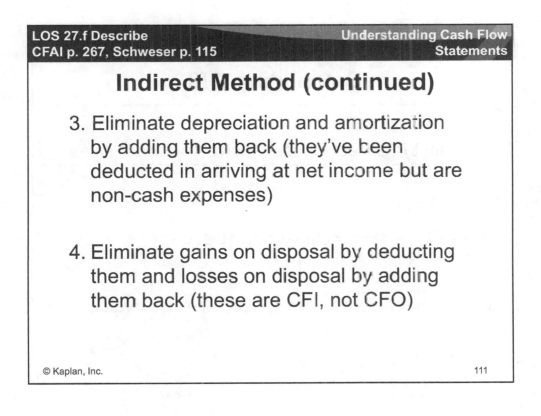

 110

LOS 27.f Describe
CFAI p. 267, Schweser p. 115

Understanding Cash Flow Statements

Indirect Method (continued)

3. Eliminate depreciation and amortization by adding them back (they've been deducted in arriving at net income but are non-cash expenses)

4. Eliminate gains on disposal by deducting them and losses on disposal by adding them back (these are CFI, not CFO)

 111

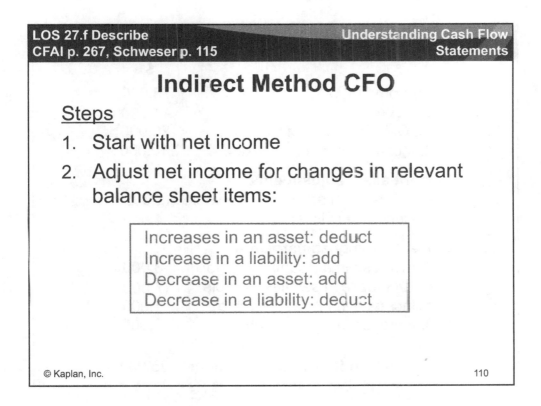

LOS 27.f Describe
CFAI p. 267, Schweser p. 115

Understanding Cash Flow Statements

Indirect Method Solution

	$
Net income	75,000
Add: Depreciation	14,000
Less: Gain from sale of PPE	(20,000)
Add: Increase in deferred taxes	10,000
Current asset adjustments	
Less: Increase in accounts receivable	(2,000)
Add: Decrease in inventory	4,000
Current liability adjustments	
Add: Increase in accounts payable	8,000
Less: Decrease in salaries payable	(7,000)
Add: Increase in interest payable	1,000
Add: Increase in taxes payable	2,000
Cash flow from operations	85,000

112 - 10

LOS 27.f Describe
CFAI p. 267, Schweser p. 115

Understanding Cash Flow Statements

Calculating CFI

CFI =

investment in assets – cash received on asset sales

Net book value =

Gross PPE – accumulated depreciation

282,000 – 84,000 = 198,000

Gain (loss) on sale = sales price – net book value

2,000

113

LOS 27.f Describe
CFAI p. 267, Schweser p. 115

Understanding Cash Flow Statements

Ecclestone CFI

Calculating NBV of asset sold

Gross Plant and Equip.		**Accumulated Depr.**	
Beginning PPE	282,000	Begin Acc. Depr.	80,000
Additions	50,000	Depr. Expense	14,000
PPE disposal	(20,000)	AD for disposal	(10,000)
Ending PPE	312,000	End Acc. Depr.	84,000

NBV of disposal = 20,000 – 10,000 = **10,000**

 114 - 6

LOS 27.f Describe
CFAI p. 267, Schweser p. 115

Understanding Cash Flow Statements

Ecclestone CFI

CFI = cash additions – cash received on disposal

	$
Sale Proceeds	30,000
– NBV of disposal	10,000
Gain (loss) on sale	20,000

CFI = –additions + proceeds

CFI = –\$50,000 + \$30,000 = –\$20,000

 115 - 3

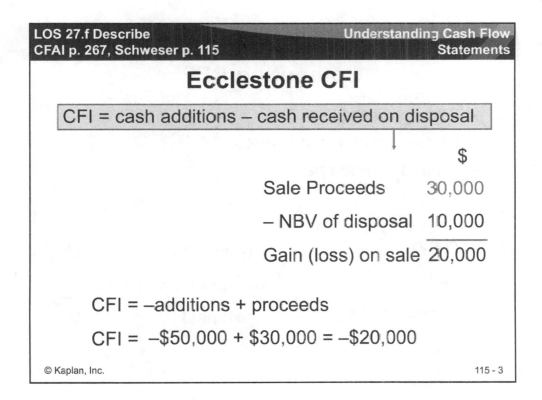

Understanding Cash Flow Statements

CFI – Problem

Last year Acme Corp. bought an asset for $72,000, depreciation expense was $15,000, accumulated depreciation increased by $5,000, and gross PPE increased by $32,000. If a gain on an asset sold during the year was $13,000, the sales proceeds on the asset sale were:

A. $30,000.

B. $43,000.

C. $48,000.

 116 - 5

LOS 27.f Describe
CFAI p. 267, Schweser p. 115

Understanding Cash Flow Statements

Computing CFF

- Change in debt
- Change in common stock
- Cash dividends paid

	$		$
Net income	X	Dividends declared	(X)
Dividends declared	(X)	ΔDividends payable	X
Δ in retained earnings	X	Cash paid	(X)

 117

LOS 27.f Describe
CFAI p. 267, Schweser p. 115

Understanding Cash Flow Statements

Ecclestone CFF

	$
▪ Change in debt	10,000
▪ Change in common stock	(20,000)
▪ Cash dividends paid	(7,000)
	(17,000)

	$		$
Net income	75,000	Dividends decl.	(17,000)
Div declared	(17,000)	Δ Div. payable	10,000
Δ in R/E	58,000	Cash div. paid	(7,000)

118 - 9

LOS 27.f Describe
CFAI p. 267, Schweser p. 115

Understanding Cash Flow Statements

Putting the Cash Flow Statement Together

	$
Cash flow from operations	85,000
Cash flow from investments	(20,000)
Cash flow from financing	(17,000)
Net increase in cash	48,000
Cash balance 12/31/X8	18,000
Cash balance 12/31/X9	66,000

119 - 3

LOS 27.g Convert
CFAI p. 267, Schweser p. 121

Understanding Cash Flow Statements

Converting an Indirect Statement to a Direct Statement of Cash Flows

Most firms use the indirect method, but the analyst may want information on the cash flows by function; some examples of this technique are:

Net sales – Δ accounts receivable + Δ advances from customers = cash collections

Cost of goods sold – Δ inventory + Δ accounts payable = cash paid for inputs

Interest expense + Δ interest payable = cash interest

 120

LOS 27.g Convert
CFAI p. 267, Schweser p. 121

Understanding Cash Flow Statements

Direct Method From Indirect CFO

1. Take each income statement item in turn (e.g., sales)
2. Move to the balance sheet and identify asset and liability accounts that relate to that income statement item—e.g., accounts receivable
3. Calculate the change in the balance sheet item during the period (ending balance – opening balance)
4. Apply the rule:

Increases in an asset: deduct
Increase in a liability: add
Decrease in an asset: add
Decrease in a liability: deduct

 121

LOS 27.g Convert
CFAI p. 267, Schweser p. 121

Understanding Cash Flow Statements

Direct From Indirect CFO

5. Adjust the income statement amount by the change in the balance sheet
6. Tick off the items dealt with in both the income statement and balance sheet
7. Move to the next item on the income statement and repeat
8. Ignore depreciation/amortization and gains/losses on the disposal of assets as these are non-cash or non-CFO items

 122

LOS 27.g Convert
CFAI p. 267, Schweser p. 121

Understanding Cash Flow Statements

Direct From Indirect CFO

9. Keep moving down the income statement until all items included in net income have been addressed applying steps 1-8
10. Total up the amounts and you have CFO

 123

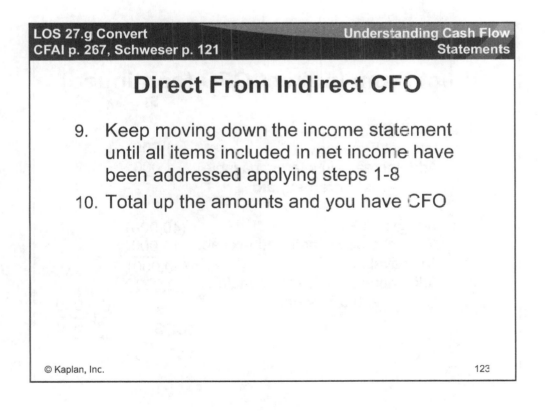

LOS 27.g Convert
CFAI p. 267, Schweser p. 121

Understanding Cash Flow Statements

Direct From Indirect CFO

Cash Inflows		
Sales	200,000	
Less: Increase in A/R	(2,000)	
Cash collected from customers		198,000
Direct cash outflows		
Cost of goods sold	(80,000)	
Add: Decrease in inventory	4,000	
Purchases	(76,000)	
Add: Increase in A/P	8,000	
Cash paid to suppliers		(68,000)
Operating expense (wages)	(10,000)	
Less: Decrease in salaries payable	(7,000)	
Cash paid to employees		(17,000)

124 - 6

LOS 27.g Convert
CFAI p. 267, Schweser p. 121

Understanding Cash Flow Statements

Direct From Indirect CFO (continued)

	$	**$**
Cash outflows		
Interest Expense	(1,000)	
Add: Increase in interest payable	1,000	
Cash interest paid		0
Tax Expense	(40,000)	
Add: Increase in deferred tax liab.	10,000	
Tax payable	(30,000)	
Add: Increase in taxes payable	2,000	
Cash taxes paid		(28,000)
	CFO	85,000

125 - 6

LOS 27.h Analyze/Interpret
CFAI p. 279, Schweser p. 124

Understanding Cash Flow Statements

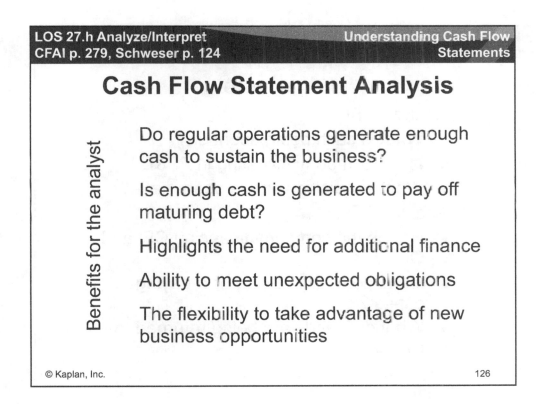

Cash Flow Statement Analysis

Benefits for the analyst

- Do regular operations generate enough cash to sustain the business?
- Is enough cash is generated to pay off maturing debt?
- Highlights the need for additional finance
- Ability to meet unexpected obligations
- The flexibility to take advantage of new business opportunities

 126

LOS 27.h Analyze/Interpret
CFAI p. 279, Schweser p. 124

Understanding Cash Flow Statements

Analysis

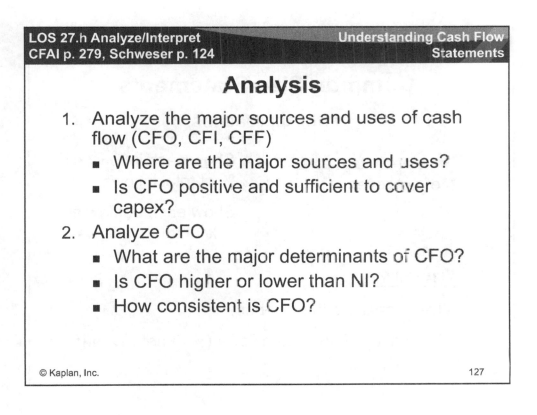

1. Analyze the major sources and uses of cash flow (CFO, CFI, CFF)
   - Where are the major sources and uses?
   - Is CFO positive and sufficient to cover capex?
2. Analyze CFO
   - What are the major determinants of CFO?
   - Is CFO higher or lower than NI?
   - How consistent is CFO?

 127

LOS 27.h Analyze/Interpret
CFAI p. 279, Schweser p. 124

Understanding Cash Flow Statements

Analysis

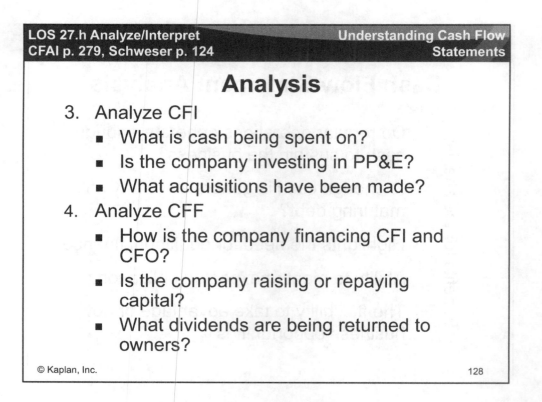

3. Analyze CFI
   - What is cash being spent on?
   - Is the company investing in PP&E?
   - What acquisitions have been made?
4. Analyze CFF
   - How is the company financing CFI and CFO?
   - Is the company raising or repaying capital?
   - What dividends are being returned to owners?

128

LOS 27.h Analyze/Interpret
CFAI p. 279, Schweser p. 124

Understanding Cash Flow Statements

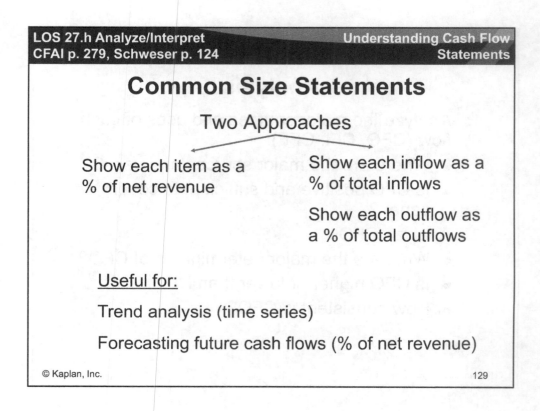

Common Size Statements

Two Approaches

Show each item as a % of net revenue

Show each inflow as a % of total inflows

Show each outflow as a % of total outflows

Useful for:

Trend analysis (time series)

Forecasting future cash flows (% of net revenue)

129

LOS 27.h Analyze/Interpret
CFAI p. 279, Schweser p. 124

Understanding Cash Flow Statements

Common Size Statements Ecclestone

Inflows

Receipts from customers	$198,000	83.2%
Sale of equipment	$30,000	12.6%
Debt issuance	$10,000	4.2%
Total	$238,000	100%

 130

LOS 27.h Analyze/Interpret
CFAI p. 279, Schweser p. 124

Understanding Cash Flow Statements

Common Size Statements Ecclestone

Outflows

Payments to suppliers	$68,000	35.8%
Payments to employees	$17,000	8.9%
Payments for interest	$0	0%
Payments for income tax	$28,000	14.7%
Purchase of equipment	$50,000	26.3%
Retirement of common stock	$20,000	10.5%
Dividend payments	$7,000	3.7%
Total	$190,000	100%

 131

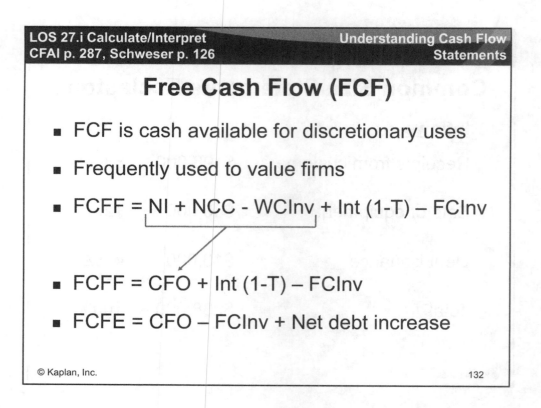

LOS 27.i Calculate/Interpret
CFAI p. 287, Schweser p. 126

Understanding Cash Flow Statements

Free Cash Flow (FCF)

- FCF is cash available for discretionary uses
- Frequently used to value firms
- FCFF = NI + NCC - WCInv + Int (1-T) – FCInv
- FCFF = CFO + Int (1-T) – FCInv
- FCFE = CFO – FCInv + Net debt increase

132

LOS 27.i Calculate/Interpret
CFAI p. 287, Schweser p. 126

Understanding Cash Flow Statements

Free Cash Flow (FCF) Ecclestone

- FCFF = CFO + Int (1 – T) – FCInv

  \$85,000 + \$1,000 (1 – 0.4) – \$20,000 = \$65,600
- FCFE = CFO – FCInv + Net debt increase

  \$85,000 – \$20,000 + \$10,000 = \$75,000
- FCFE = FCFF – Int (1 – T) + Net debt increase

  \$65,600 – \$1,000 (1 – 0.4) + \$10,000 = \$75,000

133 - 3

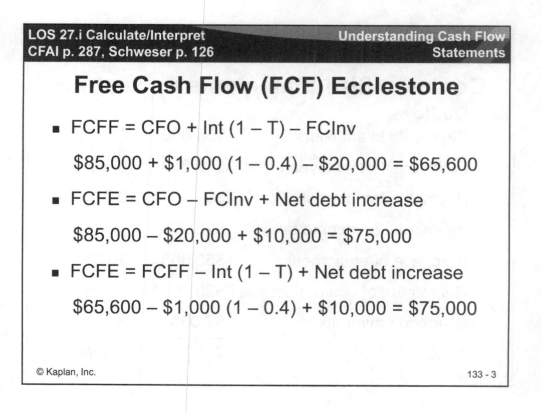

LOS 27.i Calculate/Interpret
CFAI p. 287, Schweser p. 126

Understanding Cash Flow Statements

Cash Flow Performance Ratios

Cash flow to revenue: $\frac{\text{CFO}}{\text{Net revenue}}$

Cash return on assets: $\frac{\text{CFO}}{\text{Avg total assets}}$

Cash return on equity: $\frac{\text{CFO}}{\text{Avg equity}}$

Cash to income: $\frac{\text{CFO}}{\text{Operating income}}$

 134

LOS 27.i Calculate/Interpret
CFAI p. 287, Schweser p. 126

Understanding Cash Flow Statements

Cash Flow Performance Ratios

Cash flow per share*: $\frac{\text{CFO} - \text{pref div}}{\text{\# common stock}}$

*IFRS: If dividends paid were treated as CFO, they must be added back

 135

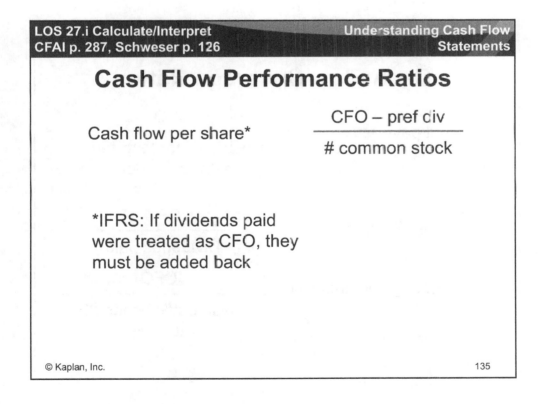

LOS 27.i Calculate/Interpret
CFAI p. 287, Schweser p. 126

Understanding Cash Flow Statements

Cash Flow Coverage Ratios

Debt coverage	$\frac{\text{CFO}}{\text{Total debt}}$
Interest coverage*	$\frac{\text{CFO + interest + tax}}{\text{Interest paid}}$
Reinvestment	$\frac{\text{CFO}}{\text{Cash paid for long-term assets}}$

*IFRS: If interest paid was treated as CFF, no addition is required

136

LOS 27.i Calculate/Interpret
CFAI p. 287, Schweser p. 126

Understanding Cash Flow Statements

Cash Flow Coverage Ratios

Debt payment	$\frac{\text{CFO}}{\text{Cash paid for long-term debt repayment}}$
Dividend payment	$\frac{\text{CFO}}{\text{Dividends paid}}$
Investing and financing	$\frac{\text{CFO}}{\text{Cash outflows for CFI \& CFF}}$

137

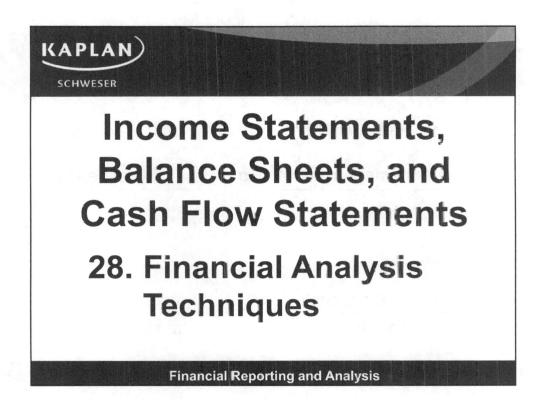

Income Statements, Balance Sheets, and Cash Flow Statements

28. Financial Analysis Techniques

Financial Reporting and Analysis

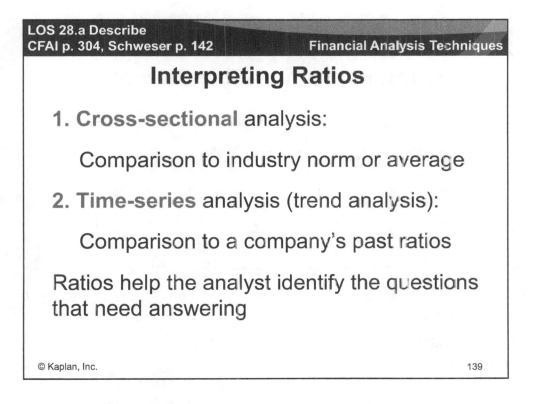

LOS 28.a Describe
CFAI p. 304, Schweser p. 142

Financial Analysis Techniques

Interpreting Ratios

1. **Cross-sectional** analysis:

   Comparison to industry norm or average

2. **Time-series** analysis (trend analysis):

   Comparison to a company's past ratios

Ratios help the analyst identify the questions that need answering

LOS 28.a Describe
CFAI p. 304, Schweser p. 142 Financial Analysis Techniques

Vertical Common-Size Statements

Income Statement

$$\frac{\text{Income statement account}}{\text{Sales}} \quad \text{e.g.,} \quad \frac{\text{Marketing expense}}{\text{Sales}}$$

Balance Sheet

$$\frac{\text{Balance sheet account}}{\text{Total assets}} \quad \text{e.g.,} \quad \frac{\text{Inventory}}{\text{Total assets}}$$

 140

LOS 28.a Describe
CFAI p. 304, Schweser p. 142 Financial Analysis Techniques

Horizontal Common-Size Statements

- Each line shown as a relative to some base year
- Facilitates trend analysis

Assets	Year 1	Year 2	Year 3
Cash	1.0	1.2	1.1
AR	1.0	1.3	1.0
Inventory	1.0	0.8	1.2
PP&E	1.0	1.5	2.0
Total	1.0	1.3	1.5

 141

LOS 28.a Describe
CFAI p. 304, Schweser p. 142 Financial Analysis Techniques

Graphs

- **Facilitate comparisons over time**
- Performance
- Financial structure
- **Communicate analyst conclusions**
- **Types**
  - Pie graph – composition of total value
  - Stacked column graph – composition of total value over time
  - Line graph – change over time

 142

LOS 28.a Describe
CFAI p. 304, Schweser p. 142 Financial Analysis Techniques

Stacked Column Graph

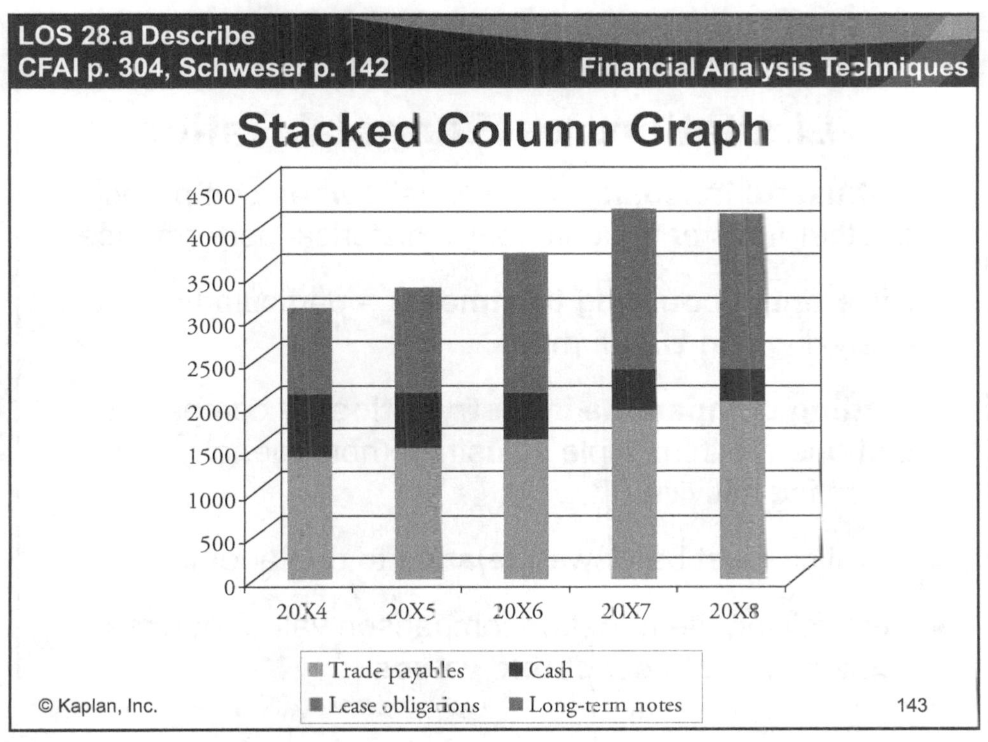

 143

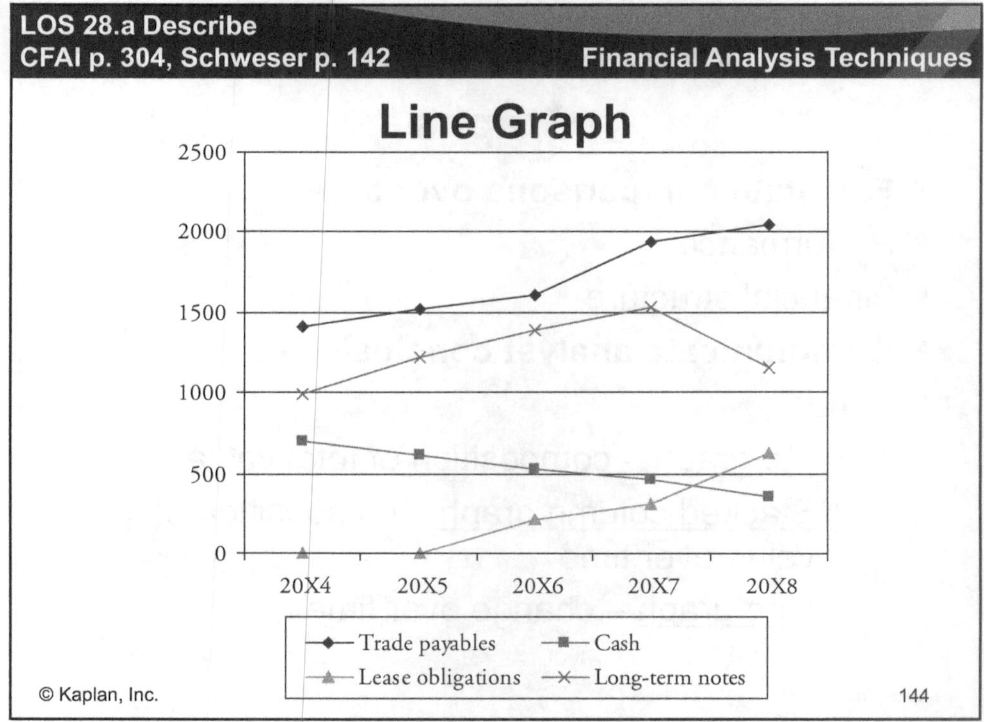

LOS 28.a Describe
CFAI p. 304, Schweser p. 142

Financial Analysis Techniques

Limitations of Financial Ratios

- **Not useful in isolation** – only valid when compared to other firms or the company's historical performance
- **Different accounting treatments** – particularly when analyzing non-U.S. firms
- **Finding comparable industry ratios** for companies that operate in multiple industries (homogeneity of operating activities)
- All ratios must be viewed **relative** to one another
- Determining the target or comparison value requires some **range of acceptable values**

145

LOS 28.a Describe
CFAI p. 304, Schweser p. 142 Financial Analysis Techniques

Common-Size Income Statement

- Expresses each income statement item as a **percentage of sales**
- Used to analyze changes in cost structure and profitability
- Used for both cross-sectional and time-series analysis

 146

LOS 28.a Describe
CFAI p. 304, Schweser p. 142 Financial Analysis Techniques

Common-Size Income Statement

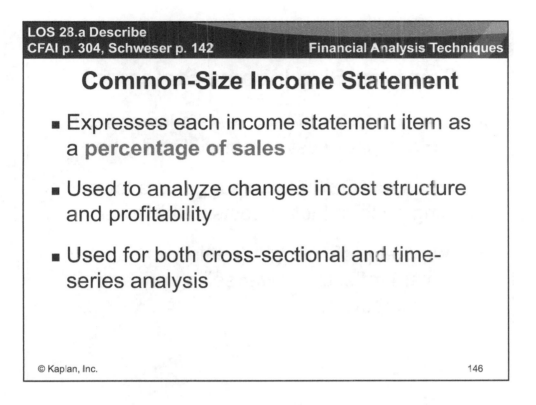

Example: Consider a common-size income statement that reveals the following (selected items only):

Income statement item	20X7	20X8	Industry Avg.
COGS	58%	62%	60%
SG&A	18%	22%	18%
Net Income	9%	8%	10%

 147

LOS 28.a Describe
CFAI p. 304, Schweser p. 142 Financial Analysis Techniques

Common-Size Income Statement

- Increased COGS% suggests a lower selling price or higher cost of material and labor
- Increased SG&A% also suggests a lower selling price or higher costs in this area
- Lower net profit margin (net income as a % of sales) reflects a lower selling price or higher expenses

 148

LOS 28.b Classify/Calculate/Interpret
CFAI p. 319, Schweser p. 148 Financial Analysis Techniques

Categories of Ratios

- **Activity** → Efficiency of day-to-day tasks/operations
- **Liquidity** → Ability to meet short-term liabilities
- **Solvency** → Ability to meet long-term obligations
- **Profitability** → Ability to generate profitable sales from asset base
- **Valuation** → Quantity of asset or flow associated with an ownership claim

 149

LOS 28.b Classify/Calculate/Interpret
CFAI p. 319, Schweser p. 148 Financial Analysis Techniques

Ratio Analysis Context

1. Company goals and strategy
2. Industry norms
   - Ratios may be **industry specific**
   - **Multiple lines** of business distort aggregate ratios
   - Differences in **accounting methods**
3. Economic conditions
   - Cyclical businesses and the **stage of the business cycle**

 150

LOS 28.b Classify/Calculate/Interpret
CFAI p. 319, Schweser p. 148 Financial Analysis Techniques

Ratio Analysis

Some general rules:

- For ratios that use only **income statement items**, use the values from the current income statement
- For ratios using only **balance sheet items**, use the values from the current balance sheet
- For ratios using **both income statement and balance sheet items**, use the value from the current income statement and the **average value for the balance sheet item**

 151

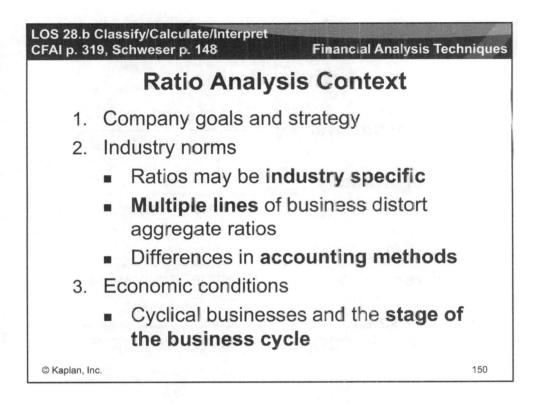

LOS 28.b Classify/Calculate/Interpret
CFAI p. 319, Schweser p. 148 Financial Analysis Techniques

Activity Ratios

Inventory turnover $= \dfrac{\text{Cost of goods sold}}{\text{Average inventory}}$

Days of inventory on hand (DOH) $= \dfrac{365}{\text{Inventory turnover}}$

Receivables turnover $= \dfrac{\text{Revenue}}{\text{Average receivables}}$

Days of sales outstanding (DSO) $= \dfrac{365}{\text{Receivables turnover}}$

 152

LOS 28.b Classify/Calculate/Interpret
CFAI p. 319, Schweser p. 148 Financial Analysis Techniques

Activity Ratios

Payables turnover $= \dfrac{\text{Purchases}}{\text{Average trade payables}}$

Number of days of payables $= \dfrac{365}{\text{Payables turnover}}$

Working capital turnover $= \dfrac{\text{Revenue}}{\text{Average working capital}}$

Working capital $= \text{Current assets} - \text{Current liabilities}$

 153

LOS 28.b Classify/Calculate/Interpret
CFAI p. 319, Schweser p. 148 Financial Analysis Techniques

Activity Ratios

Fixed asset turnover $= \dfrac{\text{Revenue}}{\text{Average net fixed assets}}$

↓ Net of accumulated depreciation

Total asset turnover $= \dfrac{\text{Revenue}}{\text{Average total assets}}$

 154

LOS 28.b Classify/Calculate/Interpret
CFAI p. 319, Schweser p. 148 Financial Analysis Techniques

Liquidity Ratios

Current ratio $= \dfrac{\text{Current assets}}{\text{Current liabilities}}$

Quick ratio $= \dfrac{\text{Cash + short term marketable securities + receivables}}{\text{Current liabilities}}$

Cash ratio $= \dfrac{\text{Cash + short term marketable securities}}{\text{Current liabilities}}$

 155

LOS 28.b Classify/Calculate/Interpret
CFAI p. 319, Schweser p. 148
Financial Analysis Techniques

Definitions: Liquidity Ratios

$$\text{Defensive interval ratio} = \frac{\text{Cash + short-term marketable investments + receivables}}{\text{Daily cash expenditure}}$$

Cash conversion cycle =

	Days
DOH	X
DSO	X
No. of days of payables	(X)
Cash conversion cycle	X

156

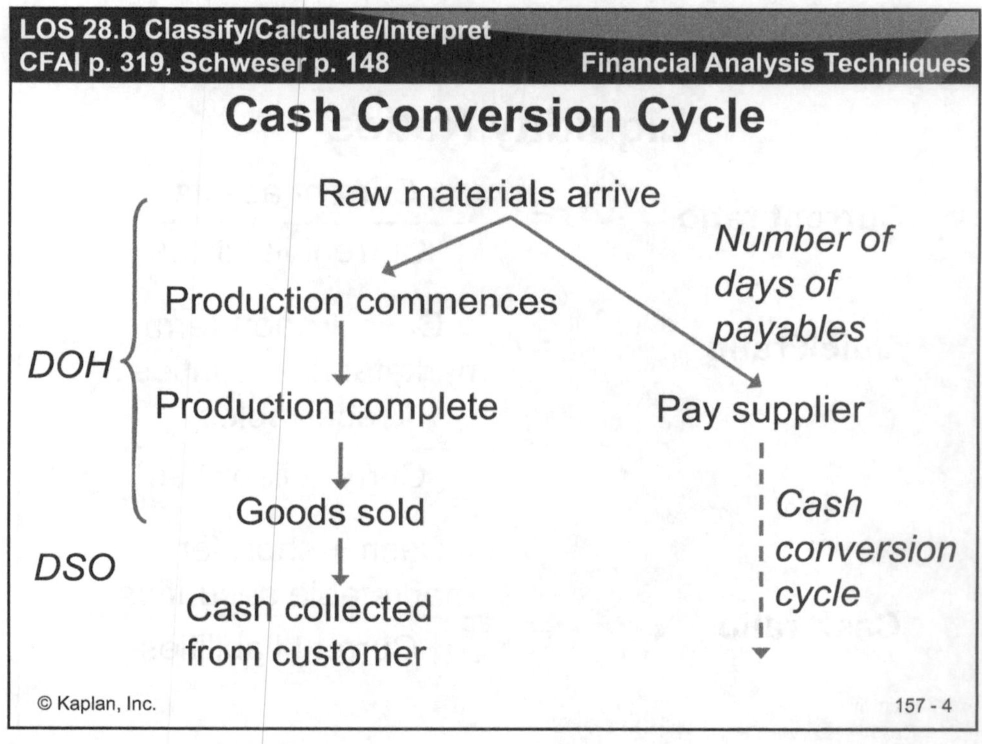

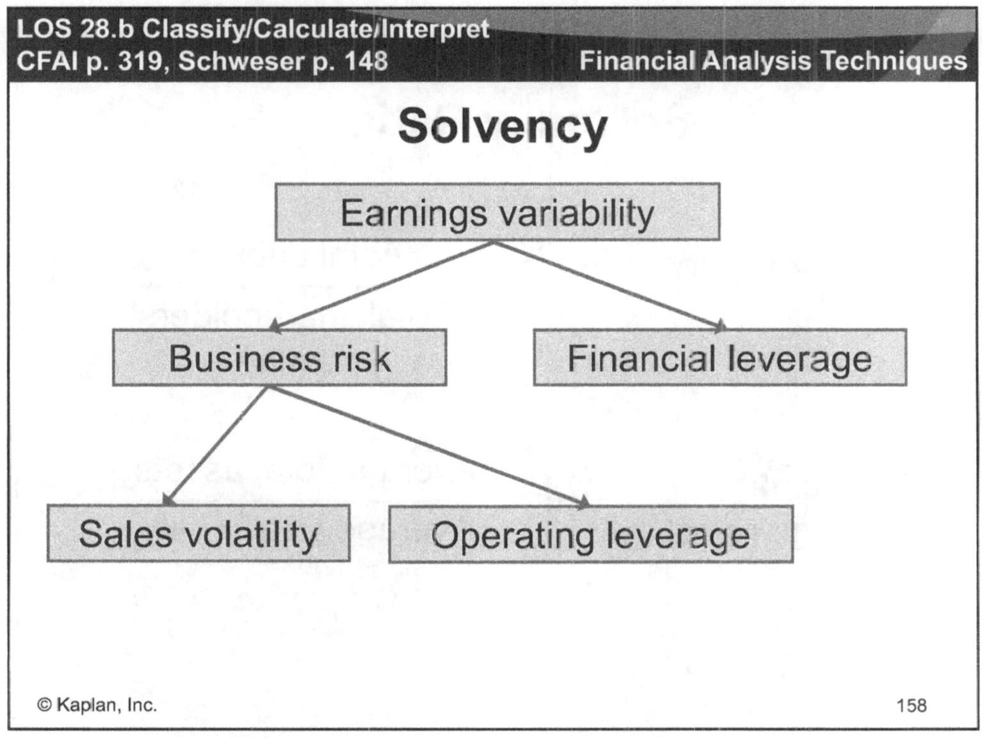
LOS 28.b Classify/Calculate/Interpret
CFAI p. 319, Schweser p. 148
Financial Analysis Techniques
Solvency
Earnings variability
Business risk
Financial leverage
Sales volatility
Operating leverage
© Kaplan, Inc.
158

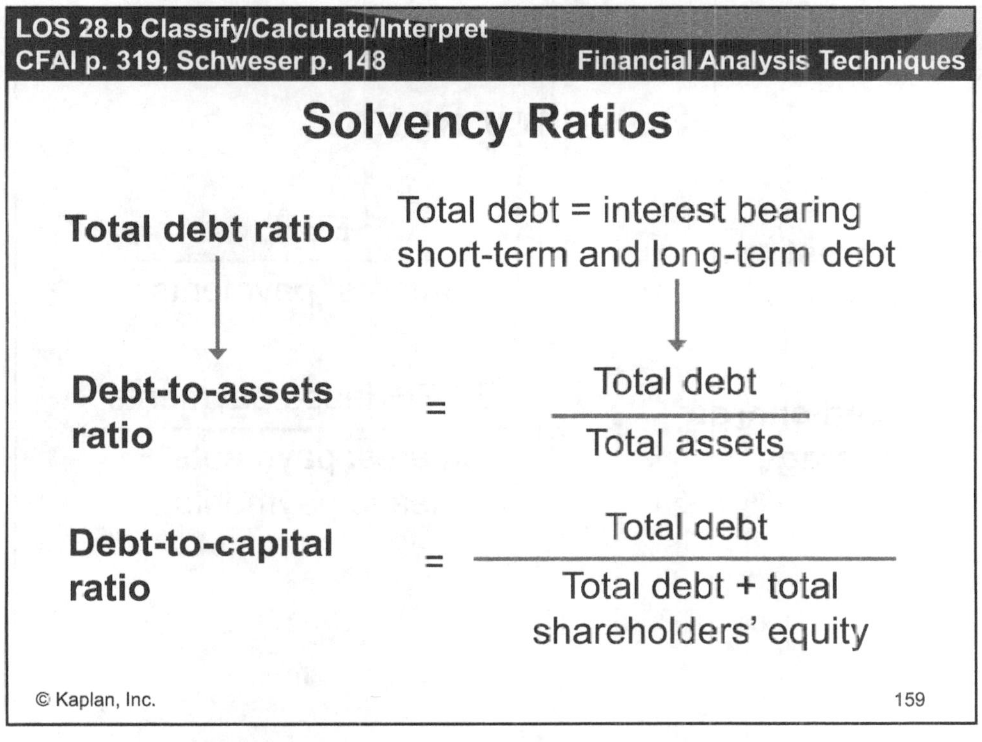
LOS 28.b Classify/Calculate/Interpret
CFAI p. 319, Schweser p. 148
Financial Analysis Techniques
Solvency Ratios
Total debt ratio
Total debt = interest bearing short-term and long-term debt
Debt-to-assets ratio
=
Total debt
Total assets
Debt-to-capital ratio
=
Total debt
Total debt + total shareholders' equity
© Kaplan, Inc.
159

LOS 28.b Classify/Calculate/Interpret
CFAI p. 319, Schweser p. 148

Financial Analysis Techniques

Solvency Ratios

Debt-to-equity ratio = $\frac{\text{Total debt}}{\text{Total shareholders' equity}}$

Financial leverage ratio = $\frac{\text{Average total assets}}{\text{Average total equity}}$

160

LOS 28.b Classify/Calculate/Interpret
CFAI p. 319, Schweser p. 148

Financial Analysis Techniques

Solvency Ratios

Interest coverage = $\frac{\text{EBIT}}{\text{Interest payments}}$

Fixed charge coverage = $\frac{\text{EBIT + lease payments}}{\text{Interest payments + lease payments}}$

161

LOS 28.b Classify/Calculate/Interpret
CFAI p. 319, Schweser p. 148 Financial Analysis Techniques

Profitability Ratios

Gross profit margin = $\frac{\text{Gross profit}}{\text{Revenue}}$

Operating profit margin = $\frac{\text{Operating income}}{\text{Revenue}}$

Operating income

Gross profit – operating costs

Approximation = EBIT

EBIT contains non-operating items (dividends rec'd and gains and losses on investment securities)

 162

LOS 28.b Classify/Calculate/Interpret
CFAI p. 319, Schweser p. 148 Financial Analysis Techniques

Profitability Ratios

Pretax margin = $\frac{\text{Earnings before tax but after interest}}{\text{Revenue}}$

Net profit margin = $\frac{\text{Net income}}{\text{Revenue}}$

Most of the return-on-sales profitability ratios are on the face of the common-size income statement

 163

LOS 28.b Classify/Calculate/Interpret
CFAI p. 319, Schweser p. 148

Financial Analysis Techniques

Profitability Ratios

Return on assets ROA $= \dfrac{\text{Net income}}{\text{Average total assets}}$

Alternatively:
Return on assets ROA $= \dfrac{\text{Net income + interest expense (1 – T)}}{\text{Average total assets}}$

Operating ROA $= \dfrac{\text{Operating income}}{\text{Average total assets}}$

164

LOS 28.b Classify/Calculate/Interpret
CFAI p. 319, Schweser p. 148

Financial Analysis Techniques

Profitability Ratios

Return on total capital $= \dfrac{\text{EBIT}}{\text{Short- + long-term debt + equity}}$

Return on equity ROE $= \dfrac{\text{Net income}}{\text{Average total equity}}$

Return on common equity $= \dfrac{\text{Net income – pref. div.}}{\text{Average common equity}}$

165

LOS 28.c Describe/Evaluate
CFAI p. 339, Schweser p. 157 Financial Analysis Techniques

Integrated Financial Ratio Approach

- Important to **analyze** all ratios **collectively**
- Use information from one ratio category to answer questions raised by another ratio
- Classic example = DuPont analysis

 166

LOS 28.c Describe/Evaluate
CFAI p. 339, Schweser p. 157 Financial Analysis Techniques

Integrated Financial Ratios – Example

	20X8	20X7	20X6
Current ratio	2.0	1.5	1.2
Quick ratio	0.5	0.8	1.0

	20X8	20X7	20X6
DOH	60	50	30
DSO	20	30	40

What can you conclude about this firm's performance?
(Note that years are presented right-to-left)

 167

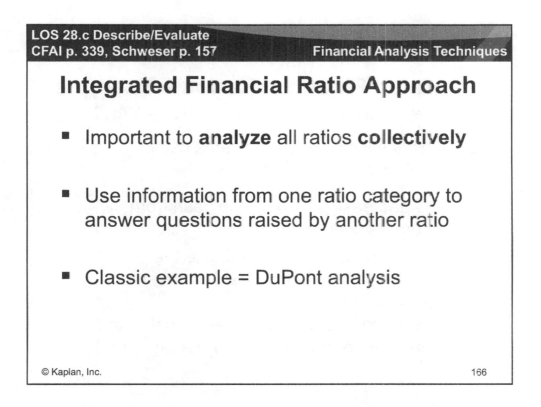

LOS 28.c Describe/Evaluate
CFAI p. 339, Schweser p. 157 Financial Analysis Techniques

Integrated Financial Ratios – Example

1. Current ratio up – Quick ratio down – Why?
2. DOH has increased – indicates rising inventory rather than low cash
3. DSO decreasing – collecting cash from customers sooner
4. Current and quick ratios indicate the collected cash is being spent on inventory accumulation
5. Appears collections have been accelerated to make up for poor inventory management

 168 - 5

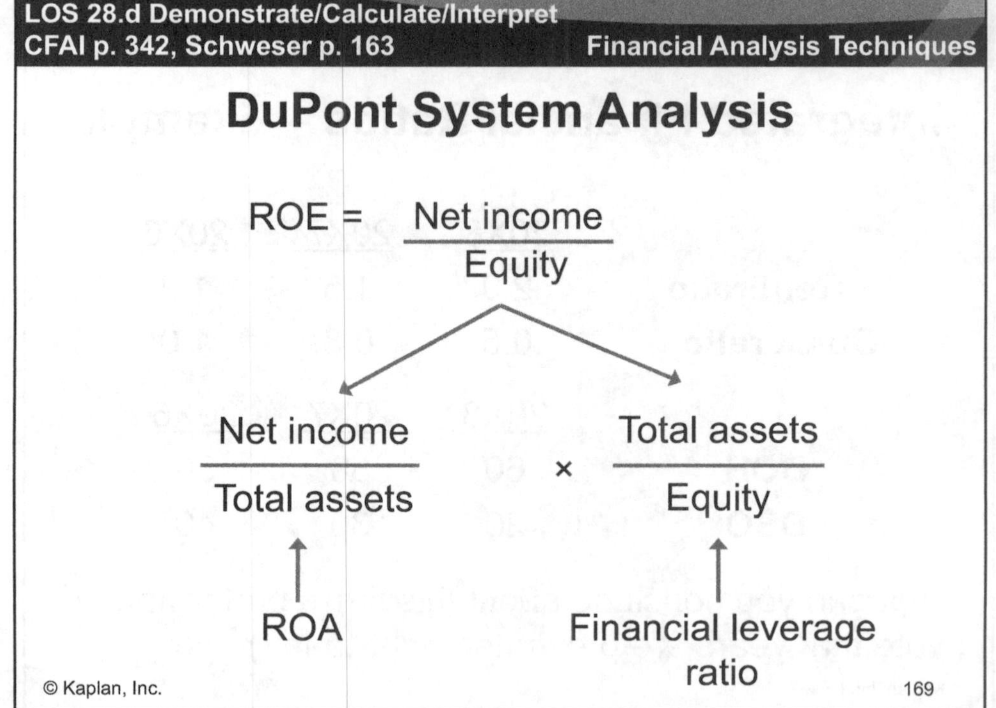

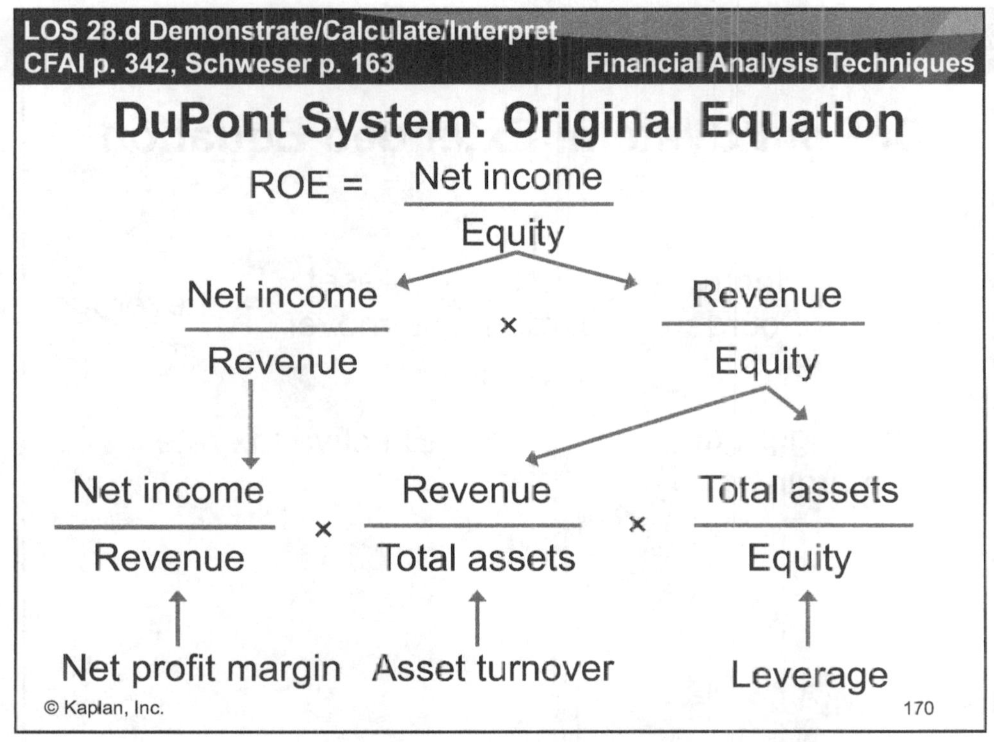
LOS 28.d Demonstrate/Calculate/Interpret
CFAI p. 342, Schweser p. 163
Financial Analysis Techniques
DuPont System: Original Equation
ROE = Net income / Equity
Net income / Revenue × Revenue / Equity
Net income / Revenue × Revenue / Total assets × Total assets / Equity
Net profit margin
Asset turnover
Leverage
© Kaplan, Inc.
170

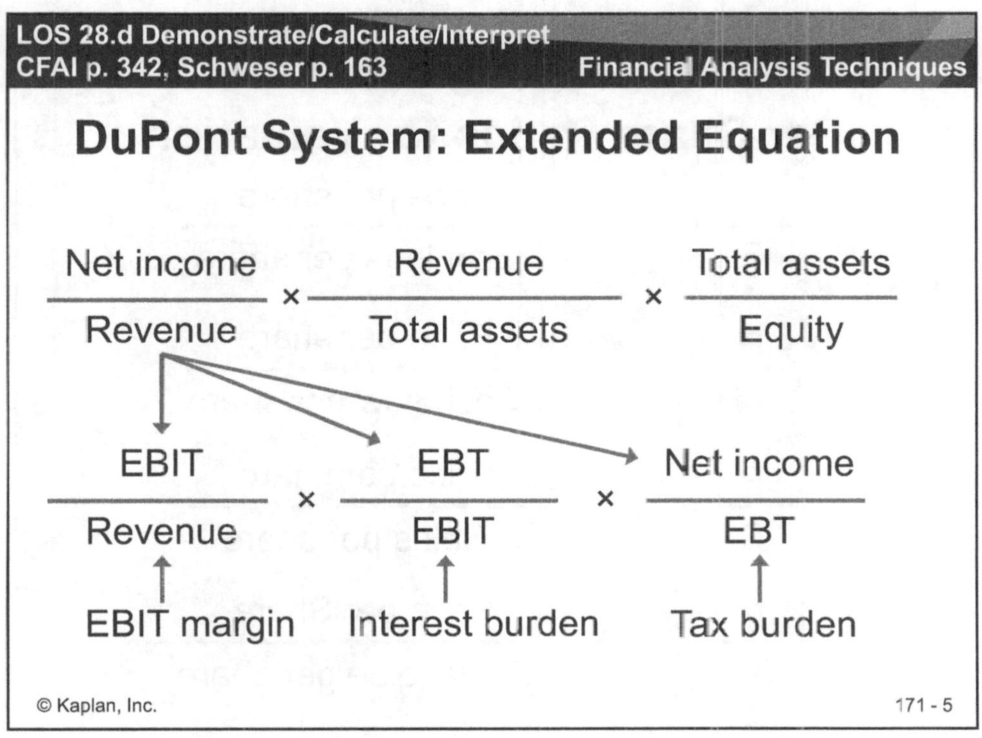
LOS 28.d Demonstrate/Calculate/Interpret
CFAI p. 342, Schweser p. 163
Financial Analysis Techniques
DuPont System: Extended Equation
Net income / Revenue × Revenue / Total assets × Total assets / Equity
EBIT / Revenue × EBT / EBIT × Net income / EBT
EBIT margin
Interest burden
Tax burden
© Kaplan, Inc.
171 - 5

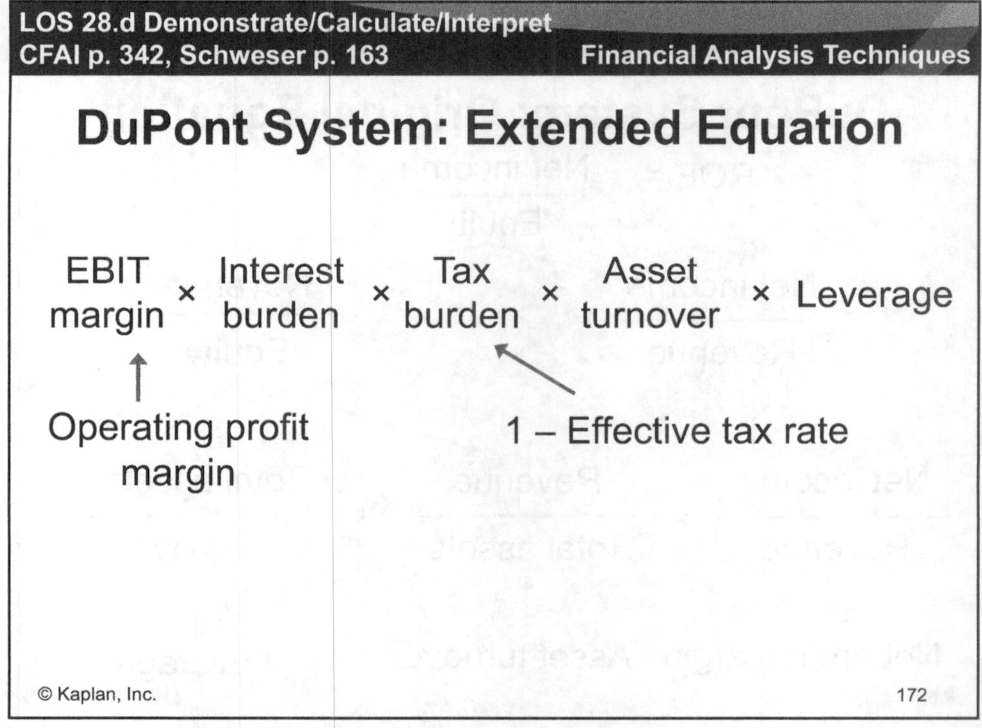

LOS 28.e Calculate/Interpret
CFAI p. 347, Schweser p. 167
Financial Analysis Techniques

Per-Share Ratios for Valuation

$$\frac{P}{E} = \frac{\text{Price per share}}{\text{Earnings per share}}$$

$$\frac{P}{CF} = \frac{\text{Price per share}}{\text{Cash flow per share}}$$

$$\frac{P}{S} = \frac{\text{Price per share}}{\text{Sales per share}}$$

$$\frac{P}{BV} = \frac{\text{Price per Share}}{\text{Book value per share}}$$

173

LOS 28.e Calculate/Interpret
CFAI p. 347, Schweser p. 167
Financial Analysis Techniques

Per-Share Quantities

Basic EPS = $\frac{\text{NI – Pref div}}{\text{Weighted avg \# ordinary shares}}$

Diluted EPS = $\frac{\text{Income adjusted for dilutive securities}}{\text{Weighted avg \# shares adjusted for dilution}}$

Cash flow per share = $\frac{\text{CFO}}{\text{Weighted avg \# shares}}$

174

LOS 28.e Calculate/Interpret
CFAI p. 347, Schweser p. 167
Financial Analysis Techniques

Per-Share Quantities

EBITDA per share = $\frac{\text{EBITDA}}{\text{Avg \# ordinary shares}}$

Dividends per share = $\frac{\text{Common dividend}}{\text{Weighted avg \# common shares}}$

175

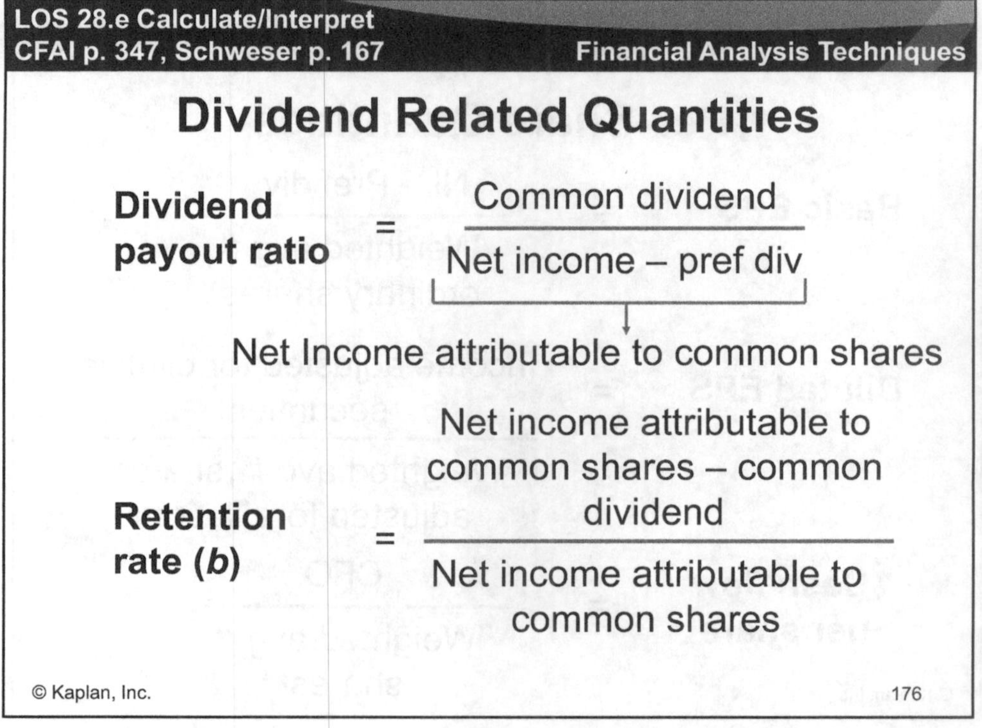
LOS 28.e Calculate/Interpret
CFAI p. 347, Schweser p. 167
Financial Analysis Techniques
Dividend Related Quantities
Dividend payout ratio
=
Common dividend
Net income – pref div
Net Income attributable to common shares
Retention rate (b)
=
Net income attributable to common shares – common dividend
Net income attributable to common shares
© Kaplan, Inc.
176

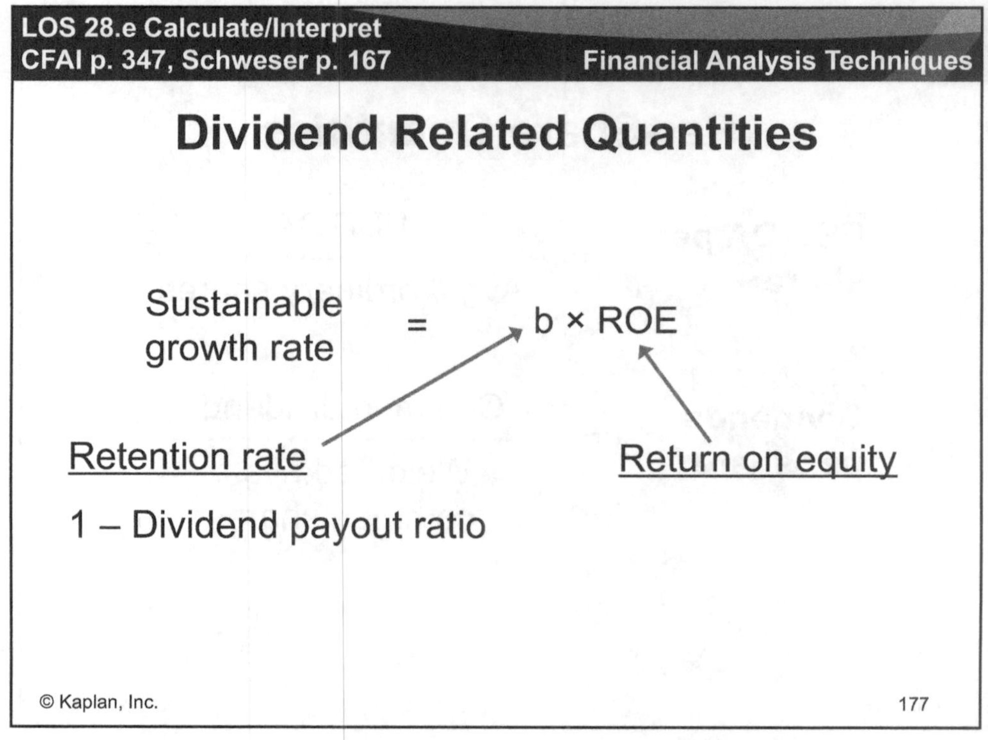
LOS 28.e Calculate/Interpret
CFAI p. 347, Schweser p. 167
Financial Analysis Techniques
Dividend Related Quantities
Sustainable growth rate
=
b × ROE
Retention rate
Return on equity
1 – Dividend payout ratio
© Kaplan, Inc.
177

Financial Analysis Techniques

Sustainable Growth Rate – Problem

A firm has a dividend payout ratio of 35%, a net profit margin of 10%, an asset turnover of 1.4, and an equity multiplier leverage measure of 1.2. Estimate the firm's sustainable growth rate.

 178 - 4

LOS 28.e Calculate/Interpret
CFAI p. 347, Schweser p. 167

Financial Analysis Techniques

Business Risk Ratios

Coefficient of variation of operating income = $\frac{\text{Operating income}}{\text{Operating income}}$

Coefficient of variation of net income = $\frac{\text{Net income}}{\text{Net income}}$

Coefficient of variation of revenue = $\frac{\text{Revenue}}{\text{Revenue}}$

 179

LOS 28.e Calculate/Interpret
CFAI p. 347, Schweser p. 167 Financial Analysis Techniques

Using Ratios for Equity Analysis

Research has found ratios (and changes in ratios) can be useful in forecasting earnings and stock returns (valuation)

Some items useful in forecasting:

% change in: current ratio • quick ratio • inventory • inventory turnover • inventory/total assets • sales • depreciation • capex/assets • asset turnover • depreciation/plant assets • total assets

ROE • Δ ROE • debt/equity • ROA • gross margin • working capital/assets • dividends/cash flow • Δ dividend • % debt repaid • operating ROA • pretax margin

 180

LOS 28.e Calculate/Interpret
CFAI p. 347, Schweser p. 167 Financial Analysis Techniques

Credit Ratings and Ratios

Assessing a company's ability to service and repay its debt:

- Interest coverage ratios
- Return on capital
- Debt-to-assets ratio
- Other ratios focus on various measures of cash flow to total debt

Also covered in SS16

Note: Adjustments are made for off-balance-sheet debt

 181

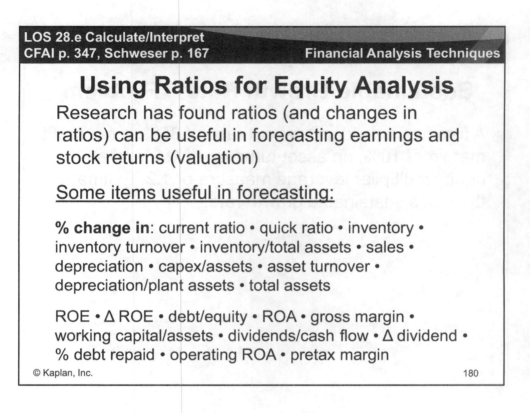

LOS 28.e Calculate/Interpret
CFAI p. 347, Schweser p. 167 Financial Analysis Techniques

Segment Reporting

Reportable business or geographic segment:

50% of its revenue from sales external to the firm, **and** at least 10% of a firm's revenue, earnings, or assets

- For each segment, firm reports *limited* financial statement information
- For primary segments, must report: revenue (internal and external), operating profit, assets, liabilities (IFRS only), capex, depreciation and amortization

 182

LOS 28.e Calculate/Interpret
CFAI p. 347, Schweser p. 167 Financial Analysis Techniques

Definitions: Segment Ratios

$$\text{Segment margin} = \frac{\text{Segment profit}}{\text{Segment revenue}}$$

$$\text{Segment asset turnover} = \frac{\text{Segment revenue}}{\text{Segment assets}}$$

$$\text{Segment ROA} = \frac{\text{Segment profit}}{\text{Segment assets}}$$

$$\text{Segment debt ratio (IFRS only)} = \frac{\text{Segment liabilities}}{\text{Segment assets}}$$

 183

LOS 28.f Describe
CFAI p. 358, Schweser p. 172

Financial Analysis Techniques

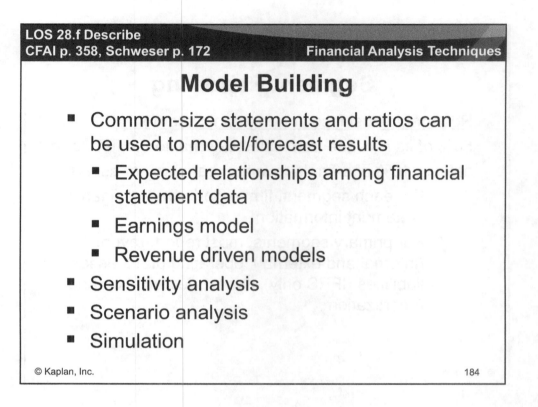

Model Building

- Common-size statements and ratios can be used to model/forecast results
  - Expected relationships among financial statement data
  - Earnings model
  - Revenue driven models
- Sensitivity analysis
- Scenario analysis
- Simulation

184

Financial Analysis Techniques

Financial Analysis – Problem

Analysis has generated the following data:

Tax rate	35%
Equity multiplier	2.7
Net profit margin	4.6%
Equity turnover	5.2

ROE is *closest* to:

A. 13%

B. 17%

C. 24%

185 - 3

Understanding Income Statements

Revenue Recognition – Solution

Project cost estimate = \$10 million; contract totals \$12 million; \$2 million of costs occur in Years 1 and 2; invoiced amounts \$4 million in Year 1 and \$3 million in Year 2; \$1 million in cash collected each year. Year 2 income under percentage of completion is:

(2/10)(12 mil – 10 mil) = \$400,000

B. \$400,000.

Understanding Income Statements

Weighted-Average Shares – Solution

Jan 1 10,000 shares
Mar 1 3,000 shares issued
July 1 20% stock dividend
Nov 1 3,000 shares repurchased

The weighted average number of shares outstanding over the year equals:

C. 14,500.

10,000(1.2)
+3,000(10/12)(1.2)
-3,000(2/12) = 14,500 sh.

Understanding Cash Flow Statements

CFI – Solution

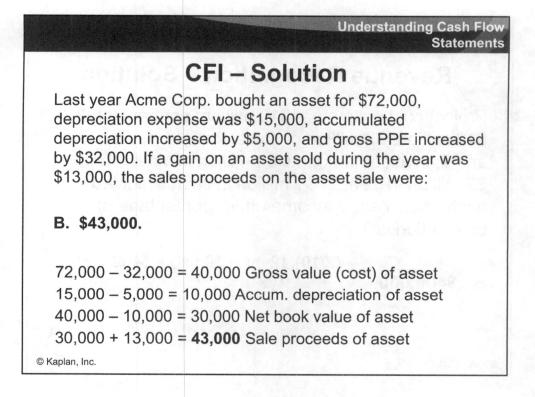

Last year Acme Corp. bought an asset for $72,000, depreciation expense was $15,000, accumulated depreciation increased by $5,000, and gross PPE increased by $32,000. If a gain on an asset sold during the year was $13,000, the sales proceeds on the asset sale were:

B. $43,000.

72,000 – 32,000 = 40,000 Gross value (cost) of asset
15,000 – 5,000 = 10,000 Accum. depreciation of asset
40,000 – 10,000 = 30,000 Net book value of asset
30,000 + 13,000 = **43,000** Sale proceeds of asset

Financial Analysis Techniques

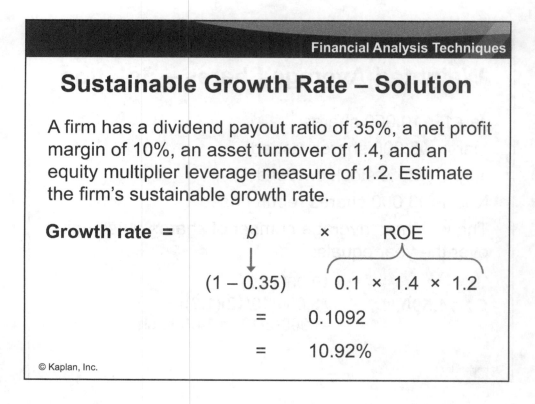

Sustainable Growth Rate – Solution

A firm has a dividend payout ratio of 35%, a net profit margin of 10%, an asset turnover of 1.4, and an equity multiplier leverage measure of 1.2. Estimate the firm's sustainable growth rate.

Growth rate = $b \times \text{ROE}$

$$(1 - 0.35) \quad 0.1 \times 1.4 \times 1.2$$

$$= 0.1092$$

$$= 10.92\%$$

Financial Analysis Techniques

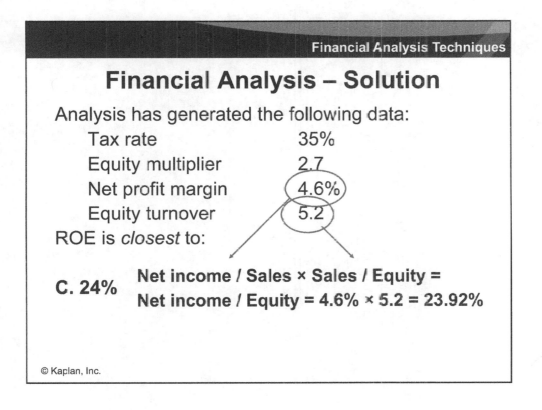

Financial Analysis – Solution

Analysis has generated the following data:

Tax rate	35%
Equity multiplier	2.7
Net profit margin	4.6%
Equity turnover	5.2

ROE is *closest* to:

C. 24%

Net income / Sales × Sales / Equity =
Net income / Equity = 4.6% × 5.2 = 23.92%